African Americans
in Science

African Americans in Science

An Encyclopedia of People and Progress

CHARLES W. CAREY JR.

VOLUME TWO

A B C • C L I O

Santa Barbara, California   Denver, Colorado   Oxford, England

Library of Congress Cataloging-in-Publication Data

Carey, Charles W.
African Americans in science : an encyclopedia of people and progress / Charles W. Carey, Jr.
p. cm.
Includes bibliographical references and index.
ISBN 978-1-85109-998-6 (hard copy : alk. paper)
ISBN 978-1-85109-999-3 (ebook)
1. African American scientists. 2. Scientists—United States. I. Title.
Q141.C2138 2008
500.896'073—dc22
2008024609

12 11 10 9 8   1 2 3 4 5 6 7 8 9 10

Editorial Manager: James P. Sherman
Submission Editors: Alex Mikaberidze and Kim Kennedy White
Production Editor: Christian Green
Production Manager: Don Schmidt
Media Editor: Ellen Rasmussen
Media Resources Manager: Caroline Price
File Management Coordinator: Paula Gerard

This book is also available on the World Wide Web as an eBook.
Visit www.abc-clio.com for details.

ABC-CLIO, Inc.
130 Cremona Drive, P.O. Box 1911
Santa Barbara, California 93116–1911

This book is printed on acid-free paper ∞
Manufactured in the United States of America

Contents

List of Entries

Institutions

Institutions have played a critically important role in the development of black scientists. In the early days, black colleges and hospitals provided African Americans seeking careers in science with the education and training they required. Although most of the historically black hospitals have passed from the scene, historically black colleges and universities (HBCUs) continue to produce an extraordinarily high number of black scientists. Since the 1960s, other institutions have played important roles as well. These institutions include historically black professional organizations, professional scientific associations, advocacy groups, and agencies of the federal government.

Whether at the undergraduate or graduate level, HBCUs have educated the majority of African American scientists. The reasons are not hard to understand. Most of the first HBCUs were founded to provide safe havens for black students to explore their intellectual capacities to the fullest, and today they provide would-be black scientists with a number of role models in the form of the black science professor/researcher. Since the 1960s, HBCUs have received significant amounts of funding from the private and public sectors so that they can improve the quality of their scientific training. Such funding also allows HBCUs to undertake state-of-the-art research projects, and today a number of HBCUs such as Delaware State University, Fisk University, Florida A&M University, Hampton University, Howard University, Morgan State University, Norfolk State University, North Carolina A&T State University, Prairie View A&M University, Texas Southern University, and Tuskegee University are in the forefront of such cutting-edge technologies as biotechnology, nanomaterials, and those related to the exploration of outer space, to name but three. At the same time, HBCUs have not turned their backs on the past; they continue to conduct research related to agriculture, the first stage of biotechnology. The 1890 land-grant institutions, which were founded as a means of providing black students with the opportunity to make farming more productive and profitable, continue to conduct research in areas such as aquaculture, forest management, pesticide development, land management and reclamation, and animal husbandry. These institutions include Alabama A&M University, Delaware State University, Florida A&M University, Fort Valley State University, Jackson State University, Kentucky State University, Langston University, Lincoln University of Missouri, North Carolina A&T State University, Prairie View A&M University, South Carolina State University, Southern University, Tennessee State University, Tuskegee University, the University of Arkansas at Pine Bluff, the University of Maryland Eastern Shore, Virginia State University, and West Virginia State University. The Tuskegee School of Veterinary Medicine is the only HBCU that conducts extensive research in areas related to veterinary medicine. Medical research has been the specialty of the four historically black medical colleges still in existence—Charles R. Drew University of Medicine and Science, Howard University College of Medicine, Meharry Medical College, and the Morehouse School of Medicine—and Xavier University of Louisiana is well known for its research programs in the pharmaceutical sciences.

Historically black hospitals were established for two reasons. One was to provide African Americans with the best possible health care, something they could scarcely hope to receive from a white-majority hospital that segregated its black patients and often provided them with minimal care. The other was to provide black physicians, surgeons, and nurses with a venue where they could learn and practice medicine. The most important of these hospitals were Freedmen's Hospital in Washington, D.C., Harlem Hospital in New York City, Homer G. Phillips Hospital in St. Louis, Mercy-Douglass Hospital in Philadelphia, and Provident Hospital in Chicago. These hospitals, and the other historically black hospitals in communities across the nation, provided a great many of the early black physicians and surgeons with their earliest training. These hospitals also served as laboratories for blacks who wished to conduct medical research, and a great many of the medical contributions of black medical researchers were made at these hospitals.

As the black hospital furthered the careers of black medical researchers, so too did the black professional scientific association further the careers of other black scientists. Some of the more important black professional scientific associations are the Association of Black Anthropologists, the Association of Black Cardiologists, the Association of Black Psychologists, Black Entomologists, the Black Psychiatrists of America, the National Association of Black Geologists and Geophysicists, the National Association of Minority Medical Educators, the National Dental Association, the National Medical Association, the National Organization for the Professional Advancement of Black Chemists and Chemical Engineers, the National Society of Black Physicists, the Network of Minority Research Investigators, the NIH Black Scientists Association, the Society of Black Academic Surgeons, and the Student National Medical Association. These groups were formed because the relevant nonminority professional scientific associations either did not admit blacks to membership or the associations did not sufficiently address the needs and concerns of its black members. During the 1960s, the nonminority associations began changing their attitudes toward black scientists, but the black associations persisted—indeed, they became stronger—because they continued to sustain and nurture their members by providing professional development opportunities such as mentoring and networking. Black professional scientific associations also work to increase their numbers by encouraging black students to become scientists. Many black youths dream of becoming scientists, but all too often they give up that dream when they fail to see other blacks practicing as scientists, either as teachers or as researchers. Thus, the black professional scientific associations seek to reassure black youths that they too can become scientists by visiting schools, hosting science enrichment programs, and funding scholarships.

Ever since the 1960s, nonminority professional scientific associations have become increasingly interested in attracting black scientists to their ranks. This change in attitude is due in no small part to the fact that the racist attitudes that caused them to exclude black members before have largely been laid to rest. Also spurring their interest in promoting the careers of black scientists, however, is the fact that the United States needs to recruit more scientists if it is to maintain its leadership position among the scientific nations of the world. To this end, the nonminority professional scientific associations seek to recruit all students who are capable of practicing science, regardless of race or any other criteria, to careers in science, also by visiting schools, hosting science enrichment programs, and funding scholarships. The nonminority professional scientific associations most interested in promoting science careers among minorities are the American Association for the Advancement of Science, the American Association for Cancer Research, the American Chemical Society, the American College of Veterinary Pathology, the American Dental Education Association, the American Geological Institute, the American Institute of Biological Sciences, the American Medical Association, the American Medical Student Association, the American Physical Society, the American Psychological Association, the American Society for Cell Biology, the American Society for Microbiology, the Association of American Medical Colleges, the Biophysical Society, the Endocrine Society, the Federation of American Societies for Experimental Biology, and the Society for Neuroscience.

Joining the black and nonminority professional scientific associations in the effort to recruit, train, and retain blacks and other minorities into careers in science are a number of advocacy groups. Such groups include the Alfred P. Sloan Foundation; Building Engineering and Science Talent; the Camille and Henry Dreyfus Foundation; Delta Sigma Theta; the Dental Pipeline; the Development Fund for Black Students in Science and Technology; the Diversity Institute; the Environmental Careers Organization; the Ford Foundation Diversity Fellowships program; the Gates Millennium Scholars program; the Health Professionals for

Diversity Coalition; the Historically Black College and University/Minority Institution Environmental Technology Consortium; the Leadership Alliance; MESA USA; the Meyerhoff Scholars Program; Minorities in Agriculture, Natural Resources and Related Sciences; the Minority Environmental Leadership Development Initiative; the National Association for Equal Opportunity in Higher Education; the National Coalition of Underrepresented Racial and Ethnic Groups in Engineering and Science; the National Consortium for Graduate Degrees for Minorities in Engineering and Science; the Partnership for Minority Advancement in the Biomolecular Sciences; the Pfizer Medical Humanities Initiative; the Quality Education for Minorities Network; Significant Opportunities in Atmospheric Research and Science; the Southern Regional Education Board; the Star Schools Program; the Thurgood Marshall College Fund; the United Negro College Fund Special Programs Corporation; and the Ventures Scholars Program. Most of these groups arose during or after the 1960s in response to increased awareness regarding racism and its effects that took place during the Civil Rights Movement.

A major partner in the effort to increase the number of black scientists is the federal government. Since the 1860s, the federal government has been a proponent of equal opportunity for African Americans, and that commitment has continued into the 21st century. The federal agencies most involved in recruiting, training, and retaining black scientists are the National Aeronautics and Space Administration, the National Institutes of Health, the National Science Foundation, and the Department of Energy. These agencies are in the forefront of the nation's efforts to fund educational and training opportunities for qualified black students, to hire them into positions where they can make the most of their education and training, and to provide professional development opportunities for black scientists throughout their careers.

Alabama A&M University

Alabama A&M University is Alabama's historically black land-grant university. In terms of scientific research, the school is best known for the work being done at its School of Agriculture and Environmental Sciences.

Alabama A&M was established in 1873, when the Alabama state legislature funded a "Colored Normal School at Huntsville" for the training of black teachers. By 1885, when the name was changed to State Normal and Industrial School of Huntsville, the curriculum had been expanded to include courses in industrial training. In 1890, the school became a land-grant college, and its site was designated as the town of Normal. In 1896, the name was changed to the State Agricultural and Mechanical College for Negroes, and in 1949, the school became known as Alabama A&M College. In 1969, it attained university status and acquired its present name.

The School of Agriculture and Environmental Sciences (SAES) operates a number of research centers, including the Center for Environmental Research and Training; the Center for Forestry and Ecology; the Center for Molecular Biology; the Plant Science Center; the Small Farm Research Center; the Food Safety and Nutrition Research Center; the Small Ruminant Research Center; and the Center for Hydrology, Soil Climatology and Remote Sensing. In addition, the school operates the Winfred Thomas Agricultural Research Center as a laboratory for the other centers, as well as a demonstration farm for Alabama farmers.

The Center for Environmental Research and Training is focused on research related to soil. Some projects address the chemical composition of soil, as well as its creation and transformation by natural and human activities. Other projects study how soil's ability to produce crops is affected by pollutants and toxic substances and how best to rid it of such substances. The center also conducts research involving water, such as how to improve its quality, how it moves through soil, and how best to safeguard wetlands.

The Center for Forestry and Ecology focuses on how to make hardwood forests more productive through the application of science. To this end, research projects address the genetics of hardwood species, the use of cloning to propagate the species, the use of biotechnology to develop new products from hardwoods, and the ecology and management of hardwood stands. Other research projects include forest protection, wildlife and ecosystem management, and integrated pest management.

The Center for Molecular Biology studies the genetics of the crops, trees, and native flora that thrive in northern Alabama and the microbes that interact with them. The Plant Science Center studies the physiology, genetics, and pathology of plants with an interest in improving methods for breeding, growing, and developing cropping systems for crops of interest to the region. The Small Farm Research Center helps small and limited resource farms sustain their operations so as to maintain the economic viability of rural communities in Alabama. Research areas include the development of alternative crops and livestock, as well as sustainable agriculture systems.

The Food Safety and Nutrition Research Center experiments with irradiation, which is the exposure to radiation as a way to preserve the freshness, nutritional content, and appealing sight and smell of poultry and to reduce the microbial levels in raw processed meats. The center also develops nutritious and safe food products from peanuts and cereals, and it seeks to understand the relationship between diet and other factors related to degenerative health and aging.

The Small Ruminant Research Center conducts basic and applied research on sheep, goats, and rabbits. Studies address breeding and genetics, feeding and nutrition, diseases and parasitism, physiology and endocrinology, and management and production studies.

The Center for Hydrology, Soil Climatology and Remote Sensing focuses on developing techniques for using data acquired by satellite and airborne microwave detection devices to measure moisture levels in soil and crops. It also uses such data to interpret and map natural resource management applications related to crop and watershed management.

The experiments and demonstrations of the Winfred Thomas Agriculture Research Center are designed to improve agricultural production and promote responsible resource management for farmers in northern Alabama. The center grows and experiments with wheat, soybeans, corn, sorghum, legumes, and triticale (a wheat-rye hybrid), and it tests various production and management techniques for livestock, including beef cattle, sheep, and goats. Other projects address the production of Christmas trees, biofuel, and other alternative crops. SAES scientists also use the center as a laboratory for many of their own experiments.

REFERENCES AND FURTHER READING

Alabama A&M University, School of Agricultural and Environmental Sciences. "Agricultural Research Centers." [Online article or information; retrieved October 29, 2007.] http://saes.aamu.edu/Research/AgResearchProgram. html.

Alabama A&M University. "Welcome to Alabama A&M University." [Online article or information; retrieved January 11, 2007] http://www.aamu.edu/.

Alabama State University

Alabama State University is one of many historically black colleges and universities located in Alabama. In terms of science, the school is best known for its research in physiology.

Alabama State was originally founded in Marion, Alabama, as the Lincoln Normal School, which specialized in training black teachers. In 1874, the name was changed to the State Normal School and University for the Education of the Colored Teachers and Students. In 1887, the school relocated to Montgomery, and two years later its name was changed again, this time to the Normal School for Colored Students. In 1929, the school was designated as State Teachers College; it awarded its first bachelor's degree two years later and its first master's degree in 1943. In 1948, it was renamed Alabama State College for Negroes, but six years later the last two words were dropped. In 1969, it attained university status and its present name.

Although Alabama State faculty and students conduct scientific research in a number of disciplines, their most prominent work is in the field of animal and human physiology. This research is made possible by funding from the National Science Foundation's Research Infrastructure in Minority Institutions (RIMI) Program. The purpose of RIMI is to provide historically black colleges and universities with the resources and technical assistance they require to train minority students to become scientists.

As of 2006, Alabama State researchers were investigating at least three areas in physiology. The first involved signaling in the mammalian vomeronasal organ, a sensory organ in the nose that helps identify the chemical substances known as pheromones. These substances are known to play a role in the reproductive behavior of mammals; for example, in the case of boars, it is known that certain pheromones in male boar urine stimulate the production in juvenile female boars of biomedical compounds that make them receptive to a male's advances, but exactly how all this happens remains unknown. Alabama State researchers are attempting to identify the precise cellular pathway by which the vomeronasal system works.

Two other RIMI-funded projects involve the roles played by various genes in the development and operation of the human immune system. One project investigates how the genes known as Hoxa3 and Pax1 affect the development of the thymus in the fetus. Located in the upper portion of the chest cavity, the thymus plays an important role in the development of a young human's immune system. The thymus, which is replaced with fat after puberty, selects the various lymphocytes (the cells that fight against infection and other invaders of the body). Alabama State researchers are particularly interested in learning how the two genes work together in the development of the fetal thymus. The other project involves the development of a vaccine against human respiratory syncytial virus (RSV). RSV, which belongs to the same family of viruses that cause measles and mumps, causes respiratory infections. Generally speaking, its symptoms are similar to those caused by the common cold, but in certain patients with autoimmune deficiencies, RSV can cause wheezing, asthma, and death. The project seeks to develop a vaccine for RSV by rearranging certain RSV genes so that they produce a protein that negates the virus's ability to infect a host organism.

See also: Research Infrastructure in Minority Institutions

REFERENCES AND FURTHER READING

Alabama State University. "Research Infrastructure in Minority Institutions at Alabama State University." [Online article or information; retrieved October 29, 2007.] http://www.alasu.edu/RIMI.

Alabama State University. "Welcome to Alabama State University." [Online article or information; retrieved August 24, 2006.] http://www.alasu.edu/.

Alfred P. Sloan Foundation

The Alfred P. Sloan Foundation is a philanthropic nonprofit institution with a strong interest in science and technology. As part of its commitment to enhancing science and science education in the United States, the foundation funds several initiatives aimed at making the world of American science more diverse.

The foundation was established in 1934 by Alfred Pritchard Sloan Jr., at the time the president and chief executive officer of the General Motors Corporation. As of 2007, the foundation's programs and interests focused on several areas: science and technology, standard of living and economic performance, education and careers in science and technology, and other selected national issues such as bioterrorism, federal statistics, and universal access to recorded knowledge. The foundation maintains a professional staff at its permanent headquarters in New York City. In terms of diversity, the foundation funds several studies designed to identify ways to attract and retain more African Americans and other underrepresented minorities into careers as scientists and science educators.

The Sloan Project for Diversity in STEM Retention grew out of the recognition that most programs for retaining minority students in academic programs leading to careers as scientists fail to understand why minority students drop out of science programs in the first place. For example, most retention programs assume that retention is best achieved by providing minorities with more minority role models or with better access to science and mathematics courses in grades K–12 when, in fact, no empirical evidence exists to show that either approach achieves measurable results. Consequently, the Sloan Project, which is conducted by the Center for Education and Work at the University of Wisconsin–Madison, investigates the academic and career development of minority undergraduates majoring in one of the STEM disciplines (science, technology, engineering, or mathematics) in an effort to understand why—or why not—they choose to pursue their studies to the point of earning a degree, all with an eye toward improving the effectiveness of existing retention programs. As of 2007, the project was still underway, but an interesting finding is that, contrary to popular belief, minorities are just as interested in STEM careers as nonminorities are but that their expectations of actually being able to achieve an education in a STEM field and then make a living in that field are significantly lower than for nonminorities. Another is that many minority STEM undergraduates attending nonminority-serving institutions feel isolated, lonely, and unwelcome and that many of them regretted the lack of opportunities to interact in a meaningful way, both socially and academically, with their nonminority classmates.

The foundation funds another initiative designed to increase the number of African Americans and other underrepresented minorities in the sciences and other STEM disciplines: the Minority PhD Program. Established in 1995 and administered by the National Action Council for Minorities in Engineering, this program offers eligible doctoral candidates the opportunity to pursue their PhD degrees with financial, mentoring, and guidance support through recognized participating faculty and departments approved by the foundation. The

Alfred P. Sloan founded the Alfred P. Sloan Foundation, a philanthropic organization that funds projects designed to recruit and retain more African Americans in careers related to science. (Library of Congress)

ultimate goal of the program is to increase the number of minorities receiving a PhD in a STEM discipline by 100 per year, but the program also supports students working toward a BS or MS degree at select departments that have demonstrated success at preparing students for doctoral work. Between 1995 and 2005, the program provided more than $5 million in direct support to almost 600 students.

The foundation also funds a number of smaller initiatives to increase the participation of minority scientists in scientific research projects of importance. Perhaps the most significant of these initiatives is the Gordon Research Conferences' Carl Storm Underrepresented Minority Fellowship. The Gordon Conferences serve as forums for the presentation and discussion of cutting-edge research in biology, chemistry, and physics, and the Storm Fellowship provides minority scientists with the financial support to attend their first Gordon Conference.

See also: Gordon Research Conferences

REFERENCES AND FURTHER READING

Alfred P. Sloan Foundation. "Programs: Education and Careers in Science and Technology." [Online article or information; retrieved May 21, 2007.] http://www.sloan.org/programs/pg_education.shtml.

Alfred P. Sloan Foundation. "Welcome." [Online article or information; retrieved October 29, 2007.] http://www.sloan.org/main.shtml.

American Association for the Advancement of Science

The American Association for the Advancement of Science (AAAS) is an international nonprofit organization dedicated to advancing science around the world. Founded in 1848, AAAS serves as a professional organization for scientists of every discipline, but it also educates the general public and advises government on issues of public policy concerning science. It publishes a number of scientific newsletters, books, and reports, including the journal *Science*, and conducts programs designed to promote a better understanding of science worldwide. One of the goals of its Directorate of Education and Human Resources is to bring more minorities into the sciences as students, teachers, and researchers.

One AAAS initiative for promoting diversity in the sciences is the Minority Writers Internship. Since 2004, two undergraduates who aspire to be science writers are hired to work as summer interns at *Science*. Under the guidance of the journal's writers and editors, they help gather information for news stories, attend scientific meetings and congressional hearings, and work on their own stories for the journal or for *Science Now*, the daily online news service of *Science*. The program is an attempt to expand the diversity of science reporting, as minorities constitute only a small fraction of the science writing community. AAAS sees diversifying this community as a necessary step toward helping minorities think about the social implications of the latest scientific developments, thus leading more minority students to decide on careers as scientists. The Minority Writers Internship is an offshoot of AAAS's Mass Media Science and Engineering Fellowship Program, a 10-week summer program that places graduate and postgraduate science, engineering, and mathematics students with media organizations nationwide.

Another AAAS diversity initiative is the Minority Scientists Network. The network is a collaborative effort between Education and Human Resources and ScienceCareers.org, AAAS's Web site for matching qualified scientists with jobs in industry, academia, and government. The network is specifically designed to help minority scientists further their careers in science.

AAAS also works for diversity by studying ways to better integrate minorities into the scientific community and workplace. For example, in 2006 AAAS released a report titled "Preparing Women and Minorities for the IT Workplace: The Role of Nontraditional Educational Pathways." The study was prompted by the discovery that the top producer of bachelor's degrees in information technology and computer sciences (IT/CS) in the Washington, D.C., metropolitan area, as well as the top producer of African Americans with IT/CS degrees, was not a four-year, government-supported research university but rather Strayer University, a privately owned and operated institution with multiple campuses. The study found that a significant number of black students receiving degrees in IT/CS are nontraditional students who were attracted to Strayer, because it offers virtually all of its courses at night, thus allowing students to work full time while studying part time. Traditional four-year programs, on the other hand, generally do not allow students this luxury. In light of this finding, the study recommended that, among other things, government and philanthropic sponsors of IT/CS education curricula reexamine their relative lack of support for IT/CS training at two-year colleges and proprietary schools, because these institutions attract a larger number of nontraditional students who have a greater tendency to be a minority and who constitute a growing number of IT/CS graduates.

In conjunction with Delta Sigma Theta Sorority, a national organization composed mostly of college-educated African American women, AAAS developed and implemented the Delta SEE (Science and Everyday Experiences) Initiative, an informal science education project funded by the National Science Foundation. This project is designed to help parents and caregivers of black children in grades K–8 help their children develop a better understanding of and appreciation for a career as a scientist. The project includes the *Delta SEE Connection*, a series of radio interviews with African American role models who are professionals in the fields of science, technology, engineering, or mathematics.

Following the 2003 school year, AAAS assumed responsibility for administering the Graduate Scholars Program of the David and Lucile Packard Foundation. The program provides financial support to graduates of historically black colleges and universities (HBCUs) who are pursuing doctoral degrees in the sciences, mathematics, and engineering. The program was established in 1992 as a complement to the foundation's HBCU Science Program, which was established in 1987 to improve the quality of undergraduate science and mathematics instruction at HBCUs and thereby increase the number of graduates who are prepared to move into leadership positions in their chosen fields.

See also: Delta Sigma Theta Sorority; Historically Black Colleges and Universities; National Science Foundation

References and Further Reading
American Association for the Advancement of Science. "AAAS: Advancing Science, Serving Society." [Online article or information; retrieved June 30, 2006.] http://www.aaas.org.

American Association for Cancer Research

The American Association for Cancer Research (AACR) is the oldest and largest scientific organization in the United States that focuses primarily on treating and curing cancer. The association serves as a clearinghouse of knowledge and ideas for cancer researchers, informs the general public about the latest developments in the treatment of cancer, and provides training opportunities for researchers who are new to the field. As part of its mission, AACR supports the recruitment and career development of minority scientists via Minorities in Cancer Research (MICR), a membership body within the association.

AACR was founded in 1907 by a group of 11 physicians and medical researchers who wanted to develop a better understanding of what causes cancer and how best to treat it. As of its hundredth anniversary in 2007, the association maintained a professional staff and a permanent headquarters in Philadelphia, and its annual meeting drew more than 17,000 medical professionals from around the country. The association convenes scientific conferences and workshops, publishes five scientific journals for researchers and a magazine for cancer survivors and their families and physicians, and offers fellowships and grants to cancer researchers who are just beginning their careers. As a means of supporting and advancing the careers of minority researchers, MICR was established in 2000 to act as an advisory body to the AACR board of directors. MICR seeks to increase the number, participation, visibility, and recognition of minority cancer researchers, to develop programs that address their needs, to provide diversity within AACR's programs and committees, and to address the disparities in cancer incidence and mortality faced by minorities.

To date, MICR has focused its efforts on making the AACR annual meeting and special conferences more accessible to minority researchers, as well as more responsive to their needs as researchers. At each AACR annual meeting, MICR presents a panel discussion and a scientific symposium that relate to the concerns of minority investigators. For example, at the 2007 meeting, the forum and the symposium addressed whether the genetic variations among races and ethnicities are sufficient to affect the efficacy of certain cancer treatments, such as certain chemotherapeutic drugs, and, if so, how these variations should influence the planning and selection of cancer therapy for populations, such as in the United States, that are ethnically diverse. The Minority-Serving Institution Faculty Scholar Awards provide financial support for faculty members at historically black colleges and universities (HBCUs) and other minority-serving institutions to participate in the annual meeting and special conferences. These awards increase the scientific knowledge base of the recipients while encouraging them and their students to pursue careers in cancer research. The Minority Scholar Awards provide the same level of support to minority researchers not affiliated with a minority-serving institution. MICR also sponsors the AACR-MIRC Jane Cooke Wright Lectureship; established in 2006 and named in honor of the famous African American cancer researcher who helped pioneer the field of chemotherapy, the lectureship recognizes an outstanding scientist who has contributed to the field of cancer research and who has, through leadership or by example, furthered the advancement of minority investigators in cancer research. In addition to receiving a cash award, the recipient is invited to give a lecture at the annual meeting.

One of MICR's most popular offerings is the Professional Development Roundtable. Presented at every annual meeting, the roundtable addresses such issues as career development and advancement, mentoring, and networking. This interactive session provides a forum in which students, postdoctoral graduates, and junior faculty can discuss important career development issues and survival skills with established senior scientists.

See also: Cancer; Historically Black Colleges and Universities; Wright, Jane C.

REFERENCES AND FURTHER READING

American Association for Cancer Research. "American Association for Cancer Research." [Online article or information; retrieved October 29, 2007.] http://www.aacr.org/default.aspx.

American Association for Cancer Research. "Minorities in Cancer Research." [Online article or information; retrieved April 30, 2007.] http://www.aacr.org/home/membership-/association-groups/minorities-in-cancer-research.aspx.

American Chemical Society

The American Chemical Society (ACS) is the leading professional association of chemists and chemical engineers in the United States. The society's Committee on Minority Affairs pursues several initiatives to bring more African Americans and other underrepresented minorities into the chemical sciences, the most important of which is the ACS Scholars Program.

The ACS was founded in 1876 to represent the professional interests of chemists and chemical engineers. By 2007, its membership had grown to more than 160,000. It maintains a professional staff and a permanent headquarters in Washington, D.C., and its programs and activities cover a broad range of professional and scientific interests. Long before that date, however, the ACS had become aware that, in order to ensure that the American economic and academic sectors would have all the chemists they would need in the future, efforts would have to be made to recruit chemists from the ranks of groups that had not historically produced a significant number of chemists. To this end, the Committee on Minority Affairs (CMA) was established to help increase the number of African Americans and other minorities receiving the basic education, encouragement, and support they needed to become professional chemists and chemical engineers.

The CMA promotes the recognition of the professional accomplishments of minorities, works to attract minority students to the profession, identifies minority-friendly educational institutions and businesses, works for the increased participation of minority chemical professionals at all levels in the

ACS, provides mentoring to minority students, and compiles best practices for the recruitment, retention, career development, and evaluation of programs for the advancement of minorities. Its Minority Affairs Program addresses three areas: student programs, member programs, and collaborations with minority advocacy organizations.

The major activity of the Minority Affairs Program is the ACS Scholars Program. Established in 1994, this program provides scholarships for minority applicants seeking a bachelor's degree in chemistry, biochemistry, or chemical engineering or a two-year degree in chemical technology. The scholarships are awarded to high school seniors who plan to major in one of the chemical sciences in college and to college freshmen, sophomores, and juniors who are majoring in chemistry, biochemistry, chemical engineering, environmental science, materials science, toxicology, or chemical technology. Individual scholarships provide up to $3,000 per academic year and are renewable as long as the recipient remains eligible for the scholarship. To help recipients succeed, every effort is made to pair each student with a mentor, usually either a professor or professional chemist, at or near the college the student attends. Since the program's inception, it has awarded more than 900 scholarships to African Americans; to date, more than 400 of them have graduated and are either in graduate school or working in a career related to chemistry. The scholarships are funded by contributions from hundreds of corporations and organizations with an interest in the future of chemistry; major contributors include the PPG Industries Foundation, the Camille and Henry Dreyfus Foundation, Glaxo-SmithKline, and Procter & Gamble. In 2007, it was estimated that the program had distributed approximately $5.5 million in scholarships during its existence. The ACS Scholars Program won the 1997 American Society of Association Executives Award of Excellence and the 2001 Presidential Award for Excellence in Science, Mathematics, and Engineering Mentoring.

The CMA presents various programs that are designed to increase the participation of minority members in the workings of the ACS. Workshops are presented at the national and regional meetings that encourage members to recruit and retain minorities and then mentor them so that they can play an active role in the affairs of the ACS. The committee also presents two awards in recognition of outstanding achievements in terms of promoting diversity within the chemistry community. The ACS Award for Encouraging Disadvantaged Students into Careers in the Chemical Sciences, which is sponsored by the Camille and Henry Dreyfus Foundation, recognizes individuals who have promoted the professional development of minorities as chemists or chemical engineers at the national level. The Stanley C. Israel Regional Award for Advancing Diversity in the Chemical Sciences recognizes individuals or institutions that have advanced diversity in the chemical sciences at the regional level.

The American Chemical Society Scholars Program pairs promising students like Jacqueline Smith (right) with mentors like Sylvester Mosley (left). (American Chemical Society/Elizabeth Woodwell)

The CMA works closely with other professional organizations that promote and support careers for minorities in the chemical sciences. In particular, the committee cosponsors activities with the National Organization for the Professional Advancement of Black Chemists and Chemical Engineers, such as receptions honoring African Americans who have received awards for scientific achievements and programs to encourage African American high school and college students to consider careers in the chemical sciences.

See also: Biochemistry; Camille and Henry Dreyfus Foundation; Chemistry; National Organization for the Professional Advancement of Black Chemists and Chemical Engineers

REFERENCES AND FURTHER READING

American Chemical Society. "ACS Department of Diversity Programs." [Online article or information; retrieved April 23, 2007.] http://portal.acs.org/portal/acs/corg/content?_nfpb=true&_pageLabel=PP_TRANSITIONMAIN&node_id=1166&use_sec=false&sec_url_var=region1.

American Chemical Society. "American Chemical Society." [Online article or information; retrieved October 29, 2007.] https://portal.acs.org/portal/acs/corg/memberapp.

American College of Veterinary Pathologists

The American College of Veterinary Pathologists (ACVP) is a professional organization that represents the interests of veterinary pathologists (doctors of veterinary medicine who specialize in the diagnosis and characterization of veterinary diseases through the examination of animal tissue and body fluids). As a means of attracting more African Americans and other underrepresented minorities to the field of veterinary pathology, the organization sponsors the ACVP/Pfizer Minority Fellowship in Veterinary Pathology.

The ACVP was founded in 1949. Its overall mission is to improve and protect both human and animal life by arriving at a better understanding of the diseases that affect animals and how those diseases can sometimes affect humans. As of 2007, the organization's members numbered more than 1,500; all members possess a degree in veterinary medicine and at least three years of postveterinary training, while many also hold doctorates in toxicology, molecular biology, or a related field. The organization also sponsors student chapters at more than 31 schools of veterinary medicine—including the nation's only historically black veterinary school, the Tuskegee School of Veterinary Medicine—throughout the United States and Canada. ACVP maintains a permanent headquarters in Madison, Wisconsin.

ACVP sponsors a number of programs to ensure that the veterinary scientists of the future receive proper training, one of which is the ACVP/Pfizer Minority Fellowship in Veterinary Pathology. The fellowship is funded by Pfizer, Inc., one of the world's leading developers and manufacturers of pharmaceutical drugs for the treatment of veterinary diseases, and it funds postdoctoral training for one minority student per year. ACVP/Pfizer fellows conduct postdoctoral research pertaining to veterinary pathology for three or more months in a Pfizer laboratory under the direction of a pathologist on the Pfizer scientific staff, and they spend the rest of their year studying anatomic or clinical veterinary pathology at an approved graduate program at a U.S. research university. To be eligible for the fellowship, an applicant must hold a doctorate of veterinary medicine (DVM). At the conclusion of their sponsored research, fellows are encouraged to publish the results in the organization's journal, *Veterinary Pathology*, and to present it at the organization's annual meeting. Each fellow receives $50,000 to be used for tuition, fees, publication costs, travel to the ACVP annual meeting, other educational expenses, and general living expenses. In certain cases, a fellowship may be renewed for an additional one or two years.

See also: Tuskegee School of Veterinary Medicine

REFERENCES AND FURTHER READING

American College of Veterinary Pathologists. "American College of Veterinary Pathologists." [Online article or information; retrieved October 29, 2007.] http://www.acvp.org/.

American College of Veterinary Pathologists. "Minority Fellowship." [Online article or information; retrieved June 11, 2007.] http://www.acvp.org/training/pfizer.php.

American Dental Education Association

The American Dental Education Association (ADEA) is the largest professional organization in the United States and Canada that represents exclusively the interests of the 66 dental schools in those two countries plus thousands of advanced dental education programs and hospital dental training programs. In addition to conducting a number of diversity programs through its Center for Equity and Diversity, ADEA administers two grant programs for increasing diversity in dental education, the Minority Dental Faculty Development Program and the Access to Dental Careers Program.

ADEA was founded in 1923 in Omaha, Nebraska, when four associations—the American Institute of Dental Teachers, the National Association of Dental Faculties, the Dental Faculties' Association of American Universities, and the Canadian Dental Faculties Association—decided to amalgamate into one body. The association was known as the American Association of Dental Schools until 2003, when it took on its present name. As of 2007, ADEA maintained a professional staff at its permanent headquarters in Washington, D.C.

In 1993, ADEA made a commitment to address diversity issues within the field of dental education by establishing the forerunner of what is now its Center for Equity and Diversity. Since then, the center has implemented several initiatives to recruit and retain more African Americans and other underrepresented minorities to careers in dentistry. In 1994, it conducted its first biennial National Minority Recruitment and Retention Conference. These conferences, sponsored by Procter & Gamble, seek to strengthen the U.S.–Canadian network of minority recruitment officers and to improve current programs for recruiting and retaining minority dental students. The center conducts regional workshops for predental advisors who belong to the National Association of Advisors of the Health Professions and others who recruit students for dental schools. It also publishes *Opportunities for Minority Students in U.S. Dental Schools, 5th* ed., American Dental Education Association, Washington, DC, 2006–2008, a biennial publication designed to attract minority students to careers in dentistry by informing them of the scholarships and other programs available at schools that are particularly interested in addressing the issue of diversity in dentistry. Lastly, the center oversees ADEA's participation in the Summer Medical and Dental Education Program (SMDEP), a six-week medical and dental school preparatory program. Founded in 1988 by the Robert Wood Johnson Foundation as the Minority Medical Education Program, SMDEP was taken over in 1993 by ADEA and the

The American Dental Education Association funds the Summer Medical and Dental Education Program to attract minority students, such as these at the University of Louisville, to careers in dentistry. (American Dental Education Association)

American Association of Medical Colleges, and it acquired its present name in 2003. Students accepted into the program attend academic enrichment sessions on organic chemistry, physics, biology, mathematics, writing, and public speaking. They also attend seminars and workshops on learning and study skills, individual and group learning, career development, and financial planning, and they receive a certain amount of exposure to clinical practice. Room, board, tuition, and course materials are paid for in full by the program. SMDEP grants are made to participating schools in the amount of $300,000 per year for four years; as of 2007, 12 schools were participating in the dental portion of the program.

In 2004, ADEA established the Minority Dental Faculty Development (MDFD) Program, which seeks to increase the number of minority faculty members at dental schools. That same year, MDFD, which is funded by the W. K. Kellogg Foundation, awarded seven grants for $250,000 apiece over the course of six years to the dental schools of the University of Oklahoma, the University of Michigan, the University of Alabama, Texas A&M University, the University of Illinois at Chicago, Howard University, and a consortium of dental schools in New York. The grants finance educational assistance programs for minority students and facilitate the training and career development of minority faculty members.

The Access to Dental Careers Program was the vehicle by which ADEA participated in the Robert Wood Johnson Foundation's Dental Pipeline. Between 2001 and 2006, this project implemented programs at 15 dental schools in the United States to reduce oral health disparities by recruiting and retaining more minorities to become dentists.

See also: Association of American Medical Colleges; Biology; Chemistry; Dental Pipeline; Howard University; Physics

REFERENCES AND FURTHER READING

American Dental Education Association. "American Dental Education Association." [Online article or information; retrieved October 29, 2007.] http://www.adea.org/.

American Dental Education Association. "Center for Equity and Diversity." [Online article or information; retrieved May 26, 2007.] http://www.adea.org/ced/default.htm.

American Geological Institute

The American Geological Institute (AGI) is a nonprofit federation of 44 professional associations (for example, the American Association of Petroleum Geologists, the National Association of Earth Science Teachers, and the Paleontological Research Institute) that represents more than 120,000 geologists, geophysicists, and other earth scientists. As part of the institute's commitment to make it possible for the maximum amount of people to embark upon careers in the geosciences, AGI administers the Minority Participation Program (MPP), which provides scholarships to African Americans, Hispanics, and other groups that are underrepresented in the geosciences.

AGI was founded in 1948 to serve the U.S. geoscience community. The organization works to enhance the professional development of the members of its member societies, serves as a link between the geoscience community and the federal government, and supports the educational, scientific, and charitable activities that benefit the entire geoscience community. AGI maintains a professional staff at its permanent headquarters in Alexandria, Virginia.

MPP was originated in 1972 in response to a growing awareness among geoscientists that their profession lacked racial and ethnic diversity; for example, less than 1 percent of all geoscientists were African American. The program's goal is to foster diversity by recruiting promising minority students and providing them with the financial assistance and mentoring they need to earn a degree and obtain a career in one of the geosciences. Recipients of AGI Minority Geoscience Scholarships are provided with financial awards ranging from $500 to $3,000 per year. Perhaps more important, MPP participants are given the opportunity to be mentored by a member of the MPP advisory committee, whose ranks are split about evenly among those who work in academia, government, and private industry. Such mentoring is crucial to making the successful transition from student to professional geoscientist.

In 2005–2006, MPP awarded scholarship funds to 27 students. Since the program's inception, more than 950 minority scholars have received millions of dollars from MPP. Much of the money for the scholarships has been provided by corporations with a vested interest in recruiting and hiring the brightest geoscientists they can find, regardless of race or ethnicity. These corporations include Exxon Mobil, Conoco Phillips, Chevron Texaco, and Marathon. Another major contributor to MPP's scholarship fund is the Seismological Society of America.

REFERENCES AND FURTHER READING

American Geological Institute. "American Geological Institute." [Online article or information; retrieved June 28, 2006.] http://www.agiweb.org/index.html.

American Institute of Biological Sciences

The American Institute of Biological Sciences (AIBS) is a nonprofit scientific organization dedicated to advancing biological research and education for the welfare of society. As part of its agenda, the organization develops programs that expand career, professional development, and service opportunities for minorities in the biological sciences.

AIBS was founded in 1947 as part of the National Academy of Sciences, but it became an independent organization shortly thereafter. As of 2007, it serves as an umbrella organization for more than 200 professional societies and scientific organizations, as well as for thousands of independent biologists. It seeks to provide services, support, and a voice for a variety of disciplines that are dedicated to research and education in biology. With a headquarters in Washington, D.C., and a professional staff of 50, AIBS promotes biological research nationally and internationally, provides scientific support services to governmental and private research and education programs, furnishes information about biological science to policy makers for better informed decisions, and publishes the peer-reviewed journal *BioScience* and the education Web site ActionBioscience.org. The organization also promotes the full participation of minorities in the biological sciences, and to this end, it sponsors several diversity programs, including the Diversity Leadership Award, the Diversity Scholars Program, and the Diversity in Biological Sciences (DIBS) coalition.

The Diversity Leadership Award was established to identify and publicize successful strategies for including more underrepresented minorities, women, and persons with disabilities in the biological sciences. Multiple awards are given each year to recognize programs that demonstrate outstanding creativity, commitment, and effectiveness in promoting diversity in biology. Nominations are solicited from scientific societies, elementary and secondary schools, colleges and universities, government entities, nonprofit organizations, and institutions such as museums and biological field stations.

The Diversity Scholars Program seeks to increase the participation of minority student biologists in AIBS programs and activities, while encouraging and supporting their professional careers. The awards are presented annually to minority graduate and undergraduate students in the biological sciences who have conducted biological research of interest to the AIBS community. Awards are presented based on the students' research experience and plans, career interests and goals, academic credentials, and letters of recommendation. Each Diversity Scholar receives $1,000 to cover the expenses of presenting their research at a meeting of one of the AIBS member societies. In addition, each receives a one-year paid membership in AIBS, and they are compensated for their traveling expenses to the annual AIBS meeting, at which they are honored. Diversity Scholars are encouraged to participate in AIBS programs and activities, to provide written feedback to the AIBS Education Office in order to share their experiences as Diversity Scholars, to contribute ideas for ongoing and future diversity programs and activities, to contribute to the AIBS diversity Web site, and to participate in the AIBS annual meeting.

The Diversity in Biological Sciences (DIBS) coalition seeks to build minority scientist networks that will link students and scientists in separate programs, thus creating more opportunities for minorities, women, and persons with disabilities in biology education and careers. As of 2007, DIBS members included representatives from AIBS, the American Association for the Advancement of Science, the Ecological Society of America, the National Council for Science and the Environment, the Quality Education for Minorities Network, the United Negro College Fund, EnvironMentors, and the National Environmental Education and Training Foundation.

See also: American Association for the Advancement of Science; Biology; Quality Education for Minorities Network; United Negro College Fund Special Programs Corporation

REFERENCES AND FURTHER READING

American Institute of Biological Sciences. "American Institute of Biological Sciences." [Online article or information; retrieved October 29, 2007.] http://www.aibs.org/core/index.html.

American Institute of Biological Sciences. "Diversity Programs and Resources." [Online article or information; retrieved January 22, 2007.] http://www.aibs.org/diversity.

American Medical Association

The American Medical Association (AMA) is the largest professional organization of physicians in the United States. Founded in 1847 as a vehicle for elevating the standard of medical education in the United States, today it represents the physician's point of view on all debates related to health care. As part of the AMA's mission to serve as an advocate for all doctors, its Minority Affairs Consortium (MAC) works to further the interests of physicians who are African American or members of other underrepresented minorities. Meanwhile, the AMA Foundation provides scholarships so that more minority students can afford to attend medical school.

An all-white organization for most of its existence, the AMA began developing a more enlightened approach to race relations in the 1960s as a result of the Civil Rights Movement. In 1963, it established a liaison with the National Medical Association, the nation's primary organization for black physicians. Five years later, the AMA declared its support for the end of racial discrimination in state and local medical societies and for increasing the number of blacks practicing medicine. In 1978, it called for policies that would increase the number of African American medical students to at least 10 percent of the total of all medical students, and in 1989, it began actively recruiting black physicians to become members of the AMA and to assume leadership roles within it. In 1992, the Advisory Committee on Minority Physicians (today the Minority Affairs Consortium) was formed to eliminate minority health disparities, educate physicians in the delivery of culturally effective health care, increase the number of blacks and other minorities in health care, and increase the membership and participation of minority physicians in organized medicine. In 2004, the AMA and the NMA agreed to cochair the Commission on Health Disparities for purposes of increasing awareness of health disparities, promoting better data gathering, promoting workforce diversity, and increasing education and training for minority medical practitioners.

Perhaps the most visible of the MAC's programs today is the Doctors Back to School Program. This program arranges for minority physicians to speak to minority students in elementary and middle schools about pursuing careers in medicine. Begun in 2002, the program is designed to help minority children realize that a need exists for more minority doctors and that they too could become physicians, surgeons, or other medical professionals. Following a short presentation by a minority physician from the local community, a typical program includes a question-and-answer period. Children frequently ask questions such as the following: "Do you have a family?" "How much money do you make?" "How do you deal with children who die?" "How long does it take to become a doctor?" "How much does it cost to become a doctor?" "What do you like most about being a doctor?" An evening's program might also include a medical terminology spelling bee, a medical scavenger hunt, and a demonstration of a piece of sophisticated medical equipment such as an EKG station to pique students' interest in a medical career. At the Daniel Hale Williams Preparatory School of Medicine in Chicago, a Doctors Back to School event in 2005 catalyzed the establishment of a Future Doctors of America Club for the school's middle and high school students.

The AMA Foundation offers several types of scholarships to African Americans and members of other underrepresented minorities to help them offset the expenses of medical school. In collaboration with MAC and with funding from the Pfizer Medical Humanities Initiative, the Foundation provides 10 Minority Scholars Awards annually. These awards are for $10,000 each and are given to medical students in their first or second year. The Physicians of Tomorrow Scholarships are presented to rising fourth-year students; funded in part by Wyeth Pharmaceuticals, by the Audio-Digest Foundation, by the Johnson F. Hammond, MD Fund, and by the Rock Sleyster, MD Fund, eight awards are made for $10,000 apiece.

See also: Daniel Hale Williams Preparatory School of Medicine; Health Disparities; National Medical Association; Pfizer Medical Humanities Initiative

REFERENCES AND FURTHER READING

American Medical Association. "AMA—Helping Doctors Help Patients." [Online article or information; retrieved October 29, 2007.] http://www.ama-assn.org/.

American Medical Association. "Minority Affairs Consortium." [Online article or information; retrieved April 26, 2007.] http://www.ama-assn.org/ama/pub/category/20.html.

American Medical Student Association

The American Medical Student Association (AMSA) is the largest association of medical students in the United States. As part of its commitment to making the medical profession as diverse as possible, AMSA sponsors the Achieving Diversity in Dentistry and Medicine (ADDM) Program.

AMSA was founded in 1950 as the student branch of the American Medical Association (AMA); its main purpose was to provide medical students the opportunity to participate in organized medicine. Over the next two decades, AMSA became considerably more interested in social issues and medical reform than the AMA, and in 1967, AMSA became an independent, student-governed organization. In 1975, the association took on its present name; today, its membership numbers 65,000, and it maintains a professional staff and a permanent headquarters in Washington, D.C.

AMSA's programming arm is the AMSA Foundation. It was founded in 1964 as a vehicle for addressing issues in medical education and making emergency loans to medical students. During the 1970s, it served as a prime recruiter for physicians to serve underrepresented minorities in the National Health Service Corps, the Bureau of Medical Services, and the Indian Health Service. Today, the foundation oversees programs that seek to eliminate health disparities, transform the culture of medicine, implement universal health care, and achieve greater diversity among the ranks of medical professionals. As part of its efforts concerning the last goal, the foundation conducts the ADDM Program. ADDM originated in 2003 as the result of a four-year contract awarded to the AMSA Foundation by the U.S. Department of Health and Human Services. The program focuses on four areas of concern: cultural competency, ethnogeriatrics, primary care leadership training, and bringing more minorities into the medical professions.

Cultural competency refers to the fact that one of the causes of health disparities is the degree to which race and ethnicity influence a person's perception of a given illness. This perception heavily influences that person's decisions regarding whether to seek health care and to what degree a physician's advice should be followed, particularly if the physician is of a different race or ethnicity. To help overcome this problem, ADDM sponsors the development of cultural competency curriculums in eight medical colleges and three dental schools. These curriculums make medical and dental students aware of how racial and ethnic differences can affect health care, and they help them learn how to communicate better about the causes and treatments of diseases and medical conditions with patients of different racial or ethnic backgrounds.

Ethnogeriatrics addresses the influence of race, culture, and ethnicity on the health and well-being of the elderly. Many ethnic older adults experience significant health disparities when compared with older adults in the general population. For instance, older African Americans are 40 percent more likely to suffer from heart disease than older whites. To address this problem, ADDM sponsors the development of ethnogeriatrics curriculums in five medical colleges and one dental school to help aspiring physicians and dentists better prepare for treating elderly patients regardless of their race or ethnicity.

Every year, the foundation sponsors the Primary Care Leadership Training Program. The program's 40 attendees receive one week of training on important issues in medical and dental primary care. In 2006, the program focused on educating medical and dental students about health disparities as they relate to the care of minority populations from the very young to the very old. Participants took part in interactive small-group discussions, met with community and academic leaders, completed hands-on projects, and learned how to develop and implement primary care projects for minority communities that are concerned about their relative lack of health care.

To help increase the number of African Americans and other underrepresented minorities pursuing careers in medicine, the foundation has developed a plan for widening the pipeline. This plan encourages medical and dental students to go out into their communities and give presentations to stimulate minority middle school and high school students to think about careers in medicine. Rather than develop a specific presentation, the foundation supports the use of a number of presentations and initiatives, such as the Kids Into Health Careers Initiative, MD Camp, and Junior Medical League, all of which have been developed by other organizations. Any medical or dental student making such a presentation may apply for financial aid from the foundation, which awards presenters up to $200 to cover the cost of materials and other expenses. The foundation also sponsors a Widening the Pipeline poster session at the AMSA national convention to encourage more dental and medical students to get involved in the program.

See also: American Medical Association; Health Disparities

REFERENCES AND FURTHER READING

American Medical Student Association. "Achieving Diversity in Dentistry and Medicine." [Online article or information; retrieved May 16, 2007.] http://www.amsa.org/addm/index.cfm.

American Medical Student Association. "American Medical Student Association." [Online article or information; retrieved October 29, 2007.] http://www.amsa.org/.

American Physical Society

The American Physical Society (APS) is the oldest professional organization in the United States devoted to advancing and diffusing a knowledge of, and an appreciation for, physics. Founded in 1899, APS holds scientific meetings, publishes several prestigious scholarly journals on physics, and advises the federal government regarding important issues related to national science policy. APS also conducts extensive programs in education and public outreach, including initiatives to end the lack of racial and ethnic diversity in the physical sciences. APS's primary vehicle for enhancing racial and ethnic diversity is the Committee on Minorities in Physics (COM).

Founded in 1972, COM advises APS about issues related to minorities in physics; suggests and administers programs and activities designed to address the problem of so few African Americans, Hispanics, and Native Americans in physics; and works closely with other organizations dedicated to achieving the

The American Physical Society sponsors a number of programs to recruit African American and other minority students to careers in physics. (American Physical Society)

same goals. COM's most notable program is the APS Scholarship for Minority Undergraduate Physics Majors. This scholarship, which began in 1980, has the goal of increasing the number of African American and other minority students who receive bachelor's degrees in the physical sciences. Any African American, Hispanic American, or Native American who is a U.S. citizen or permanent resident, who is majoring or planning to major in physics, and who is a high school senior, college freshman, or sophomore is eligible to apply for the scholarship. Perhaps more important, scholarship winners also "win" a mentor, usually a COM member and/or a faculty member at the student's institution of higher learning or another one nearby. Such mentoring is crucial to making the successful transition from student to professional physicist. In addition to providing funding and mentoring to an individual student, COM also contributes funds to the student's physics department to be used to enhance the education of minority students in general.

COM maintains a speakers bureau of minority physicists and provides travel grants to physics departments who wish to bring in these speakers. COM also works closely with the National Society of Black Physicists in support of that organization's initiatives to foster diversity in the physical sciences.

See also: National Society of Black Physicists; Physics

REFERENCES AND FURTHER READING

American Physical Society. "APS Physics." [Online article or information; retrieved October 29, 2007.] http://www.aps.org/.

American Physical Society. "Committee on Minorities in Physics Annual Report for January 2006–December 2006." [Online article or information; retrieved October 29, 2007.] http://www.aps.org/about/governance/committees/commin/upload/COM_AnnualReport_2006.pdf.

American Psychological Association

The American Psychological Association (APA) is the primary professional organization for psychologists in the United States and the largest association of psychologists in the world. Founded in 1892, by the early 21st century, the APA boasted 148,000 members, a professional staff, and a permanent headquarters in Washington, D.C. It sponsors a number of initiatives to increase diversity in the field of psychology, most of which are conducted under the auspices of its Office of Ethnic Minority Affairs (OEMA).

The OEMA was established in 1979 as a means to increase the scientific understanding of how culture pertains to psychology and how ethnicity influences behavior. To these ends, the OEMA promotes opportunities that recruit, train, and retain African Americans and other underrepresented minorities in the field of psychology. It also works to ensure that ethnic minority communities receive psychological services that are culturally appropriate, encourages all psychologists to develop some minimal levels of multicultural competence, and strives to develop public policies that address the concerns of ethnic minority psychologists and their communities.

The major programs by which OEMA seeks to accomplish these goals are the Diversity Project 2000 and Beyond (DP2KB); the Psychology in Ethnic Minority-serving Institutions (PEMSI) Initiative; and the Commission on Ethnic Minority Recruitment, Retention and Training in Psychology (CEMRRAT2 Task Force). DP2KB encourages ethnic minority students attending community college to consider careers in psychology, as either practitioners, educators, or researchers. For two days before and after the APA annual convention, selected community college students are brought to the site of the convention at APA expense, where they take part in leadership and mentoring sessions. Many of these students come to the attention of the DP2KB program through their involvement in the PEMSI program, which promotes careers in psychology by strengthening the psychology departments and programs at two- and four-year institutions that cater primarily to African Americans and other ethnic minorities. The CEMRRAT2 Task Force works to promote and improve multicultural education and training, as well as to recruit and retain more ethnic minority faculty and students. In addition, OEMA administers federally funded projects related to the prevention of school violence, the integration of mental health into public primary health care settings, and the elimination of health disparities as they pertain to psychology.

The OEMA also administers the Minority Fellowship Program (MFP), a scholarship program for minorities who are pursuing doctoral degrees in psychology and neuroscience. The Mental Health and Substance Abuse Services (MHSAS) Fellowship, which is funded by the Substance Abuse and Mental Health Services Administration, supports the training of mental health service providers or practitioners in the field of substance abuse treatment or prevention. The Mental Health Research Fellowship supports students pursuing careers in research psychology related to ethnic minority mental health. The HIV/AIDS Fellowship supports students pursuing careers as research psychologists specializing in HIV/AIDS. The MHSAS Postdoctoral Fellowship supports recent doctoral recipients who seek careers in mental health services research. The Diversity Program in Neuroscience (DPN), which is funded by the National Institute of Mental Health (NIMH) and is coadministered by the APA and the Association of Neuroscience Departments and Programs, offers predoctoral and postdoctoral fellowships to research psychologists who wish to conduct research in areas that are important to NIMH.

See also: HIV/AIDS; National Institute of Mental Health

REFERENCES AND FURTHER READING

American Psychological Association. "American Psychological Association." [Online article or information; retrieved October 29, 2007.] http://www.apa.org/.

APA Online. "Ethnic Minority Affairs Office." [Online article or information; retrieved April 26, 2007.] http://www.apa.org/pi/oema/aboutus.html.

American Society for Cell Biology

The American Society for Cell Biology (ASCB) represents the interests of a wide range of researchers active in the life sciences, all of whom are involved in endeavors that focus on the biological functions of cells. The society's efforts to achieve greater diversity among this group are overseen by the Minority Affairs Committee (MAC).

ASCB was founded in 1960 as a means of advancing the relatively new field of cell biology. By 2007, the society's membership had grown to more than 11,000, the vast majority of them holders of doctorates or equivalent degrees, and it maintained a professional staff and a permanent headquarters in Bethesda, Maryland. Part of ASCB's mission to promote and develop the field of cell biology involves providing training and career development opportunities to graduate students and life sciences researchers just beginning their careers, but especially to students and postdoctoral researchers who are African Americans or members of other underrepresented minorities. To this end, MAC was established in 1985 with George M. Langford serving as its first chair. Today, many of MAC's activities are funded by the National Institute of General Medical Sciences through its Minority Access to Research Careers program.

MAC promotes research opportunities for minority cell biologists in several ways. The committee sponsors summer courses for minority students at the Marine Biological Laboratory (MBL) at Woods Hole, Massachusetts, and Friday Harbor Laboratories at the University of Washington. These sites offer investigators the opportunity to experiment with a wide range of aquatic and wetlands life-forms, and their facilities are used extensively by many of the nation's leading cell biologists. Consequently, not only are students in the summer courses afforded the opportunity to conduct cutting-edge research, but also they are afforded the opportunity to network with some of the most important senior practitioners in their field. MAC also sponsors the MBL Scholars Lunch, an annual summer luncheon and career development workshop for junior faculty, including Linkage Fellows, and for students attending summer courses at MBL. The luncheon gives attendees yet another opportunity to network with senior cell biologists who conduct research, either part time or full time, at MBL. The MAC Visiting Professorship Awards Program makes it possible for faculty from historically black colleges and universities and other minority-serving institutions that focus on teaching rather than on research to spend 8 to 10 weeks during the summer conducting research in the laboratory of a sponsoring ASCB member. In some cases, the program also supports minority faculty who wish to continue their research for an additional summer.

MAC programs also help increase the number of students who are drawn to careers in the life sciences. The Linkage Fellows Program helps junior faculty at minority-serving institutions promote cell biology at the local level by mentoring their undergraduates who are promising candidates to become cell biologists, and thus linking those students to ASCB and MAC. Each year, up to six Linkage Fellows receive up to $7,500 per year for professional and student development activities such as bringing themselves and one or two students to the ASCB annual meeting, encouraging those students to present posters at the ASCB annual meeting, publicizing MAC programs and awards for faculty and students at their home institutions, and conducting outreach programs at neighboring minority-serving institutions. At the Annual Biomedical Research Conference for Minority Students, MAC conducts an exhibit booth and presents cash awards for the best posters and research projects related to cell biology.

The committee sponsors several activities at the ASCB annual meeting such as a mentoring symposium, a poster competition, an awards lunch, and the E. E. Just Lecture. The E. E. Just Lectureship, named after the prominent African American cell biologist, was established in 1993. This award is presented each year at the annual meeting to an outstanding minority cell biologist; not only does it recognize the recipient's scientific contributions, but it also provides minority students with additional role models and publicizes to the scientific community at large the contributions of minority scientists. In addition to receiving a cash award, the recipient presents a lecture at the annual meeting.

To bring minority students and junior faculty to the annual meeting so that they can participate in these activities, MAC offers travel awards to pay the expenses of transportation and lodging. In 2006, for example, these awards helped 58 minorities, 9 of them from historically black colleges or universities, attend the annual meeting. As part of the award, awardees make presentations at the Minority Poster Session, which gives them an opportunity to meet the ASCB's executive officers and council, thus providing the presenters with an excellent opportunity to network with prominent cell biologists.

See also: Historically Black Colleges and Universities; Just, Ernest E.; Langford, George M.; National Institute of General Medical Sciences

REFERENCES AND FURTHER READING

American Society for Cell Biology. "The American Society for Cell Biology." [Online article or information; retrieved October 29, 2007.] http://www.ascb.org/.

American Society for Cell Biology. "The Minority Affairs Committee." [Online article or information; retrieved May 4, 2007.] http://www.ascb.org/index.cfm?navid=90.

American Society for Microbiology

Founded in 1899, the American Society for Microbiology (ASM) is the world's largest scientific society of individuals interested in the microbiological sciences. By the 21st century, ASM's members numbered more than 43,000, and the society supported a professional staff at its permanent headquarters in

Washington, D.C. As part of its commitment to diversity, ASM supports the activities of several committees dedicated to increasing the involvement of underrepresented minorities in the life sciences.

The Committee on Minority Education promotes the recruitment, education, mentoring, and retention of African American faculty and students, as well as faculty and students of other underrepresented minorities. In addition to holding roundtable sessions at the ASM general meeting, the committee sponsors predoctoral and postdoctoral fellowships for minorities. The Robert D. Watkins Graduate Research Fellowship offers students enrolled in PhD programs who have completed their coursework, as well as recent recipients of PhDs, the opportunity to conduct three years of research on a topic related to microbiology. In addition to receiving $57,000 ($19,000 per year, paid out in six equal payments), recipients also gain the opportunity to present their findings at the annual ASM general meeting and to attend one summer session of the Kadner Institute, the ASM's summer institute for graduate students and postdoctoral researchers preparing for careers in microbiology. The ASM Minority Undergraduate Research Fellowships offer undergraduates pursuing careers in microbiology the opportunity to conduct research for 10 weeks during the summer under the supervision of an ASM member at either the student's home institution, the ASM member's institution, the Tufts University School of Medicine in Massachusetts, or the Albert Einstein College of Medicine in New York. In addition to receiving up to $5,850, recipients also gain the opportunity to present the results of their research at the Annual Biomedical Research Conference for Minority Students and the ASM general meeting.

The Committee on Underrepresented Members serves to ensure that ASM members of minority ethnic groups are recognized as valuable members of ASM and are included in all aspects of its operations. Perhaps the most important of its activities is the Minority Mentoring Program. This program gives minority members the opportunity to form a professional relationship with a more experienced member of the organization in a way that facilitates the professional and career development of the mentee. The program provides minority members with career advice, informal feedback on projects and publications, and enhanced opportunities to participate in research. The committee also administers the ASM General Meeting Minority Traveling Grant. Postdoctoral scholars or faculty at HBCUs or other minority-serving institutions who are also ASM members may receive up to $1,500 to defray the costs of their expenses to attend the ASM annual convention.

The Committee on Diversity works to increase the visibility and participation of underrepresented minority scientists in the American Academy of Microbiology, the honorific leadership group within ASM. The committee encourages nominations of minority scientists for study at the academy, for

ASM awards and leadership positions, and for participation in the academy's colloquia. It also administers the William A. Hinton Research Training Award, which honors outstanding contributions that foster the research training of minority undergraduates in microbiology, thus increasing the number of minority microbiologists. The award includes a $2,000 cash prize and all expenses paid to the ASM general meeting.

The Committee on Microbiological Issues Impacting Minorities ensures that relevant issues affecting minority populations or minority microbiologists are addressed in the society's public policy positions and statements. It also monitors the status of minority microbiologists in the profession and in ASM, and it interacts and collaborates with similar committees or groups in other scientific organizations. The committee publishes the *Minority Microbiology Mentor Newsletter* for ASM's minority members and their mentors. This newsletter contains information such as career advice, networking tips, unique funding and career opportunities, news about how microbiological issues affect minorities or how minority issues affect microbiologists, and scientific articles published by minority microbiologists or minority-serving institutions.

In addition to these activities, ASM manages the Annual Biomedical Research Conference for Minority Students (ABRCMS). Sponsored by the National Institute of General Medical Sciences, ABRCMS (formerly known as the MARC/MBRS Symposium) is the largest professional conference for biomedical students in the country. First held in 2001, the conference's participants include more than 2,500 undergraduate and graduate students, postdoctoral scientists, and faculty members from more than 275 colleges and universities. The three-day conference is an opportunity for student presenters to demonstrate the results of their biomedical research in poster or oral presentations. The conference is a networking opportunity for promising minority students pursuing careers in biomedicine, because it allows them to meet administrators from universities and government and private institutions who can help them further their careers.

See also: Hinton, William A.; Microbiology; National Institute of General Medical Sciences

REFERENCES AND FURTHER READING

American Society for Microbiology. "American Society for Microbiology." [Online article or information; retrieved October 29, 2007.] http://www.asm.org/.

American Society for Microbiology. "Underrepresented Minority Groups in the Life Sciences." [Online article or information; retrieved April 27, 2007.] http://www.asm.org/general.asp?bid=16715.

Association of American Medical Colleges

The Association of American Medical Colleges (AAMC) is a nonprofit association of medical schools, teaching hospitals, and academic societies whose missions are closely related to medical education. The association seeks to improve the nation's health by enhancing the effectiveness of academic medicine. To enhance the diversity of medical education in the United States, AAMC seeks to attract more African Americans and other underrepresented minorities to enroll in medical college, to support minority students who attend medical school, and to further the professional development of minority faculty and administrators.

AAMC was founded in 1876 as a vehicle for advancing medical education in the United States by establishing common policies for managing medical colleges and teaching hospitals. Although still vitally interested in those areas, today's AAMC also seeks to enhance the biomedical research that has come to form such an important part of a modern medical education, as well as to improve the American health care system. To these ends, AAMC has committed itself to working for increased diversity in the American medical community, particularly by producing more physicians and other medical professionals from the ranks of underrepresented minorities. Its Division of Diversity Policy and Programs has implemented the following initiatives: the Summer Medical and Dental Education Program, the Minority Student Medical Career Awareness Workshop, the Medical Minority Application Registry, and the Herbert W. Nickens Medical Student Scholarships and Faculty Fellowships. AAMC also maintains Web sites for prospective minority medical students and conducts career development seminars for minority faculty members.

The Summer Medical and Dental Education Program (SMDEP) is a six-week medical and dental school preparatory program. Founded in 1988 by the Robert Wood Johnson Foundation as the Minority Medical Education Program, SMDEP was taken over by AAMC and the American Dental Education Association in 1993, and it took on its present name in 2003. SMDEP grants are made to participating schools in the amount of $300,000 per year for four years. The program is free to accepted applicants, who receive free room, board, tuition, and course materials. Participants attend academic enrichment sessions on organic chemistry, physics, biology, mathematics, writing, and public speaking. They also attend seminars and workshops on learning and study skills, individual and group learning, career development, and financial planning, and they receive limited exposure to clinical practice.

The Minority Student Medical Career Awareness Workshop program sponsors annual career fairs for high school and college students and recent college graduates who are interested in medical careers. These fairs allow students to meet with minority affairs officers, admissions officers, and financial aid professionals from a variety of medical colleges, to find out more about other AAMC programs such as SMDEP and to learn about other medical school application and preparation programs. In 2007, AAMC held career fairs specifically for minorities, in conjunction with the AAMC annual meeting, at Hampton University and other minority-serving institutions, and in Washington, D.C.

The Medical Minority Application Registry (Med-MAR) program provides minority applicants to medical school with additional help in getting through the application and admission process, as well as guidance as to which schools are particularly interested in admitting minorities as medical students. Anyone taking the standardized medical school application test (MCAT) who self-identifies as an underrepresented minority can register for Med-MAR. Biographical information and test scores of registrants are distributed to AAMC member schools that wish to diversify their applicant pool, which then send the registrants the information they need to complete a successful applications package. Med-MAR registrants are also given copies of *Minority Student Opportunities in United States Medical Schools* (Washington, DC: Association of American Medical Colleges, 2005), an AAMC publication describing medical school programs that provide special opportunities, such as academic enrichment programs and financial aid, for underrepresented minorities.

The Nickens scholarships and fellowships recognize medical students and junior faculty members who have demonstrated leadership in the effort either to enhance diversity in medical education or to eliminate disparities in health care. Each year, five $5,000 Medical Student Scholarships are presented to third-year medical students, and one $15,000 Faculty Fellowship is awarded.

AAMC operates two Web sites for prospective minority medical students. Aspiring Doc.org provides information for minorities who are considering a career as a physician but who are unsure that a medical career is right for them. A prominent feature of the Web site is stories about real-life minority physicians who discuss candidly the difficulties they faced as medical students and as young professionals, how they overcame them, and the joys and rewards they have reaped as a result of their medical careers. Minorities in Medicine (http://www.aamc.org/students/minorities/start.htm) provides prospective students with information about how to apply to medical school, how to obtain financial aid, and how to prepare for the intense education experience that is medical school.

AAMC conducts career development seminars for minority junior faculty members who are considering careers in academic medicine. The program helps participants identify their professional development goals; develop career paths for achieving those goals; understand the realities of academic appointment, promotion, and tenuring; develop techniques for overcoming the special challenges faced by minorities in academia; gain insight into the grant-making process employed by the National Institutes of Health and other

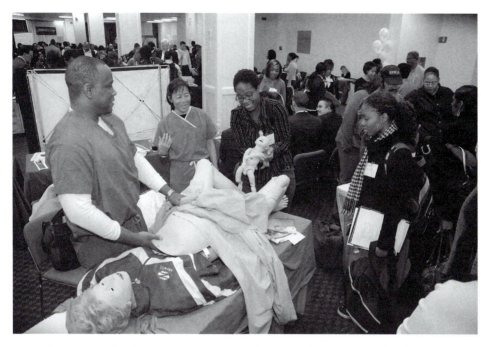

Attendees at a medical career awareness workshop and recruitment fair for minorities, sponsored by the Association of American Medical Colleges, use an obstetrical patient simulator to practice delivering a baby. (Association of American Medical Colleges)

federal agencies and foundations; and learn some of the ins and outs of writing a successful grant proposal.

See also: American Dental Education Association; Biology; Chemistry; Hampton University; Physics

REFERENCES AND FURTHER READING

Association of American Medical Colleges. "Association of American Medical Colleges." [Online article or information; retrieved October 29, 2007.] http://www.aamc.org/.

Association of American Medical Colleges. "Diversity." [Online article or information; retrieved April 28, 2007.] http://www.aamc.org/diversity/start.htm.

Association of Black Anthropologists

Anthropology is the science that deals with the origins, physical and cultural development, racial characteristics, and social customs and beliefs of humankind. To this end, most anthropologists study native peoples, many of whom still live in a primitive state. All too often, these people are people of color who have been, and in many cases still are, the victims of exploitation, oppression, and discrimination. The Association of Black Anthropologists (ABA) was founded to publicize the victimization of people of color to explain the socio-economic and political causes by which they are victimized, to analyze and critique social science theories that misrepresent the realities of their victimization, and to construct more sophisticated theories for interpreting the social dynamics with which they must cope. Over the years, the association broadened its scope to include the promotion of research on black people around the globe, particularly those living in modern societies, with an emphasis on how different people of color experience white supremacy. Other ABA goals include mentoring young black anthropologists and all students who study blacks, in addition to promoting the development of black leadership in anthropology.

The ABA began as an ad hoc group of black anthropologists within the American Association of Anthropologists (AAA) who felt a need to be heard, engaged, and understood. In 1970, this group formed the Minority Caucus, an informal group within the AAA. Eventually it became known as the Caucus of Black Anthropologists, and in 1975, it was formally constituted as the ABA. Despite the forces that led to the creation of the ABA, it remained throughout its existence a section of the AAA, with which it maintains a cordial relationship. By 2000, when it held its first conference separate from the AAA in Havana, Cuba, the ABA's membership had grown to approximately 300.

One of the major activities of the ABA is to publish a scholarly journal, *Transforming Anthropology: The Journal of the ABA*. The journal began as a newsletter, called *News from the Natives*, in 1973. Over time, it became known as *Notes from the ABA* and in 1990, as *Transforming Anthropology*. As the title suggests, the journal publishes articles that critique mainstream anthropology by developing black and other marginal anthropological perspectives. The journal also publishes articles that reflect the ABA's rejection of mainstream anthropology's insistence on the separation of subject and investigator and its embracing of political activism within the context of research. Although this activism generally attempts to expose and investigate racism, sexism, economic exploitation, and all forms of oppression, it is most often concerned with exploring the nature and persistence of white skin privilege and post-colonialism throughout the world with an eye to eventually dismantling these structures and negating their effects. The ABA also sponsors the publication of books that promote its viewpoint and the contributions of black anthropologists, such as *African American Pioneers in Anthropology* (Urbana: University of Illinois Press, 1999), edited by Ira E. Harrison and Faye V. Harrison.

See also: Anthropology

REFERENCES AND FURTHER READING

Association of Black Anthropologists. "Association of Black Anthropologists." [Online article or information; retrieved October 29, 2007.] http://www.indiana.edu/~wanthro/candice1.htm.

Association of Black Cardiologists

African Americans, indeed all people of color, are disproportionately susceptible to cardiovascular disease (CVD, medical conditions that affect the heart
and circulatory system). The Association of Black Cardiologists (ABC) was
founded as a means of rectifying this situation, while serving as a vehicle for
promoting the careers of black heart specialists and for encouraging black
medical students to consider careers in cardiology.

The ABC was founded in 1974 by Richard A. Williams and 16 other black
cardiologists. One of them, Elijah Saunders, would later become a charter
member of the International Society on Hypertension in Blacks, which also
concerns itself with the high incidence of cardiovascular disease among people of color. By 2006, the organization had grown to include more than 600
health care professionals and was maintaining a permanent headquarters in
Atlanta.

The ABC conducts three annual programs that are designed to increase the
scientific knowledge of cardiologists. These programs are the Annual Scientific Session, first held in 1987, the Annual Cardiology Fellows program, first
held in 1990, and the Regional Program Series, first held in 1992. The ABC also
conducts other programs on a nonannual basis such as the Cardiovascular
Summit and Congress of the Treatment of Cardiovascular Diseases in African
Americans, first held in 1995, and the Symposium on Cardiovascular Disease
in Women, first held in 1999. These programs include topics in the basic sciences, clinical medicine, the practice management and legal risk management
of physicians, and the impact of managed care on the practice of medicine.
In 1995, the ABC was accredited by the Accreditation Council for Continuing
Medical Education to provide continuing medical education for physicians.
Since 2002, all of the ABC's professional development programs have been
conducted by its Center for Excellence in Continuing Education and Program
Development. The ABC also funds two other centers of excellence. The Center for Epidemiology, which was founded in 2000, participates in a number of
clinical trials and provides community education. In 2003, for example, the
center provided the principal investigators for the African American Heart Failure Trial (which tested the safety and efficacy of a vasodilator known as BiDil
when used in conjunction with standard CVD therapy), for the Home AED
Trial [which evaluated the impact on treating sudden cardiac arrest of a home
automatic external defibrillator (AED), which could be used before the arrival
of an EMS team], and ARIES (which evaluated the safety and efficacy of two
pharmaceutical drugs for reducing high cholesterol in African Americans). In
terms of community education, the center conducts CHOICES (Changing
Health Outcomes by Improving Cardiovascular Education and Screenings),
whereby African Americans are taught and screened about CVD through their
local churches, and REACH (Racial and Ethnic Approaches to Community

Health) for Wellness, which extends the activities of CHOICES into beauty salons and barber shops.

The Center for Women's Health was also founded in 2000, following a three-year study of the high rate of incidence of CVD, diabetes, and stroke among women of color. Its many programs include ABC's of Nutrition and Exercise, a program designed to address obesity in children through education about proper nutrition and the importance of daily physical activity. The center also maintains an online case library where physicians can locate materials related to assessing coronary artery disease in women and gender differences in atherosclerosis (hardening of the arteries), among other topics.

To encourage CVD scholarship, the ABC sponsors a number of awards. The Dr. Richard Allen Williams Scholarships are awarded annually to stimulate the interest of minority medical students to pursue careers in cardiology. The Dr. Walter M. Booker, Sr. Health Promotion Award is presented annually to the individual who has pioneered programs and innovative thinking that improve the health status in African American communities. The Dr. Herbert Nickins Epidemiology Award is presented annually for outstanding contribution to the promotion and reduction of cardiovascular risks for minority populations. The Dr. Daniel D. Savage Memorial Scientific Award is given annually based on scientific achievement in cardiovascular disease research. The CIT (Cardiologists in Training) Award is presented to a senior ABC member who has demonstrated commitment and loyalty to mentoring cardiology fellows. The Dr. Jay Brown Memorial CIT Award is presented to a leading cardiologist in training for the best abstract presentation delivered at the Annual Scientific Session. The Fourth Year Cardiology Subspecialty Fellowship awards are annual scholarships that provide minority cardiology fellows with fully funded fourth-year fellowships to universities with electrophysiology and interventional subspecialty training programs.

See also: Cardiovascular Disease; Diabetes; International Society on Hypertension in Blacks; Obesity

REFERENCES AND FURTHER READING
Association of Black Cardiologists. "Association of Black Cardiologists, Inc." [Online article or information; retrieved October 29, 2007.] http://www.abcardio.org/.

Association of Black Psychologists

The Association of Black Psychologists (ABPsi) was founded in San Francisco, in 1968, by a number of black psychologists from across the country. Under the leadership of their first president, Charles W. Thomas, they set out to build a professional organization capable of addressing the problems facing black psychologists and to affect positively the mental health of the national black community. By 2006, ABPsi had grown from a handful of concerned professionals into an independent, autonomous organization of over 1,400 members.

ABPsi was particularly concerned by the negative effects of the hurricane season of 2005, which resulted in the displacement of much of the Gulf Coast's black community by Hurricane Katrina. The group denounced the use of pejorative terms such as *refugees* and *looters* that the national media applied to many of the black survivors of the hurricane on the grounds that such terms are psychologically damaging as well as counterproductive in terms of obtaining relief and assistance for Katrina's survivors. Additionally, the group established programs to provide the survivors with culturally appropriate assistance in the form of career counseling, job readiness training, and long-term psychological counseling.

REFERENCES AND FURTHER READING

Association of Black Psychologists. "The Association of Black Psychologists." [Online article or information; retrieved February 11, 2006.] http://www. abpsi.org/index.htm.

Association of Research Directors, 1890 Land Grant Universities

The Association of Research Directors (ARD), 1890 Land Grant Universities coordinates most of the agricultural research being conducted at the 1890 land-grant colleges and universities that is funded by the U.S. Department of Agriculture (USDA). ARD also cooperates with other federal agencies and national associations in developing and monitoring legislation affecting research, extension, teaching, and international programs at the 1890 schools, all of which are historically black colleges and universities.

The Morrill Act of 1862 created a system of federally funded, land-grant colleges throughout the United States. African Americans, however, were prohibited from attending the land-grant schools situated in the segregated South, so the Second Morrill Act of 1890 created a second group of land-grant colleges to serve the educational needs of African Americans. These schools are Alabama A&M University, Alcorn State University in Mississippi, Delaware State University, Florida A&M University, Fort Valley State University in Georgia, Kentucky State University, Langston University in Oklahoma, Lincoln University of Missouri, North Carolina A&T State University, Prairie View A&M University in Texas, South Carolina State University, Southern University in Louisiana, Tennessee State University, the University of Arkansas at Pine Bluff, the University of Maryland Eastern Shore, Virginia State University, and West Virginia State University. Tuskegee University in Alabama is also considered to be an 1890 school, because it performs a role identical to the other 17 schools.

Historically, most of the agricultural research funded by the federal government has been conducted at the nation's land-grant schools. However, research funding for the 1890 schools was administered by the 1862 schools; so, for the 80 years of their existence, the 1890 schools received very little money for research projects. To remedy this situation, ARD was founded in 1972 to secure for the 1890 schools a piece of the federal research pie. Within five years, ARD achieved success with passage of the Evans-Allen Act, the popular name for Section 1445 of the National Agricultural Research, Education, and Teaching Policy Act (NARETPA) of 1977. Evans-Allen created the Evans-Allen Program Formula Fund, a source of funding for agricultural research at the 1890 schools that was administered directly to the 1890 schools by the USDA. ARD also played a major role in securing passage of other federal acts that have contributed hundreds of millions of dollars to the 1890 schools for agricultural research.

Generally speaking, the research coordinated by ARD falls under one of seven categories. Farm and foreign agricultural service research ensures the well-being of U.S. agriculture through the timely delivery of farm programs, the strengthening of crop insurance and other risk management programs, and the improvement of trade opportunities to raise farm income. Rural development research improves the quality of life for rural residents. Food, nutrition, and consumer service research provides children and needy families with access to a more healthy diet through food assistance programs and comprehensive nutrition education efforts. Natural resources and environmental research promotes the conservation and sustainable use of natural resources on private land and in the national forests. Food safety research ensures that the nation's meat, poultry, and egg supplies are safe, wholesome, and properly labeled. Education and economics research discovers and disseminates knowledge concerning the biological, physical, and social sciences related to agricultural research, economic analysis, statistics, extension, and higher education. Marketing and regulatory programs research facilitates the domestic and international marketing of U.S. agricultural products, ensures the health and care of animals and plants, and improves market competitiveness for the benefit of both consumers and American agriculture.

Today, ARD serves as the recognized voice of the research programs of the 1890 schools. It maintains a permanent headquarters in Orangeburg, South Carolina, on the campus of South Carolina State University. Voting membership is open to the research directors of the 1890 schools, and associate (nonvoting) membership is open to the USDA regional, associate, and assistant research directors, to former 1890 school research directors, and to representatives from affiliated organizations. Ex officio membership is open to certain employees of the USDA's Cooperative State Research, Education and Extension Service, the agency that administers Evans-Allen funds. ARD holds two business meetings every year, and from time to time it also hosts an approximately biennial research symposium (the last three were held in 1997, 2000, and 2005). ARD otherwise encourages excellence in scientific research by awarding the Morrison/ Evans Outstanding Research Scientist Award, the B. D. Mayberry Young Scientist Award, and awards for outstanding research papers.

See also: Alabama A&M University; Delaware State University; Evans-Allen Program Formula Fund; Florida A&M University; Fort Valley State University (FVSU); Historically Black Colleges and Universities; Kentucky State University; Langston University; Lincoln University of Missouri; North Carolina A&T State University; Prairie View A&M University; South Carolina State University; Southern University and A&M College System; Tennessee State University; Tuskegee University; University of Arkansas at Pine Bluff; University of Maryland Eastern Shore; Virginia State University; West Virginia State University

REFERENCES AND FURTHER READING
University of Maryland Eastern Shore. "Association of Research Directors, Inc." [Online article or information; retrieved January 5, 2007.] http://www. umes.edu/ard.

Beta Kappa Chi
Beta Kappa Chi (BKX) is a national scientific honor society affiliated with the Association of College Honor Societies. Although membership in the society is open to anyone who meets the academic qualifications, most of its members are African Americans and all of its chapters are located at historically black colleges and universities (HBCUs).

BKX was founded in 1923 at Lincoln University, an HBCU in Pennsylvania. Its founders were undergraduate science majors who had been denied admission to other scientific honor societies because of their race. The society grew slowly at first, and after 20 years, it could boast of only eight chapters. Over the next 10 years, however, the society added an additional eight chapters, and in the 10 years following that, it added another 10 chapters. As of 2007, BKX had 60 chapters, all of them at HBCUs in the 17 southern states, Ohio, Pennsylvania, and the District of Columbia, and it had initiated more than 15,000 student scientists into its ranks, of whom 700 were active members.

BKX's motto is "Science holds the golden key to the Royal Palace of Knowledge," and its purpose is to emphasize the importance of scientific training as part of a liberal arts education. It does this by encouraging and promoting original research and high scholarship in the pure and applied sciences through the activities of its local chapters and at its annual convention. At the convention (the 2008 convention was hosted by Jarvis Christian College in Hawkins, Texas), undergraduate and graduate research papers are presented and the best of this research is recognized and rewarded.

Undergraduate students are eligible for membership in BKX if they rank in the upper fifth of their class, have completed at least 64 semester hours of course work and at least 17 semester hours in the pure and applied sciences, and possess a GPA of at least 3.0 in the science area as well as overall. Graduate students are eligible if they have completed at least 15 semester hours in one of the pure or applied sciences and have received an A in at least one-third of those hours and at least a B in the remaining two-thirds.

See also: Historically Black Colleges and Universities; North Carolina A&T State University

REFERENCES AND FURTHER READING

Beta Kappa Chi. "Beta Kappa Chi (BKX) National Scientific Honor Society." [Online article or information; retrieved January 17, 2007.] http://www. betakappachi.org.

Biophysical Society

The Biophysical Society encourages the development and dissemination of knowledge about biophysics, the branch of biology that studies the physical properties governing the functions within cells and the interactions among cells. The society promotes diversity within its field through the activities of its Minority Affairs Committee (MAC).

The Biophysical Society was founded in 1957 as a means of advancing the relatively new field of biophysics. Today, its members number more than 7,000, and it maintains a professional staff and a permanent headquarters in Bethesda, Maryland. Because its annual meeting is the largest congregation of biophysicists in the world, the Minority Affairs Committee focuses most of its efforts on promoting diversity in the field of biophysics and on bringing students and junior faculty who are African Americans or members of other underrepresented minorities to the annual meeting and involving them in its activities. The society also cosponsors the Herman R. Branson Summer Honors Course in Biophysics.

Drawing largely on funding from the Federation of American Societies for Experimental Biology (FASEB) and the National Institute of General Medical Sciences' Minority Access to Research Careers (MARC) program, the MAC helps defray travel expenses for minority attendees of the annual meeting. The Student Travel Award presents awardees with up to $500, to be used for airfare, and the Minority Biophysicists Travel Grant awards up to $1,000 for airfare and lodging. In both cases, awardees must be members of the society; a student's recommending advisor must also be a member; and the awards to minority biophysicists, who frequently are the mentors of student awardees, are made on the basis of scientific merit. Awardees are also afforded the opportunity to make oral or poster presentations at the annual meeting, and the best of these presentations receive cash awards courtesy of FASEB/MARC.

The society sponsors two summer courses in biophysics for minorities. In conjunction with the National Society of Black Physicists, the society serves as an organizer of the Herman R. Branson Summer Honors Course in Biophysics. This program is a 10-week summer program that includes a formal introductory course in biophysics at a major research university (frequently Florida A&M University) and a placement in the university's biophysics research lab. Enrollment in the course is limited to 12 rising juniors or seniors who are majoring in biology, chemistry, physics, or mathematics. Students who successfully complete the course receive academic credit and a stipend for participating in research. In conjunction with the University of North Carolina at Chapel Hill and the National Institute of General Medical Sciences, the society offers an 11-week course for junior and senior undergraduates pursuing a major in biochemistry, biology, chemistry, computer science, or physics. The course includes mentored research experience in a biophysics laboratory.

See also: Biology; Branson, Herman R.; Chemistry; Federation of American Societies for Experimental Biology; Florida A&M University; Minority Access to Research Careers; National Institute of General Medical Sciences; National Society of Black Physicists; Physics

REFERENCES AND FURTHER READING

Biophysical Society. "Biophysical Society." [Online article or information; retrieved October 29, 2007.] http://www.biophysics.org/about/.
Biophysical Society. "Minority Resource Center." [Online article or information; retrieved May 7, 2007.] http://www.biophysics.org/minority/.

Black Entomologists

Black Entomologists (BE) is a professional organization for entomologists (biologists who study insects and related organisms). BE was founded in 2000 in Montreal, by a small group of black entomologists who were attending the annual meeting of the Entomological Society of America (ESA). The purpose of the group is to serve the professional, scientific, social, and cultural interests and needs of its members. Membership is not limited to African Americans, but rather is open to Africans, Caribbeans, Hispanics, Native Americans, and other professionals who are interested in furthering the goals of the organization. These goals include improving communication among black entomologists; organizing meetings and events for black entomologists during annual meetings of ESA (with which BE is affiliated); assisting in the recruitment, retention, and advancement of blacks in entomology graduate programs and careers; promoting the science of entomology in the developing black world; and facilitating the advancement of entomology-related careers among people of color. While most members of BE focus their research activity on entomology, others conduct research in related fields such as plant pathology, the study of the diseases that affect plants, and nematology (the study of certain types of worms).

By 2006, BE's membership had grown to 56. At that time, the group had made significant progress toward developing a scholarship fund to promote the study of insects among underrepresented minority K–12 and undergraduate students. That same year, the group held its first symposium, a program at the ESA's annual meeting to honor the memory of Professor Thomas R. Odhiambo (1934–2003), one of Africa's eminent entomologists and founding director of the International Centre for Insect Physiology and Ecology. More informally, the group continues to promote careers in entomology among gifted undergraduates by recruiting minorities into graduate programs by professors who are members of BE. Should the recruiter have no immediate funding or placement in his or her own program, then the applicant is recommended to other BE members at other colleges.

REFERENCES AND FURTHER READING
Black Entomologists. "Black Entomologists." [Online article or information; retrieved October 29, 2007.] http://www.blackentomologists.org/.

Black Psychiatrists of America

The Black Psychiatrists of America (BPA) represents the mental health interests of the African American community. Despite being a voluntary organization without a paid staff or permanent headquarters, BPA has made some important contributions to the advancement of black professionals in psychiatry, as well as to a better understanding of psychiatry as it pertains to African Americans.

BPA originated as an outgrowth of the Section of Psychiatry and Neurology of the National Medical Association, the professional organization of African American physicians. In 1969, Chester M. Pierce, one of the section's leaders, persuaded the American Psychiatric Association (APA) to establish the Committee of Black Psychiatrists (CBP) as a subgroup of the APA devoted to black psychiatry. In addition to serving as the membership of the Committee of Black Psychiatrists, the members also formed the Executive Council of the Black Psychiatrists of America, but with an additional mission. That mission was to get the nation's medical community, particularly the part that is funded by the federal government, to acknowledge that virtually all psychiatric studies at the time systematically excluded blacks from being subjects. Consequently, these studies were not applicable to the black community, a situation that BPA sought to change.

That same year, BPA persuaded the National Institute of Mental Health (NIMH) to establish the Center for Minority Group Affairs under the direction of James Ralph, a black psychiatrist. Immediately, the center began distributing grant money to black psychiatrists for the purpose of studying black subjects. For example, one of the first studies that the center funded involved an investigation by Harold M. Rose and Ruth Dennis of the phenomenon of high rates of black homicide. Over time, the center's studies presented the psychiatric community with a number of revelations, such as the fact that antidepressants are much less effective on African Americans than they are on middle-class whites, the only subjects on whom they had been tested previously.

Meanwhile, BPA was busy encouraging and supporting the work of black psychiatrists in other ways. In the early 1970s, it established the Solomon Carter Fuller Award. Named in honor of one of the first black psychiatrists, the Fuller Award is presented annually to someone who has made a significant contribution to better understanding the mental health of African Americans. The BPA also established the Solomon Carter Fuller Traveling Fellowship, which provided funding for young black psychiatrists to be mentored by veteran black psychiatrists, thus providing a network for nurturing the African American psychiatrists of the future.

In 1976, BPA formally established itself as an entity separate from the APA. Meanwhile, the APA continued to support the Committee of Black Psychiatrists as its own subgroup devoted to black psychiatry, while the NMA split off the Section of Psychiatry from Neurology. Consequently, most black psychiatrists belonged to more than one of these organizations, and in time, the BPA would conduct its annual business meeting at the annual meeting of either the NMA or the APA.

Perhaps BPA's most important achievement since becoming independent is the establishment of Black Psychiatrists International, a group that supports and encourages black psychiatrists around the world, but especially in Africa, where the number of black psychiatrists is surprisingly small. In addition, BPA produces a very informative quarterly newsletter and also helps substantially with the annual Transcultural Seminars in the Caribbean. As of 2006, BPA's membership numbered approximately 1,200, virtually all of the black psychiatrists practicing in the United States.

See also: Fuller, Solomon C.; National Institute of Mental Health; National Medical Association; Pierce, Chester M.

REFERENCES AND FURTHER READING

Pierce, Chester M. "The Formation of the Black Psychiatrists of America." In *Racism and Mental Health; Essays*, edited by Charles V. Willie, Bernard M. Kramer, and Patricia P. Rieker. Pittsburgh, PA: University of Pittsburgh Press, 1973.

Spurlock, Jeanne, ed. *Black Psychiatrists and American Psychiatry*. Washington, DC: American Psychiatric Association, 1999.

Building Engineering and Science Talent

Building Engineering and Science Talent (BEST) is a public-private partnership that seeks to redress the demographic imbalance of the U.S. technical workforce by bringing more African Americans and other underrepresented groups into it. It works to identify practices and programs that increase the number of women and minorities in scientific and technological careers and then to implement these practices nationally.

BEST arose out of the establishment by the U.S. Congress, in 1998, of the Commission on the Advancement of Women and Minorities in Science, Engineering and Technology Development (CAWMSET). CAWMSET was the brainchild of Congresswoman Constance A. Morella (R-MD), who was concerned because women, African Americans, Hispanic Americans, and American Indians comprised two-thirds of the nation's workforce but held fewer than one-quarter of the technical jobs, particularly the jobs most closely tied to innovation. This imbalance threatened not only the economic future of women and minorities, but also the economic future of the nation, because it promised to lead to a shortfall of science, engineering, and technology workers in the near future, thus compromising the United States' ability to compete in the global economy. To avoid this dilemma, CAWMSET sought ways to improve the recruitment, retention, and advancement of women, minorities, and persons with disabilities in fields related to science, engineering, and technology. Its recommendations were published in 2000 in a report titled "Land of Plenty: Diversity as America's Competitive Edge in Science, Engineering and Technology."

"Land of Plenty" proposed many changes in the way science is taught in the nation's elementary and secondary schools, particularly those with a significant number of African American children. One called-for change was the implementation of a major public relations campaign to heighten the image of the scientist in minority communities. Another was for the federal and state governments to invest more money in historically black colleges and universities, which award more than 85 percent of the undergraduate degrees in science earned by African Americans, and in community colleges, which have demonstrated the willingness and ability to train women and minorities for scientific careers. Lastly, the report recommended the establishment of a permanent body to continue the commission's work by developing, coordinating, and overseeing action plans for bringing the commission's recommendations to fruition.

In 2001, the Council on Competitiveness, a nonprofit, nonpartisan policy action group based in Washington, D.C., established Building Engineering and Science Talent (BEST), Inc., to serve as the permanent body for implementing CAWMSET's recommendations. Headquartered in San Diego, BEST also makes recommendations above and beyond those made by CAWMSET. Furthermore, it seeks to encourage industry, government, and academia to take ownership of the recommendations that they are best suited to fulfill, to coordinate the fulfillment of the recommendations, to obtain the funding for seeing the recommendations through to fulfillment, and to monitor progress by compiling and analyzing data relevant to diversity in the scientific/technological workplace.

In 2001, BEST assembled three blue-ribbon panels to develop the best possible methods for implementing CAWMSET's recommendations as they apply to elementary and secondary education, higher education, and the workforce. In 2002, these panels shared their initial findings with Congress in a series of congressional hearings, and in 2004, each panel released its own final report. "What It Takes: Pre-K–12 Design Principles to Broaden Participation in Science, Technology, Engineering and Mathematics" is focused on what works in elementary and secondary education to encourage young people to consider careers in science and engineering, and then outlines the basic design principles these programs have in common. "A Bridge for All: Higher Education Design Principles to Broaden Participation in Science, Technology, Engineering and Mathematics" studies the university-based programs that have enjoyed the greatest success at diversifying the nation's talent pool in science and technology. It concludes, however, that "higher education alone cannot provide the impetus to create favorable conditions for change" but that "national leadership, fresh incentives and additional pressure [are required] to secure the engagement of the nation's colleges and universities" (33). "The Talent Imperative: Diversifying America's Science and Engineering Workforce" identifies four design principles—(1) the sustained commitment to change at every level of the organization, (2) the incorporation of diversity into an organization's operating structure and culture, (3) the holding of managers accountable for achieving diversity targets, and (4) the continuous effort to improve diversity based on internal and external benchmarks—that must underlay any effort to increase the participation of women and minorities in the scientific/technological workplace. The report also calls for "employers' full engagement . . . to move beyond piecemeal and uncoordinated efforts into transformational change" (39).

See also: Historically Black Colleges and Universities

REFERENCES AND FURTHER READING

BEST: Building Engineering and Science Talent. "The BEST Initiative." [Online article or information; retrieved January 26, 2007.] http://www.bestwork-force.org.

National Science Foundation. "Commission on the Advancement of Women and Minorities in Science, Engineering and Technology Development (CAWMSET)." [Online article or information; retrieved January 26, 2007.] http://www.nsf.gov/od/cawmset.

Camille and Henry Dreyfus Foundation

The Camille and Henry Dreyfus Foundation makes awards to academic and other institutions for the purpose of stimulating progress in chemistry and chemical engineering. One of these awards is the American Chemical Society Award for Encouraging Disadvantaged Students into Careers in the Chemical Sciences.

Camille and Henry Dreyfus were Swiss-American chemists who invented a method for manufacturing cellulose acetate fiber (a synthetic fiber similar to rayon). They founded the Celanese Corporation to manufacture the fiber, and they managed the firm's operations in the United States, Canada, and Great Britain. In 1946, Camille Dreyfus, wishing to honor the memory of his brother Henry, established the Dreyfus Foundation "to advance the science of chemistry, chemical engineering and related sciences as a means of improving human relations and circumstances around the world." To that end, the foundation seeks to identify and address the needs and opportunities of the chemical sciences as they are practiced in the United States. The foundation is particularly interested in improving diversity in the chemical sciences.

The American Chemical Society (ACS) Award for Encouraging Disadvantaged Students into Careers in the Chemical Sciences was established in 1993. It is awarded annually to an individual who has significantly stimulated or fostered the interest of minority and/or economically disadvantaged students in chemistry, thereby promoting their professional development as chemists or chemical engineers and/or increasing their appreciation of chemistry as the central science. Recipients are chosen by the American Chemical Society, which presents the award at its annual meeting. The award consists of $5,000 and a certificate to the individual winner, and a grant of $10,000 to the academic institution designated by the recipient so that the institution might better serve the needs of minority and/or economically disadvantaged students who wish to become chemists or chemical engineers. Past recipients include Henry C. McBay (1995), Samuel P. Massie (1996), and Slayton A. Evans Jr. (2000).

The foundation also contributes generously to the ACS Scholars Program. This program provides scholarships to minority undergraduates who are majoring in one of the chemical sciences. Since 1994, when the program was initiated, the foundation has contributed more than $200,000.

See also: American Chemical Society; Chemistry; Evans, Slayton A., Jr.; Massie, Samuel P., Jr.; McBay, Henry C.

REFERENCES AND FURTHER READING

Camille and Henry Dreyfus Foundation. "The Camille & Henry Dreyfus Foundation, Inc." [Online article or information; retrieved October 29, 2007.] http://www.dreyfus.org/.

Carver Research Foundation

For 50 years, the Carver Research Foundation (CRF) was one of the nation's foremost independent research centers, particularly for projects involving agricultural science. Nevertheless, the foundation always struggled to fund itself, and eventually it became a subsidiary of the institution that housed and supported it throughout its existence, Tuskegee Institute (later Tuskegee University).

CRF was founded by its namesake, the renowned agricultural scientist George Washington Carver. Carver, for many years a professor at Tuskegee and the director of the state agricultural experimental station at Tuskegee, wanted to dispose of his estate in such a way that would support the continuation of his agricultural research. He was specifically interested in improving the lot of the average Southern farmer by improving the quality of Southern soil, much of which had been stripped of its nutrients by almost 150 years of growing cotton. Accordingly, in 1940, he founded the George Washington Carver Foundation, as CRF was originally known, with almost $33,000 of his own money. In addition to supporting agricultural research and rural development, the foundation was to build and maintain a museum where the results of its work could be displayed publicly. Although the foundation was set up to be a distinct entity in and of itself, it was housed on the Tuskegee Institute campus and made use of Tuskegee personnel and facilities throughout its existence.

From 1940 to 1943, Carver, in addition to his other duties, served as CRF's director. His primary task during these years was to increase the foundation's funding, which he addressed in several ways. First, he commissioned a biography of himself, with the proceeds going to the foundation. Second, he signed a contract with the Carvoline Company to help it manufacture various cosmetic products from peanut oil. Third, he signed a number of contracts with other companies to conduct agricultural research on their behalf; a typical contract involved a fiber research project for the Savannah Sugar Refining Company. Fourth, he encouraged and supported a number of different fund-raising efforts, most notably a campaign by Hollywood movie stars to raise funds for CRF. Upon his death in 1943, he contributed further to the foundation's endowment by leaving to it the bulk of his estate, thus making his total personal contribution a little more than $60,000.

Carver was succeeded as director of CRF by his longtime assistant, Austin W. Curtis Jr. Although Curtis served in this position for only one year, he managed to further the aims of the foundation by bringing Henry Ford Sr., head of Ford Motor Company, onto CRF's board of directors. Curtis also recruited several prominent American businesspeople, including Frank Gannett, head of the Gannett newspaper chain, to serve as trustees.

In 1944, Curtis relinquished his position as CRF director to Russell W. Brown, who served in that capacity for the next 14 years. Under Brown, CRF funded modest research projects to develop inexpensive building materials for home construction from native materials, industrial solvents from fermented sweet potatoes, and paper and paperboard from agricultural by-products, to name three. Brown's major task, however, was to increase CRF's funding, because the interest accruing from Carver's endowment was far too little to support all the projects that the foundation wanted to pursue. Consequently, Brown expanded the amount of industrial research CRF conducted. This research included the development of specialized inks for the Parker Pen Company, halogenated ethers for the Research Corporation, synthetic biochemicals having potential chemotherapeutic properties for the Upjohn Company, and poultry feed for Swift and Company. The money that CRF earned from these projects allowed it to provide research fellowships and other financial support to a modest number of graduate assistants.

By the end of his tenure in 1958, Brown had taken on research projects for a number of leading companies, as well as several agencies of the federal government, including the Department of Agriculture, the Public Health Service, and the Office of Naval Research. The most important project conducted during Brown's directorship, however, was the HeLa Project. This project, conducted for the National Foundation for Infantile Paralysis, produced more than 600,000 cell cultures, which were then used to evaluate the effectiveness and safety of the Salk vaccine, the first vaccine against poliovirus.

In 1958, Brown was replaced as CRF director by Clarence T. Mason, who held that position for the next 10 years. During his directorship, two major changes took place at CRF: an increase in the number of graduate students conducting research under its auspices and a major shift in how CRF conducted research in general. Mason had joined CRF as a research associate in 1944, when only two graduate students were working at CRF as researchers. By the beginning of his tenure, that figure had increased to approximately one dozen. One of the main thrusts of his administration was to increase that figure further, and by the time of his death in 1968, the number had increased to 88, of whom 45 were Carver Fellows, which meant that their research was fully funded by CRF.

From its inception, CRF had conducted its own research, but a chronic lack of funding forced it to do so by using the resources and facilities provided to it by Tuskegee. In fact, CRF and Tuskegee had become so closely intertwined that in 1963, CRF was designated as the school's research arm on an experimental basis. In this capacity, CRF deemphasized its own research and took responsibility for coordinating, promoting, and administering all research conducted at Tuskegee, including overseeing all proposal and grant writing. Consequently, the scope of the research in which CRF was now involved grew to include engineering, veterinary medicine, applied sciences, education, behavioral sciences, arts and sciences, nursing, and human resources development. In essence, the focus of CRF's activities had shifted from research to research administration, with CRF becoming responsible for all grants, contracts, promotions, and related activities regarding research conducted at Tuskegee. This arrangement worked so well over the next six years that it was formalized in 1969, the year after J. H. M. Henderson took over as CRF director. In conjunction with this fundamental change in the foundation's role, its formal name changed, too, to the Carver Research Foundation of Tuskegee Institute.

During the first five years of his tenure as CRF director, Henderson increased the number of contracts managed by the foundation from 19 to 90. Nevertheless, by 1979, when he relinquished his position to Margaret M. Tolbert, it was clear that CRF's role as Tuskegee's research administration unit was causing confusion for both CRF and Tuskegee. In terms of its effects on CRF, the arrangement prevented the foundation from developing a coherent research program that was consistent with the desires of its founder. Accordingly, in 1982, the name of the foundation was changed to the Carver Research Center and it resumed its original mission: to conduct original research in the field of agricultural science with a focus on rural development.

In 1990, the Carver Research Center, by then under the direction of B. D. Mayberry, ceased to exist as an independent entity and became instead a subsidiary of Tuskegee University. In this capacity, it continued to conduct agricultural research, although once again the scope of such research expanded beyond rural development. One of the center's major projects was operating the Center for Food and Environmental Systems for Human Exploration of Space (CFESH), which is sponsored by the National Aeronautics and Space Administration (NASA). CFESH's research addresses problems associated with growing foods, particularly sweet potatoes and peanuts, in closed environments for both long- and short-term space missions.

See also: Carver, George Washington; National Aeronautics and Space Administration; Tolbert, Margaret Mayo; Tuskegee University

References and Further Reading
Mayberry, B. D. *The History of the Carver Research Foundation of Tuskegee University, 1940–1990.* Tuskegee, AL: Tuskegee University Press, 2003.

HELA PROJECT

In 1952, Jonas Salk developed a vaccine to protect children from the crippling effects of the poliovirus. Before it could be administered, however, it had to be tested extensively on living cells to determine both its effectiveness and its safety. The HeLa Project, which was conducted at Tuskegee University by the Carver Research Foundation (CRF), provided the cells on which the Salk vaccine was tested.

The HeLa Project derived its name from the first two letters of the first and last names of Henrietta Lacks. Lacks, a black woman, was being treated for cervical adenocarcinoma, a tumor affecting one of the glands of the neck, at Johns Hopkins University Hospital in Baltimore, when she died in 1951. Before her death, however, George O. Gey and several other Johns Hopkins physicians removed some of the tumor's epithelial cells and preserved them in a cell culture in vitro (in a test tube). By 1953, Gey had discovered that the so-called HeLa cells were a particularly hardy strain; they preserved their properties in cell culture in vitro, traveled well from one laboratory to another, and began to multiply immediately upon being given the appropriate nutrition. They also discovered that HeLa cells are particularly susceptible to infection by poliovirus, which at the time was crippling hundreds of thousands of children around the world annually.

Meanwhile, Salk had developed his polio vaccine, and now it required extensive testing before it could be administered. At first, it was intended that testing would be conducted on cells from rhesus monkeys, but when Gey made his discoveries concerning HeLa cells, it was decided to conduct the tests on HeLa cells instead. After considering a number of facilities where HeLa cells could be produced in mass quantities under laboratory conditions, the National Foundation for Infantile Paralysis, which sponsored Salk's research, chose CRF to prepare the thousands of cell cultures needed by the 23 testing laboratories around the country that would play a role in evaluating the effectiveness and safety of Salk's vaccine.

With CRF director Russell W. Brown serving as principal investigator, the HeLa Project got underway in April 1953. Within two months, CRF personnel had developed the capacity to produce HeLa cell cultures in significant numbers. By the following February, the project's staff of 35 full-time employees was preparing and shipping 10,000 cultures per week. By the time the project was concluded in 1955, more than 600,000 separate cultures had been produced.

The project's success permitted the speedy completion of the Salk polio vaccine evaluation program, and in 1955, the Salk vaccine was administered to the general public. Although by 1961 it had given way to a vaccine developed by Albert Sabin that was easier to administer, it is estimated that more than 200 million doses of the Salk vaccine had been administered in the United States alone, thus reducing the incidence of polio in this country by 96 percent.

See also: Carver Research Foundation; Tuskegee University

REFERENCES AND FURTHER READING

Mayberry, B. D. *The History of the Carver Research Foundation of Tuskegee University, 1940–1990.* Tuskegee, AL: Tuskegee University Press, 2003.

Central State University

Central State University is one of two historically black colleges in Ohio. In terms of scientific research, Central State is best known for its work in the fields related to water resources management.

Central State came into being in 1887 as the Combined Normal and Industrial Department at Wilberforce University in Wilberforce, Ohio. Wilberforce had been founded in 1856 by the African Methodist Episcopal Church as a college for training black ministers, but the department was created and funded by the Ohio state legislature for the purpose of educating black teachers and skilled laborers. The department offered only two-year programs until 1941, when it achieved college status. Six years later, it became independent of Wilberforce and was renamed the College of Education and Industrial Arts at Wilberforce. In 1951, it became known as Central State College, and in 1965, it achieved university status.

Central State's most important research institution is the International Center for Water Resources Management (ICWRM). The center's state-of-the-art research facility was completed in 1994, and its laboratories and work areas are devoted to water chemistry, to water quality instrumentation, to limnology (the study of lakes, ponds, and rivers), to hydrology (the study of the movement, distribution, and quality of water), and to hydraulics (the study of the mechanical properties of liquids). Since then, the center has conducted a number of projects for the U.S. Army Corps of Engineers' Huntington District (West Virginia). These projects include regular soil sampling and hydrometer testing of the river beds of the Ohio, Monongahela, and Illinois rivers to assess the effects of storms on watersheds, as well as a habitat study of the Kanahwa River's Marmet Pool. Other domestic research projects include the control of acid mine drainage in southeastern Ohio for the Ohio Department of Natural Resources and the adaptation of the National Aeronautics and Space Administration's Simple Biospheric Model so that it can predict evapotranspiration (the movement of water to the air from various sources such as soil, vegetation, and bodies of water) from agricultural areas using satellite data.

ICWRM has played a leading role in several overseas research projects funded by the U.S. Agency for International Development. Two such projects evaluated the potential of groundwater resources in arid regions of Egypt to provide that country with sources of water other than the Nile River. The first studied the surface hydraulics of flash floods in Wadi El Assiuti in eastern Egypt, and the second evaluated the feasibility of irrigating 190,000 acres of arid land in the Eastern Oweinat region of southern Egypt with subsurface groundwater. The center also collaborated with the University of Science and Technology in Kumasi, Ghana, in a study of the environmental impact of gold mining in Ghana's Obuasi region. The study considered the effects of contamination by arsenic and mercury (used in the ore extraction process) and the distribution of these and other contaminants by ordinary and extraordinary hydrologic events.

See also: National Aeronautics and Space Administration

REFERENCES AND FURTHER READING

Central State University. "Central State University." [Online article or information; retrieved October 29, 2007.] http://www.centralstate.edu/.

Central State University. "Water Resources Management." [Online article or information; retrieved October 29, 2007.] http://www.centralstate.edu/academics/bus_ind/water_res/wrm/index.html.

Charles R. Drew University of Medicine and Science

The Charles R. Drew University of Medicine and Science in Los Angeles is the only major medical school west of the Mississippi River dedicated to providing medical training to blacks and minorities. Its research efforts are dedicated to closing the gap in health disparities among underserved and ethnic minority populations.

Following the assassination of Dr. Martin Luther King Jr. in 1968, the black neighborhood of Watts in Los Angeles erupted into some of the worst rioting ever seen in this country. To his credit, the governor of California, Edmund G. "Pat" Brown, suspected that the rioting was not simply a response to Dr. King's death but was also motivated by a number of underlying racial factors; so he appointed a commission to identify those factors. Known as the McCone Commission, because its chair was John A. McCone, former director of the Central Intelligence Agency, the commission discovered that Watts was woefully underserved in terms of medical care. The closest hospital was inaccessible by public transportation from Watts, while the next closest was a two-hour bus ride away. In addition, Watts residents were found to suffer from every major disease at a significantly higher rate than other Los Angelenos. The state Department of Public Health concluded from the report that only 21 percent of Watts's hospital needs were being met and recommended that a general hospital be constructed in that section of the city. The result was the Los Angeles County-Martin Luther King, Jr. General Hospital, which opened its doors in 1972.

While plans were afoot to build King General, other plans were being laid to staff the hospital with minorities, because it was believed that minority physicians are more likely than white physicians to care for poor and minority patients and to practice in areas like Watts, where medical sciences are scarce. A group calling itself the Charles R. Drew Medical Society began working to establish a medical school in Watts that would cater to the educational needs of African Americans, Hispanics, and other minorities. Working in conjunction with the medical schools at the University of California at Los Angeles and the University of Southern California, in 1966, the society succeeded in founding the Charles R. Drew Postgraduate Medical School as the academic arm of King General. The overall plan was for Drew Postgraduate to take minority graduates of medical schools, with a preference shown for graduates from inner cities and other economically depressed areas, and provide them with intern and residency programs at King General, thus providing further for the medical needs of Watts's residents. King General and Drew Postgraduate worked cooperatively but independently of each other until 1982, when they were officially joined as the King-Drew Medical Center (KDMC). In 1987, Drew Postgraduate became known officially as the Charles R. Drew University of Medicine and Science.

By 2005, Drew University was operating two schools, the College of Medicine and the College of Science and Health. The College of Medicine awards the MD degree and provides specialty training in the areas of anesthesia, dermatology, emergency medicine, family medicine, general dentistry, internal medicine, obstetrics/gynecology, ophthalmology, oral maxillofacial surgery, orthopedics, otolaryngology, pediatrics, and psychiatry. The College of Science and Health awards AS and BS degrees in biomedical science, clinical coding, diagnostic medical sonography, health information technology, nuclear medicine technology, pharmacy technology, physician assistant, radiography, substance abuse counseling, and urban public health; it also awards a master's degree in public health.

Drew focuses its research programs on bringing attention to health issues and diseases that disproportionately affect minorities and the poor. Major areas of importance include diabetes, hypertension, cancer, reproductive health, chronic kidney disease, neuropsychiatric disorders, and HIV/AIDS. As of 2005, the majority of Drew's research was being conducted under the auspices of five research centers.

The Center for Natural Medicine and Prevention was established to scientifically investigate the prevention and treatment of the major chronic diseases

Students and faculty outside the W. M. Keck Foundation building at the Charles R. Drew University of Medicine and Science. (Charles Drew University of Medicine and Science)

of our time through multidisciplinary collaborative research, demonstration programs, and prevention-oriented natural health care. Its research programs focus on the effects of integrative medicine, primarily from the approach of consciousness, with an emphasis on cardiovascular health and the quality of life in underserved, high-risk populations. One of its more interesting programs demonstrated the efficacy of transcendental meditation on disease prevention and health promotion, specifically in terms of preventing and treating cardiovascular disease, hypertension, certain forms of arteriosclerosis (commonly known as hardening of the arteries), and aging.

The International Health Institute conducts research and offers support related to health care initiatives in developing nations. Past projects have included HIV/AIDS prevention in Angola; disaster preparedness in India; and cervical cancer screening, education, and treatment in rural Guatemala. One of the institute's more interesting programs is the Students for Tropical Medicine and International Health, which was founded by motivated medical students as a means of addressing health care issues such as the parasitic, bacterial, and viral infections that are specific to the tropical regions of the world.

The Biomedical Research Center (BRC) hosts a number of innovative initiatives that address health care disparities between minorities and nonminorities.

The Urban Telemedicine Center of Excellence uses telemedicine technology, which historically has been used to bring specialty care to remote or rural settings, to increase access to specialty care, improve quality of care, and reduce the cost of care for underserved minority populations in Los Angeles County's so-called remote inner city. Although the project provides all sorts of medical support, it focuses on ophthalmology, asthma/allergy, cardiology, and dentistry. The Collaborative Alcohol Research Center operates two substance abuse clinical research centers in South-Central Los Angeles; in addition to conducting clinical studies of substance abuse in pregnant and parenting women and their children, including those with fetal alcohol syndrome, these centers provide treatment and counseling programs for families affected by alcohol and drug abuse. BRC also operates centers for AIDS research, education, and services, and diabetes research. One of BRC's more interesting projects involves the establishment of a DNA/molecule medicine laboratory, which will assist associated investigators in their search for alterations in gene structure, organization, and expression that cause genetic diseases relevant to minority populations.

In 2005, Drew was presented with a major challenge to its mission when the King Drew Medical Center lost its national accreditation because of a number of health and safety violations. Consequently, several of Drew's residency programs also lost their accreditation. The following year, the school severed its ties with the hospital and terminated its support of almost 250 medical residents. Threatened with the loss of accreditation, the school voluntarily relinquished accreditation. In 2007, it passed a curriculum review and announced plans to reorganize itself as a part of the University of California System.

See also: Asthma; Cancer; Diabetes; Health Disparities; HIV/AIDS

REFERENCES AND FURTHER READING

Charles R. Drew University of Medicine and Science. "Welcome to Drew." [Online article or information; retrieved November 21, 2005.] http://www.cdrewu.edu/_022/_html/.

Organ, Claude H., and Margaret Kosiba, eds. *A Century of Black Surgeons: The U.S.A. Experience.* Norman, OK: Transcript Press, 1987: 377–426.

Clark Atlanta University

Clark Atlanta University is a historically black institution of higher learning located in downtown Atlanta. It was founded in 1988 as a result of the merger of Clark College, a four-year liberal arts college (which offered only undergraduate degrees) and Atlanta University (which offered only graduate degrees). In the early 21st century, Clark Atlanta's School of Arts and Sciences conducts a plethora of scientific research projects in the Research Center for Science and Technology.

Clark College was founded in 1869 as Clark University by the Freedmen's Aid Society of the Methodist Episcopal Church (later the United Methodist Church). Named for Bishop Davis W. Clark, the first president of the Freedmen's Aid Society, the school was intended to serve as the flagship of all the other Methodist Episcopal churches providing education for freedpeople in the South. Atlanta University was founded in 1865 by the American Missionary Association as an undergraduate school for blacks, and by the end of the 19th century, it was turning out a significant number of African American teachers and librarians. In 1929, it implemented graduate programs in the social and natural sciences, and in the 1940s, it added professional programs in social work, library science, and business administration. Between 1929 and 1988, the university was loosely affiliated with Clark, Morehouse, Morris Brown, and Spelman colleges in what was known as the Atlanta University System, serving as the semiofficial graduate school for Atlanta's other historically black colleges and universities.

As part of Clark Atlanta's commitment to further the development of science, the university operates the Research Center for Science and Technology. The center facilitates interdisciplinary and collaborative research between the university and national and federal laboratories, other universities, and industry, including small and minority high-technology companies. As of 2006, the center's research was being conducted in more than a dozen component centers, laboratories, institutes, and major programs. The Army Center of Excellence in Electronic Sensors and Combat and the Army Center for Research in Information Science conduct basic physical research that can be translated into the technology for tracking targets, as well as for sending and processing signaling data on the battlefield. The Center for Environmental Policy, Education and Research is dedicated to developing solutions to environmental problems and issues. The Center of Excellence in Microelectronics and Photonics is devoted to research into the fundamental properties of compound semiconductors and their development for applications in microelectronics and integrated optics. The Center for Surface Chemistry and Catalysis focuses on research, development, and applications of new materials for the transformation of one chemical species to another. The Center for Theoretical Studies of Physical Systems studies atomic and molecular physics, mathematical physics/applied mathematics, signal and image processing, and molecular dynamics. The Earth Systems Science Program seeks to understand how the urban and regional environments impact living conditions and human activities. The Environmental Justice Resource Center works to educate professional and community leaders so that they can make informed decisions on environmental issues. The High Performance Computing Research Partnership Program develops sophisticated computing methods for application in the fields of fluid dynamics, structural mechanics, chemistry, materials science, environmental science modeling, and signal and image processing. The High Performance Polymers and Composites Center concerns itself with the synthesis, processing, modeling, fabrication, and testing of polymers and composites. The Laboratory for Advanced Signal and Image Processing develops new techniques for multidimensional signal analysis and the processing of data for military, medicine, and remote sensing applications. The Laboratory for Electro-Optical Materials focuses on the development of nonlinear optical, photorefractive, and photoresponsive materials. The Center for Cancer Research and Therapeutic Development focuses on understanding the cellular and molecular bases of the types of cancers that disproportionately affect African American and other minority populations. The Biomedical Research and Training Program offers training for graduates and undergraduates in the biological sciences, chemistry, computer science, and physics.

See also: Historically Black Colleges and Universities

REFERENCES AND FURTHER READING

Clark Atlanta University. "Clark Atlanta University." [Online article or information; retrieved October 29, 2007.] http://www.cau.edu/.

Clark Atlanta University. "Research Programs: Research Centers." [Online article or information; retrieved August 6, 2006.] http://www.cau.edu/acad_prog/default.html.

Council for Chemical Research

The Council for Chemical Research (CCR) promotes basic research and quality education in chemistry and chemical engineering. The council recognizes outstanding efforts to diversify the community of chemical researchers with its annual Diversity Award.

CCR was founded in 1979 as a vehicle for bringing together interested parties in industry, academia, and government for purposes of furthering the development of chemical research in the United States. By the early 21st century, CCR's membership included such leaders as department chairs or deans in academia and managers or directors of research in industry and government laboratories from more than 200 companies, universities, and government agencies with a major stake in maintaining the nation's global position in chemical technology. CCR maintains a professional staff at its permanent headquarters in Washington, D.C.

As part of CCR's commitment to making the U.S. chemical research workforce the best it can be, the council looks for ways to enhance the diversity of that workforce. One way it achieves this goal is with the CCR Diversity Award. Established in 2002, this award is presented annually to an individual in a leadership position who has contributed in a visionary way to changing the individual's organization in terms of how it promotes diversity in chemical research or education. For example, the first winner of the award was Freeman Hrabowski, president of the University of Maryland Baltimore County (UMBC). With financial assistance from the Robert and Jane Meyerhoff Foundation, Hrabowski established at UMBC the Meyerhoff Scholars Program. This innovative program has helped more than 500 African American students and students belonging to other underrepresented minorities obtain undergraduate and graduate degrees in biochemistry, chemical engineering, chemistry, and other sciences. The award consists of a $3,000 donation to the program of the awardee's choice that has demonstrated significant achievements in advancing and promoting diversity.

See also: Biochemistry; Chemistry; Meyerhoff Scholars Program

REFERENCES AND FURTHER READING
Council for Chemical Research. "CCR Diversity Award." [Online article or information; retrieved October 29, 2007.] http://www.ccrhq.org/about/Diversityaward.htm.

Council for Chemical Research. "The Council for Chemical Research." [Online article or information; retrieved October 29, 2007.] http://www.ccrhq.org/.

Daniel Hale Williams Preparatory School of Medicine

The Daniel Hale Williams Preparatory School of Medicine (DHW) is a charter school in Chicago dedicated to preparing African Americans and members of other underrepresented minorities for careers in medicine. Although dozens of medical charter schools exist throughout the United States, DHW is perhaps the only one that was established specifically to serve people of color.

DHW was founded in 2005 by the Chicago Public Schools as a way to address a major issue related to health disparities: the steadily declining rate of black applicants to medical school. It was named in honor of Daniel Hale Williams, the renowned black physician, surgeon, and hospital administrator. Located on the campus of Jean Baptiste Point DuSable High School in Chicago's South Side, the school is funded in part by a five-year, $500,000 grant from the Bill & Melinda Gates Foundation. It is also supported by the Midwestern University Chicago College of Osteopathic Medicine in a school partnership arrangement.

By 2011, when the school graduates its inaugural class, DHW's student body is expected to consist of approximately 500 students (85 each in grades 7 through 12). Each year, the first 85 students to apply who are at grade level in reading and mathematics and who agree to complete the six-year program will be accepted into the 7th grade, and higher-grade students will be accepted until the grade maximum of 85 is met. With the student-to-teacher ratio at 22 to 1, the curriculum can be focused on preparing every student to perform well as an undergraduate, particularly in a premed course. Upon the completion of the 11th grade, a student will have taken mathematics courses in prealgebra, algebra, advanced algebra, precalculus, calculus, and trigonometry; science courses in biology, chemistry, physics, and environmental science; and Latin for two to four years. Students choosing the science career path will also study earth science and physiology. The 12th grade is dedicated to college-level courses in mathematics, science, and writing, as well as to participating in internships at the College of Osteopathic Medicine.

Not surprisingly, DHW students are active in science fairs, and in the 2006 Chicago regional science fair, they took home four gold medals and four silver medals—a very impressive accomplishment for a student body that numbered only 85. Also in 2006, the school formed a branch of the Future Doctors of America Club, with 27 inductees. The club is sponsored by the Department of Family Medicine of Provident Hospital of Cook County, the historically black hospital founded by the school's namesake.

See also: Biology; Chemistry; Health Disparities; Physics; Provident Hospital and Training School; Williams, Daniel H.

REFERENCES AND FURTHER READING

Daniel Hale Williams Preparatory School of Medicine. "Welcome to Our School!" [Online article or information; retrieved May 21, 2007.] http://www.wpsm.cps.k12.il.us/.

Delaware State University

Delaware State University is the only historically black institution of higher learning in Delaware. In terms of scientific research, the school is best known for its research in optics and biotechnology.

In 1891, the Delaware state legislature established the Delaware State College for Colored Students to educate African Americans in several fields, including agriculture, chemistry, and engineering. Located in Dover, the state capital, in 1947, the school's name was shortened to Delaware State College. The school underwent major changes in the 1960s, when the state spent millions of dollars to upgrade its buildings and facilities. In 1993, the college became a university and took its present name. Today, Delaware State offers a number of graduate degrees, including master of science degrees in biology, chemistry, and physics. Faculty and students conduct research in a number of scientific fields, but the most notable research takes place under the auspices of the Applied Optics Center and the Delaware Biotechnology Institute.

The Applied Optics Center focuses on research related to nonlinear optics (which investigates the behavior of light at very high light intensities) and laser spectroscopy (the use of lasers to study matter via the unique spectrum of electromagnetic radiation emitted by a specific atom or molecule). Nonlinear optical behavior is best observed in the light produced by pulsed lasers (lasers that project very high-intensity light in short bursts like a strobe light); so the center's goal is to develop spectroscopy systems and other end uses based on laser light sources. To this end, the center experiments with a titanium sapphire laser, several argon ion lasers, and a variety of red, orange, and green helium neon lasers, some of which are capable of projecting laser light in bursts of such short duration they can be measured in femtoseconds (one millionth of one billionth of a second). Many of the finds made by the center have been published in such prestigious scientific journals as the *Journal of Applied Physics, Applied Physics Letters, Journal of Chemical Physics, Physical Review, European Physical Journal*, and *Annales de Physique*.

The center's largest and longest running research project involves blue laser wavelength generation. Pulsed light from the blue and near-ultraviolet bands of the electromagnetic radiation spectrum are suitable for a wide range of applications from optical data storage to medical diagnostics; however, the methods used to develop such wavelengths have been largely unsatisfactory. Consequently, the center is experimenting with new methods for generating blue laser wavelength by doubling wavelengths of red and near-infrared light through the use of various laser-beam-generating crystals, particularly ones made from potassium-titanyl phosphate.

The center conducts much of its research in collaboration with private industry, professional associations, and the federal government. For example, as of 2006, the center was conducting two projects with DadeBehring, a biomedical company located in Newark, Delaware. Both projects involved enhancing the detection method in biomedical equipment that Dade Behring manufactures for diagnosing trace elements or compounds in biological solutions, such as blood and urine, by designing and developing solid-state laser devices for use as the equipment's light sources. Another collaborative project supported the American Dental Association's Pfaffenbarger Research Center efforts to find a better method for curing the various dental polymers used to fill cavities. The method that was being used, a standard curing lamp, often shrank the polymers so much that the filling detached from the tooth cavity walls; so researchers were looking for ways to use pulsed laser light so that the polymers can be cured with a minimum of shrinking. The center was also collaborating with the National Aeronautics and Space Administration (NASA) on a laser amplification project. As part of its Mission Planet Earth Strategic Enterprise Plan, NASA sought a better method for making measurements from outer space. In support of this effort, the center was working to develop an ultraviolet laser system, the first of its kind, with both the high energy output and the high spectral quality such measurements require. This system will also be incorporated into NASA's transmitter technology for the remote sensing of ozone, water vapor, and aerosols in the atmospheres of distant planets and stars.

The Delaware Biotechnology Institute is a consortium of government, academic, and private industry research laboratories located across the state of Delaware. Headquartered at Delaware State, the institute seeks to serve as a center of excellence in biotechnology and the life sciences. Established in 1999, the institute coordinates the activities of more than 50 laboratories and faculty research groups in five focus areas: plant molecular biology (the study of plant genetics), avian genetics, computational biology and computer science, proteomics (the study of the structures and functions of protein), and biomolecular materials (also known as biomaterials).

The institute's plant biologists focus on using modern biotechnology methods to learn more about how plant processes occur at the molecular level. They are particularly interested in how the expression of a plant's genes are regulated by messenger ribonucleic acid (mRNA), which carries genetic coding from deoxyribonucleic acid (DNA) to a cell's ribosomes, where it initiates the production of proteins. Current research focuses on how mRNA is broken down after its work is done and how this process is controlled. So far, this line of investigation has led to interesting disclosures about the role played by certain ribonucleases (the enzymes that break down mRNA) in regulating the permeability or integrity of the cell membrane. It has also shed much light on structure and function of so-called hidden genes (RNA genes that do not produce protein) and is now investigating the role played by such genes in plant physiology. The institute's researchers hope that the results of these and similar investigations will lead to a better understanding of how to enhance crop production, as well as how to develop novel traits in plants.

Institute researchers who are involved in avian genetics are primarily concerned with developing a better understanding of the illnesses that affect poultry. They are particularly interested in Marek's disease, a herpesvirus-induced lymphoma that causes tumors in chickens. Marek's disease is particularly insidious, because it continually mutates, rendering vaccines useless after only a short period. Researchers hope to learn more about how the disease alters white blood cells in infected chickens so that a vaccine can be developed that interferes with the herpesvirus's ability to infect the host cell. Other projects related to avian genetics include analyzing the avian genome (the complete set of avian chromosomes) and studying the role genetics plays in regulating the production of growth hormone in chickens.

In terms of computational biology, institute researchers use sophisticated computer programs to study the growing database of the genomes of various organisms. A major research interest is to develop computer tools for detecting single nucleotide polymorphisms (the small but important variations among the genetic material of individual organisms of the same species). The institute's computational biologists also develop 3-D, interactive maps to detect patterns within and among genomes and to develop computer simulations of biological processes.

In terms of proteomics, institute researchers are studying the soil bacteria known as rhizobia, which fix nitrogen in certain legumes after becoming established inside the root nodules of the legumes. (Nitrogen fixation is the process by which nitrogen is taken from its inert molecular form, N_2, in the atmosphere and converted into nitrogen compounds, such as ammonia, nitrate, and nitrogen dioxide, that are used in various biochemical processes.) Another interesting project involves studying proteins from extremeophiles (organisms that thrive under extreme conditions of temperature, pressure, and/or pH). From understanding how these proteins maintain their structures and functions under extreme conditions, researchers hope to synthesize proteins with enhanced stability and durability for industrial, biotech, and environmental applications.

A major focus of biotechnology is the development of new materials, either from living organisms themselves or by exploiting their bioprocesses. To this end, institute researchers work to develop biosurface modifications for promoting or preventing protein absorption, to create methods for separating and sensing proteins rapidly, to engineer cells and tissues, to synthesize new protein structures that change conformation as a function of pH and temperature, and to develop integrated "lab-on-a-chip" devices for directing the molecular evolution of enzymes. One particularly innovative field involves bio-optoelectronics research, which draws on optics, electronics, and biology to create next-generation, so-called smart fiber optics, biosensors, and DNA-based transistors.

See also: Biology; Chemistry; National Aeronautics and Space Administration; Physics

REFERENCES AND FURTHER READING

Delaware State University. "Delaware State University." [Online article or information; retrieved October 29, 2007.] http://www.desu.edu/.

Delaware State University, Office of the Associate Provost for Research. "Research Administration and Centers." [Online article or information; retrieved October 29, 2007.] http://www.desu.edu/research.

Delta Sigma Theta Sorority

Delta Sigma Theta Sorority (Delta) is a private, nonprofit organization whose purpose is to provide services and programs to promote human welfare.

Founded in 1913 by 22 undergraduate women at Howard University, Delta boasts a membership of more than 200,000 women, most of whom are African American and college-educated. As of 2006, Delta had more than 900 chapters located in the United States, Japan, Germany, Bermuda, the Bahamas, and Korea and a permanent, professional staff located at its international headquarters in Washington, D.C. One of Delta's major program areas is educational development, and to this end, the sorority established and conducts the Science and Everyday Experiences (SEE) Initiative, a community-based science program for black children in grades K–8.

Established in 2002 in conjunction with the Delta Research and Education Foundation (DREF) and the American Association for the Advancement of Science (AAAS), SEE helps the parents and caregivers of black children to help their children develop a better understanding of science and how it affects everything we do, big and small. Specifically, the program trains Delta members to organize and present informal science education activities and events for children and families. Upon completing the leadership workshop, Delta volunteers are able to organize science fairs at local schools; organize field trips to science museums, zoos, planetariums, and botanical gardens; and set up informal science activity tables at church events, community fairs, libraries, scouting events, PTA meetings, family reunions, shopping malls, grocery stores, hair salons, and barber shops. The activities stress how science is connected to everyday experiences, and Delta volunteers encourage families to "play science" on their own at home and to keep an informal journal of their at-home science activities. To further help parents with this part of the program, SEE maintains a Web site where parents can learn how to conduct a wide range of interesting and fun science activities for their children.

Another component of SEE is the Delta SEE Connection, a science radio talk show whose guests are African Americans who are professionally involved in either science, technology, engineering, or mathematics. These interviews highlight cutting-edge scientific research being conducted by blacks at private institutions and research colleges across the nation. Delta SEE Connection is broadcast over Radio One, a conglomerate of 51 radio stations in urban and African American markets, and on Science Update, an AAAS radio program. The purpose of Delta SEE Connection is to get black children to see black scientists, engineers, and mathematicians as suitable role models and therefore consider careers in science and technology.

See also: American Association for the Advancement of Science; Howard University

REFERENCES AND FURTHER READING

Delta Sigma Theta. "Delta Sigma Theta Sorority, Inc." [Online article or information; retrieved October 29, 2007.] http://www.deltasigmatheta.org/cms/.

SEE Science and Everyday Experiences. "Delta Sigma Theta and DREF Implement SEE." [Online article or information; retrieved June 30, 2006.] http://www.deltasee.com.

Dental Pipeline

The Pipeline, Profession & Practice: Community-Based Dental Education Program, more commonly known as the Dental Pipeline, is a five-year collaborative effort among 15 U.S. dental schools to improve the oral health of African Americans and other underserved minorities. The program recruits and retains minorities who are underrepresented in the field of dentistry and trains them to become dentists in community-based clinical education programs.

The Dental Pipeline was initiated in 2001 by the Robert Wood Johnson Foundation. The program establishes dental care facilities in minority communities, which double as clinical education centers. In this way, minority dental students complete a significant part of their studies near their homes and, in the process, provide inexpensive oral health care to minority communities who would otherwise be underserved by dentists. The Dental Pipeline was implemented in response to *Oral Health in America: A Report of the Surgeon General* (2000, http://profiles.nlm.nih.gov/NN/B/B/J/T/segments.html), which made it clear that minority communities are underserved in terms of dental care. Two major contributors to this problem, according to the report, were the facts that minorities comprise a miniscule percentage of the students attending dental school and that the cost of a dental education had become virtually unaffordable for most potential minority dental students.

In 2003, the Robert Wood Johnson Foundation recruited 11 schools to participate in the Dental Pipeline: Boston University, Howard University, Meharry Medical College, Temple University, Ohio State University, the University of North Carolina at Chapel Hill, the University of California at San Francisco, the University of Connecticut Health Center, the University of Illinois at Chicago, the University of Washington, and West Virginia University. Later that same year, The California Endowment provided funding for four more schools in California to participate: Loma Linda University, the University of California at Los Angeles (UCLA), the University of the Pacific, and the University of Southern California.

Schools participating in the Dental Pipeline establish community-based clinical education programs in minority communities. They also revise the curricula of their dental education programs so that community-based practice and training in cultural competency (how culture affects one's perception of and responsiveness to health care in general) become major portions of the course work. In addition, they implement programs to recruit students living in such communities to enter and then remain in the program until they earn a degree in dentistry. In turn, it is hoped that the graduates of these programs will set up practices in the same or similar communities, thus increasing the access of minority populations to quality oral health care. Assistance in establishing the community-based facilities is provided by the Columbia University Medical Center's Center for Community Health Partnerships, and the UCLA School of Public Health evaluates the overall success of the project.

The Dental Pipeline assigns senior dental students who are clinically competent to community clinics and private practices in or near minority communities, where they treat underserved patients. By the time they complete the program, students have spent approximately 60 days in a community setting, thus enhancing their clinical experience and cultural competency for providing minority patients with the best possible oral health care. In theory, the program also makes nonminority students feel more comfortable treating minority patients. It is hoped that one result of this aspect of the program will be a heightened interest on the part of nonminority graduates to open practices in minority communities or, at least, to practice part time in minority communities. Classroom training focuses on preparing students for the clinical practice portion of the training, so that students receive more clinical training than in a more traditional dental education program.

As of 2007, the Robert Wood Johnson Foundation had provided $15 million to the 11 schools it funds, with each school receiving up to $1.5 million, and The California Endowment had provided $5 million to the four schools it funds, with each school receiving up to $1.3 million. In addition, The California Endowment and the W. K. Kellogg Foundation have provided more than $1.5 million for scholarships to students enrolled in the program; these scholarships are administered by the American Dental Education Association. The program was scheduled to expire in 2007, at which point it was hoped that the community-based programs could continue with alternate sources of funding.

See also: American Dental Education Association; Howard University; Meharry Medical College

REFERENCES AND FURTHER READING

Dental Pipeline. "About Us." [Online article or information; retrieved May 30, 2007.] http://www.dentalpipeline.org/au_aboutus.html.

Department of Energy

The U.S. Department of Energy (DOE) is responsible for domestic energy production, energy conservation, and energy-related research, but it is also responsible for the nation's nuclear weapons program, nuclear reactor production for the U.S. Navy, and the disposal of radioactive waste.

Consequently, the department oversees a number of the nation's major research laboratories, and it is one of the largest federal supporters of basic research. DOE supports a number of programs designed to bring more African Americans and other underrepresented minorities into the ranks of working scientists. These programs include the Minority Educational Institution Student Partnership Program, the Mickey Leland Energy Fellowship Program, the National Energy Technology Laboratory's Historically Black Colleges and Universities and Other Minority Institutions Program, the DOE Faculty and Student Team Program at the Oak Ridge National Laboratory, the Minority Institutions Biological and Environmental Student Research Participation Program, and the Office of Civilian Radioactive Waste Management Minority Service Institution Undergraduate Scholarship Program.

DOE attained cabinet-level status in 1977, but its origins go back to World War II and the Manhattan Project, the federal government's effort to build an atomic bomb. As of 2007, the department oversaw the activities of 25 national laboratories whose research activities include the development of fuel cells and advanced batteries for hybrid electric cars, solar energy, clean coal research, nuclear reactor design and safety, the storage and elimination of radioactive waste from commercial nuclear reactors, and the development of innovative technologies for identifying, extracting, and exploiting alternative sources of fossil fuels. DOE also supports basic scientific research in areas such as advanced scientific computing, biology and environmental research, high-energy physics, basic energy sciences, fusion energy research, nuclear physics, and the development of nanoscale materials. The DOE mission requires that it support the education and professional development of the future's scientists, and to this end, it promotes diversity programs that prepare African Americans and other underrepresented minorities for careers in its science and engineering workforce.

One vehicle for accomplishing this mission is the Minority Educational Institution Student Partnership Program (MEISPP), a summer internship program. The program offers selected undergraduates, who are majoring in biology, computer science, information technology, geology, microbiology, or physics, the opportunity to participate in ongoing research projects at DOE's national laboratories. As an intern for an eight-week period during the summer, each student works closely with a mentor who guides the student through practical work experiences that are related to the student's overall professional goals. Interns also participate in workshops that are designed to develop well-rounded leaders and successful project managers of scientific research efforts. Workshops address such issues as time management, the development of a professional identity, and effective communications skills. The program also gives students the opportunity to network with experts in their chosen field throughout the department and its laboratories, thus developing important contacts for the future. MEISSP internships are excellent preparation for future careers in the department and often lead to full-time employment after graduation.

Successful applicants must have completed their sophomore year and demonstrated leadership potential, a commitment to public service, an interest in energy-related issues, and strong written and verbal communications skills. In terms of financial support, the program offers a salary, lodging, and reimbursement of travel expenses to and from the location of the internship. Each participating office within the department selects its own MEISSP interns based on its needs, qualifications, and interests of the applicants.

The duties and responsibilities of interns vary according to the office of assignment. For instance, interns may write reports on environmental management issues; assist with clean air policy and technology; help develop and advance oil, coal, and natural gas technologies; or work with issues such as energy efficiency, international nuclear safety, cyber security, and waste management. Research duties assigned to interns are anything but routine; for example, one intern researched a new boride semiconductor that is able to absorb beta radiation without damage under space flight conditions with Plutonium–238, the nuclear fuel of choice for space missions. Another intern ran experiments that tested the density of nickel chloride, a compound commonly used in organic syntheses and electroplating, in solutions at various temperatures, pressures, and concentrations, and then used this data to calculate thermodynamic information. Still another intern wrote a comparison report of three high-temperature superconductor cable projects.

The Mickey Leland Energy Fellowship Program is a summer internship program that provides minority college students the opportunity to conduct research related to fossil fuel energy at one of DOE's national laboratories. Originally known as the Minority Education Initiative, in 2000, the program was renamed to honor the memory of the distinguished African American congressman from Texas. The program began with a focus on geology, specifically how to develop innovative methods for discovering large concentrations of fossil fuels. It quickly expanded, however, to include all scientific and engineering disciplines related to the research efforts of the DOE Office of Fossil Energy. Undergraduates who are majoring in the geosciences, physics, chemistry, or engineering are eligible for the program. Since its renaming, the program offers more than 100 internships per year. Upon completing their college education, interns receive special consideration for employment opportunities with DOE.

The National Energy Technology Laboratory (NETL) in Pittsburgh is the DOE's only national laboratory devoted to fossil energy research. Since 1984, NETL and its predecessors have sponsored the Historically Black Colleges and Universities and Other Minority Institutions (HBCU/OMI) Program. The program serves as a vehicle for involving African Americans and other

Students from North Carolina Agricultural and Technical State University participate in the faculty and student teams program at the Department of Energy's Argonne National Laboratory (Department of Energy)

underrepresented minorities in the development of innovative methods for exploiting coal, petroleum, and natural gas that are energy efficient and environmentally sound. Specifically, the program encourages and supports faculty and students at HBCUs and other minority-serving institutions to conduct research related to NETL's mission by offering research grants to such institutions. As a result, the program facilitates the transfer of technologies developed at minority-serving institutions to the private sector, and it strengthens ties between minority institutions and private industry so as to promote careers for minorities as scientists, engineers, technicians, and managers, in endeavors related to the extraction and development of fossil fuels.

Through the Oak Ridge National Laboratory (ORNL) in Oak Ridge, Tennessee, DOE supports the Oak Ridge Institute of Science and Education (ORISE). ORISE administers a number of DOE scientific education projects, including several intended specifically for minority students and faculty at HBCUs. The DOE Faculty and Student Team Program at ORNL brings teams from HBCUs and other minority-serving institutions to ORNL to conduct research concerning energy, the environment, and the basic sciences for 10 weeks during the summer. Teams consist of a faculty member and two or three students, all from the same school, whose discipline/major is related to computer science, earth science, environmental science, biology, biomedicine, or physics, among others. The Minority Institutions Biological and Environmental Student Research Participation Program is a 10-week summer program for students interested in conducting research related to health and the environment. The program is open to graduate students whose research is related to atmospheric science, biochemistry, biology, biophysics, bioremediation, biostatistics, chemistry, ecology, genetics, genomics, marine science, molecular and cellular biology, measurement science, molecular nuclear medicine, nuclear medicine, pathology, physics, physiology, radiation biology, structural biology, the earth sciences, or toxicology, among others. The DOE Office of Civilian Radioactive Waste Management (OCRWM) Minority Service Institution Undergraduate Scholarship Program offers scholarships to undergraduates pursuing careers of interest to the OCRWM. Juniors and seniors majoring in science, engineering, engineering technology, or mathematics are eligible for one of 12 two-year scholarships.

See also: Biology; Computer Science; Historically Black Colleges and Universities; Microbiology; Physics

REFERENCES AND FURTHER READING

Haas Center for Public Service. "Mickey Leland Energy Fellowship: A Summer Internship Program Providing Energy Opportunities for Minority Students." [Online article or information; retrieved June 6, 2007.] http://haas. stanford.edu/external_fellowships/fellowship.php?ef_id=142&.

National Energy Technology Laboratory. "Advanced Research: Historically Black Colleges and Universities and Other Minority Institutions (HBCU/ OMI) Program." [Online article or information; retrieved June 18, 2007.] http://www.netl.doe.gov/technologies/coalpower/advresearch/hbcu.html.

U.S. Department of Energy. "Minority Educational Institution Student Partnership Program." [Online article or information; retrieved June 6, 2007.] http://www.doeminorityinternships.org/.

U.S. Department of Energy. "U.S. Department of Energy." [Online article or information; retrieved October 29, 2007.] http://www.energy.gov/.

Development Fund for Black Students in Science and Technology

The Development Fund for Black Students in Science and Technology (DFBSST) is a nonprofit, tax-exempt organization that provides scholarships to African American undergraduates who are majoring in scientific or technical fields of study at historically black colleges and universities (HBCUs).

DFBSST was established in 1983 by five black technical professionals living in Washington, D.C. Health physicists Hattie Carwell and Julian Earls, computer specialist James Hicks, builder and construction contractor James Jones, and civil engineer Knox Tull realized that it is essential to provide financial assistance to talented black students who choose to pursue scientific or technical careers. Their goal was to support such students at HBCUs, where it has been demonstrated that African American students experience the highest rates of retention and graduation. Moreover, HBCUs have trained almost 90 percent of the African American scientists who have received their professional training in the United States since the 1920s. Since the beginning of the DFBSST, the founding five have been joined by a number of other black technical professionals, most of whom contribute at least $1,000 annually to the organization's endowment fund.

As of 2007, DFBSST had provided more than $240,000 in scholarships to more than 100 students in fields such as astrophysics, biology, chemistry, computer science, physics, aerospace engineering, and chemical engineering. Each scholarship provides a student with up to $2,000 per year for up to four years. Recipients are students at HBCUs who have been identified by their respective deans and faculty members as being worthy of financial support. Scholarships are awarded based on academic achievement, career goals, and faculty recommendations, although some are awarded on the basis of financial need.

DFBSST is incorporated in Washington, D.C. Its affairs are conducted by a volunteer board of directors; so it maintains no permanent offices or paid staff. Its funding comes from annual donations by members, contributions from other interested parties, and the Combined Federal Campaign of the National Capital Area.

See also: Astronomy and Astrophysics; Biology; Chemistry; Computer Science; Historically Black Colleges and Universities; Physics

REFERENCES AND FURTHER READING
Development Fund for Black Students in Science and Technology. "Development Fund for Black Students in Science and Technology." [Online article or information; retrieved October 29, 2007.] http://dfbsst.dlhjr.com/.

Diversity Institute

The Diversity Institute was a professional development program for faculty and graduate students in the STEM disciplines (science, technology, engineering, and mathematics). Its purpose was to teach STEM faculty, both present and future, how to teach science and related subjects to students of diverse backgrounds so as to improve the chances that students from all backgrounds, but especially African Americans and members of other underrepresented minorities, will continue on to graduate school and earn PhDs in the STEM disciplines.

The institute was established in 2004 by the Center for the Integration of Research, Teaching and Learning (CIRTL). It was headquartered at the University of Wisconsin–Madison's Wisconsin Center for Education Research and funded by the National Science Foundation. The institute was established in response to a growing concern that African Americans and other underrepresented minorities were embarking on careers in the STEM disciplines at a rate that was alarmingly lower than for students from privileged backgrounds and that this fact was contributing to an overall shortage of Americans holding PhDs in the STEM disciplines. In response, the institute's staff and consultants set out to develop an intellectual foundation for inclusive teaching and to generate new teaching tools for those who teach the STEM disciplines at the college level.

The backbone of the program was the institute's consultants, known as Diversity Scholars. The Diversity Scholars were faculty members from the three schools that support CIRTL (Wisconsin–Madison, Pennsylvania State University, and Michigan State University) who are experts in diversity issues in STEM teaching and learning and who are interested in incorporating diversity in STEM classrooms and laboratories. From 2004 to 2005, the Diversity Scholars reviewed and provided feedback to the institute's staff on hundreds of abstracts, articles, and manuscripts addressing inclusive teaching practices and their impact on students, diversity in the classroom, classroom climate, and the profile of underrepresented students pursuing STEM majors. They also met with the staff to discuss strategies for encouraging inclusion in STEM teaching and learning. The staff used this input to generate four pieces of work: a literature review, a resource book, a case book, and a self-guided workshop. In 2005, the institute presented this work to the public at the CIRTL Forum 2005, Addressing the Student Learning Experience: Achieving Diversity in STEM Disciplines, in Madison, Wisconsin.

The forum brought together more than 200 administrators, faculty, and graduate students from almost 60 major research universities to discuss ways to train faculty, but especially future faculty, to become more sensitive to issues related to diversity in the STEM classroom. In particular, it focused on improving the STEM classroom experience for women and underrepresented minorities by developing inclusive learning environments. Several studies have shown that underrepresented minorities often do not complete their studies in a science or science-related major, because they do not feel welcome in the classroom or the department, but that they are encouraged to complete such studies when students and faculty, regardless of background, are able to work together well. Both the forum and the institute's work were designed to give faculty and future faculty new tools for creating classrooms where students and teachers "work together well."

The institute's literature review presents readers with the latest research on inclusive teaching techniques and information about the challenges that minority students still face. The review cites more than 130 abstracts, articles, and manuscripts that the Diversity Scholars found most useful. The resource book, *Reaching All Students: A Resource Book for Teaching in Science, Technology, Engineering and Mathematics (STEM)* (2nd ed., Madison, WI: Diversity Institute, 2007), contains articles that emphasize effective instructional models, strong communication with all students, student learning styles and preferences, effective assessment of one's teaching, and awareness of student demographics. The case book, *Case Studies in Inclusive Teaching in Science, Technology, Engineering and Mathematics (STEM)*, is a workbook for facilitating discussions about diversity among faculty, administrators, and graduate students. The heart of the workbook is a series of one-page case studies of challenging educational situations, usually involving a white professor and a minority student. The self-guided workshop, *Unmasking Inequality: A Self-Guided Workshop on Educational Success*, is designed to enhance awareness of fundamental issues surrounding diversity and thus enable professors to help students from all backgrounds nurture and fulfill their interest in becoming scientists.

Although the institute's work ended in 2005, the Diversity Scholars continued to disseminate the results of that work at national meetings and conferences. In addition, the literature review, the resource book, the case book, and the self-guided workshop were published in print form and made available online (2004).

See also: National Science Foundation

REFERENCES AND FURTHER READING

CIRTL Diversity Institute. "Mission, Goals & Strategy." [Online article or information; retrieved May 22, 2007.] http://cirtl.wceruw.org/Diversity Resources/about/mission/.

Endocrine Society

The Endocrine Society is the world's largest professional organization of endocrinologists and related biomedical researchers. The society works to make the field of endocrinology more diverse through the activities of its Minority Affairs Committee.

The Endocrine Society was founded in 1917 as a vehicle for promoting sound research concerning the endocrine glands (which secrete hormones and other biochemical mediators for regulating the activities of virtually every human organ and tissue). Originally known as the Association for the Study of Internal Secretions, the society took on its present name in 1952. By 2007, its membership had risen to 13,000, and it maintained a professional staff and a permanent headquarters in Chevy Chase, Maryland. Today, it supports the study not only of the endocrine glands and their secretions, but also of the many diseases and conditions associated with them, such as diabetes, infertility, osteoporosis, thyroid disease, obesity, and pituitary tumors. The society also works to foster a greater understanding of endocrinology among the general public and to promote the interests of all endocrinologists at the national level. To this end, the society seeks to increase the diversity of its membership, and of endocrinologists in general, by means of a number of programs, the most important of which is the teaching of so-called Shortcourses in Endocrinology at historically black colleges and universities (HBCUs) and other minority-serving institutions.

The Shortcourses program was inaugurated in 1996 as a way to introduce endocrinology as a field of scientific endeavor to undergraduate students at minority-serving institutions and to educate them on the number and types of opportunities open to researchers in that field. Funded by a grant from the National Institute of General Medical Sciences (NIGMS), Shortcourses can be integrated into a basic or advanced biology class, presented as a stand-alone workshop, incorporated into a school symposium, offered as a seminar to science students, used to present cutting-edge research, or structured in a number of other ways to meet the needs of the host institution. Each year, volunteer members of the society present dozens of Shortcourses free of charge. During the 2004–2005 academic year, for example, 42 Shortcourses were presented to approximately 3,000 students at minority-serving institutions, including the following HBCUs: Benedict College, Florida A&M University, Grambling State University, Jackson State University, Johnson C. Smith University, Lane College, Lemoyne-Owen College, Lincoln University of Missouri, Meharry Medical College, North Carolina A&T State University, Savannah State University, Southern University, Talladega College, Tennessee State University, Tougaloo College, the University of the Virgin Islands, Virginia State University, and Xavier University of Louisiana. In addition to teaching Shortcourses, the volunteer presenters remain on campus for several days to participate in existing biology courses, appear on radio talk shows, give television interviews, lecture about endocrine disorders, and advise interested students about graduate and professional schools.

To follow up on the success of Shortcourses, the society offers travel grants to students and faculty who participate in the program so that they may attend the society's annual meeting. In 2005, such grants were awarded to five faculty members and 25 students from HBCUs. While at the annual meeting, these grantees were invited to participate in the Minority Mentoring Reception. Attendees are invited to discuss with senior endocrinologists a variety of topics such as the availability of careers related to endocrinology in science education, administration, industry and biotechnology, choosing and planning a career path, obtaining tenure, and writing successful grant applications.

In addition to Shortcourses, the society offers the Summer Research Opportunity (SRO) Program for Minority Students. Funded by the Federation of

American Societies for Experimental Biology and NIGMS's Minority Access to Research Career (MARC) Program, SRO provides undergraduates the opportunity to conduct research related to endocrinology during an eight-week period in the summer. Research is conducted at the laboratory of a sponsoring society member, and the program pays for some if not all of the students' travel and living expenses. Not only does the program allow students to gain valuable experience in scientific research, but it also affords them the opportunity to network with senior practitioners in the field.

See also: Biology; Diabetes; Florida A&M University; Historically Black Colleges and Universities; Jackson State University; Lincoln University of Missouri; Meharry Medical College; National Institute of General Medical Sciences; North Carolina A&T State University; Obesity; Southern University and A&M College System; Tennessee State University; Tougaloo College; University of the Virgin Islands; Virginia State University; Xavier University of Louisiana

REFERENCES AND FURTHER READING

Endocrine Society. "Minority Activities." [Online article or information; retrieved May 8, 2007.] http://www.endo-society.org/minorityactivities/.
Endocrine Society. "The Endocrine Society." [Online article or information; retrieved October 29, 2007.] http://www.endo-society.org/.

Environmental Careers Organization

The Environmental Careers Organization (ECO) is a national, nonprofit organization that provides professional training for those seeking careers in the environmental field. ECO seeks to enhance the training of college students and recent graduates who focus their studies on the environmental sciences with paid internships with various corporations, nonprofit organizations, and government agencies that play an active role in environmental affairs. ECO is committed to increasing the number of African Americans and other minorities in the environmental field, and to this end, it operates the Diversity Initiative.

ECO was founded in Boston, in 1972, where it maintains a professional staff and a permanent headquarters. Since then, the organization has been placing as many as 500 highly trained individuals per year in internships with sponsoring organizations that enhance their abilities as environmentalists. ECO interns, known as associates, receive on-the-job office, laboratory, and field training in such facets of the environmental sciences as resource conservation, hazardous waste management, public policy, environmental education, community sustainability, and climate change, to name but a few. Associates are employed from between 12 weeks to two years, and they earn between $400 and $800 per week, in addition to allowances for relocation, housing, travel, and career development. Many associates are hired by their sponsors immediately upon completion of their internships.

In 1990, ECO became concerned about the relative paucity of African Americans and other underrepresented minorities seeking careers as environmentalists. That same year, the organization implemented the Diversity Initiative as a means of redressing this problem. One step was to achieve greater diversity among the ECO staff. Another step was to investigate environmental issues affecting people of color and their current status in the environmental movement, the results of which were published by ECO in *Beyond the Green: Redefining and Diversifying the Environmental Movement* (Boston: Environmental Careers Organization, 1992). Then ECO began developing recruitment programs and support groups to encourage and assist African Americans and other minorities to consider careers that involve protecting and enhancing the environment.

As of 2007, ECO has taken on more than 2,000 minorities, many of them African American, as associates and placed them with more than 500 public, private, and nonprofit organizations. As part of this effort, ECO developed multiyear cooperative agreements with several agencies of the federal government, including the Environmental Protection Agency, the Fish and Wildlife Service, and the Forest Service. In addition, ECO has raised more than $15 million in support of the Diversity Initiative, including more than $5 million from major corporate sponsors such as Ford Motor Company, DuPont, and IBM. ECO also sponsors the National Roundtables on Diversity in the Environment as part of the Diversity Initiative.

REFERENCES AND FURTHER READING

Environmental Careers Organization. "Diversity Initiative." [Online article or information; retrieved February 27, 2007.] http://www.eco.org/site/c.dnJLKPNnFkG/b.942795/k.122B/Diversity_Initiative.htm.

Environmental Careers Organization. "Welcome to ECO!" [Online article or information; retrieved October 29, 2007.] http://www.eco.org/site/c.dnJLKPNnFkG/b.795025/k.AA86/The_Environmental_Careers_Organization.htm.

Evans-Allen Program Formula Fund

The Evans-Allen Program Formula Fund provides federal funding for agricultural research at 18 historically black colleges and universities (HBCUs). Evans-Allen research generally falls under one of eight categories: animal science, aquaculture, biomedicine, food and nutrition, international development, natural resources, plant and soil science, and rural development. Administered by the Department of Agriculture's Cooperative State Research,

Education and Extension Service, the fund has provided more than $1 billion for agricultural research at HBCUs since its inception in 1977, and it has served to attract other funding for scientific research conducted at HBCUs.

The fund was created by the Evans-Allen Act, the popular name for Section 1445 of the National Agricultural Research, Extension and Teaching Policy Act (NARETPA) of 1977. The purpose of the act was to provide federal funding for the land-grant institutions established by the Second Morrill Act of 1890, all of which are state-supported HBCUs. These schools include Alabama A&M University, Alcorn State University in Mississippi, Delaware State University, Florida A&M University, Fort Valley State University in Georgia, Kentucky State University, Langston University in Oklahoma, Lincoln University of Missouri, North Carolina A&T State University, Prairie View A&M University in Texas, South Carolina State University, Southern University in Louisiana, Tennessee State University, the University of Arkansas at Pine Bluff, the University of Maryland Eastern Shore, Virginia State University, and West Virginia State University. In addition, Tuskegee University was included under the auspices of the act, because it performs a role identical to the other 17 schools.

While the land-grant institutions established by the Morrill Act of 1862 were given land as part of their endowment, the land-grant schools established in 1890 were given only cash, and precious little of that. Moreover, prior to 1977, all federal funding for research at the 1890 schools had been funneled through the 1862 schools. The result was a gross underfunding of research projects at public HBCUs. The Evans-Allen Act changed this situation by providing money for agricultural research directly to the 1890 schools. Although annual allocations in the first several years rarely exceeded $50,000 per school, over time the amount of money provided yearly to each of the 1890 schools exceeded $1 million. For example, in fiscal year 2004, funding ranged from a low of $1,015,561 (Delaware State) to a high of $3,161,411 (Prairie View A&M), and the total dispersed to the 18 schools that year exceeded $33 million. Today, the total amount of Evans-Allen money distributed to the 18 schools exceeds $1 billion. To a certain degree, the Evans-Allen Program Fund provides HBCUs with even more money than that, because the act requires schools receiving Evans-Allen money to provide matching funds equal to 50 percent from nongovernment sources, thus providing school administrators with a tool and an incentive to raise funds for scientific research from private benefactors and industry.

Evans-Allen funds have served as the foundation and lifeblood of HBCU agricultural research programs, because they provided funds for upgrading research facilities and for attracting top-notch research faculty. As a result, the 1890 schools are able to conduct first-class research, which in turn induces the federal government and private industry to fund other types of scientific research at HBCUs.

See also: Alabama A&M University; Delaware State University; Florida A&M University; Fort Valley State University (FVSU); Historically Black Colleges and Universities; Kentucky State University; Langston University; Lincoln University of Missouri; North Carolina A&T State University; Prairie View A&M University; South Carolina State University; Southern University and A&M College System; Tennessee State University; Tuskegee University; University of Arkansas at Pine Bluff; University of Maryland Eastern Shore; Virginia State University; West Virginia State University.

REFERENCES AND FURTHER READING

U.S. Department of Agriculture, Cooperative State Research, Education and Extension Service. "Evans-Allen Program Formula Grant." [Online article or information; retrieved January 3, 2007.] http://www.csrees.usda.gov/business/awards/formula/evansallen.html.

Federation of American Societies for Experimental Biology

The Federation of American Societies for Experimental Biology (FASEB) is an association of scientific societies whose missions focus on conducting biological research and then promoting and disseminating information about the results. In terms of diversity, FASEB seeks to attract more African Americans and members of other underrepresented minorities to the ranks of biological researchers through the FASEB Minority Access to Research Careers (FASEB MARC) Program, which is funded by the National Institute of General Medical Sciences (NIGMS).

FASEB was founded in 1912 by three societies as a means of establishing uniform policies and protocols for conducting research in the biological sciences. By the early 21st century, the federation's membership has grown to 21 societies, and it maintains a professional staff and a permanent headquarters in Bethesda, Maryland. Meanwhile, its original focus has expanded to incorporate advocacy for government research policies that promote scientific research in the biological sciences. As part of its commitment to expand and improve the kinds of research activities of particular interest to NIGMS, FASEB encourages and assists minority students in obtaining doctorates in the biomedical and behavioral sciences. These activities include granting travel awards to minority students and faculty members so that they can attend the annual meetings, scientific conferences, and summer research programs of FASEB's constituent societies and those of other scientific societies; funding travel by visiting scientists who give career development presentations at historically black colleges and universities (HBCUs) and other minority-serving institutions; and presenting seminars and workshops on how to write successful grant applications.

There are several types of FASEB MARC travel awards. The Faculty/ Mentors and Students Travel Award provides funding for one faculty member and for one or two students from an HBCU or other minority-serving institution who are majoring in a biological science; the purpose of the funding is to participate in a national meeting or conference related to biomedical research. These assemblages do not have to be sponsored by one of FASEB's constituent societies; for example, the award also funds faculty and students who wish to attend the Annual Biomedical Research Conference for Minority Students (ABRCMS). The award may be used to pay for registration fees, travel expenses, and food and lodging during the meeting. The Poster/Platform (Oral) Presenter Travel Award provides funding for undergraduate, graduate, or postgraduate students and postdoctoral fellows to attend national meetings or conferences at which they will be making either oral or poster presentations of their research.

Since 1982, FASEB has sponsored a number of summer research conferences, at which prominent scientists make presentations concerning cutting-edge biomedical research to other scientists with similar research interests. To encourage minority researchers to attend one of the 30 or so research conferences held each summer, FASEB MARC offers Program Travel Awards to help defray part or all of the travel expenses incurred by minority faculty, post-doctorates, and advanced graduate students. A related program is the Summer Research Opportunity Program (SROP), which covers travel and living expenses for minority students who wish to spend from 4 to 12 weeks during the summer conducting research at the laboratory of a sponsoring FASEB senior scientist. SROP awards include funding for students to travel to the upcoming meeting of ABRCMS or to the annual meeting of a FASEB member society so that they can present their findings. The number of institutions that participate in SROP varies from year to year; in 2007, for example, 16 sponsors, including Rockefeller and Johns Hopkins universities, hosted SROP students.

To assist minority faculty and students with their career choices and professional development, FASEB MARC conducts the Career Development Seminars at Minority Institutions program. Minority-serving institutions that host the program can choose from a number of topics that they would like the seminar to be focused on; topics include "Networking: A Required Skill for Success," "Mentoring: A Proven Strategy for Developing Students," and "Becoming a Scientist: Considerations for the Minority Student in Choosing a Career in Science."

FASEB MARC offers minority researchers two programs to help them write better grant proposals. Under contract to the National Institutes of Health, Grant Writers' Seminars and Workshops LLC conducts a program in Bethesda, Maryland, called Write Winning Grants. This program helps grant writers enhance their abilities to generate research ideas that are novel and innovative and then express those ideas clearly and persuasively in their grant applications. To encourage minority grant writers to attend this program, FASEB MARC offers 75 travel grants of up to $750 each to pay for transportation, food, lodging, registration fees, and course materials. Awardees must be actively engaged in research and possess a PhD in their chosen discipline. For those who are unable or unwilling to travel to Bethesda, FASEB contracts with Grant Writers' to conduct one-day seminar versions of Write Winning Grants at various HBCUs and other minority-serving institutions around the country.

See also: Historically Black Colleges and Universities; National Institute of General Medical Sciences; National Institutes of Health

REFERENCES AND FURTHER READING

Federation of American Societies for Experimental Biology. "Federation of American Societies for Experimental Biology." [Online article or information; retrieved October 29, 2007.] http://www.faseb.org/.

Federation of American Societies for Experimental Biology. "Minority Access to Research Careers." [Online article or information; retrieved May 9, 2007.] http://marc.faseb.org/.

Fisk University

Fisk University is one of the foremost historically black colleges and universities. Founded as a school for training African Americans who wished to be preachers and/or teachers, Fisk boasts a long and proud history as a top-notch scientific institution, as well as a first-rate liberal arts institution. Although Fisk scientists have made important contributions in a number of disciplines, the school is best known for its contributions to physics.

Fisk was founded in 1866 in Nashville, Tennessee, by the United Church of Christ as a school for freedpeople. In 1871, it began offering college courses, and in 1875, it awarded its first bachelor's degree. In 1967, it attained university status. In 2006, the Newsweek-Kaplan survey, a prestigious college evaluation survey, named it one of the top 25 universities in the United States, and *Peterson's*, a prestigious college evaluation publication, regularly ranks it as one of the nation's top colleges for science. A recent National Science Foundation study revealed that Fisk alumni have received more doctorate degrees in the natural sciences (biology, chemistry, and physics) than the alumni of any other single college or university in the nation. Elmer S. Imes, the famous physicist, was a Fisk alumni, as was the chemist St. Elmo Brady, while Percy L. Julian, the famous chemist, taught at Fisk and served on its board of trustees.

The history of Fisk's contributions to physics begins in 1929, when Elmer Imes returned there to found its physics department. Imes had published several papers concerning the use of infrared spectroscopy, the study of the bands (spectra) of infrared light emitted by atoms and molecules, as a tool for studying the structures of atoms and molecules, and, upon returning to Fisk, he continued this pioneering research. His interest in infrared spectroscopy was shared by his eventual successor as department chair, James Lawson. In 1948, Lawson obtained a custom-built infrared spectrometer of research quality from the University of Michigan, where Lawson and Imes had received their doctoral degrees.

Lawson left Fisk the following year, but his successor, Nelson Fuson, continued the work of Imes and Lawson by founding the Fisk Infrared Spectroscopy Research Laboratory. In short order, Fuson and his graduate students began publishing the results of their research regarding atomic and molecular structure in the journals of the American Physical Society (APS) and the American Chemical Society (ACS). More important, these same students began reporting their findings at regional meetings of both organizations, which until that time had been segregated affairs. But the brilliance of the presentations and the findings of the Fisk students caused both the APS and the ACS to begin holding their regional meetings for the Southeastern states at hotels that welcomed blacks. In 1956, Fisk hosted the Southeastern Section meeting of the APS, the first time any national scientific organization had met at a historically black college or university. More than 100 scientists from across the South, most of them white, attended the three-day meeting, during which they stayed in Fisk dormitories. Thus, in addition to making some valuable contributions to physics and chemistry, Fisk faculty and students used science to strike important blows for integration years before the Civil Rights Movement got underway.

Having recognized that it was doing cutting-edge work in infrared spectroscopy, in 1953, the staff of the Fisk Infrared Spectroscopy Research Laboratory decided to hold a weeklong seminar on how to use infrared spectroscopy to analyze materials of interest to physicists, chemists, and biologists in both academia and industry. Instrument manufacturers were also invited to demonstrate their spectrometers, because these devices were just beginning to be made available commercially. The seminar, known as the Fisk Infrared Institute, was so popular that it attracted scientists from around the world and continues to be held into the 21st century. Over the years, the institute has included other analytical techniques such as gas chromatography, visible spectroscopy, Raman spectroscopy, and pollution analysis.

As of 2006, the Fisk physics department was conducting research in a number of areas. The Chemical Physics Group focuses on two distinct areas. One is nanotechnology (to give some example of how incredibly small nanoscale materials are, a human hair is approximately 70,000 nanometers thick). Nanotechnology involves the fabrication and discovery of novel phenomena, the properties and functions of materials at nanoscale, and the understanding and

Since 1929, Fisk University has produced a number of the nation's foremost black physicists. (Library of Congress)

control of matter at dimensions of roughly 1 to 100 nanometers, where unique phenomena lead to novel applications.

The other is the research and development of explosive, biological, and chemical detection applications at trace level as a means of enhancing homeland security. The Optical Materials Group is involved in the development of new optical materials for applications in the areas of lasers, waveguide devices, and biosensors. The Materials Science and Applications Group is involved in the crystal growth of novel materials. These materials include electronic materials that are the basis for radiation detectors and optical crystals that are useful for infrared lasers. The Center for Photonic Materials and Devices researches and develops technologies for the National Aeronautics and Space Administration (NASA) in the field of photonics (the science and technology of generating and controlling photons), particularly in the visible and near infrared spectrum (a photon is the smallest unit of light energy).

As of this writing, Fisk was establishing the Center for Physics and Chemistry of Materials. The purpose of the center is to provide undergraduate and graduate students with intense, cutting-edge training in a number of the areas just listed. The center will also serve as Fisk's stepping-stone in being able to grant PhD degrees in physics (at the present time it can award only the BS and the MS degrees).

See also: American Chemical Society; American Physical Society; Biology; Brady, St. Elmo; Chemistry; Historically Black Colleges and Universities; Imes, Elmer S.; Julian, Percy L.; National Aeronautics and Space Administration; National Science Foundation; Physics

REFERENCES AND FURTHER READING

Fisk University. "Fisk University." [Online article or information; retrieved October 29, 2007.] http://www.fisk.edu/.

Fisk University. "Natural Sciences and Mathematics." [Online article or information; retrieved October 29, 2007.] http://www.fisk.edu/page.asp?id=185.

Florida A&M University

Founded in the late 19th century as a training school for black teachers, Florida Agricultural and Mechanical University (FAMU) has developed into one of the largest historically black colleges and universities in the country. Its alumni include LaSalle Leffall, the prominent oncological surgeon. In terms of scientific research, FAMU is best known for its College of Pharmacy and Pharmaceutical Sciences.

FAMU, located in Tallahassee, Florida, began its institutional life in 1887 as the State Normal College for Colored Students. Four years later, it was designated Florida's land-grant institution for teaching the agricultural and mechanical arts to African Americans. In 1905, it was designated an institution of higher learning, and in 1910, the year after it was renamed the Florida Agricultural and Mechanical College for Negroes, it began awarding bachelor's degrees. In 1953, the school attained university status and changed its name to Florida Agricultural and Mechanical University, and in 1971, it was made part of Florida's state university system.

FAMU operates research programs in a number of scientific disciplines, but most of its cutting-edge research is being conducted under the aegis of the College of Pharmacy and Pharmaceutical Sciences (COPPS). COPPS originated as the School of Pharmacy in 1951 after community health care leaders and health professionals on campus recognized the need for pharmaceutical services in underserved African American communities across the country. In 1985, it took on its present name and acquired the power to grant PhD degrees, and in 1989, it became FAMU's first school to award a PhD. Today, COPPS is one of the largest colleges of pharmacy in the country.

As of 2006, COPPS was conducting biomedical research in several research centers. The AIDS Research Center works to develop, synthesize, and test new pharmaceutical agents, such as anti-inflammatory steroids, for attacking HIV, the virus that causes AIDS. It also works to increase the number of black investigators conducting AIDS-related research.

The Center for the Study of Cardiovascular Disease investigates atherosclerosis (hardening of the arteries). In a heart affected by atherosclerosis, plaque (a combination of fats, cholesterol, blood cells, and calcium deposits) builds up in the blood vessels that provide blood to the heart, thus blocking the passage of blood and leading to a heart attack. By arriving at a better understanding of atherosclerosis, the center's researchers ultimately hope to be able to develop a pharmaceutical treatment for the disease. The Drug Abuse Research Center, in conjunction with the National Institute on Drug Abuse, studies the effects of cocaine and other types of drug addiction on individuals, as well as the impact of drug addiction on minority communities. The center also works with local organizations and law enforcement officials to combat drug abuse–related problems in Tallahassee. The Center for Drug Delivery seeks to optimize the effectiveness of pharmaceutical drugs in general by developing new drug delivery approaches. Specifically, the center investigates ways to link drugs to biomedical carriers, which can target them to the site of action; to incorporate polymeric delivery systems, which can deliver the drug at specified times and controlled rates; and to disperse a drug in semisolid and solid matrices, such as biodegradable gels and tablets, to produce sustained action. One of the most interesting of these projects involves the use of propellant-based aerosol products for the delivery of anticancer medications. Under contract to the National Aeronautics and Space Administration (NASA), the center is developing a patch for administering the sleep agent melatonin to astronauts during space travel. The Neuroscience Research Center focuses on arriving at a better understanding of the aging brain and the process of neurodegeneration (the process by which the aging brain gradually loses its ability to function).

The Center for Minority Prostate Cancer Training and Research works to eliminate the disproportionate prostate cancer morbidity and mortality experienced by African American men in Florida. To this end, the center conducts prostate cancer research while maintaining a series of support networks and activities to assist the African American community.

See also: Cancer; Historically Black Colleges and Universities; Leffall, LaSalle D., Jr.; National Aeronautics and Space Administration; National Institute on Drug Abuse

REFERENCES AND FURTHER READING

FAMU College of Pharmacy and Pharmaceutical Sciences. "Research Centers and Programs." [Online article or information; retrieved August 13, 2006.] http://pharmacy.famu.edu/Research.asp.

Florida A&M University. "Florida A&M University." [Online article or information; retrieved October 29, 2007.] http://www.famu.edu/.

Ford Foundation Diversity Fellowships

The Ford Foundation Diversity Fellowships seek to increase the number of African Americans and members of other underrepresented minorities who teach science and other research-based courses at the nation's colleges and universities. The Diversity Fellowships program supports education and training for minority professors who are committed to using diversity as a resource for enriching the education of all students.

The Diversity Fellowships for Achieving Excellence in College and University Teaching, as they are known in full, are an initiative of the Ford Foundation. Founded in 1936 by Edsel Ford and two executives of the Ford Motor Company as an independent, nonprofit, nongovernmental charitable organization, the foundation has demonstrated a strong and continued interest in matters related to science and education. The Diversity Fellowships program is administered by the National Research Council, a constituent member of the National Academies, from its headquarters in Washington, D.C.

Diversity Fellowships are awarded to African Americans and members of other underrepresented minorities who are committed to a career in teaching and research at the college or university level, who are enrolled in or are planning to enroll in a suitable research-based program leading to a PhD or ScD (doctor of science) degree at a U.S. institution, who have not earned any other doctoral degrees, who are committed to embracing and responding positively to the learning needs of students from diverse backgrounds, and who are willing and able to sustain an extended personal engagement with students and faculty from backgrounds that are underrepresented in academia. The fellowships support students in the fields of astronomy, chemistry, computer science, the earth sciences, the life sciences, physics, and psychology, among others.

The foundation provides Diversity Fellowships at three levels: predoctoral, dissertation, and postdoctoral. Undergraduates in their senior year, recent graduates, and individuals who have completed some graduate work are eligible for predoctoral fellowships. Doctoral candidates who have completed their course work but have yet to complete the dissertation are eligible for dissertation fellowships. Postdoctoral fellowships are awarded to individuals who have earned the PhD or ScD and who wish to conduct full-time research at an appropriate nonprofit institution of higher learning or research, including universities, government or national laboratories, privately sponsored nonprofit institutes, government chartered nonprofit research organizations, and centers for advanced study. Each year, the Diversity Fellowships program awards approximately 60 predoctoral awards, 35 dissertation awards, and 20 postdoctoral awards. Predoctoral award winners receive $20,000 per year for up to three years, while dissertation and postdoctoral award winners receive a one-time award of $21,000 and $40,000, respectively.

In addition to the cash awards, fellowship recipients are provided with a stipend to cover the expenses of attending the annual Conference of Ford Fellows, which offers attendees unparalleled access to networking and mentoring opportunities. At the conference, fellows are afforded the opportunity to network with other current and former fellows; to meet with representatives of university and academic presses; and to attend workshops on getting published, finishing the dissertation, planning and advancing an academic career, and writing grant applications.

See also: Astronomy and Astrophysics; Chemistry; Computer Science; Physics

REFERENCES AND FURTHER READING

The National Academies. "Welcome to the Ford Foundation Diversity Fellowships Home Page." [Online article or information; retrieved May 24, 2007.] http://www7.nationalacademies.org/fordfellowships/.

Fort Valley State University (FVSU)

Fort Valley State University (FVSU) is Georgia's historically black, land-grant university. In terms of scientific research, it is best-known for its work in agriculture.

Fort Valley State resulted from the 1939 merger of two schools in Fort Valley, Georgia. Fort Valley High and Industrial School had been founded in 1895 as a vocational school for African Americans, and State Teachers and Agricultural College of Forsyth had been founded in 1902 to train blacks for careers as teachers and farmers; together, they formed Fort Valley State College. In 1996, the school attained university status and acquired its present name.

Much of FVSU's agricultural research is conducted under the auspices of the school's Agricultural Research Center. The center's researchers seek to improve the ability of farmers, particularly those with limited resources, to produce crops that are both affordable and profitable. To this end, research projects focus on testing and developing chemicals, food, and feed products for use on small farms. The center's farm also serves as a laboratory for research being conducted by FVSU researchers in the College of Agriculture, Home Economics, and Allied Programs, particularly in the areas of animal science, plant science, and agricultural engineering.

Animal science researchers seek to produce value-added meat and dairy products by studying physiology, biotechnology, parasitology, and endocrinology as they apply to meat- and dairy-producing animals. Current plant science research focuses on improving crops by using genetic engineering and biotechnology techniques; one particularly interesting project involves developing and producing genetically engineered plants that can serve as the sources of an edible vaccine. Research in agricultural engineering focuses on detecting and controlling the harmful microbes found in farm products and developing better methods for storing food products after harvest.

References and Further Reading
Fort Valley State University. "College of Agriculture, Home Economics and Allied Programs." [Online article or information; retrieved October 29, 2007.] http://www.ag.fvsu.edu/.

Fort Valley State University. "Fort Valley State University." [Online article or information; retrieved October 29, 2007.] http://www.fvsu.edu/.

Freedmen's Hospital

Freedmen's Hospital in Washington, D.C., was established during the Civil War to address the needs of thousands of runaway slaves who had made their way to the nation's capital in search of freedom. Established by the federal government as a means of addressing the health care needs of freedpeople, it was eventually incorporated into Howard University. By 1975, when it was renamed Howard University Hospital, it had developed into one of the nation's finest teaching hospitals and the most important facility in terms of providing medical training to blacks.

Freedmen's was founded in 1862 on the grounds of a Union Army base, Camp Barker. The first director of the 278-bed facility was Alexander T. Augusta, a black army physician. Later on, Freedmen's would be headed up by other prominent black physicians such as Daniel Hale Williams (one of the first surgeons to operate successfully on the human heart) and Charles R. Drew (developer of the first blood bank). In 1869, Freedmen's was relocated to the Howard University campus, and for more than 100 years thereafter, it served as the teaching hospital for the Howard University College of Medicine.

Because of its connection with Howard, Freedmen's served as a training ground for a number of black interns and residents in the United States between the Civil War and the Cold War. Black medical school graduates who were accepted into the hospital's intern program were offered clinical instruction in anesthesiology, cardiology, community health and family practice, dermatology, emergency and trauma, medicine, neurology, neurosurgery, obstetrics and gynecology, ophthalmology, pathology, pediatrics and child health, physical medicine and rehabilitation, psychiatry, radiology, and surgery. For most of its existence, Freedmen's was one of only 10 hospitals in the country to provide such training to black doctors. Five of the others were, like Freedmen's, hospitals that catered to blacks: Meharry Medical College's Hubbard Hospital in Nashville, Tennessee; Provident Hospital and Training School in Chicago; Homer G. Phillips Hospital in St. Louis; Kansas City Hospital No. 2; and Mercy-Douglass Hospital in Philadelphia. The remaining four were pre-

Much of the early medical research conducted by African Americans was performed at Freedmen's Hospital in Washington, D.C. (Library of Congress)

dominantly white hospitals that admitted black patients: Cook County Hospital in Chicago; Harlem Hospital and Bellevue Hospital in New York City; and Cleveland City Hospital. But, because Howard University College of Medicine was the preeminent facility in the United States for training black physicians, Freedmen's helped train the majority of African American doctors who entered medical practice during the years of its existence, as either medical students, interns, or residents.

In 1975, Freedmen's ceased to exist, and its departments were transferred to a newer facility, Howard University Hospital (HUH). Nevertheless, the services provided by Freedmen's to the black medical students, interns, and residents continue to be provided by HUH. In addition, HUH conducts a number of scientific and clinical research programs through its centers of excellence. These centers include the Cancer Center, the National Minority Organ and Tissue Transplant Education Program, and the Center for Sickle Cell Disease.

See also: Drew, Charles R.; Harlem Hospital; Homer G. Phillips Hospital; Howard University; Howard University College of Medicine; Howard University Hospital; Mercy-Douglass Hospital; Provident Hospital and Training School; Sickle Cell Disease; Williams, Daniel H.

REFERENCES AND FURTHER READING

Cobb, W. Montague. "The First Hundred Years of the Howard University College of Medicine." *Journal of the National Medical Association* Issue 57 (1967): 408–420.

Howard University College of Medicine. "Howard University College of Medicine." [Online article or information; retrieved July 4, 2006.] http://www.med.howard.edu.

Gates Millennium Scholars (GMS)

The Gates Millennium Scholars (GMS) program awards scholarships to outstanding African American students and to other minority students who are pursuing or intend to pursue graduate degrees in science and related fields. The program encourages and supports minority students who are completing their undergraduate studies to earn master's and doctoral degrees in mathematics, science, engineering, education, library science, and public health, disciplines in which their ethnic and racial groups are currently underrepresented.

Headquartered in Fairfax, Virginia, Gates Millennium Scholars was founded in 1999 by Bill Gates, the founder of Microsoft Corporation. Today, GMS is funded by the Bill & Melinda Gates Foundation, which works to reduce inequalities in the United States and around the world, and it is administered by the United Negro College Fund (UNCF). To reach, coordinate, and support all targeted groups, UNCF works with the American Indian Graduate Center Scholars, the Hispanic Scholarship Fund, and the Organization of Chinese Americans to assist in implementing the initiative. Since its inception, the program has paid college costs not covered by other programs and scholarships for more than 10,000 students, thus permitting them to attend the schools of their choice. GMS's goal is to provide $1 billion in scholarships to 20,000 students during the lifetime of the program.

To receive a GMS scholarship, an eligible student must be nominated by a principal, teacher, guidance counselor, tribal higher education representative, or other professional educator who is familiar with the student's outstanding academic qualifications in general, and particularly with the student's ability to excel at mathematics, science, engineering, education, library science, or public health. Since the program also seeks to build up a cadre of minority professionals who can further the recruitment efforts of GMS, nominees must also have strong leadership potential and a demonstrated commitment to community service.

See also: United Negro College Fund Special Programs Corporation

REFERENCES AND FURTHER READING

The Gates Millennium Scholars. [Online article or information; retrieved January 26, 2007.] "About GMS." http://www.gmsp.org/publicweb/aboutus.aspx.

Gordon Research Conferences

The Gordon Research Conferences (GRC) serve as forums for the presentation and discussion of cutting-edge research in biology, chemistry, and physics, as well as their various branches and related technologies. As part of its effort to diversify the greater scientific community, GRC operates the GRC Underrepresented Minority (URM) Diversity Initiative.

The first Gordon Research Conference was initiated in 1931 by Neil Gordon, a professor of chemistry at Johns Hopkins University. Gordon wished to establish a more direct form of communications between and among chemists than that provided by the formal symposium or the scientific journal. Instead, he wanted practitioners of the chemical sciences to meet informally so that they could discuss casually their thoughts about the leading research topics of the day and to exchange ideas as to how those topics might best be addressed. In the mid-1930s, Gordon's conferences became affiliated with the American Association for the Advancement of Science and became known as the AAAS-Gibson Island Chemical Research Conferences, after the location in Maryland where most of the early conferences were held. Following Gordon's retirement in 1946, the conferences were moved to New Hampshire and incorporated under their present name. Today, the conferences are held at a number of sites in New England and California, as well as at several international venues. Meanwhile, the list of topics covered by the five-day summer conferences continued to expand, and in 2007, GRC presented conferences on 182 different topics ranging from the biology of aging to X-ray physics.

Attendees at a GRC event are chosen by the conference chair from a list of applicants. Successful applicants are those who impress the chair as being willing and able to contribute in a meaningful way to the discussions at hand, whether they be senior scientists, junior faculty, postdoctoral researchers, or graduate students. Because of the nature of the discussions and the participants, a GRC conference is not only an excellent source of state-of-the-art information about an attendee's specialty, but it also affords attendees the opportunity to expand their professional networks, thus enhancing their ability to enter into fruitful research collaborations in the future.

At some point, Carl Storm, a GRC director for many years, recognized the lack of diversity at GRC conferences and realized that minority researchers were being denied a valuable opportunity to develop their research and their careers as a result. Consequently, he devoted much of his effort as a director to establishing the GRC URM Diversity Initiative, whereby scientists who are African Americans or members of other underrepresented minorities are encouraged to apply to attend a GRC conference, and then supported during the conference itself. In recognition of Storm's efforts, GRC established the Carl Storm Underrepresented Minority Fellowship. This fellowship, which is supported financially by the Alfred P. Sloan Foundation, awards $600 to any minority scientist attending his/her first GRC conference to help defray registration fees and transportation expenses. These awards are presented on a first-come-first-served basis and are available to graduate students, postdoctoral researchers, junior faculty, and senior scientists alike. Final funding is contingent upon acceptance by the chair of the applicant's conference of choice.

See also: Alfred P. Sloan Foundation; American Association for the Advancement of Science; Biology; Chemistry; Physics

REFERENCES AND FURTHER READING

Gordon Research Conferences. "Gordon Research Conferences." [Online article or information; retrieved October 29, 2007]. http://www.grc.org/.

Gordon Research Conferences. "The GRC Underrepresented Minority (URM) Diversity Initiative." [Online article or information; retrieved May 9, 2007.] http://www.grc.org/diversity.aspx.

Hampton University

Hampton University is the oldest historically black institution of higher learning in Virginia. In terms of scientific research, it is best known for its work in support of the various missions of the National Aeronautics and Space Administration (NASA).

Hampton University grew out of the educational outreach of Mary S. Peake, who began teaching freedpeople under the Emancipation Oak in Elizabeth City County (today the City of Hampton) in 1861. In 1868, a formal school for freedpeople was established by various church groups and former Union Army officers who had served in the Hampton area during the Civil War. The campus combined a nearby plantation with the plot of ground on which the Emancipation Oak still grows. In 1870, the school was chartered as Hampton Normal and Agriculture Institute, and its curriculum focused on teaching African Americans to teach and farm. One of its first students was Booker T. Washington, who went on to become one of the most famous African American educators of all time. In 1930, the school shortened its name to Hampton Institute, and in 1984, it gained university status and took on its present name. As of 2006, the school awarded MS degrees in applied mathematics, biology, chemistry, computer science, medical science, and physics and PhD degrees in physics, medical physics, and pharmacy.

The university's physics research programs take advantage of the school's close proximity to Langley Research Center (LaRC). Also located in Hampton, LaRC is one of NASA's main research centers. As of 2006, Hampton researchers were supporting LaRC's involvement with the International Coordination Group on Laser Atmospheric Studies (ICLAS), a working group of the International Radiation Commission. ICLAS promotes international research on the development, improvement, and use of an advanced laser technology known as lidar (an acronym for light detection and ranging) as a tool for measuring concentrations of ozone, water vapor, pollutants, and other chemical compounds in the atmosphere. Hampton researchers were also partnering with LaRC, Centre National d'Etudes Spatiales (CNES, the French Space Administration), the Institut Pierre Simon Laplace, and Bell Aerospace & Technologies Corporation in support of the Cloud-Aerosol Lidar and Infrared Pathfinder Satellite Observation (CALIPSO) satellite. Launched in 2006, CALIPSO gathers data pertinent to the role played by clouds, atmospheric aerosols, and other airborne particles in the regulation of Earth's weather, climate, and air quality. CALIPSO combines an active lidar instrument with passive infrared and visible imagers to probe the vertical structure and properties of thin clouds and aerosols over the globe.

LaRC also funds a number of aerospace research projects at the Center of Aeropropulsion (CAP), part of Hampton University's School of Engineering and Technology. Established in 2003, CAP conducts research and development in aerospace science and technology, including aerodynamics, propulsion, aeroacoustics (the noise generated by flying vehicles), hypersonic engine and vehicle systems, novel sensors for aerospace applications, and other projects related to the human exploration and development of space. CAP also serves as a focal point for training and encouraging the participation of underrepresented minorities and persons with disabilities in areas of interest to NASA. To this end, CAP fosters interdisciplinary research collaborations among historically black colleges and universities, major universities, other research institutions, and industry.

Hampton University's physics research centers conduct research for a number of clients other than NASA. The Center for Atmospheric Studies investigates ozone trends and chemistry, polar stratospheric and mesospheric clouds, and the effects of aerosols and solar variability on the Earth's atmosphere for both NASA and the National Oceanic and Atmospheric Administration (NOAA). The Center for Advanced Medical Instrumentation conducts research for the Department of Energy in the development of various gamma ray detection devices for use in nuclear medicine. Current research focuses on the development of small field-of-view systems for breast imaging to assist in breast cancer detection. Established by the National Science Foundation in 2001 as one of four Physics Frontier Centers, the Center for the Study of the Origin and Structure of Matter addresses such issues as the nature of gravity; the strong nuclear force (the force that binds quarks, the fundamental building blocks of all matter) dark matter (matter that neither emits nor reflects enough electromagnetic radiation, such as visible light or X-rays, to be detected directly); dark energy (a hypothetical form of energy that

In its early days, Hampton University students studied such subjects as the science of cheesemaking, but today they participate in a wide range of cutting-edge research projects, including much of the aerospace research conducted at NASA's nearby Langley Research Center. (Library of Congress)

theoretically permeates all of space and acts in opposition to gravity at large scales); and the possible existence of dimensions other than length, width, and height in outer space. Lastly, university researchers are conspicuously active in the research programs of the Thomas Jefferson National Accelerator Facility (Jefferson Lab) in nearby Newport News. Funded by the Department of Energy, Jefferson Lab explores the nature of matter by conducting basic research concerning the role played by gluons (the subatomic particles that theoretically "glue" quarks together by acting as carriers of the strong nuclear force in much the same way that electrons carry electromagnetism).

See also: Biology; Chemistry; Computer Science; Department of Energy; Historically Black Colleges and Universities; National Aeronautics and Space Administration; National Science Foundation; Physics

REFERENCES AND FURTHER READING

Hampton University. "Hampton University." [Online article or information; retrieved October 29, 2007.] http://www.hamptonu.edu/.

Hampton University. "Hampton University Research." [Online article or information; retrieved November 27, 2006.] http://www.hamptonu.edu/research/.

Harlem Hospital

Harlem Hospital was the first major hospital in the United States to appoint a black physician to its staff. As a direct result of that appointment, Harlem Hospital became a leading center for testing antibiotic and chemotherapy drugs. In time, it also became an important center for conducting research concerning asthma as well as for training African American physicians.

Founded by the City of New York in 1887, Harlem Hospital was originally a small receiving hospital for prisoners and charity cases awaiting transfer to other city hospitals. By 1919, it had grown to 390 beds and had become the primary care facility for the residents of Harlem, a bustling black neighborhood on the east side of Manhattan Island. The hospital's medical staff, however, was all white and probably would have stayed that way indefinitely had it not been for World War I. When the United States became involved in the war, many of the hospital's attending physicians left; so in 1919, the hospital superintendent appointed a black physician, Louis T. Wright, as a clinical assistant visiting surgeon, the lowest rank to which a physician could be appointed. Wright was certainly qualified for the position, having served as a medical officer in France during the war, but his appointment caused such a furor that the superintendent who appointed him was immediately transferred. Political pressure from Harlem's black leaders, however, kept Wright himself from being dismissed.

Those same leaders pushed successfully for further appointments of qualified blacks to Harlem Hospital's staff. In the early 1920s, other black physicians were appointed to the outpatient staff; in 1925, Wright and four other physicians were appointed to the inpatient staff; and in 1926, the hospital took on its first black interns. In 1930, the hospital staff became fully integrated following the appointment of a completely new medical board. The new board removed a number of white physicians from the medical staff and replaced them with 12 black physicians, bringing the total to 19; the new board also assigned black physicians to positions according to their qualifications. Consequently, Wright was promoted to full attending surgeon and named secretary of the medical board.

During the 1930s, Harlem Hospital began developing a reputation as a clinical research center. Given the oftentimes rough-and-tumble nature of many of Harlem's residents, the hospital staff had ample opportunity to investigate the area of soft tissue trauma. Under Wright's direction, a number of studies resulting in published papers were conducted on subjects such as penetrating stab and gunshot wounds of the abdomen and abdominal wall and traumatic sub-cutaneous rupture of the spleen.

In the late 1940s, Harlem Hospital began conducting research concerning various types of pharmaceutical drugs. Once again as a result of Wright's insti-gation, the hospital became the first center to test the effects on humans of aureomycin, one of the first antibiotic drugs. This effort led to the testing of other antibiotics, as well as the development of treatment programs involving these drugs. For example, Harlem Hospital staff developed an antibiotic treat-ment for lymphogranuloma venereum (a sexually transmitted disease that is carried by the bacterium *Chlamydia trachomatis*) that utilizes the antibiotic drugs chlortetracycline and chloramphenicol.

In 1948, Harlem Hospital also became a research center for studying the effects of chemotherapy drugs on cancer. That same year, the hospital received a grant from the National Cancer Institute to establish the Cancer Research Foundation, and for the next seven years, its staff investigated the effects of some of the first chemotherapy drugs. Their earliest efforts focused on folic acid antagonists, biochemical agents that retard the development of cells. Since one of the hallmarks of cancer is rapid cellular growth, it was hoped that these agents might have important therapeutic properties. Other compounds studied included triethylene melamine (a hydrogen mustard com-pound that was originally developed for use in chemical warfare), Thio-Tepa (a nitrogen mustard derivative), aureomycin and actinomycin D (two of the first antibiotics), derivatives of folic acid (essential to cell growth), and A-methopterin (also known as methotrexate), which interferes with the ability of folic acid to enhance cell growth.

Although the Harlem staff's efforts met with little success, they did develop some of the earliest protocols for conducting chemotherapy research. To pub-licize the results of their work, they established the *Harlem Hospital Bulletin*, with Wright as editor. The foundation's activities at Harlem ceased in 1955, when Jane C. Wright, Wright's daughter and his successor as head of the foun-dation, moved it to New York University (NYU) Medical School so that it could have access to better facilities, equipment, and staffing.

In 1991, Harlem Hospital opened the Asthma Center, one of only six such clinical research centers in the country. Harlem residents are five times more likely to suffer from asthma than the general U.S. population; so the Harlem Asthma Research Team, a group of doctors and scientists from the Harlem Center for Health Promotion and Disease Prevention, began to identify the reasons why. The Asthma Prevention Project, one result of that initiative, involves a series of clinical studies designed to identify risk factors; to exam-ine frequent emergency department asthma care; and to determine the roles of stress, emotions, and cultural health practices on asthma morbidity.

Harlem Hospital operates two other innovative research and treatment centers. The Comprehensive Sickle Cell Center, one of America's oldest, provides diagnosis, prenatal diagnosis, counseling, and genetic counseling. The Tuberculosis Clinic, one of only three in the nation, helped reduce active tuberculosis cases in Harlem by 75 percent between 1992 and 2005. In addition to performing cutting-edge research, Harlem Hospital is also an important center for training African American physicians. As a teaching institution affiliated with Columbia University's College of Physicians and Surgeons, the hospital operates one of the nation's largest intern and residency programs for black physicians.

See also: Asthma; Cancer; National Cancer Institute; Wright, Jane C.; Wright, Louis T.

REFERENCES AND FURTHER READING

HHC-Harlem Hospital Center. "Harlem Hospital Center." [Online article or information; retrieved November 17, 2005.] http://www.ci.nyc.ny.us/html/hhc/html/facilities/harlem.shtml.

Organ, Claude H., and Margaret Kosiba, eds. *A Century of Black Surgeons: The U.S.A. Experience*. Norman, OK: Transcript Press, 1987: 149–196.

Health Professionals for Diversity Coalition

The Health Professionals for Diversity Coalition brings together a number of organizations that represent health care providers, medical researchers, educators, students, and others who are actively engaged in training workers for the health professions. In addition to promoting diversity in the health professions, the coalition works to end health disparities, which result in large part from the lack of diversity in the nation's health care workforce.

The coalition was formed in reaction to the wave of antiaffirmative action initiatives in the mid-1990s that threatened to terminate a number of programs intended to increase the participation of African Americans and other underrepresented minorities in the health care fields. These initiatives were of particular concern to those dedicated to the delivery of quality health care because of the number of reports concerning disparities in health care that also began to circulate, culminating with the release in 2004 of the Institute of Medicine's *In the Nation's Compelling Interest: Ensuring a Diverse Health-Care Workforce* (Washington, DC: National Academies Press, http://www.iom.edu/CMS/3740/4888/18287.aspx) and the Sullivan Commission on Diversity in the Healthcare Workforce's *Missing Persons: Minorities in the Health Professions* (http://www.kaisernetwork.org/health_cast/uploaded_files/092004_sullivan_diversity.pdf). These reports documented the benefits of diversity, examined challenges to promoting diversity, and offered policy recommendations to more effectively promote diversity. According to both reports, African Americans and other ethnic minorities were receiving health care that was demonstrably inferior to that received by the nation's white majority population, in large part because of a lack of trained medical professionals willing to live and work in minority communities. Previously, it had been hoped that affirmative action programs that gave preference to minority applicants to medical, dental, and veterinary schools would go a long way toward eliminating health disparities. The reasoning was that minority physicians, dentists, veterinarians, and other health care professionals would be much more likely to reside and practice in minority communities where they are most needed. The groups that formed the coalition saw the end of such affirmative action programs as instruments for perpetuating health disparities, a situation they deemed to be unacceptable. Since the nation's nonwhite population is expected to become the majority by the year 2050, the coalition's members considered disparities in health care to be a threat to the health care of the entire nation, not to just a few groups or communities.

The coalition serves as a forum for its member organizations to communicate and coordinate their activities concerning diversity. The coalition's members include a number of national organizations, particularly those that were most involved in using affirmative action to recruit and retain minorities at schools and colleges providing health care training. These organizations include the American Association of Colleges of Nursing, the American Association of Colleges of Osteopathic Medicine, the American Association of Colleges of Pharmacy, the American Association of Colleges of Podiatric Medicine, the American Dental Education Association, the Association of Academic Health Centers, the Association of American Medical Colleges, the Association of American Veterinary Medical Colleges, the Association of Professors of Medicine, the Association of Schools and Colleges of Optometry, the Association of Schools of Public Health, the Hispanic Serving Health Professions Schools, and the National Association of Medical Minority Educators. Other national organizations that were members of the coalition in 2007 included the American Academy of Family Physicians, the American College of Physicians, the American Physical Therapy Association, the American Psychological Association, the National Association of Advisors for the Health Professions, and the National Association of Public Hospitals and Health Systems. At present, the coalition, along with other members of the health care community, is in the process of studying ways to implement the recommendations of the reports of the Institute of Medicine and the Sullivan Commission on Diversity in the Healthcare Workforce.

See also: American Dental Education Association; Association of American Medical Colleges; Health Disparities; Institute of Medicine; Sullivan Commission on Diversity in the Healthcare Workforce

REFERENCES AND FURTHER READING

Health Professionals for Diversity Coalition. "About Health Professionals for Diversity." [Online article or information; retrieved May 30, 2007.] http://www.hpd-coalition.org/about.htm.

Historically Black College and University/Minority Institution Environmental Technology Consortium

The Historically Black College and University/Minority Institution Environmental Technology (HBCU/MI ET) Consortium conjoins 17 universities, 12 of them HBCUs, for the purpose of encouraging African Americans and other minorities to pursue careers in the environmental sciences and related areas. The consortium also works to increase environmental awareness among minorities, to promote environmental justice as it applies to minority neighborhoods, to increase the number of minority-owned, environmental technology-based businesses, and to foster research related to environmental technology.

The consortium was founded in 1990 to help its members participate in federally funded environmental programs. It is managed by Howard University in collaboration with the National Association for Equal Opportunity in Higher Education, and since 2002, it has been funded by the Department of Energy (DOE). Its other HBCU members are Alabama A&M University, Clark Atlanta University, Florida A&M University, Hampton University, Jackson State University, North Carolina A&T State University, Prairie View A&M University, Southern University, Texas Southern University, Tuskegee University, and Xavier University of Louisiana. Its non-HBCU members, all of which are Hispanic-majority institutions, are Florida International University, New Mexico Highlands University, Northern Arizona University, Texas A&M University–Kingsville, and the University of Texas at El Paso.

Consortium schools train undergraduate and graduate students for careers in various areas of environmental technology, including materials management; environmental restoration; environmental health; and hazardous, solid, and mixed waste handling. The consortium also promotes institutional development in environmental education at its member schools, and it works to increase interaction between its member schools and other universities, corporations, and interest groups with similar interests. In terms of environmental justice, the consortium works closely with the U.S. Environmental Protection Agency's Office on Environmental Justice to ensure that minority communities, which have been particularly victimized by neighboring factories and refineries that contaminate local drinking water, air, and soil with toxic wastes and emissions, are protected under environmental laws. To this end, it has assisted four member schools to establish research centers to work directly with minority communities that are adversely affected by environmental problems.

A major aspect of DOE funding has been the increase in research conducted by the consortium's member schools. Recent research projects include a study of sediment composition and its effects on hazardous metal ion sorption (Prairie View); a study of the biogeochemical dynamics of microbial degradation of pesticides, mixed wastes, and other organic materials (Tuskegee); a study of the biomarkers of lead-induced toxicity in channel catfish (Jackson State); the development of fluorescent probes for environmental sensing and detection of heavy metals (Clark Atlanta); an investigation of heavy metal interactions with biomaterials (Hampton); the manipulation and decontamination of chemical and biological solutions and solid surfaces via electrical discharges (Alabama A&M); urban air and water quality studies (Texas Southern); the evaluation of a novel permeable barrier system for immobilizing radionuclides and metals (Howard); evaluating the role of certain fungi and phosphate-mediating bacteria in arsenic-tolerant and arsenic-hyperaccumulating plants (Tuskegee); the use of portable immunoassays to measure uranium and other heavy metals (Xavier); the detection and control of microorganisms in indoor environments (Alabama A&M); surface studies of chromium sorption on natural particles (Prairie View); the mechanisms and consequences of adhesion of chemolithotrophic bacteria to mineral surfaces (Prairie View and Xavier); and the development of a portable biosensor (Xavier).

See also: Alabama A&M University; Clark Atlanta University; Department of Energy; Florida A&M University; Hampton University; Howard University; Jackson State University; North Carolina A&T State University; Prairie View A&M University; Southern University and A&M College System; Texas Southern University; Tuskegee University; Xavier University of Louisiana

REFERENCES AND FURTHER READING

National Association for Equal Opportunity in Higher Education. "HBCU/MI Environmental Technology Consortium." [Online article or information; retrieved January 31, 2007.] http://www.nafeo.org/etc/index.html.

Historically Black Colleges and Universities

Historically black colleges and universities (HBCUs) are institutions of higher learning that were established specifically to provide African Americans with a college education. As of 2007, there were 114 HBCUs in the United States, all but five of them in states and former territories where slavery had been legal in 1860. Ironically, three of the five non-Southern schools—Cheyney University (Pennsylvania), Lincoln University (Pennsylvania), and Wilberforce

University (Ohio)—were the first three colleges to be established as HBCUs.

As non-HBCUs slowly increased their enrollment of black students after the U.S. Supreme Court ruled against segregated schools in *Brown v. Board of Education* (347 U.S. 483) in 1954, HBCUs saw their own enrollments drop off somewhat. Nevertheless, HBCUs continue to train a significant proportion of black professionals who are educated in this country, particularly in terms of science. It has been estimated that, though approximately 20 percent of all black college students attend or have attended HBCUs, as many as 90 percent of this country's black scientists received their scientific training at an HBCU, either as an undergraduate or as a graduate student.

The first HBCUs, particularly those in the South, focused on training African Americans to become better farmers, mechanics, and teachers. Later, HBCUs established professional and graduate programs for training doctors and lawyers. Not until the last several decades have HBCUs expanded their focus to include the production of scientists. But by 2007, with the help of private organizations and federal agencies, HBCUs were developing the ability to conduct cutting-edge research and, in the process, turn out top-notch scientists. This article outlines some of the scientific research being conducted at HBCUs in the early 21st century.

In terms of scientific research, the most important HBCUs are Clark Atlanta University, Fisk University, Florida A&M University, Howard University, North Carolina A&T State University, Prairie View A&M University, and Tuskegee University. The broad range of research conducted at these schools can best be illustrated simply by citing the names of the major research centers and programs at each.

Clark Atlanta operates the Army Center of Excellence in Electronic Sensors and Combat, the Army Center for Research in Information Science, the Center of Excellence in Microelectronics and Photonics, the Center for Surface Chemistry and Catalysis, the Center for Theoretical Studies of Physical Systems, the Earth Systems Science Program, the Environmental Justice Resource Center, the High Performance Computing Research Partnership Program, the High Performance Polymers and Composites Center, the Laboratory for Advanced Signal and Image Processing, the Laboratory for Electro-Optical Materials, the Center for Cancer Research and Therapeutic Development, the Biomedical Research and Training Program, and the Center for Environmental Policy, Education and Research.

Fisk is best known for the Fisk Infrared Spectroscopy Research Laboratory, the Center for Photonic Materials and Devices, and the Center for Physics and Chemistry of Materials.

Florida A&M University's College of Pharmacy and Pharmaceutical Sciences operates the AIDS Research Center, the Center for the Study of Cardiovascular Disease, the Drug Abuse Research Center, the Center for Drug Delivery, the Neuroscience Research Center, and the Center for Minority Prostate Cancer Training and Research.

Howard conducts its most important research in the Center for the Study of Terrestrial and Extraterrestrial Atmospheres, the Center for Nanomaterials Characterization Science and Processing Technology, the Materials Science Research Center of Excellence, and the NASA NSCORT Center of Excellence in Advanced Life Support.

North Carolina A&T State operates the Center for Advanced Materials and Smart Structures, the Center for Composite Materials Research, the Center for Cooperative Systems, and the Center for Energy Research and Technology.

Prairie View A&M operates the Center for Applied Radiation Research, the Center of Excellence for Communication Systems Technology Research, the Future Aerospace Science and Technology Center, the Texas Gulfcoast Environmental Data Center, the Thermal Science Research Center, the Cooperative Agriculture Research Center, and the Prairie View Solar Observatory.

Tuskegee researchers conduct their investigations under the auspices of the Center for Advanced Materials, the Center for Computational Epidemiology and Risk Analysis, the Center for Food and Environmental Systems for Human Exploration and Development of Space, the George Washington Carver Agricultural Experiment Station, and the Center for the Integrated Study of Food, Animal and Plant Systems.

While the larger HBCUs are able to conduct research across the broad spectrum of science, the smaller HBCUs tend to focus their research efforts in one or two areas. For example, Alabama A&M University focuses on agriculture and the environment. Its research centers include the Center for Environmental Research and Training, the Center for Forestry and Ecology, the Center for Molecular Biology, the Plant Science Center, the Small Farm Research Center, the Food Safety and Nutrition Research Center, the Small Ruminant Research Center, the Center for Hydrology, Soil Climatology and Remote Sensing, and the Winfred Thomas Agricultural Research Center. On the other hand, Hampton University focuses on physics. Its research centers include the Center of Aeropropulsion, the Center for Atmospheric Studies, the Center for Advanced Medical Instrumentation, and the Center for the Study of the Origin and Structure of Matter. Meanwhile, Jackson State University emphasizes research related to medicine and health. Its research centers include the Computational Center for Molecular Structure and Interactions, the Jackson Heart Study Coordinating Center, the Center of Excellence in Minority Health, the Center for Environmental Health, and the National Center for Biodefense Communications for Rural America.

Agriculture/aquaculture are the specialties of Alabama State University, Fort Valley State University, Kentucky State University, Langston University, Lincoln University of Missouri, Southern University, the University of Arkansas at Pine

Bluff, and Virginia State University. Biotechnology/biomedicine are the specialties of Delaware State University, Norfolk State University, North Carolina Central University, Spelman College, Texas Southern University, and Winston-Salem State University. Morgan State University, the University of Maryland Eastern Shore, and the University of the Virgin Islands specialize in marine biology. Central State University specializes in water resources, Tennessee State University focuses on space science, the University of the District of Columbia specializes in renewable energy, West Virginia State University focuses on anaerobic digestion, and Xavier University of Louisiana specializes in basic pharmaceutical science.

All four of the historically black medical colleges—Charles R. Drew University of Medicine and Science, Howard University College of Medicine, Meharry Medical College, and Morehouse School of Medicine—conduct research related to disease and medical conditions. Much of this research focuses on the diseases and medical conditions that contribute the most to health disparities, such as asthma, cardiovascular disease, cancer, diabetes, HIV/AIDS, obesity, and sickle cell disease. Last but not least, the nation's only historically black school of veterinary medicine, the Tuskegee School of Veterinary Medicine, conducts research related to large and small animal medicine and surgery, pathology, parasitology, and microbiology.

See also: Alabama A&M University; Alabama State University; Asthma; Biology; Biotechnology; Cancer; Cardiovascular Disease; Central State University; Charles R. Drew University of Medicine and Science; Clark Atlanta University; Delaware State University; Diabetes; Fisk University; Florida A&M University; Fort Valley State University (FVSU); Hampton University; Health Disparities; HIV/AIDS; Howard University; Howard University College of Medicine; Jackson State University; Kentucky State University; Langston University; Lincoln University of Missouri; Meharry Medical College; Morehouse School of Medicine; Morgan State University; Norfolk State University; North Carolina A&T State University; North Carolina Central University; Obesity; Physics; Prairie View A&M University; Sickle Cell Disease; Southern University and A&M College System; Spelman College; Tennessee State University; Texas Southern University; Tuskegee School of Veterinary Medicine; Tuskegee University; University of Arkansas at Pine Bluff; University of the District of Columbia; University of Maryland Eastern Shore; University of the Virgin Islands; Virginia State University; West Virginia State University; Winston-Salem State University; Xavier University of Louisiana

REFERENCES AND FURTHER READING

The HBCU Network, "The History of HBCUs." [Online article or information; retrieved August 21, 2007.] http://www.hbcunetwork.com/The_History_Of_HBCUs_Timeline.cfm.

Homer G. Phillips Hospital

Homer G. Phillips Hospital (HGPH) in St. Louis was one of the six most important teaching hospitals for the training of African American physicians and nurses. From 1937 to 1979, Homer G.—as HGPH was affectionately known in the black community of St. Louis—provided black doctors and nurses with postgraduate medical training, as well as a place in which to practice their professions.

Historically, black St. Louisans have had little difficulty receiving medical treatment. Provisions had been made for them to be treated at the city's Max C. Starkloff Hospital (later known as City Hospital No. 1) and the Washington and St. Louis university hospitals, and in 1894, Provident Hospital, later renamed The Peoples Hospital, was founded to serve the medical needs of St. Louis's indigent population, black and white. Medical care at all of these hospitals, however, was provided by white medical personnel exclusively, because black physicians and nurses were excluded from having any meaningful presence in any of the city's hospitals.

This situation changed somewhat in 1919, when a petition from black leaders induced the city to open City Hospital No. 2. Dedicated to the care of black St. Louisans, City No. 2 granted black physicians the status of associate staff members, enabling them to visit their patients in the 177-bed hospital. The full-time staff, however, remained all white, with the result that black doctors could not receive the training necessary to become specialists, although some so-called black house officers were permitted to serve as surgical assistants. Moreover, City No. 2 quickly became overcrowded and outdated, and by the 1930s, it was no longer serving the needs of the black community in St. Louis.

The drive to replace City No. 2 with a "modern" facility that would provide employment opportunities for black medical professionals began in 1922. A St. Louis attorney, Homer G. Phillips, spearheaded a bond drive that raised more than $1 million for City No. 2's replacement, while a generous contribution from the Rosenwald Fund and financial support from the federal government provided the necessary additional funding. After more than 10 years of wrangling over various political issues such as where the new hospital should be located, construction of the 685-bed Homer G. Phillips Hospital began in 1933, and it opened for business four years later.

Like City No. 2, HGPH's attending staff included a number of white physicians; unlike City No. 2, it included a number of black physicians as well, thus giving African American doctors and nurses a place to practice medicine. Just as important, HGPH provided black graduates of medical schools with a place to complete internships and residencies, thus allowing them to develop proficiency in a medical specialty. To this end, HGPH provided intern and residency training in general surgery, obstetrics/gynecology, orthopedics, urology, otolaryngology (ears, nose, and throat), neuropsychiatry, internal medicine, and ophthalmology. After 1940, this training was provided by the faculty of St. Louis's Washington University School of Medicine, although some programs were offered at institutions outside St. Louis. These programs filled such a huge need in the black medical community that in the late 1930s and early 1940s, it has been estimated that they attracted approximately half of all the black medical school graduates in the United States.

In addition to postgraduate medical training, HGPH also offered programs in medical research. In conjunction with researchers from Washington University, HGPH interns and residents conducted research on wound healing and burn treatment. They also performed much of the initial testing of amigen (a protein prepared by predigesting hog pancreas and milk with various enzymes) that is administered intravenously to treat malnutrition and widespread burns and to aid convalescence after surgery.

Ironically, *Brown v. Board of Education* (347 U.S. 483), the Supreme Court decision of 1954 that ordered the desegregation of public schools, marked the beginning of the end of HGPH as a top-notch training facility for black physicians. The following year, the city of St. Louis decided to integrate its hospitals, after which HGPH received less and less funding. By 1970, black medical graduates were being accepted into internships and residencies at formerly all-white hospitals, and the need for hospitals like HGPH declined precipitously. The facility was closed for good in 1979, as was City Hospital No. 1 six years later; the two facilities were replaced by a single hospital, Regional, shortly thereafter.

REFERENCES AND FURTHER READING

Organ, Claude H., and Margaret Kosiba, eds. *A Century of Black Surgeons: The U.S.A. Experience.* Norman, OK: Transcript Press, 1987: 197–249.

Howard University

Howard University is the flagship of the nation's historically black colleges and universities. Originally founded as a school for training freedpeople to be educators or ministers, it gradually evolved into an important scientific research center as well. By the 21st century, Howard researchers were conducting investigations in virtually all of the scientific disciplines.

Howard was founded in 1867 in Washington, D.C., and named after Oliver O. Howard, a Union general and head of the Freedmen's Bureau. Although its original designation was The Theological and Normal Institute, it quickly achieved university status, with schools devoted to education, theology, medicine, law, and agriculture. Today, Howard offers 27 PhD programs, 30 master's degree programs, and 9 MD/PhD programs, and its Office of Research Administration (ORA) oversees a vast array of scientific research projects.

Howard University's Thirkield Hall, which in 1923 (when this photo was taken) housed the school's department of physics and astronomy. (Library of Congress)

Much of Howard's scientific research is conducted under the aegis of various research centers, which are parceled out among the Graduate School, the Howard University College of Medicine (HUCM), and Howard University Hospital (HUH). The centers operated by HUCM and HUH are discussed in separate entries devoted to those entities; so this article is focused on the centers operated by the Graduate School that are related to scientific investigation.

The Center for the Study of Terrestrial and Extraterrestrial Atmospheres is an interdisciplinary research unit with 17 participating faculty from the departments of chemistry, physics, electrical engineering, mechanical engineering, and the Materials Science Research Center of Excellence. Established in 1992, the center supports the mission of the National Aeronautics and Space Administration (NASA) by studying the atmosphere of Earth as well as the atmospheres of planets, moons, and stars throughout the galaxy and beyond. Specific research topics include aerosol detection, the growth of electronic materials, and the development of chemical sensors for atmospheric gases.

The Center for Nanomaterials Characterization Science and Processing Technology operates under a grant from the National Science Foundation's Centers of Research Excellence in Science and Technology program. It focuses on the exploration of the fundamental science and engineering necessary for designing nanoscale materials (materials smaller than 100 nanometers, or 100 billionths of a meter) for molecular recognition. Research activities include the synthesis and characterization of new materials that are capable of bonding with a specific form of molecule and then the evaluation and application of these materials for use as sensors, drug delivery vehicles, or separation media for water treatment, to name but three applications.

The Materials Science Research Center of Excellence seeks to achieve a better understanding of the semiconductor materials, such as aluminum gallium arsenide, aluminum arsenide, gallium arsenide, and silicon carbide, that are used in the fabrication of microwave transistors and solar cells. This multidisciplinary program includes faculty from electrical and chemical engineering and the departments of physics and chemistry.

The NASA NSCORT Center of Excellence in Advanced Life Support investigates an important range of key advanced life support issues that are critical to sustaining life in outer space. These issues include solid waste, water, and air processing and revitalization, in addition to related resource recovery, food production and safety, and systems engineering.

See also: Historically Black Colleges and Universities; Howard University College of Medicine; Howard University Hospital; National Aeronautics and Space Administration; National Science Foundation

REFERENCES AND FURTHER READING

Howard University. "Howard University." [Online article or information; retrieved October 29, 2007.] http://www.howard.edu/.

Howard University Office of Research Administration. "Research Centers and Institutes." [Online article or information; retrieved August 14, 2006.] http://ora.howard.edu/centers/int.htm\#top.

Howard University College of Medicine

No institution in the United States has turned out more African American physicians than the Howard University College of Medicine (HUCM). The first medical school founded primarily for training black doctors, HUCM continues to serve as the flagship of the four historically black medical schools still in operation in the early 21st century. Although HUCM is devoted primarily to training physicians who will deliver care in underserved communities, the school also conducts a number of important medical research programs.

HUCM first opened its doors in 1868 as the medical department of what is today known as Howard University. Slavery having been ended by the actions of the federal government just a few years earlier, freedpeople were flocking in droves to Washington, D.C., in search of opportunity. It was quickly realized that there were not nearly enough doctors to serve Washington's growing black population. Howard's founders concluded that the best people to serve this community would be black physicians, and so the earliest version of HUCM was established.

At the time of its founding, HUCM included degree programs in medicine and pharmacy, and a degree program in dentistry was introduced in the 1880s. Prior to 1904, all classes were offered only at night, because the vast majority of HUCM students had to work during the day. Because the medical curriculum was three years in length and the pharmacy program two years, HUCM's first graduate was a pharmacy student, James T. Wormley, who received his degree in 1870. The first medical students to graduate did so the following year.

Although a number of other medical schools for blacks opened in the decades following HUCM's establishment, all but one had failed by the 1920s. This situation resulted from the Flexner Report, which established such high standards for medical programs in the United States and Canada that, of all the all-black schools, only HUCM and Meharry Medical College could meet them. Consequently, between its founding and the Civil Rights Movement, HUCM produced more than half of the African American physicians, with almost all of the rest coming from Meharry. Ironically, Abraham Flexner, whose report was responsible for the closing of most black medical schools, later accepted the position of chair of Howard University's board of trustees.

One reason Flexner did not condemn HUCM was that its students had access to a first-class hospital, Freedmen's Hospital. Freedmen's had been founded in 1862 to care for the medical needs of former slaves, and in 1869, it was relocated to the Howard campus so that it could serve as the teaching hospital for HUCM. This arrangement continued until 1975, when Freedmen's was replaced by Howard University Hospital.

As of 2006, HUCM offered its students the complete range of biomedical and clinical training. Today, its basic science departments provide instruction in anatomy, biochemistry, biophysics, microbiology, molecular biology, pharmacology, and physiology. Its clinical departments provide instruction in anesthesiology, cardiology, community health and family practice, dermatology, emergency and trauma, medicine, neurology, neurosurgery, obstetrics and gynecology, ophthalmology, pathology, pediatrics and child health, physical medicine and rehabilitation, psychiatry, radiology, and surgery.

As part of its mission to educate physicians, HUCM operates the Center for Continuing Medical Education. The center provides information on the latest medical developments for physicians, community health professionals, and others seeking this assistance through conferences, special lectureships, courses, workshops, videotapes, the Internet, telemedicine, and other distance learning techniques. The center also provides hands-on participation at HUCM and at various sites off campus.

Although HUCM's focuses on turning out physicians and other medical professionals to serve the African American community, it also maintains a world-class center of excellence devoted to cancer research. The Cancer Center conducts a number of studies regarding cancers that particularly affect African Americans. Generally speaking, these studies can be divided into two groups: those that seek the causes of certain types of cancer and those that conduct clinical trials of possible treatments for those cancers. One example of the former is the African American Hereditary Prostate Cancer Study, which is designed to determine whether there is a genetic basis in regard to prostate cancer in African American men. Another study investigates how high levels of stress in black women diminish their bodies' production of lymphocytes (killer cells that destroy tumors before they can develop), thus leading to the development of breast cancer. Another group of studies investigates the impact of various factors such as hormones, dietary fat, and cooking practices on the development of breast cancer in young African American women.

In terms of clinical trials, the Cancer Center is most involved in investigating protocols that promise to treat or prevent the development of breast cancer, colorectal cancer, lung cancer, prostate cancer, and bone cancer. For example, one clinical trial investigated ways to reduce the morbidity associated with the removal of lymph nodes in early-stage breast cancer patients.

HUCM also heads up a national program in science education for the general public. The program, the National Minority Organ and Tissue Transplant Education Program (MOTTEP), is designed to increase the donation of organs and tissue for transplant by minorities. The program achieves this goal by conducting educational programs concerning the facts about organ/tissue donation. For example, prior to MOTTEP, many blacks had refused to sign organ donor cards, because they believed that medical personnel did not work as hard to save organ donors and that only whites receive transplanted organs. The program is also designed to decrease the number of minorities in need of transplants. This goal is achieved by addressing the diseases and behaviors that lead to the need for transplantation such as diabetes, hypertension, alcohol and substance abuse, poor nutrition, and lack of exercise. Headquartered at HUCM, MOTTEP maintains sites in 15 other U.S. cities.

See also: Biochemistry; Freedmen's Hospital; Howard University; Howard University Hospital; Meharry Medical College

REFERENCES AND FURTHER READING

Cobb, W. Montague. "The First Hundred Years of the Howard University College of Medicine." *Journal of the National Medical Association* 57 (1967): 408–420.

Howard University College of Medicine. "Howard University College of Medicine." [Online article or information; retrieved July 4, 2006.] http://www.med.howard.edu.

FLEXNER REPORT ON MEDICAL EDUCATION

The period between 1868 and 1910 was the heyday of the black medical college, wherein African Americans were trained, often by black professors, to become physicians. Issued in 1910, the Flexner Report brought that era to an end by forcing most black medical colleges to either upgrade their instruction and facilities, which most were unable to do, or close their doors.

Prior to the Civil War, most African Americans who wished to become physicians went to Europe for their medical training, where racial discrimination was virtually nonexistent. After the Civil War, however, seven medical colleges were founded to provide medical education for blacks, and these seven schools trained approximately 85 percent of all black doctors practicing medicine as of 1905. More important, these doctors demonstrated a greater willingness than graduates of other schools to practice medicine in rural communities, particularly in poor black communities in the South. The economic situation of these schools, however, was always unstable, so they could not always afford to provide their students with the best instructors or facilities for learning medicine.

The death knell for five of these schools was sounded in 1910, when the Flexner Report on Medical Education was published. Known officially as *Medical Education in the United States and Canada: A Report to the Carnegie Foundation for the Advancement of Teaching* (New York: Arno Press), the report had been set in motion two years earlier by the American Medical Association's Council on Medical Education. The council had requested the Carnegie Foundation for the Advancement of Teaching to conduct a survey of medical education in the United States. To head up the survey, the foundation recruited Abraham Flexner, a high school principal who had written a report regarding the status of American higher education. Moreover, Flexner had been highly recommended to the foundation by his brother, Simon Flexner, a noted professor of medicine at Johns Hopkins University, whose medical school was considered by many to be the best in the nation. By 1910, Abraham Flexner had visited each one of the more than 150 medical schools in the United States and Canada.

Using Johns Hopkins as his model, Flexner evaluated each school in terms of five criteria, which he judged to be essential to a medical school's ability to turn out qualified physicians: (1) entrance requirements, (2) number and training of faculty, (3) size of endowment and tuition, (4) quality of laboratories, and (5) availability of a teaching hospital. Whenever a school failed to meet Flexner's criteria, he recommended that it be closed. Obviously, such criteria favored large, well-established schools while penalizing the small, new schools. In particular, the report penalized black medical colleges, most of which struggled constantly to recruit and compensate qualified professors, construct buildings, and equip laboratories, not to mention gain access to teaching hospitals for their students. In fact, such factors had already contributed to the closing of Chattanooga National Medical College in 1908. The Flexner Report had an immediate and negative effect on the ability of most of the remaining black medical schools to attract contributions, faculty, and students. Knoxville Medical College closed its doors in 1910, followed by Flint Medical College in 1911 and Leonard Medical School in 1914. The University of West Tennessee College of Physicians and Surgeons managed to hang on until 1923, but then it too was forced to cease operations. Only Howard Medical College (today Howard University College of Medicine) and Meharry Medical College, which met the criteria set by Flexner, survived the wave of closings.

The Flexner Report is credited with bringing about some much needed reforms in how medicine is taught in the United States and Canada. As a result of the report, medical schools in both countries now stress the biomedical sciences and hands-on clinical training. However, the report had a deleterious effect on black medical education, because it made it difficult, if not impossible, for many would-be black physicians to obtain the necessary training. It also had a negative effect on the health care of blacks in general and of rural blacks in particular, many of whom depended entirely on the graduates of black medical colleges for all of their health care needs.

Although his report had a serious negative effect on black medical education, Flexner seems not to have targeted black medical schools for extermination. A great many schools that enrolled only white students were also forced to close as a result of his report. Interestingly, Flexner was later offered (and accepted) the position of chairman of the board of trustees at Howard University, the nation's flagship institution of higher education for blacks.

See also: American Medical Association; Howard University; Howard University College of Medicine; Meharry Medical College

REFERENCES AND FURTHER READING

Bonner, Thomas N. *Iconoclast: Abraham Flexner and a Life in Learning.* Baltimore, MD: Johns Hopkins University Press, 2002.

Hiatt, Mark D., and Christopher G. Stockton. "The Impact of the Flexner Report on the Fate of Medical Schools in North America After 1909." [Online article or information; retrieved October 30, 2007.] http://www.jpands.org/vol8no2/hiattext.pdf.

Howard University Hospital

Howard University Hospital (HUH) was founded in 1975 as a replacement facility for Freedmen's Hospital in Washington, D.C. Since then, it has served as the teaching hospital for Howard University and as an important primary care facility for Washington's black population. HUH also conducts a number of scientific research projects through its various centers of excellence.

Freedmen's had been established during the Civil War to serve Washington's growing number of African Americans, many of whom had fled the South looking for freedom and economic opportunity. By 1975, it had developed into one of the nation's most important teaching hospitals for training black physicians. At the same time, it was realized that Freedmen's had outgrown its facility, and so the decision was made to close it down and build a state-of-the-art facility nearer to Howard University College of Medicine (HUCM). This new facility was christened Howard University Hospital. As of 2006, HUH offered HUCM students clinical training in anesthesiology, cardiology, community health and family practice, dermatology, emergency and trauma, medicine, neurology, neurosurgery, obstetrics and gynecology, ophthalmology, pathology, pediatrics and child health, physical medicine and rehabilitation, psychiatry, radiology, and surgery. It also maintains several centers of excellence devoted to biomedical research and education.

The Cancer Center conducts a number of studies regarding cancers that particularly affect African Americans. Established in 1972, it grew out of the research efforts of Jack E. White, founder of the Freedman's Hospital Tumor Clinic and Cancer Teaching Project, and it was transferred from Freedmen's to HUH. The center conducts a number of studies into the causes of certain types of cancer, such as the African American Hereditary Prostate Cancer Study, which seeks to determine the genetic basis, if any, for the development of prostate cancer in African American men. Other studies investigate the impact of various factors such as stress, hormones, dietary fat, and cooking practices on the development of breast cancer in African American women. Lastly, the center conducts clinical trials of potential treatments for breast cancer, colorectal cancer, lung cancer, prostate cancer, and bone cancer.

HUH also serves as the national headquarters for the National Minority Organ and Tissue Transplant Education Program (MOTTEP), an effort to increase the donation of organs and tissue for transplant by minorities. In addition to conducting educational programs aimed at minorities to acquaint them with the facts concerning organ and tissue donation, MOTTEP seeks to decrease the number of minorities in need of transplants.

HUH operates several other biomedical research centers as well. The Center for Drug Abuse Research is sponsored by the National Institute on Drug Abuse (NIDA) as a way to increase the involvement of historically black colleges and universities (HBCUs) in federally supported drug abuse research. The center provides research development activities to support and strengthen the capacity of HBCUs to participate in NIDA drug abuse research programs. The Child Development Center provides the Washington community with quality comprehensive care for children and youth from birth to 18 years, but it also conducts studies on, for example, chromosome analysis, on amino acid and other chemical analysis related to inborn errors of metabolism, and on other metabolic and genetic disturbances. In addition, the center diagnoses and treats problems related to speech, language, and hearing. The Collaborative Alcohol Research Center examines the causes of alcoholism and its effects on human life within the African American community and other minority populations. The center's researchers seek to arrive at a better understanding of the molecular mechanisms of alcohol action at the cellular level so that new therapeutic approaches to reduce the incidence of alcohol abuse and alcoholism can be developed. The General Clinical Research Center conducts clinical tests related to various medical conditions and treatments; as of 2006, it was focusing on kidney disease and hypertension in African Americans, an antihypertensive and lipid-lowering treatment to prevent heart attacks, evaluating and reducing the risk factors for cardiovascular disease, and understanding the ethnic factors in alcohol abuse among African Americans. The Transplant Center offers consultation for renal, liver, and pancreas transplantation, for vascular access for dialysis patients, and for general surgery. Since its inception in 1973, the center has transplanted more than 400 kidneys and 40 livers. The Center for Sickle Cell Disease studies and treats sickle cell disease in Washingtonians. The hospital's branch of the National Human Genome Center seeks to learn more about DNA sequence variation and its interaction with the environment so that medical researchers can use such knowledge to prevent or treat diseases common in African Americans.

See also: Cardiovascular Disease; Freedmen's Hospital; Howard University; Howard University College of Medicine; National Institute on Drug Abuse; Sickle Cell Disease

REFERENCES AND FURTHER READING

Cobb, W. Montague. "The First Hundred Years of the Howard University College of Medicine." *Journal of the National Medical Association* 57 (1967): 408–420.

Howard University College of Medicine. "Howard University College of Medicine." [Online article or information; retrieved July 4, 2006.] http://www.med.howard.edu.

Institute of Medicine

The Institute of Medicine (IOM) provides evidence-based, authoritative information and advice on health and science policy, particularly as the policy affects biomedical science and medicine, to government officials, health care professionals, and the general public. To this end, the institute has issued two important reports, *The Right Thing to Do, the Smart Thing to Do: Enhancing Diversity in Health Professions: Summary of the Symposium on Diversity in Health Professions in Honor of Herbert W. Nickens, MD* (Washington, DC: National Academies Press, 2001) and *In the Nation's Compelling Interest: Ensuring Diversity in the Health Care Workforce* (Washington, DC: National Academies Press, 2004), concerning the need to increase the number of African Americans and other underrepresented minorities pursuing careers as health care professionals.

IOM was chartered in 1970 by the National Academy of Sciences; today, those two organizations, along with the National Academy of Engineering and the National Research Council, comprise the National Academies. IOM's membership is composed of the nation's most outstanding physicians, researchers, and other practitioners of medicine, as well as nonmedical professionals whose expertise relates directly to medicine and health, who are elected to the institute on the basis of their professional achievements and their commitment to service. Once elected, they volunteer to serve without pay on committees and other study groups that investigate important matters concerning health in the United States. These groups issue approximately 50 reports each year.

Since the turn of the century, IOM has taken an active interest in increasing the number of African Americans and other underrepresented minorities pursuing careers as physicians, dentists, medical researchers, and other health care professionals. It has also worked to eliminate disparities in health care between communities of minorities and nonminorities. In 2001, IOM issued *The Right Thing to Do, the Smart Thing to Do.* The symposium provided a forum for policy makers, educators, researchers, and others involved in the nation's health care system to address three related problems: (1) the continued underrepresentation of African Americans and other minorities in the health professions, (2) the growth of minority populations in the United States and the growing need to address their health care needs, and (3) the legislative and legal challenges to affirmative actions that threaten to limit even further the ability of minorities to become medical professionals. As the report indicates, these problems are interconnected. Nonminority physicians and dentists are often reluctant, for a number of reasons, to practice in minority communities. A shortage of minority health care professionals, therefore, results in a shortage of quality health care for minority communities. Should this situation persist, it is conceivable that epidemics will originate in minority communities and then spread to nonminority communities. On the other

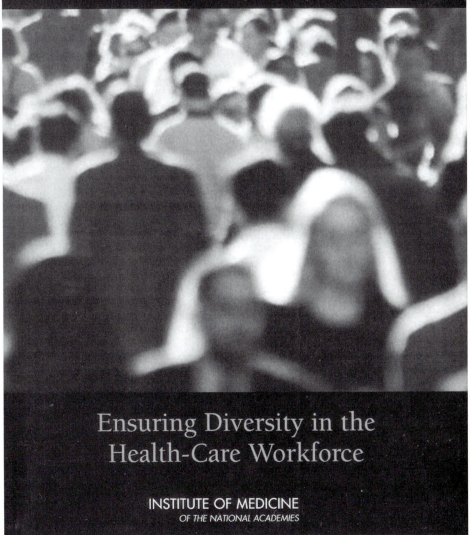

IN THE NATION'S
COMPELLING
INTEREST

Ensuring Diversity in the
Health-Care Workforce

INSTITUTE OF MEDICINE
OF THE NATIONAL ACADEMIES

The Institute of Medicine issued In the Nation's Compelling Interest *to call attention to the lack of black medical researchers.* (Reprinted with permission from National Academy of Sciences) hand, minority physicians and dentists have no problem practicing in minority communities, and so a sufficient number of health care professionals from minority backgrounds ensures the continued good health of minority communities and, by extension, the nation at large. *The Right Thing to Do* illustrates the efforts of government, the health care industry, and the health care professions to address these three problems, but it also calls for innovative efforts to achieve parity for all Americans in terms of the ability to receive quality health care and to earn one's living as a health care professional.

By 2004, the situation as outlined in *The Right Thing to Do* had changed hardly at all. That same year, IOM issued a related report, *In the Nation's Compelling Interest*. *The Right Thing* had documented the efforts being made by educational institutions, private foundations, and state and federal government agencies to prepare and motivate more minorities for health care occupations and then to recruit and retain them into medical education programs such as medical and dental schools. In 2004, *Compelling Interest* focused on developing strategies to identify and reduce the institutional and policy-level barriers that prevent minorities from becoming health care professionals. For example, the report called for new admissions policies to medical schools that recognize the value of diversity in medical education and that then assesses each applicant in terms of background, experience, and multilingual ability, for example, in addition to prior academic achievement and standardized test scores. The report called on the federal Health Resources and Services Administration, which provides funding to a number of health training programs, to evaluate the programs it funds to ensure their effectiveness in terms of increasing the number of minorities who graduate from those programs, and it encouraged Congress to increase funding for the programs that are most effective. The report called on state and local governments, as well as private businesses and foundations, to support efforts to bring more minorities into the health care professions through loan forgiveness, tuition reimbursement, loan repayment, and other initiatives. Lastly, the report called on the Department of Education to encourage entities that accredit medical schools, dental schools, and other health care training programs to develop standards for producing minority health care professionals and then to monitor the progress of each school or program toward meeting those standards as part of the accreditation process.

REFERENCES AND FURTHER READING

Institute of Medicine of the National Academies. "About." [Online article or information; retrieved June 8, 2007.] http://www.iom.edu/CMS/About IOM.aspx.

International Society on Hypertension in Blacks

One of the medical conditions to which African Americans are more susceptible than European Americans is hypertension (high blood pressure). Many
initiatives to deal with this problem have been forthcoming from the black
medical community, but one of the most effective organizations in this respect
has been the International Society on Hypertension in Blacks (ISHIB). By
2006, ISHIB had broadened its objectives beyond investigating hypertension
among African Americans to treating and preventing all forms of cardiovascular disease and related medical conditions such as diabetes, stroke, lipid disorders, and kidney disease, among ethnic minority populations around the
world. In 2006, ISHIB's membership included hundreds of medical
researchers, physicians, physician assistants, nurses, pharmacists, dieticians,
nutritionists, public health professionals, medical students, social workers,
and other health care providers, with permanent headquarters in Atlanta.

ISHIB was the brainchild of three physicians: W. Dallas Hall, Neil B. Shulman, and Elijah Saunders. Like many black physicians, they were concerned
with the disproportionate occurrence of high blood pressure among African
Americans, and they explored the causes of this phenomenon and its prevention in their 1985 book, *Hypertension in Blacks: Epidemiology, Pathophysiology and Treatment* (Chicago: Year Book Medical Publishers). The
following year, they carried their efforts to a higher level by founding ISHIB.
The group's charter officers included Shulman as chairman of the board of
trustees, Saunders as president, and Hall as secretary-treasurer.

During its early years, ISHIB sought to make the medical community aware
of the latest methods for preventing hypertension by sponsoring annual
research conferences. The first conference was held in Kenya. After attending
seminars where attendees learned firsthand about how to prevent high blood
pressure, the attendees then went into local villages to disseminate that knowledge by working with local doctors and nurses. This conference was so successful that subsequent conferences, held in Puerto Rico, Ontario, South
Carolina, Michigan, England, Louisiana, the U.S. Virgin Islands, Ohio,
Cameroon, California, Maryland, Brazil, and Georgia, followed the same model.

In addition to the annual conference, ISHIB implemented a number of
other strategies for addressing high blood pressure in blacks. In 1987, it established three annual awards to recognize and therefore encourage outstanding
contributions to the treatment and prevention of hypertension: Distinguished
Researcher, Distinguished Young Researcher, and Outstanding Community
Service. In 1991, it began publishing a monthly journal, *Ethnicity & Disease*,
which provides original reports, book reviews, and expert commentary
regarding disease patterns in ethnic minority populations throughout the
world. In 1993, it inaugurated the Worship Site Blood Pressure Education Program, an innovative method for identifying and treating African Americans

with high blood pressure by conducting screening sessions at predominantly black churches. In 1994, it published an important monograph, *Emerging Perspectives in Hypertension: Focus on the African-American Patient*. This monograph was followed by *AII: A Target in Hypertensive Disease in African-American Patients* (1995), *Meet the Experts: Effective Use of Combination Drug Therapy in the Treatment of Minority Hypertensive Populations* (1997), *The Effective Use of Calcium Antagonists* (1997), *Expert Panel: On the Effective Use of Low-Dose Combination Therapy in African-American Patients* (1998), and *Landmark Guidelines to Raise Bar for Treatment of African Americans with High Blood Pressure* (2003).

In 1996, ISHIB participated in a clinical trial to evaluate the efficacy of Accupril, the key ingredient of which is an angiotensin-converting enzyme (ACE) inhibitor. Angiotensin is a biomolecule that causes blood vessels to narrow, thus increasing blood pressure. ACE enables angiotensin to function by converting it to its activated form (called angiotensin II, or AII); thus, ACE inhibitors prevent the formation of AII and therefore hold down blood pressure. This clinical trial was followed by a 1996 clinical trial of calcium antagonists, which reduce the amount of calcium entering the muscle cells of the arteries, causing them to relax and widen, and a 1998 clinical trial of the angiotensin receptor blocker (ARB) Teveten (rather than prevent the formation of AII, ARBs lower blood pressure by keeping angiotensin from attaching to blood vessel walls). Between 1996 and 2000, ISHIB sponsored seminars concerning the use of ACE inhibitors, the role of the renin-angiotensin-aldosterone system (a hormone system that helps regulate long-term blood pressure and blood volume in the body) in hypertension and the injury of certain organs, and the development of a unified model for treating cardiovascular disease in the urban ethnic patient.

In 2003, ISHIB developed disease/lifestyle councils for diabetes/metabolic syndrome, heart failure, kidney disease, lipids, obesity, and stroke in order to focus the organization's attention on these important aspects of cardiovascular disease. ISHIB also works closely with major pharmaceutical manufacturers, including Merck, Biovail, Forest Laboratories, Abbott Laboratories, and Pfizer, to develop new treatments for hypertension and cardiovascular disease.

See also: Cardiovascular Disease; Diabetes

REFERENCES AND FURTHER READING

International Society on Hypertension in Blacks. "About ISHIB." [Online article or information; retrieved February 15, 2006.] http://www.ishib.org/AI_index.asp.

Jackson State University

Jackson State University is the foremost historically black college or university (HBCU) in Mississippi. Officially designated the Urban University of Mississippi, Jackson State's scientific research centers investigate a broad range of topics in a number of areas.

Jackson State was founded in 1877 in Natchez, Mississippi, by the American Baptist Home Mission Society. Originally known as the Natchez Seminary, the school was intended to provide training to freedpeople who wished to become pastors. In 1882, the school was relocated to Jackson, the state capital, where it became known as Jackson College. It continued to operate as a private church school until 1940, when the State of Mississippi converted it into a teacher's college for African Americans. Shortly thereafter, the school's name was changed to Jackson State College, and in 1944, it awarded its first bachelor's degrees. The school expanded its facilities and curriculum over the next 30 years, and in 1974, it achieved university status and took on its present name. Today, it offers MS degrees in biology, chemistry, environmental science, and science education and PhD degrees in chemistry and environmental science.

In 1980, Jackson State became the first HBCU in the nation to offer a BS degree in meteorology. Since then, it has trained approximately 25 percent of the black meteorologists and atmospheric scientists educated in the United States. The program's research focuses on the development of computer simulations for predicting and studying such atmospheric phenomena as thunderstorms, sea breezes, lake effect snowstorms, squall lines, and tropical cyclones.

As of 2006, Jackson State supported two centers for studying nonhealth-related scientific phenomena: the Computational Center for Molecular Structure and Interactions (CCMSI) and the Trent Lott Geospatial and Visualization Research Center. Researchers at CCMSI, which is funded by the National Science Foundation, develop computer models for studying the structures and properties of a wide range of molecules. A particular emphasis is placed on the study of large biomolecules, from which a great many of the biochemical compounds are formed. Other research projects include developing models to predict such phenomena as electric response properties in conjugated chains and to study the dynamics of ureic compound, the conformational properties of esters and amides, and the interactions between nucleic and acid bases and polar solvents. The Trent Lott Center is a centralized research facility that supports the High Performance Visualization Center Initiative of the U.S. Naval Meteorology and Oceanography Command. The center provides an infrastructure of technology, data, people, and institutional linkages that enables the discovery, evaluation, and application of geospatial and visual data to meteorological and oceanographic research. To this end, the center's laboratories provide researchers with state-of-the-art facilities in terms of geographic information systems, remote sensing, and scientific visualization.

Jackson State also supports a number of centers that focus on various aspects of health and medicine. These centers include the Jackson Heart Study Coordinating Center, the Center of Excellence in Minority Health, the Center for Environmental Health, and the National Center for Biodefense Communications for Rural America.

The Jackson Heart Study Coordinating Center oversees the Jackson Heart Study, which examines the factors that influence the development of cardiovascular disease in African American men and women. The study helps African Americans in the Jackson metropolitan area reduce the risk factors associated with cardiovascular disease, such as obesity, hypertension, and lack of physical activity, but it is also the first large-scale cardiovascular disease study in African Americans. In addition to enhancing the community's awareness and understanding of cardiovascular disease through seminars and workshops on cardiovascular disease, diabetes, hypertension, cholesterol, and nutrition, the study provides greater insight on specific research in areas such as high blood pressure, obesity, diabetes, physical activity, and lifestyle changes.

The Center of Excellence in Minority Health seeks to address and eliminate the health inequalities affecting minorities through innovative programs in community outreach and information sharing, as well as research on the causes of health disparities. The center's research focuses on two areas: cancer and cardiovascular disease. As of 2006, cancer research sought to determine the ability of *Vernonia amygdalina* (a leafy vegetable known as ndole in West and Central Africa) to inhibit the growth of breast cancer cells, and cardiovascular disease research investigated ways to promote fitness activities among Jackson's inner-city residents and to change negative dietary practices.

The Center for Environmental Health studies the basic mechanisms by which toxic substances compromise health. One project studies the herbicides arsenic and atrazine in terms of their toxicokinetics (a substance's ability to become more toxic as the time of exposure to the substance lengthens), histopathology (a substance's ability to kill tissue), and genotoxic effect (a substance's ability to cause genetic mutations and to contribute to the development of tumors). Another project studies the effects of ultraviolet radiation on the cornea and lens of the human eye. Another evaluates the ability of certain aromatic hydrocarbons to induce DNA photocleavage (the damage caused by compounds whose excited states can initiate a series of chemical reactions that ultimately lead to nucleic acid cleavage). DNA photocleavage is a promising approach for the development of new antitumor and antiviral therapeutic strategies. Yet another project assesses alcohol and p-nitrophenol as risk factors in the development of breast cancer. (P-nitrophenols are used in the manufacture of dyes, leathers, rubber, and pesticides/fungicides, and they have a poisonous effect on the nervous system, which is strengthened in connection with alcohol.)

The National Center for Biodefense Communications for Rural America seeks to develop methods for identifying significant risks to the health of humans, animals, and crops resulting from acts of bioterrorism perpetrated in the rural United States. To this end, the center conducts basic research regarding the acts of bioterrorism most likely to succeed, develops systems for the early detection and reporting of such acts, and develops and conducts training programs for volunteer fire departments, sheriff's departments, hospital emergency room staffs, and other personnel most likely to arrive first on the scene. One current project involves enhancing the Mississippi State Animal Disease Tracking (MSADT) System so that it supports the surveillance, tracking, and reporting of animal disease data from veterinary clinics to the State Veterinarian's Office and to and from the State Animal Diagnostic Laboratories. Another project is a pilot research study on the knowledge of policies and procedures regarding treatment protocols for chemical agents on the part of hospital medical personnel in Jackson.

See also: Biology; Cancer; Cardiovascular Disease; Chemistry; Diabetes; Historically Black Colleges and Universities; National Science Foundation; Obesity

REFERENCES AND FURTHER READING

Jackson State University. "Jackson State University." [Online article or information; retrieved October 29, 2007.] http://www.jsums.edu/.

Jackson State University, Office of Vice President for Research Development & Federal Relations. "Centers & Institutes." [Online article or information; retrieved November 28, 2006.] http://www.jsums.edu/~ordsfr/centers.htm.

John A. Andrew Clinical Society

The John A. Andrew Clinical Society was an organization of black surgeons affiliated with the Surgical Section of the National Medical Association (SSNMA), the national organization for black surgeons. The society's primary activity was to sponsor an annual surgical clinic for black physicians at the John A. Andrew Memorial Hospital in Tuskegee, Alabama. The purpose of the clinic was to give black physicians a chance to expand their knowledge about surgery by talking to expert surgeons from around the country and observing them operate. The clinic, which lasted for several days, consisted of patient evaluation and operations performed by leading black surgeons with the assistance of other surgeons eager to improve their surgical skills. Although the SSNMA sponsored similar clinics around the country, none was more prestigious than the John A. Andrew Clinical Society's.

The society was formally organized in 1918, although it had begun holding clinics six years earlier. The society was named after the John A. Andrew Hospital, the teaching hospital of Tuskegee Institute (today Tuskegee University) in Alabama, which was itself named after John A. Andrew, governor of Massachusetts during the Civil War who had accepted black volunteers into the state's armed forces. Andrew was a champion of civil rights, and his granddaughter, Elizabeth Mason, donated $55,000 to Tuskegee Institute to help build a hospital, which opened in 1913. The society was the idea of John A. Kenney, a physician who had attended a meeting of the National Medical Association (NMA) at Hampton Institute (today Hampton University) in 1917 and who, at the meeting, formally invited the NMA to hold its next meeting at Tuskegee. The society was begun as the local organizing committee for the NMA meeting, and the program included a number of surgical clinics at John A. Andrew Hospital.

More than 400 patients were treated at these weeklong clinics, during which three dozen surgical procedures were demonstrated. The clinics were so well received by Southern physicians, who had little chance to observe a surgeon at work, that the society continued to hold them on a yearly basis. The clinics were held from 1912 to 1954, and they ended not because they had lost their popularity but for other reasons. For one, state laws eventually prohibited out-of-state surgeons from performing surgery in Alabama without proper licensure, and the standards for granting temporary licenses to perform surgery became tougher. Also, medical insurers refused to provide liability coverage for the clinic. Meanwhile, other methods for teaching surgery, such as motion pictures and videotape presentations, had proven to be almost as effective a teaching tool as the clinics themselves.

See also: Hampton University; National Medical Association; Tuskegee University

REFERENCES AND FURTHER READING

Organ, Claude H., and Margaret Kosiba, eds. *A Century of Black Surgeons: The U.S.A. Experience*. Norman, OK: Transcript Press, 1987.

Julius Rosenwald Fund

The Julius Rosenwald Fund served as a major source of funding for Tuskegee Institute (today Tuskegee University), thus contributing to the education of many African American scientists. It also played an important role in the establishment of the United Negro College Fund, and it contributed millions of dollars to construct schools for African American children throughout the South.

The fund was established in 1917 by Julius Rosenwald, a Chicago merchant who had made a fortune from his dealings with Sears, Roebuck & Company,

The Julius Rosenwald Fund, founded by Julius Rosenwald, contributed generously to Tuskegee University and the United Negro College Fund. (Library of Congress)

one of the nation's largest retailers. Originally a supplier of men's clothing to Sears, Rosenwald served as treasurer and vice president of Sears from 1895 to 1907, as president from 1908 to 1924, and as chairman of the board from 1924 until his death in 1932.

Rosenwald's philanthropic activities began well before he established the fund that bore his name. Convinced that the greatest social problem facing the United States in the early 20th century was racism, in 1910, he offered to provide $25,000 to any community that would put up $75,000 toward the construction of a Young Men's Christian Association (YMCA) facility for African Americans. Eventually, 25 communities took up Rosenwald on his offer. After a friend introduced him to Booker T. Washington, the legendary head of Tuskegee Institute, in 1912, Rosenwald accepted a position on Tuskegee's board of trustees, a position he held for the rest of his life. That same year, he pledged enough of his own money to purchase the building materials for six schools in rural Alabama for African American children, provided that the children's parents would provide the labor to build the schools. Over time, Rosenwald and his fund donated more than $4 million in matching funds for the construction of thousands of so-called Rosenwald Schools in rural, predominantly black communities in 15 Southern states, and in each case, his money was matched or exceeded by local parents.

One of the most important contributions the fund ever made was the seed money it contributed to Tuskegee's endowment fund. This donation made it possible for Washington to devote most of his energy to making Tuskegee a first-class instructional and research institution, rather than spending it on fund-raising activities. Moreover, the money provided by the endowment over the years has permitted Tuskegee to maintain its reputation as one of the foremost historically black colleges and universities in terms of its commitment to scientific research. Another important contribution was the one that helped establish the United Negro College Fund, which provides scholarships to African Americans pursuing degrees in science and other fields.

Unlike most philanthropists who establish charitable foundations, Rosenwald insisted that the fund should spend all of its money within 25 years of his death. This decision reflected his own insistence that future generations should and could solve their own problems, as well as his own conviction that the present generation should do everything in its power to solve its own problems. Consequently, the fund exhausted its capital in 1948, but not before it had contributed more than $63 million to the philanthropies it supported.

See also: Historically Black Colleges and Universities; Tuskegee University

REFERENCES AND FURTHER READING

Embree, Edwin R., and Julia Waxman. *Investment in People: The Story of the Julius Rosenwald Fund.* New York: Harper, 1949.

Granat, Diane. "America's 'Give While You Live' Philanthropist." *APF Reporter*, 21, 1 (2003). [Online article or information; retrieved February 2, 2007.] http://www.aliciapatterson.org/APF2101/Granat/Granat.html.

Kentucky State University

Kentucky State University (KSU) is Kentucky's foremost historically black institution of higher learning. In terms of scientific research, the school is best known for its Division of Aquaculture and Aquatic Sciences, which focuses on the rearing of aquatic organisms under controlled or semicontrolled conditions.

Kentucky State was founded in 1887 in Frankfort, Kentucky. Originally known as the State Normal School for Colored Persons, it was intended to serve as a training school for black teachers. Three years later, the institution became a land-grant college, and the departments of home economics, agriculture, and mechanics were added to the curriculum. In 1902, the name was changed to Kentucky Normal and Industrial Institute for Colored Persons, in 1926, to Kentucky State Industrial College for Colored Persons, and in 1938, to Kentucky State College for Negroes. The phrase "for Negroes" was dropped in 1952, and in 1972, the school became one of Kentucky's public universities and acquired its present name. Today, Kentucky State has one of the most diverse student bodies and faculties in the nation; the student body is equally divided between black and white students, and the faculty is composed of 35 percent African Americans, 50 percent whites, and 15 percent from other ethnic groups.

The Division of Aquaculture and Aquatic Sciences focuses on raising freshwater species commercially, with a focus on shrimp (prawn), trout, catfish, largemouth bass, paddlefish, hybrid striped bass, baitfish, walleye, common carp, yellow perch, tilapia, crappie, red claw, crayfish, hybrid bluegill, and sturgeon. The division's graduate students gain a knowledge of the production and reproduction of primary aquaculture species, basic physiology and nutrition of aquatic vertebrate and invertebrate culture species, the mechanics and operation of primary production methods, the causes and controls of pathogenic organisms, the function and manipulation of biological and chemical cycles in ponds, and the design and analysis of experiments.

Much of the division's research is conducted at the KSU Aquaculture Research Center. Over the last several years, the center's faculty and graduate students have conducted research in a number of areas: the impact of different management technologies on the production, population structure, and economics of freshwater prawn culture in temperate climates; the effects of different feeding frequencies on growth, body composition, and fillet composition of juvenile sunshine bass; the effects and interactions of stocking density and added substrate on production and population structure of freshwater prawns; the effect of culture temperature on the growth, survival, and biochemical composition of yellow perch; induced gynogenesis in black crappie, whereby the embryo contains only maternal chromosomes due to the failure of the sperm to fuse with the egg; the cryopreservation of paddlefish, whereby cells or whole tissues are preserved by cooling to subzero temperatures; the effects of low-protein diets, with and without the amino acids methionine and lysine, on the growth of catfish; and the use of hemp seed meal, poultry by-product meal, and canola meal in diets for sunshine bass.

REFERENCES AND FURTHER READING

Kentucky State University. "Kentucky State University." [Online article or information; retrieved October 29, 2007.] http://www.kysu.edu/.

Kentucky State University Aquaculture. "KSU's Program of Distinction." [Online article or information; retrieved October 29, 2007.] http://www.ksuaquaculture.org/.

Langston University

Langston University is the only historically black college/university (HBCU) in Oklahoma. In terms of science, the school is best known for its research programs in goat husbandry and aquaculture.

Chartered in 1897, Langston University was originally known as Oklahoma Colored Agricultural and Normal University, because its purpose was to train African Americans to farm and teach. By 1941, when the name was changed to Langston University in honor of John Mercer Langston (the first African American ever elected to public office and the first dean of Howard University Law School), the curriculum had broadened considerably. The main campus is located in rural Langston, with branches in Oklahoma City and Tulsa. The university is home to the internationally acclaimed E (Kika) de la Garza Institute for Goat Research, one of the world's foremost institutions for the study of goats.

The primary research thrust of the de la Garza Institute is dairy goat nutrition. Nutrition studies are primarily aimed at determining the nutrient requirements of goats, with a special emphasis on the high-producing dairy goat. Facilities include a 150-goat dairy, a creamery, and special laboratories for milk analysis. The milk analysis laboratory also provides analysis for the goat Dairy Herd Improvement (DHI) program. It is the only DHI laboratory that calibrates instruments with goat milk standards, and it services goat milk producers throughout the United States. Past and present research projects include using cool season perennial grasses and low-input forage systems for goat pasturage; evaluating and modeling extended lactations in dairy goats; studying mammary gland health and mastitis in dairy goats; and determining the quality, safety, and shelf life of dairy goat products in the U.S. market.

The scope of the institute's research includes Angora, meat, and cashmere goats. For example, past scientific studies include determining the amino acid requirements of Angora goats for fiber production and developing standards for selecting and manipulating animals to maximize the production of cashmere wool. Present research includes using goats for sustainable vegetation management in U.S. grazing lands, determining the ability of goats to withstand harsh nutritional environments, and determining the effects of acclimatization on the energy requirements of goats. Facilities include special laboratories for fiber and stable isotope analysis and a field demonstration building where the Oklahoma Angora Buck evaluation is conducted each year.

The institute also conducts research concerning ruminants (cloven-hoofed, cud-chewing quadrupeds) other than goats. This research covers such topics as tethering for detailed study of grazing ruminants, studying diet selection and performance by sheep and goats grazing mixed pastures, characterizing the energy requirement for activity by grazing ruminants, and determining the amount of energy expended by free-ranging ruminants. Research results from all of the institute's studies are published regularly in *The Journal of Animal Science, Small Ruminant Research, Journal of Dairy Science, Canadian Jour-*

Students on the campus of Langston University, a historically black university in Langston, Oklahoma. (Langston University)

nal of Animal Science, Sheep and Goat Research Journal, and *Animal Feed Science and Technology.*

The Langston University Aquaculture Facility provides Oklahoma fish farmers with the latest scientifically based aquaculture techniques applicable to the Southwestern United States. The facility consists of 46 research ponds, a fish hatchery, and a research laboratory, and its research is founded on an ecological understanding of the region's aquatic environment. For example, a sustainable system of aquaculture in arid Oklahoma requires the maximization of water use. Large quantities of water are often in short supply or expensive to obtain, and the consequences of global warming only increase the uncertainty of water supplies available for aquaculture production. Consequently, research projects focus on ways to enhance water conservation, energy conservation, and water quality, and the information generated by these projects is presented to fish culturists through the Aquaculture Extension Program. In addition, fish production systems involving more than one species of fish are investigated for their ability to increase yields, improve water quality, and reduce production costs by maximizing the use of available nutrient inputs from fish feeds, while new fish species are tested for their ability to control common fish farm parasites.

See also: Historically Black Colleges and Universities

REFERENCES AND FURTHER READING

Langston University. "Langston University." [Online article or information; retrieved October 29, 2007.] http://www.lunet.edu/.

Langston University. "Research & Extension." [Online article or information; retrieved November 29, 2006.] http://www.luresext.edu/index.htm.

Leadership Alliance

The Leadership Alliance is a consortium of colleges and universities that seek to increase the number of African Americans and other underrepresented minorities in various academic fields, but especially in those related to the life sciences and physical sciences. The alliance pursues this goal by sponsoring summer research programs for minorities at its member institutions and corporate sponsors and by granting fellowships to minority graduate students so that minorities can better compete for science-related positions in academia.

The alliance was founded in 1992 by 23 colleges and universities in response to their growing awareness of the lack of African Americans and other underrepresented minorities pursuing careers as professors and administrators in biology, chemistry, and physics. During the next 15 years, the number of member institutions grew to 32, and the group's focus expanded to include recruiting and developing minority educators and administrators in all of the sciences, including the social sciences, at the college and university level. Nevertheless, in 2007, the bulk of the alliance's efforts addressed issues related to the lack of minorities in the biological and physical sciences. As of 2007, member institutions included 11 historically black colleges and universities (HBCUs): Claflin University, Delaware State University, Dillard University, Howard University, Morehouse College, Morgan State University, Prairie View A&M University, Southern University, Spelman College, Tougaloo College, and Xavier University of Louisiana. Other member institutions included Brooklyn College, Brown University, Columbia University, Cornell University, Dartmouth College, Harvard University, Hunter College, Johns Hopkins University, Montana State University, New York University, Princeton University, Stanford University, Tufts University, the University of Colorado at Boulder, the University of Maryland Baltimore County, the University of Miami (Florida), the University of Pennsylvania, the University of Puerto Rico, the University of Virginia, Vanderbilt University, and Yale University. The alliance maintains a professional staff and a permanent headquarters in Providence, Rhode Island, on the campus of Brown University.

As a means of increasing the number of opportunities for minority students to conduct meaningful research in scientific fields, the alliance developed the Summer Research Early Identification Program (SR-EIP). Selected undergraduate students may conduct research for 8 to 10 weeks during the summer at most of the alliance's non-HBCU institutions, in addition to Delaware State and Howard, under the guidance of a mentor. Students who have completed an SR-EIP summer program may apply for an internship with Eli Lilly and Company, one of the alliance's corporate sponsors. By working one-on-one with a practicing scientist, students broaden their practical knowledge and improve their skills in terms of academic research and scientific experimentation. Program participants are also given the opportunity to improve their scientific writing skills by preparing a report concerning their research. SR-EIP provides students with funding for travel, room, and board. To be eligible, a student must be a rising sophomore, junior, or senior and demonstrate the ability and willingness to work toward a graduate degree in the life sciences or physical sciences.

The culmination of each summer's SR-EIP is the Leadership Alliance National Symposium (LANS). At the symposium, all of the SR-EIP participants give oral or poster presentations about their recently completed research before an audience consisting of faculty, administrators, students, and representatives of private corporations and public agencies. Held annually since 2001, LANS's program also includes workshops and panels on topics related to graduate school, career opportunities, networking, and career development.

The Alliance provides financial assistance to selected graduate students nearing the completion of their doctoral studies in the life sciences or physical sciences. Established by a grant from the Schering-Plough Corporation in 2003, these fellowships are awarded to approximately 10 students each year so they can participate in career development programs. Since its establishment, Leadership Alliance/Schering-Plough Fellowships have been awarded to students pursuing PhDs in biology, biomedical science, cell biology, chemistry, clinical psychology, ecology, high-energy physics, human services psychology, immunobiology, marine biology, molecular biology, neurobiology, parasitology, pathobiology, pathology, and pharmacology.

See also: Biology; Chemistry; Delaware State University; Howard University; Morgan State University; Physics; Prairie View A&M University; Southern University and A&M College System; Spelman College; Tougaloo College; Xavier University of Louisiana

REFERENCES AND FURTHER READING

Leadership Alliance. "The Leadership Alliance." [Online article or information; retrieved May 14, 2007.] http://www.theleadershipalliance.org/matriarch/default.asp.

Lincoln University of Missouri

Lincoln University of Missouri is the second-oldest historically black institution of higher education in Missouri. In terms of scientific research, the school is best known for its work in the areas of animal science, environmental science, and human nutrition.

Lincoln University was founded in 1866 in Jefferson City, the state capital, by the former members of the 62nd and 65th U.S. Colored Infantry regiments, which had served with the Union Army during the Civil War. Originally known as Lincoln Institute, the school's mission was to provide freedpeople with the training they needed to become better farmers, mechanics, and teachers. In 1870, Lincoln began receiving aid from the state of Missouri, which assumed ownership of the school nine years later. Lincoln offered its first college courses in 1877, and in 1890, it became a land-grant institution. In 1921, the school was designated a university and took on its present name, and in 1940, it began offering graduate courses.

Most of Lincoln University's scientific research is conducted under the auspices of the Cooperative Research Program. Research within the program, which was established in 1972, is conducted at both fundamental and applied levels, with the general intention of improving the quality of life of minorities, persons with limited resources, and small farm families throughout Missouri.

Animal science researchers focus on topics such as livestock, fertility, grazing impacts, and reproductive biotechnology. Current projects include addressing the demand for protein-based food by the state's aquaculture industry and evaluating the effects of diet changes on the nutrient constituents of swine excreta and its treatment for odor control and environmental protection. The results of the swine study will not only help improve the treatment of swine waste as it relates to environmental protection, but also swine health and growth.

The university's environmental researchers work with communities in southeastern Missouri to help address their concerns about environmental quality in general and water quality in particular. Current projects include investigating the occurrence of persistent pesticides in soil and water samples from these rural communities.

Lincoln's human nutrition team conducts research on diet and human health issues such as obesity, the role of vitamins in human health, and hypertension. Current research focuses on the nutrition, exercise, and health risks associated with obesity. Researchers are particularly interested in developing a better understanding of how obesity contributes to cardiovascular disease, as well as ways to modify unhealthy lifestyles that contribute to obesity. One project studies the effectiveness of nutrition education and physical exercise as ways to improve the eating habits and body mass index in children 8 to 12 years of age. Research volunteers are recruited through the Jefferson City Boys and Girls Club to participate in an after-school program involving nutrition education and physical activity. Another project studies the effects of race and obesity on the various risk factors of cardiovascular disease. Specifically, this study examines the efficacy of increased physical activity, adjusted dietary energy and saturated fat intake, and increased fruit and vegetable consumption as ways to reduce the weight of women aged 40 to 60. A third studies the effects of diet energy levels and exercise on energy balance and biomarkers of cardiovascular health in diet-induced obese rats. Subjects are fed a high-fat diet for 12 weeks and then given 10 weeks of diet and exercise treatment. Following the treatment program, blood samples are analyzed for lipids (from which fatty acids are derived), C-reactive protein (a plasma protein associated with an increased risk for diabetes, hypertension, and cardiovascular disease), and leptins (protein hormones that play a key role in regulating energy intake and expenditure, including the regulation of appetite and metabolism).

See also: Cardiovascular Disease; Diabetes; Obesity

REFERENCES AND FURTHER READING

Lincoln University of Missouri. "Cooperative Research." [Online article or information; retrieved December 4, 2006.] http://www.lincolnu.edu/pages/375.asp.

Lincoln University of Missouri. "Lincoln University of Missouri." [Online article or information; retrieved October 29, 2007.] http://www.lincolnu.edu/pages/1.asp.

Meharry Medical College

Meharry Medical College, located in Nashville, Tennessee, is the largest private, comprehensive historically black institution for educating health care professionals and scientists in the United States. It is believed that, between Reconstruction and the Civil Rights Movement, Meharry produced more than half of the black MDs trained in the United States. Meharry continued to be an important center for training physicians, as well as for conducting minority-related medical research, well into the 21st century. Since 1970, Meharry has conferred more than 10 percent of the PhD degrees awarded nationally to African Americans in all of the biomedical sciences.

Meharry received its name from the Meharry brothers—Samuel, Hugh, David, Jesse, and Alexander. In 1875, the Meharrys provided more than $30,000 in cash and property for the building of a medical school for blacks at Central Tennessee College in Nashville, which had been established several years earlier by the Freedmen's Aid Society of the Methodist Episcopal Church. Allegedly, the Meharrys' motivation originated in 1826, when Samuel was treated hospitably by a slave family after his wagon became mired in a swamp; having no money with which to repay the family, Samuel vowed that someday he would "do something for your race." Additional funding was provided by the Freedmen's Aid Society and the John F. Slater Fund, and in

1876, the Medical Department of Central Tennessee College was opened. In 1900, the college was renamed Walden University, and the medical department became known as Meharry Medical College of Walden University. Fifteen years later, Meharry was granted a charter by the state of Tennessee making it an independent institution, which it has remained ever since. Today, Meharry includes schools of medicine, dentistry, graduate studies and research, and allied health professions. It also operates George W. Hubbard Hospital (founded in 1917), two health centers, and the Harold D. West Basic Sciences Center.

The oldest and largest of Meharry's four schools is the School of Medicine. As of 2005, the school was admitting an average of 80 medical students each year, most of whom are either African American, Hispanic, Asian, or Native American. The majority of Meharry's graduates establish practices in family medicine, internal medicine, pediatrics, or obstetrics and gynecology in minority communities that are generally underserved by other physicians. In addition to offering the MD degree to its medical students, the school also provides, through Hubbard Hospital, training for about 30 residents annually in family practice, internal medicine, occupational medicine, preventive medicine, obstetrics and gynecology, and psychiatry. Additionally, the school trains graduate students for the MS degree in public health offered through Meharry's School of Graduate Studies and Research and for the PhD degree in biochemistry, microbiology, pharmacology, and physiology. Finally, the school provides significant training to students from Meharry's Schools of Dentistry and Allied Health Professions.

The Meharry School of Dentistry was founded in 1886. As of 2005, it was accepting approximately 55 students each year into its Doctor of Dental Surgery (DDS) program. Like Meharry's medical graduates, most dental graduates establish practices in minority communities that were previously underserved by other dentists. In addition to providing basic dental training, the school sponsors a postdoctoral program in oral and maxillofacial surgery and a general practice residency program at Hubbard Hospital; the latter program emphasizes public health service and care for physically and/or mentally compromised patients. The school also operates a Regional Research Center for Minority Oral Health, one of four in the United States. The purpose of the center is to improve the oral health of ethnic minorities by enhancing the ability of minority dental schools to conduct basic research on oral health.

The Meharry School of Graduate Studies and Research began in 1938 as a series of short courses in the basic and clinical sciences. In 1947, an MS degree program was implemented as the first graduate degree. A PhD program was established in 1972, and an MD/PhD program was inaugurated in 1982. By 2005, the school was overseeing the activities of a number of research centers. The Asthma Disparities Center, which is affiliated with the National Institutes of Health, focuses on understanding why minorities, low-income groups, and pregnant women tend to suffer disproportionately from asthma and related conditions. The Center for Molecular and Behavioral Neurosciences conducts research calculated to understand and reduce health disparities in the areas of neurological disease, mental health, and drug and alcohol abuse and addiction. The Clinical Research Center was established in 1981 by the National Institutes of Health as a vehicle for making Meharry one of the leading clinical research institutions among generalist-producing, comprehensive health centers in this country, with an emphasis on conducting clinical research that improves the health care of disadvantaged and minority populations. The Center for Health Disparities conducts research aimed at understanding how society, economics, culture, behavior, and biology contribute to disproportionately high occurrences among minorities and low-income groups of a variety of medical conditions, including respiratory disease, cancer, cardiovascular disease and stroke, diabetes, infant mortality, intentional and unintentional injury, teen pregnancy, kidney failure, and mental health, and the Center for Health Disparities Research in HIV focuses specifically on HIV/AIDS. The Sickle Cell Center provides clinical care, education, genetic counseling, and laboratory services to patients with sickle cell disease and other hemoglobin-related deficiencies while conducting basic research on these conditions.

Meharry's School of Allied Health Professions was established in 1974 through a formal agreement between Meharry and Tennessee State University. The school's establishment was the first time a private medical college and a public land-grant university combined to provide access to training in the health-related professions for minority students. As of 2005, the school offered degree programs in cardiorespiratory care science, dental hygiene, health care administration and planning, health information management, medical technology, occupational therapy, physical therapy, and speech pathology and audiology.

See also: Asthma; Biochemistry; Cancer; Cardiovascular Disease; Diabetes; HIV/AIDS; Microbiology; National Institutes of Health; Sickle Cell Disease; Tennessee State University; West, Harold D.

REFERENCES AND FURTHER READING

Meharry Medical College. "Meharry Medical College." [Online article or information; retrieved October 29, 2007.] http://www.mmc.edu/.

Organ, Claude H., and Margaret Kosiba, eds. *A Century of Black Surgeons: The U.S.A. Experience.* Norman, OK: Transcript Press, 1987: 103–148.

Tennessee State University Digital Library. "Meharry Medical College (1876–)." [Online article or information; retrieved October 25, 2005.] http://www.tnstate.edu/library/digital/meharry.htm.

Mercy-Douglass Hospital

Prior to 1948, the health care needs of African Americans in Philadelphia were served by two small hospitals, Douglass and Mercy. The two separate facilities struggled financially, however, and in 1948, they merged to form Mercy-Douglass Hospital. This hospital served Philadelphia's African American community until 1973, when it closed its doors.

In 1895, Douglass Memorial Hospital, named in honor of the black abolitionist Frederick Douglass, was opened in Philadelphia to provide a place for black men and women to practice medicine, and it had one of the first nursing schools for African American women in the country. Almost from the beginning, however, Douglass was unable to take care of all the patients who wished to avail themselves of its services; so in 1907, Mercy Hospital was opened. In addition to providing an alternative source of health care for black Philadelphians, Mercy also operated a nursing school that catered to the needs of black students. Although the hospitals managed to make ends meet, both struggled financially. Neither was able to grow any larger than 110 beds, making if difficult for each to develop up-to-date facilities. This situation changed in the early 1940s, when the two hospitals began to consolidate some of their operations. This project was completed in 1948, when the two hospitals became known officially as Mercy-Douglass Hospital.

One reason for the merger was to make it easier for hospital personnel to conduct medical research. In fact, in the early 1940s, Douglass's Frederick D. Stubbs had implemented a research program on the surgical management of tuberculosis. One of the first projects undertaken by the program involved closed intrapleural pneumolysis (the surgical separation of lesions, or patches of diseased tissue, between a tuberculous lung and the surrounding chest wall). By 1947, Stubbs and his collaborators had described the two most common complications that arise from this procedure. One is bronchopleural fistula (the development of abnormal tubes between the bronchi and the pleura, the membrane that enfolds the lungs), and the other is cardiac standstill resulting from stimulation by the vagus nerve (the cranial nerve connecting the abdomen to the brain). By making the surgical community aware of these complications, as well as of ways to avoid them, the Douglass researchers succeeded in getting closed intrapleural pneumolysis adopted by an increasing number of thoracic surgeons as a means of treating pulmonary tuberculosis.

Given the combined resources of the two hospitals, the tuberculosis research program begun at Douglass would almost surely have yielded other important contributions to thoracic surgery. Unfortunately, it ended with Stubbs's death in 1947. His untimely demise seems to have left Mercy-Douglass without a dedicated research leader, for little was done in terms of medical research at the hospital thereafter.

Despite the merger, Mercy-Douglass Hospital struggled financially. The school of nursing closed in 1960, and the hospital closed in 1973. The building was torn down two years later, but in 1986, the Woodland Avenue Health Center was constructed on its site.

See also: Stubbs, Frederick D.

REFERENCES AND FURTHER READING

Minton, R. F. "The History of Mercy-Douglass Hospital." *Journal of the National Medical Association* 43, 3 (May 1951): 153–159.

Organ, Claude H., and Margaret Kosiba, eds. *A Century of Black Surgeons: The U.S.A. Experience.* Norman, OK: Transcript Press, 1987: 444–448.

MESA USA

MESA USA is a partnership of middle school, high school, and community college programs that are focused on helping African Americans and other minorities improve academically in science and related subject areas. The program's goal is to help minorities earn bachelor's degrees in science, mathematics, and engineering.

MESA (Mathematics, Engineering, Science Achievement) is an academic enrichment model that includes academic planning, community service, family involvement, academic enrichment, hands-on activities involving the application of scientific principles, career advising, field trips, competitions, and workshops. It was developed in 1970 at the University of California at Berkeley (Cal-Berkeley) and introduced into California's public schools that same year. Over the next 15 years, MESA programs were adopted by Arizona, Colorado, Maryland, New Mexico, Oregon, Utah, and Washington, and in 2004, pilot programs were established in the community college systems of Florida, Georgia, Illinois, New Jersey, and New York. Although the various state programs are variations on the model developed at Cal-Berkeley, the establishment of MESA USA allows the states to share resources and to compare notes on which aspects of their individual programs work best.

MESA provides academic support in science, mathematics, and engineering through two programs: the MESA Schools Program (MSP) and the MESA Community College Program (MCCP). The MESA Schools Program (MSP) helps middle school and high school students excel in science and mathematics so that they can not only gain admission to college but also major in a science-related discipline. Students are selected to participate in MSP through a process that involves teachers at participating schools and locally based MESA personnel, and schools enter the program with the consent of local school boards and state departments of education. Most MSPs are affiliated with education departments at nearby state universities, whose faculty members often serve as MESA consultants.

The success of MSP results directly from its multifaceted program. Individual academic plans allow counselors to monitor the progress of individual students, who receive special training in study skills. MESA periods, held during the regular school day, allow advisors, usually science or mathematics teachers, to work with students on MESA activities, and MESA Day Academies allow students to show off their knowledge and skills in regional science and mathematics competitions. Guest speakers and field trips make students aware of the various options available to them concerning college, as well as the wide range of career opportunities in science and related disciplines. MESA incorporates strategies to help parents contribute in a material way to their children's academic success, and it provides teachers with new tools for teaching science and mathematics. Perhaps the most important of these tools are the Learning Loop and the Mathematics-Physics-Technology Institutes. The Learning Loop is an innovative method for teaching mathematics. The Mathematics-Physics-Technology Institutes are annual two-week professional development programs that instruct MESA teachers of grades 8–12 how to integrate science and mathematics learning by using technology as the cohesive ingredient between the two subject areas. As of 2007, MSP was generating some impressive results. In Arizona, for example, 90 percent of MESA graduates went on to college, and more than 60 percent of them majored in science or a related field.

The MESA Community College Program (MCCP) replicates MSP but with a number of modifications to make it more appropriate for students in two-year colleges. The program establishes academic-based community centers at campuses where most students are commuters and where opportunities for peer support and information-sharing are scarce. At many campuses, MCCP is supported by a variety of local industries, so students learn firsthand about career options, scholarships, internships, and special programs.

Like MSP, MCCP incorporates many facets. MESA students are scheduled into the same science and mathematics courses, which in essence are also academic excellence workshops. Students in these courses learn how to achieve good grades through group study, as well as other survival skills to help them graduate from a four-year program in science, mathematics, or engineering. They are made aware of the various career options for holders of degrees in science and related disciplines by guest speakers and mentors from local industries, field trips, job shadowing, career fairs, company tours, and internship opportunities. They receive instruction in writing a resume, doing well in a job interview, and finding summer and part-time employment. Students participate in workshops and field trips that help them select and then transfer to a four-year school. Most of these activities are originated by the MESA community center, which serves as a student study center and a clearinghouse for information about colleges and careers.

REFERENCES AND FURTHER READING

University of California Office of the President. "MESA USA." [Online article or information; retrieved May 24, 2007.] http://mesa.ucop.edu/about/mesausa.html.

Meyerhoff Scholars Program

The Meyerhoff Scholars Program supports high-achieving, African American undergraduates attending the University of Maryland Baltimore County (UMBC) who intend to earn doctoral degrees in the sciences or engineering. The program has been widely recognized as a national model for addressing the imbalance in the number of African Americans pursuing high-level careers in science and technology.

The Meyerhoff Scholars Program was created in 1989 at UMBC via a substantial grant from the Robert and Jane Meyerhoff Foundation. Robert Meyerhoff was a civil engineer turned philanthropist from Baltimore, who had received his professional training at the Massachusetts Institute of Technology (MIT). He and his wife, Jane, were concerned about the acute shortage of black scientists and engineers. At first, they provided financial support for a few black undergraduates at his alma mater, but it eventually became obvious that MIT was unable to provide the community support that minority students needed to successfully complete their degrees. At that point, the Meyerhoffs decided to redouble their efforts by partnering with UMBC, a state university in their hometown which was founded in 1966 as a historically diverse institution. In its first eight years, the program graduated more than 400 students majoring in biochemistry, bioinformatics (the use of techniques from applied mathematics, statistics, and computer science to solve biological problems), biology, chemical engineering, chemistry, computer engineering, computational biology, computer science, mathematics, mechanical engineering, molecular biology, physics, and statistics.

To be considered for the Meyerhoff Scholars Program, students must be nominated by their high school administrators, guidance counselors, or teachers. Students are selected based on academic performance, standardized test scores, letters of recommendation, community service, and a demonstrated desire to pursue a PhD or combined MD/PhD degree in the sciences or engineering.

In addition to providing individual scholarships from between $5,000 and $22,000 per year for four years, the Meyerhoff Scholars Program provides students with a considerable amount of academic and community support. At the start of their freshman year, all Meyerhoff Scholars attend an accelerated six-week residential program, called Summer Bridge, which includes course work, cultural explorations, and meetings with leaders in science and technology. Summer Bridge helps students establish the work and study habits necessary for success at UMBC and the typical science-based doctoral program. Meyerhoff Scholars also receive counseling and academic advising from Meyerhoff staff, as well as from their regular departmental academic advisors. In the first two years, students meet regularly with program staff for general academic advising, and in their junior and senior years, advising is focused on preparing students to apply for graduate and professional schools. The program also helps its scholars to develop mentoring relationships with leading scientists, physicians, and engineers in the larger community; these mentors help to shape and reinforce students' long-term career goals while offering insight concerning a given field. As part of the mentoring program, Meyerhoff Scholars participate in meaningful research throughout their undergraduate careers in order to gain hands-on experience and to develop a clear understanding of what a career in science entails. To date, Meyerhoff Scholars have had the results of their research published in more than 50 scholarly articles in major scientific publications.

Perhaps most important, Meyerhoff Scholars form a tight-knit support community that helps to reinforce each scholar's accomplishments. Rather than fostering a climate of competition, the program stresses cooperation and collaboration. Scholars rely on mutual support, which includes continually challenging each other to do more, creating a positive learning environment. Students are encouraged to form informal study groups and take advantage of university and departmental tutoring resources, and many Meyerhoff Scholars serve as peer tutors.

While the Meyerhoff Scholars Program is focused on undergraduates, the Meyerhoff Fellows Program involves graduate students. This program is funded by a grant from the National Institutes of Health's Minority Biomedical Research Support initiative, and it provides similar support for students pursuing a PhD in biochemistry, biology, chemistry, chemical and biochemical engineering, mechanical engineering, molecular and cell biology, neuroscience, psychology, or toxicology.

See also: Biochemistry; Biology; Chemistry; Computer Science; Physics

REFERENCES AND FURTHER READING

University of Maryland Baltimore County. "The Meyerhoff Scholarship Program." [Online article or information; retrieved February 2, 2007.] http://www.umbc.edu/meyerhoff/.

Minorities in Agriculture, Natural Resources and Related Sciences

Minorities in Agriculture, Natural Resources and Related Sciences (MANRRS) is a national society dedicated to fostering and promoting careers in the agricultural sciences and related fields among African Americans and other underrepresented minorities. Its activities include mentoring college students and recent graduates, promoting job opportunities and internships in the agricultural sciences, and providing a support network for African American scientists and other professionals whose work relates to agriculture.

MANRRS grew out of a student initiative at Michigan State University (MSU) to establish a support group for minority students in that university's agricultural programs. This group, established in 1982 as the Minority Agriculture and Natural Resources Association (MANRA), at first served only the MSU campus. Three years later, MANRA helped start a similar organization, Minorities in Agriculture (MIA) at Pennsylvania State University (PSU); a major difference between the two groups was that MIA consisted largely of professionals, whereas MANRA consisted mostly of students. In 1986, MANRA and MIA jointly sponsored the First Annual Conference of Minority Students in Agriculture and Natural Resources at MSU, which was attended by students from several other colleges as well. At the third annual conference, hosted by the University of Maryland Eastern Shore in 1988, MANRA and MIA officially combined to form the nucleus of MANRRS. Also at the meeting were representatives from all of the land-grant colleges, including those founded in 1890 for the express purpose of providing African Americans with college-level training in the agricultural sciences, as well as from several government organizations and private firms. The following year, the organization expanded to 11 chapters, and by 2007, it boasted 53 chapters at college and university campuses across the country, with a professional staff and a permanent headquarters at MSU.

The chief service provided by MANRRS continues to be the annual Career Fair and Training Conference. In addition to workshop sessions and keynote addresses by prominent minority practitioners of the agricultural sciences, the conference conducts a career fair where employers from government agencies and private corporations related to agricultural and natural resources discuss internships and full-time employment opportunities within their respective organizations. The annual conference also serves as a medium for professionals to develop networks other than the ones provided by the professional societies in their specialties, as well as a smaller circle of relationships to circumvent some of the exclusionary impacts of established professionals' lines of communication. MANRRS also sponsors regional workshops in each of its six regions that focus primarily on professional and leadership development for students.

MANRRS has developed partnerships with a number of private companies and government agencies. Many of these entities have become national sponsors, allowing MANRRS to offer internships and cooperative training experiences for its student members, as well as professional and scholarly development opportunities for its professional members. The society also publishes a quarterly newsletter, *The Network: MANRRS Today*, and maintains a Web site. These tools serve as vehicles for disseminating information about scholarships, internships, and employment opportunities. As of 2007, the organization was proceeding with plans to implement an educational endowment fund to provide scholarships to undergraduate members, an ambassadors program and a research apprenticeship program to recruit underrepresented minorities into careers in the agricultural sciences, and a research support endowment fund to finance professional members' research and professional development.

See also: University of Maryland Eastern Shore

REFERENCES AND FURTHER READING

Minorities in Agriculture, Natural Resources and Related Sciences. "Welcome to MANRRS." [Online article or information; retrieved April 9, 2007.] http://preview.manrrs.org/manrrs_index.aspx.

Minority Access to Research Careers

Minority Access to Research Careers (MARC) is an initiative of the National Institute of General Medical Sciences. The program seeks to increase the number and competitiveness of African Americans and other underrepresented minorities engaged in biomedical research by strengthening the science curricula at historically black colleges and universities (HBCUs) and other minority-serving institutions and by increasing the research training opportunities for students and faculty at these institutions. To these ends, MARC offers assistance in the form of Undergraduate Student Training in Academic Research (U*STAR) Awards; Post-Baccalaureate Research Education Program (PREP) Awards; fellowships for predoctoral students, predoctoral faculty, and senior faculty; and ancillary training activities.

U*STAR Awards provide financial support for undergraduate biomedical programs at HBCUs and other minority-serving institutions that offer bachelor's degrees in the biomedical sciences. The schools receive the awards—approximately $11,000 per student per year—and then use them to support juniors and seniors who are honor students majoring in the biomedical sciences, who have expressed an interest in a biomedical research career, and who intend to complete their education by obtaining a PhD in a biomedical science (for example, bioinformatics, biological chemistry, biophysics, cell biology, computational biology, developmental biology, genetics, pharmacology, or physiology). However, schools may also use the awards to strengthen the biomedical teaching faculty and/or improve their biomedical course curriculum, research training programs, or research infrastructure. As of 2007, the HBCUs participating in the U*STAR program were Alcorn State University, Clark Atlanta University, Delaware State University, Grambling State University, Jackson State University, Morgan State University, North Carolina Central University, Savannah State University, Tennessee State University, University of Maryland Eastern Shore, University of the Virgin Islands, Virginia Union University, and Xavier University of Louisiana.

Post-Baccalaureate Research Education Program (PREP) Awards encourage minority students with bachelor's degrees in the biomedical sciences to pursue a doctorate related to biomedical research. Like U*STAR Awards, PREP Awards are awarded to schools, which then use them to support the minority scholars of their choice. PREP scholars are assigned to work as apprentice scientists in a mentor's laboratory and are paid a salary of $21,000 per year for up to two years. At that point, scholars are expected to apply for admission to a university or research institution with a graduate program in the biomedical or behavioral sciences.

Unlike U*STAR and PREP Awards, MARC fellowships are awarded to individuals, not schools. Individual National Research Service Awards (NRSA) are given to outstanding graduates of the U*STAR program to help them pursue a graduate degree in the biomedical sciences, and Individual Predoctoral Kirschstein-NRSA Fellowships are awarded to individuals pursuing research training leading to the PhD or equivalent degree in one of the behavioral, biomedical, clinical, or health services sciences. As of 2007, recipients of either award received $20,772 per year for up to five years. Faculty Predoctoral Fellowships are awarded to faculty members of HBCUs and other minority-serving institutions to enable them to obtain a research doctorate in a biomedical science. Recipients receive up to $38,976 per year for up to five years, after which they are expected to return to their home institution to teach and conduct research. Faculty Senior Fellowships are awarded to eligible faculty at HBCUs and other minority-serving institutions to give them the opportunity to update their research skills and/or move into new areas of research through a year-long period of intensive research in a state-of-the-art research environment. Recipients receive up to $51,036 for up to two years. Ancillary training activities sponsored by MARC include support for meetings, conferences, technical workshops, and similar training activities that enhance the research skills or competitiveness of minorities seeking careers in biomedical research.

See also: Clark Atlanta University; Delaware State University; Historically Black Colleges and Universities; Jackson State University; Morgan State University; National Institute of General Medical Sciences; North Carolina

Central University; Tennessee State University; University of Maryland Eastern Shore; University of the Virgin Islands; Xavier University of Louisiana

REFERENCES AND FURTHER READING
National Institute of General Medical Sciences. "Minority Access to Research Careers." [Online article or information; retrieved February 3, 2007.] http://www.nigms.nih.gov/minority/marc.html.

Minority Biomedical Research Support

Minority Biomedical Research Support (MBRS) is an initiative of the National Institute of General Medical Sciences (NIGMS), part of the National Institutes of Health (NIH). The program seeks to increase the competitiveness of African Americans and other underrepresented minorities engaged in biomedical research (for example, bioinformatics, biological chemistry, biophysics, cell biology, computational biology, developmental biology, genetics, pharmacology, or physiology) at historically black colleges and universities (HBCUs) and other minority-serving institutions. Toward this end, MBRS supports research by faculty members, strengthens the institutions' biomedical research capabilities, and provides opportunities for students to work as part of a research team.

The NIH Revitalization Act of 1993 encouraged NIH to increase the number of underrepresented minorities participating in biomedical and behavioral research. Consequently, in 1996, NIGMS established the MBRS Program as a vehicle for supporting HBCUs and other minority-serving institutions and their faculty and students. To these ends, MBRS offers assistance with the Support of Competitive Research (SCORE) Program, the Research Initiative for Scientific Enhancement (RISE) Program, and the Initiative for Maximizing Student Diversity (IMSD) Program.

The SCORE Program supports faculty and institutional development at HBCUs and other minority-serving institutions. As of 2007, SCORE offered three levels of support to individual researchers, as well as a level of support for institutions themselves.

The Research Advancement Award supports faculty researchers who are engaged in state-of-the-art biomedical or behavioral research and who have published their results in peer-reviewed publications, but who need further assistance until they can obtain funding from sources other than NIH. Each year, MBRS awards between 30 and 35 Research Advancement Awards, which total approximately $7 million; recipients also receive specialized training in how to write successful grant applications. The Pilot Project Award supports faculty researchers who have started to conduct their own research or who are generating preliminary data for more experienced researchers but who wish to switch to a different line of inquiry. Each year, MBRS awards between 20 and 25 Pilot Project Awards, which total approximately $2.2 million. Research Continuance Awards support senior faculty researchers who have been engaged in scholarly research and who are published but who seek to continue their research on a more limited scope. Each year, MBRS awards between 40 and 50 Research Continuance Awards, which total approximately $3 million. Institutional Development Awards support institutional research activities that improve the institution's research facilities and/or enhance the ability of their faculty researchers to conduct competitive biomedical and behavioral research. Each year, MBRS awards between 25 and 30 Institutional Development Awards, which total approximately $2.5 million.

The RISE Program supports student development at HBCUs and other minority-serving institutions that award undergraduate or graduate degrees in a biomedical or behavioral science. RISE grants are made directly to such institutions, which in turn use them to develop programs that will increase the number of minorities receiving PhDs in the biomedical sciences. Such programs include laboratory research experiences, specialty courses that help develop critical thinking and other research skills, collaborative learning experiences, research career seminars, scientific reading comprehension and writing skills, tutoring for excellence, and travel to scientific meetings. Institutions that are awarded a RISE grant receive up to $1 million per year for up to four years.

The IMSD Program supports student development at universities and other institutions that conduct a significant amount of biomedical research and whose student bodies include a significant number of minorities. Like RISE grants, IMSD grants are made directly to the institutions, which may then use the funds as they see fit to initiate new programs or to expand existing ones that prepare minority students for careers as biomedical researchers. Institutions that are awarded an IMSD grant receive up to $550,000 per year for up to four years.

See also: Historically Black Colleges and Universities; National Institute of General Medical Sciences; National Institutes of Health

REFERENCES AND FURTHER READING
National Institute of General Medical Sciences. "Minority Biomedical Research Support." [Online article or information; retrieved February 6, 2007.] http://www.nigms.nih.gov/minority/mbrs.html.

Minority Environmental Leadership Development Initiative

The Minority Environmental Leadership Development Initiative (MELDI) is a project of the University of Michigan School of Natural Resources and Environment (SNRE). Established in 2003, MELDI seeks to enhance the leadership and career development opportunities available to African American students and professionals, not only at SNRE but throughout the country, and to students and professionals of other minorities who are underrepresented in the environmental sciences.

MELDI was founded on the premise that career and leadership development enhance the ability of minorities to make careers for themselves in the environmental sciences, where traditional types of relationships and networks continue to be important factors in one's career advancement. To this end, MELDI seeks to identify outstanding minority environmental professionals and publicize their accomplishments; to identify and publicize the most effective diversity initiatives in the environmental field; to host conferences and other career and leadership development activities; and to provide a clearinghouse for information about diversity initiatives, internships and volunteer openings, networking opportunities, job postings, and current events as they relate to diversity in the environmental field. In conjunction with the University of Michigan's Rackham School of Graduate Studies, the organization sponsors the MELDI Fellowship, which provides one or more of SNRE's minority graduate students with a stipend to cover tuition and health insurance costs for one or more semesters.

In terms of career and leadership development conferences, MELDI sponsors conferences such as the 2005 National Summit on Diversity in the Environmental Field, the 2006 Environmental Justice Research Symposium, and the 2007 Faculty Diversity and Environmental Justice Research Symposium. In addition to addressing diversity in academia and environmental justice as it applies to minority communities in the United States and overseas, these conferences bring together faculty members, postdoctoral fellows, and students to discuss their research and to interact with policy makers, environmental justice practitioners, and grant makers from various public agencies and private organizations that are active in the environmental field. As part of its commitment to publicize the work of minority environmentalists, to serve as an information clearinghouse, and to help students and recent graduates establish themselves in environmentally related careers, MELDI publishes *The Paths We Tread: Profiles of the Careers of Minority Environmental Professionals*, *MELDI Career Resource Guide to Environmental Jobs*, and *MELDI Guide to Negotiating the Job Market* (Ann Arbor: University of Michigan, School of Natural Resources and Environment, 2005. http://www.umich.edu/~meldi/PDF/ProfilesBook_0605.pdf).

REFERENCES AND FURTHER READING
Minority Environmental Leadership Development Initiative. "Minority Environmental Leadership Development Initiative." [Online article or information; retrieved April 9, 2007.] http://www.umich.edu/~meldi/index.html.

Minority Opportunities in Research

Minority Opportunities in Research (MORE) is a division of the National Institute of General Medical Sciences (NIGMS). MORE administers research and research training programs aimed at increasing the number of African Americans and other underserved minorities conducting research in the biomedical sciences (for example, bioinformatics, biological chemistry, biophysics, cell biology, computational biology, developmental biology, genetics, pharmacology, or physiology). To this end, MORE oversees the Minority Access to Research Careers (MARC) program, the Minority Biomedical Research Support (MBRS) program, and the Bridges to the Future programs, while administering a number of fellowships and supplemental awards for fostering career development and research. The MARC and MBRS programs are covered in separate articles; this article focuses on MORE's other initiatives.

The Bridges to the Future Programs includes the Bridges to the Baccalaureate Degree and the Bridges to the Doctoral Degree initiatives. The baccalaureate program helps minority students make the transition from two-year junior or community colleges that have demonstrated an outstanding ability to prepare minority students for completing their undergraduate degrees to four-year colleges and universities that offer undergraduate degrees related to the biomedical or behavioral sciences. The program encourages the development of partnerships between one or more two-year institutions and one or more four-year institutions; the four-year schools must use the funds to develop support programs for the minority students who transfer in from the junior and community colleges. The doctoral program helps minority students make the transition from universities offering the MS degree as the terminal degree in the biomedical sciences to universities offering the PhD degree. As with the baccalaureate program, the doctoral program encourages the development of partnerships between one or more MS-granting institutions, each of which must have a proven track record of graduating significant numbers of minority students, and one or more PhD-granting institutions; also, the PhD-granting institutions must use the funds to develop support programs for the minority students who transfer in from the MS-granting institutions. As of 2007, awards for both Bridges initiatives provided funding of up to $600,000 per four-year school (or schools, if more than one in a partnership) for up to three years.

MORE provides fellowships and supplemental awards to institutions with substantial minority enrollments to permit them to enhance their research and research training capabilities. The Faculty Development Award funds faculty members with a PhD degree in a biomedical science who wish to spend either two to five consecutive summers or a full academic term conducting biomedical research at a research-intensive laboratory. Recipients may enroll in one course per academic term in fields directly related to the research in order to update their theoretical backgrounds. In addition to enhancing the recipients' research opportunities, the award seeks to develop long-term collaborations between recipients and the faculties of the research laboratories. As of 2007, recipients received up to $50,000 per year.

Fellowship Awards for Minority Students support highly qualified minority students working toward a PhD degree in the biomedical or behavioral sciences and who intend to embark on careers in biomedical research. Recipients receive an annual stipend of $20,772 and an allowance for tuition and fees.

Institutional Research and Academic Career Development Awards (IRACDA) support postdoctoral researchers who are also teaching at a historically black college or university (HBCU) or other minority-serving institution so as to promote linkages between research-intensive institutions and minority-serving institutions that can lead to further collaborations in research and teaching. The annual dollar amount of such awards, which are limited to five years, vary, but they cover salary, fringe benefits, tuition, fees, books, and related career development expenses. Research Supplements to Promote Diversity in Health-Related Research provide additional funding to researchers who already hold grants from NIGMS to encourage them to include minority students and researchers on their research teams. Because the nature and duration of such research projects vary tremendously, so too do the terms of the Research Supplements.

See also: Historically Black Colleges and Universities; Minority Access to Research Careers; Minority Biomedical Research Support; National Institute of General Medical Sciences

REFERENCES AND FURTHER READING

National Institute of General Medical Sciences. "Minority Programs." [Online article or information; retrieved February 3, 2007.] http://www.nigms.nih. gov/minority.

Minority Science and Engineering Improvement Program

The Minority Science and Engineering Improvement Program (MSEIP) provides financial assistance to historically black colleges and universities (HBCUs) and other minority-serving institutions so that they may make sustainable improvements in their science and engineering education programs. The overall goal of the program is to increase the number of African Americans and other underrepresented minorities pursuing careers in science and engineering.

MSEIP is a descendant of the Minority Institutions Science Improvement Program (MISIP), which was created by one of the provisions of the National Science Foundation Act of 1950. MISIP was administered by the National Science Foundation until authority for the program was transferred to the Department of Education by the Department of Education Reorganization Act of

1979. For a time, the program was known as the Minority Science Improvement Program. As of 2007, MSEIP was administered by the Department's Institutional Development and Undergraduate Education Service.

MSEIP funds support a broad range of activities that eliminate or reduce the barriers preventing African Americans and other minorities from embarking on careers in science and technology. Grants are generally made directly to HBCUs and other minority-serving institutions of higher learning, but they are also made to nonprofit science-oriented organizations and professional scientific societies that provide such institutions with a service such as in-service training for project directors. MSEIP funds are not used for student scholarships; rather, they are used to establish or strengthen an institution's ability to produce minority scientists and engineers. To this end, MSEIP funds may be spent to purchase, rent, or lease scientific or laboratory equipment for educational, instructional or research purposes; to construct, maintain, renovate, or improve classroom, library, laboratory, and other instructional facilities; to purchase or rent telecommunications technology equipment or services; to purchase library books, periodicals, technical and other scientific journals, microfilm, microfiche, and other educational materials, including telecommunications program materials; to establish or improve a development office to strengthen and increase contributions from alumni and the private sector; to help establish or maintain an institutional endowment to facilitate financial independence; and to acquire computer equipment, including software, for use in strengthening financial management and management information systems.

Eligible institutions and organizations may apply for MSEIP funding annually. Recipients who demonstrate sustainable improvement in their science and engineering programs for minorities may apply to have their grants extended for an additional year. Total awards in fiscal year 2006 equaled almost $8.7 million given to 80 schools, including 24 HBCUs and a number of other colleges and universities with significant African American enrollments.

See also: Historically Black Colleges and Universities; National Science Foundation

REFERENCES AND FURTHER READING

U.S. Department of Education. "Minority Science and Engineering Improvement Program." [Online article or information; retrieved February 10, 2007.] http://www.ed.gov/programs/iduesmsi/index.html.

Minority University–Space Interdisciplinary Network

The Minority University–Space Interdisciplinary Network (MU-SPIN) helps to develop the scientists and engineers whom the National Aeronautics and Space Administration (NASA) will need in the future. MU-SPIN does so by providing historically black colleges and universities (HBCUs) and other minority-serving institutions with state-of-the-art computers and computer networks, as well as the training programs to use the networks competently, so that the institutions can train scientists and engineers capable of working on NASA projects. As such, MU-SPIN forms a part of NASA's Minority Undergraduate Research and Education Programs.

MU-SPIN was established in 1990 by NASA's Office of Equal Opportunity Programs. At the time, most HBCUs and other minority-serving institutions were not connected to the Internet, because they lacked the technology; so MU-SPIN's first mission was to help these institutions buy and/or build computers for classroom use. In 1996, MU-SPIN shifted its focus to helping HBCUs and other minority schools develop networks for maximizing the potential of their computers. The result was the establishment of Network Resources and Training Sites (NRTS), which built on the training accomplishments of the prior years and improved research infrastructure, thereby increasing opportunities to participate in and benefit from NASA and other federal funding programs. Institutions chosen for the NRTS project were those that had not historically received major amounts of funding from NASA and that were judged capable of implementing the NRTS vision. In the first year alone, approximately 4,000 people from 87 different institutions attended NRTS workshops, and more than 150 computer labs were either created or enhanced with equipment and/or network connectivity. Other aspects of the NRTS initiative included developing and implementing strategic management guidelines; creating an income stream independent of federal funding that significantly enhanced the ability of these institutions to become magnet institutions of education, research, and technology innovation; and emphasizing the importance of publishing and marketing research results.

By 2003, with the NRTS vision largely achieved, MU-SPIN shifted its focus once again. This time, the goal was to create a virtual project, whereby each NRTS and their collaborating institutions were connected via the Internet to each other and to the rest of the country. Seven NRTS schools were selected to become Expert Institutes, five of which are HBCUs: Elizabeth City State University, Morgan State University, Prairie View A&M University, South Carolina State University, and Tennessee State University. Each Expert Institute was encouraged to identify its own area of technological expertise and then to develop that expertise to the fullest extent. In so doing, MU-SPIN hoped to create a virtual university of more than 80 HBCUs and other minority-serving institutions to which the Expert Institutes would contribute a broader range of curriculum and programs that would otherwise be unobtainable to any single school. The Expert Institutes initiative also promoted technology transfer and commercialization as a means to develop alternate sources of income beyond federal funding so as to contribute to the economic growth of the

NRTS network. Finally, the Expert Institutes initiative promoted NASA faculty/ student summer research aimed at providing direct interaction with NASA scientists, thus creating an additional method of tracking the student participation and career advancement of African Americans and other minorities.

See also: Historically Black Colleges and Universities; Morgan State University; National Aeronautics and Space Administration; Prairie View A&M University; South Carolina State University; Tennessee State University

REFERENCES AND FURTHER READING

National Aeronautics and Space Administration, Goddard Space Flight Center. "Minority University–Space Interdisciplinary Network." [Online article or information; retrieved February 10, 2007.] http://muspin.gsfc.nasa.gov/.

Morehouse School of Medicine

The Morehouse School of Medicine (MSM) in Atlanta trains primary care physicians, especially from underrepresented minority and disadvantaged backgrounds, to provide high-quality health care to underserved and minority communities. Along with the Howard University College of Medicine and Meharry Medical College, MSM has trained a significant percentage of the African American physicians practicing medicine in this country. MSM has also become a major center for research on health issues pertinent to the African American community.

The assassination of Martin Luther King Jr. in 1968 triggered a spate of riots across the country, including Atlanta. Many state officials suspected that the underlying cause of the riots was the unequal treatment of blacks by whites, and so the state appointed a number of commissions to see what could be done to address these inequalities and thus prevent further rioting. One commission, the Georgia Comprehensive Health Planning Council's Task Force for Physician Manpower, discovered that, while 27 percent of Georgia's population was black, only 3 percent of its physicians were black. Not surprisingly, the task force also discovered that black Georgians were forced to deal with restricted access to health care. To remedy this situation, the task force recommended that the state provide increased opportunities for African Americans to become physicians. One result of this recommendation was a study to determine the feasibility of founding a medical school at Atlanta's historically black Morehouse College. With financial assistance from the U.S. Department of Health, Education and Welfare's Health Resources Administration, the Carnegie Foundation, and the state of Georgia, in 1978, the Morehouse School of Medicine admitted its first class, 24 students who enrolled in a two-year basic medical sciences program. Three years later, MSM was granted a charter by the state making it independent of Morehouse College. In 1985, MSM awarded its first MD degrees. By 2005, it was also awarding the PhD degree in biomedical sciences and MS degrees in public health and clinical research to approximately 60 graduates annually. More than 80 percent of MSM's graduates practice medicine in previously underserved communities, most of them as primary health care providers rather than specialists.

One of the first programs established at MSM was a family practice residency program. In conjunction with three Atlanta hospitals, the Tuskegee Veterans Administration Hospital, and the Atlanta-based Centers for Disease Control and Prevention, the program began training residents at the three hospitals to treat the various medical conditions a physician would typically encounter while administrating to the health needs of a small, rural Georgia community. In 1986, MSM added a residency program in public health and preventive medicine. By 2005, its residents could also receive training in general surgery, internal medicine, obstetrics/gynecology, and psychiatry.

In addition to its medical education programs, MSM has made a major commitment to conducting medical research, particularly in areas of special importance to African Americans. The Cardiovascular Research Institute was established in 1999 as part of a National Institutes of Health initiative to develop cardiovascular research centers at historically black colleges and universities. The Clinical Research Center seeks to improve health care for the African American community by conducting clinical trials on outpatients in the areas of cardiovascular disease, cancer, clinical pharmacology, and HIV/AIDS. The Cork Institute on Alcohol and Other Addictive Disorders conducts research concerning the physiology of drug and alcohol addiction and serves as the national headquarters for the Historically Black Colleges and Universities Substance Abuse Consortium, an organization established to primarily address the issues of increasing the number of African American and other minority professionals in the field of substance-related disorders.

The Space Medicine and Life Sciences Research Center supports the achievement of routine space travel and the enrichment of life on Earth through the use of space technology and the application of biomedical knowledge. The center's space flight and gravitational biology research program investigates the effects of space travel and microgravity on the cardiovascular and musculoskeletal systems, on tissue, on the circadian rhythm (the cyclical 24-hour period of human biological activity), and on signal transduction (the sending of nervous impulses to and from the brain).

The Neuroscience Institute conducts research related to the functional organization of the nervous system while seeking ways to reduce suffering brought about by neurological disorders, and in 2005, the institute's researchers were investigating a broad range of cellular and molecular neuroscience projects. Several projects included the molecular biology and physiology of circadian rhythm, signal transduction and modulation in the basal ganglia (the gray mass of nerve tissue at the base of the brain), and the toxic effect of HIV infection on the behavior of neurons (the fundamental units of nerve tissue, each consisting of a nerve cell and its connections). Others sought to understand the effect of transient hypoxia (the temporary deficiency of oxygen) on sensory neurons that are sensitive to a specific neurotransmitting chemical, the role played by neuregulin (a protein that performs multiple essential functions in development) in certain types of neurological activity, the effects of hormones and neuropeptides (nerve proteins that regulate almost all life processes on a cellular level) on aggressive behavior, the regeneration of neurons in the central nervous system at the cellular level, and the roles played by thyroid hormone and the protein prohibitin in the sexual development of mammals.

The Prevention Research Center conducts research aimed at increasing health care awareness among African Americans by providing them with better access to health care information. In 2005, the center was engaged in projects designed to heighten the awareness of heterosexually active men and women about the dangers of HIV infection; to increase the cancer prevention rate, particularly among black men in their 50s who are susceptible to colorectal cancer; to provide indigent teenagers and their parents with computer access to health care information; and to help change the dietary and other lifestyle habits of people who are likely to suffer from heart disease, stroke, or lung cancer.

See also: Cancer; Cardiovascular Disease; Historically Black Colleges and Universities; HIV/AIDS; Howard University College of Medicine; Meharry Medical College; Tuskegee Veterans Administration Hospital

REFERENCES AND FURTHER READING

Morehouse School of Medicine. "About MSM." [Online article or information; retrieved November 19, 2005.] http://www.msm.edu/aboutmsm/index. htm.

Organ, Claude H., and Margaret Kosiba, eds. *A Century of Black Surgeons: The U.S.A. Experience.* Norman, OK: Transcript Press, 1987: 427–432.

Morgan State University

Morgan State University is Maryland's foremost historically black institution of higher learning. In terms of scientific research, the school is best known for its Estuarine Research Center, which seeks to develop a better understanding of the Chesapeake Bay and its tributaries and the aquatic life that lives therein.

Morgan State was founded in Baltimore, in 1867, as the Centenary Biblical Institute, and its original mission was to train young black men to be ministers. In 1890, it was renamed Morgan College in honor of the Reverend

Lyttleton Morgan, the first chairman of its board of trustees, who donated land to the college, and five years later, it awarded its first bachelor's degree. In 1939, the school was acquired by the state of Maryland, and over the next several decades, it evolved into the state's four-year liberal arts college for blacks. In 1975, the college was designated a university, and in 1988, it became part of the state university system.

Baltimore is the largest city on the Chesapeake Bay, the nation's largest estuary; so it is only natural that Morgan State researchers take an interest in the bay. To this end, the school established the Estuarine Research Center, which studies the bay from four different perspectives: invertebrate population ecology, plankton biology, hyperspectral remote sensing, and estuarine ecology.

The center's invertebrate population ecology studies are focused on crabs and oysters, both of which are of tremendous importance to Maryland's commercial fisheries. From 1968 to the present, shortly before the Calvert Cliffs Nuclear Power Plant was constructed, the center's researchers have been studying the effects of the plant's thermal discharge on the bay's blue crab population. Over the years, the data compiled by this study has indicated several changes that appeared to be undesirable for the crab fishery closest to Calvert Cliffs, as well as for the bay's entire crab population. The center's researchers also seek to understand why oyster harvests in recent years have been so poor, despite the state's oyster recovery activities since 1993. Experimental oyster studies conducted during drought conditions in the early 2000s revealed extremely high mortalities of a standard strain of native oyster. To determine whether survivorship can be improved, the center is evaluating the performance of two disease-tolerant varieties of native oyster against a standard strain in field experiments in the Patuxent River by examining growth, mortality, and disease acquisition rates and status.

The center's plankton biology studies focus on phytoplankton ecology, specifically the relationships between water quality parameters and the distribution and composition of phytoplankton (the photosynthetic or plant constituent of plankton, mainly unicellular algae). Having monitored the bay's phytoplankton ecology since 1984, the center's researchers have recently developed a phytoplankton index of biotic integrity for assessing the habitat condition of the phytoplankton community. This index is being incorporated into an ecosystem index that will facilitate the assessment of the water and habitat quality of Chesapeake Bay.

The center also studies algal blooms (relatively rapid increases in the population of phytoplankton algae in an aquatic system). When algal blooms involve certain harmful species of algae, they sometimes disrupt higher links in the local food chain; as the algae die and decompose, they stimulate the growth of bacteria, which deplete the oxygen levels in the water, leading to fish kills or the replacement of certain species with less valuable ones that are more tolerant of higher phosphorus and lower oxygen levels. Because of the threat that harmful algal blooms pose to the bay's ecosystem, center researchers study them by using hyperspectral remote sensing (HRS), also known as imaging spectroscopy, a relatively new technology that allows researchers to detect and identify minerals, vegetation, and human-made materials at large spatial scales. At present, the center is developing a method for using hyperspectral remote sensing for monitoring nutrient enrichment of the bay and its watershed, which researchers suspect is the primary cause of algal blooms.

The center's work with estuarine ecology focuses on two areas: (1) the interactions between predator and prey and (2) the effects of the alteration of natural shoreline habitats by human activity on the bay's ecology. One of the largest human-made effects on the bay's ecology is the use of bay water for cooling purposes by coastal power plants. To ensure that such activity does not impinge harmfully on the aquatic ecosystem, center researchers monitor the power plants to make sure they comply with all pertinent Environmental Protection Agency (EPA) regulations.

REFERENCES AND FURTHER READING

Morgan State University. "Morgan State University." [Online article or information; retrieved October 29, 2007.] http://www.morgan.edu/.

Morgan State University Estuarine Research Center. "Research Programs." [Online article or information; retrieved August 15, 2006.] http://www.morgan.edu/erc/research.html.

National Aeronautics and Space Administration

Perhaps the most spectacular scientific achievement in the history of American science has been the success of the U.S. space program. Under the direction of the National Aeronautics and Space Administration (NASA), Americans have been in the forefront of humankind's efforts to learn more about the universe we live in. At the same time, NASA has also played a leading role in aeronautic research. Many of NASA's noteworthy achievements in aeronautical engineering and space exploration can be credited directly to the efforts of black scientists and administrators. It is not possible to describe the careers that all of them enjoyed with NASA, but the following examples serve to underscore the width and breadth of the African American contribution to NASA's many missions.

One of the first blacks to go to work for NASA was Katherine G. Johnson. After teaching high school mathematics for several years, in 1953, she joined the staff at Langley Research Center in Hampton, Virginia, one of the nation's foremost centers for aeronautical research. Her first assignment was as a so-called computer, a human who performed by hand the many tedious and time-consuming calculations required by engineering studies. When NASA was formed in 1958, Langley became part of the new agency, and Johnson became a NASA employee. Over the next 30 years, she developed and solved equations concerning space navigation such as mapping out orbits for satellites while helping to develop a highly sophisticated ground tracking system for the manned flight missions of the 1960s. Later, she served in the Lunar Spacecraft and Operations Division, where she performed many of the critical calculations related to the various lunar landings.

Annie Easley went to work for NASA in much the same way that Johnson did. Easley did not have a college degree when she went to work in 1955 for the National Advisory Committee on Aeronautics (NACA) at the Lewis Flight Propulsion Laboratory (today NASA's John H. Glenn Research Center) in Cleveland. Nevertheless, she possessed excellent mathematical computational skills, and so she too was hired as a computer. In 1958, NACA became NASA, and shortly thereafter, Easley was assigned to Lewis's Flight Software Section as a mathematician and computer engineer. In this capacity, she used binary code, which uses only zeroes and ones, to write computer programs for measuring the velocity and direction of solar winds; for controlling the Centaur, a rocket booster that was used to put communications satellites into orbit; and for quantifying the efficiency of energy conversion systems.

Like Easley, Julian M. Earls spent his entire NASA career at Lewis/Glenn. Hired in 1965 as a nuclear radiation specialist, he eventually became involved in health physics. In 1983, he entered the ranks of management by becoming division chief of the Health, Safety, and Security Office. Over the next 20 years, he served in increasingly challenging positions with distinction, and in 2003, he was named director of the Glenn Research Center, with direct responsibility for its more than 3,200 personnel and $773 million annual budget.

Vance Marchbanks was the chief flight surgeon during John Glenn's first mission, the first space flight to orbit the Earth. Marchbanks, a graduate of Howard University College of Medicine, had joined the Army Air Corps (later the U.S. Air Force) during World War II and served as a flight surgeon for the Tuskegee Airmen. After the war, he became an expert in aeromedical research and aerospace medicine. He designed an improved device for testing the oxygen masks used by high-altitude pilots that became a standard item of air base equipment, and he developed a system for measuring how the stress related to high-altitude air travel affected the crews of B-52 bombers. This system worked so well that it was eventually used to measure the effects of stress on astronauts. After retiring from the air force in 1964, he was recruited by NASA to serve as a flight surgeon for the Project Mercury missions, which sent only one human at a time into space. By the time of Glenn's mission, he had advanced to the position of head physician for Project Mercury. In this capacity, he oversaw a team of 11 medical specialists who monitored Glenn's vital signs before, during, and after the mission. Marchbanks also played an important role in the Project Apollo missions, which eventually put a man on the moon, by overseeing the testing of the moonsuit and backpack that the Apollo astronauts used.

Robert Shurney designed a number of tools and techniques for living and working in the weightless conditions of space. Shurney's first space inventions addressed the simple problem of eating and drinking under zero-gravity conditions. To prevent solid foods from drifting off their plates and into a piece of equipment or control console where they might disrupt the entire operation of the spacecraft, he designed special zero-gravity utensils and trays that keep solid food from floating away and containers that enable astronauts to suck liquids or pasty solids through a small tube. He also designed the lightweight aluminum tires used on the first lunar rover (moon buggy) that was used to transport astronauts on the surface of the moon in 1971. The most significant feature of these tires is their unique chevron tread, which enabled the moon buggy to navigate through the dust that coats the lunar surface without spraying the astronauts with dust.

Nichelle Nichols was an actress, not a scientist, but she played a crucial role in attracting African Americans to become space shuttle astronauts. In 1976, NASA announced that it would begin training a large corps of astronauts to fly aboard its fleet of space shuttles, and it was particularly interested in recruiting minorities to serve as astronauts. However, very few African Americans applied for the program, mostly because NASA had recruited only two black astronauts to that point; one, Edward Dwight, had been discharged for no good reason, and the other, Robert Lawrence, was killed during a training exercise. Moreover, the fact that Lawrence's parachute had failed to open while the parachute of his white training partner had worked fine caused many blacks to question NASA's commitment to putting African Americans into space. At this point, NASA recruited Nichols to help recruit more blacks for the astronaut program. Nichols had portrayed Lieutenant Uhura, the only black crew member on the starship *Enterprise*, on *Star Trek*, an incredibly popular television program during the 1960s and 1970s. Nichols made a number of television commercials and personal appearances to encourage blacks to apply for the astronaut program. Her efforts were directly responsible for attracting to the astronaut program the first three African Americans to fly in space, Guion S. Bluford Jr., Ronald E. McNair, and Frederick D. Gregory.

In addition to Bluford, McNair, and Gregory, 10 other African Americans have flown in space as NASA shuttle astronauts: Charles F. Bolden Jr., Mae C.

Jemison, Bernard A. Harris, Robert L. Curbeam Jr., Michael P. Anderson, Winston E. Scott, Joan E. Higginbotham, Stephanie D. Wilson, B. Alvin Drew, and Leland D. Melvin.

After completing his tour of duty as an astronaut, Gregory became NASA's associate administrator for the Office of Safety and Mission Assurance. He later served as associate administrator for the Office of Space Flight and as NASA deputy administrator. Shortly before retiring in 2005, he served for a few months as acting administrator, making him the highest-ranking black to work for NASA.

George E. Alcorn Jr. made important contributions to NASA as a researcher and as an administrator. In the late 1970s, he developed a new type of imaging X-ray spectrometer for determining the elemental composition of the stars and other distant bodies and a chemical ionization mass spectrometer that can detect the presence of amino acids, a sure sign of life, on other planets. In 1984, he left research to become deputy project manager for the International Space Station (ISS) mission, and in this capacity, he oversaw the development of advanced technologies for use on the ISS. Later, as project manager for the Airborne LIDAR Topographic Mapping System (ALTMS), he oversaw the development of this technology into a tool for determining the elevation of various landforms on the solar system's planets and moons by seeing through soft but thick layers of dust. He also served as assistant director for standards and excellence in NASA's Applied Engineering and Technology Directorate.

Like Alcorn, James King Jr. contributed to the space program as a researcher and manager. During the 1960s, he served as a research chemist at NASA's Jet Propulsion Laboratory in California, and his primary achievement in this capacity was to describe the physical chemistry of atomic hydrogen, a key ingredient in rocket propellant. Understanding the behavior of atomic hydrogen is crucial, because its ability to react with the other elements in rocket propellant depends on minute variations in its electrical charge and initial energy state. As a manager, in the 1970s, he directed NASA's space shuttle environmental effects program, which sought to prevent shuttle flights from polluting the atmosphere, and its upper atmospheric research program. He also served as assistant laboratory director for JPL's technical divisions, which focus on developing the systems and technologies necessary for traveling beyond the solar system.

Isaac T. Gillam IV began his NASA career in 1963 as a resources management specialist at NASA headquarters in Washington, D.C. Before long, he was named director of the program to design and develop the Delta rocket booster, which NASA used to put a number of small satellites into orbit, and then program manager of small launch vehicles. In 1976, he became director of shuttle operations at the Dryden Flight Research Center in California, and in this capacity, he oversaw the flight testing of the various space shuttles. He later served as director of all of Dryden's operations, special assistant in the Office of Science and Technology Policy, and assistant associate administrator of NASA.

Emmett W. Chappelle joined the research staff at NASA's Goddard Space Flight Center in Greenbelt, Maryland, in 1966. He devoted his entire NASA career to research on exobiology (the search for possible life-forms on other planets) via astrochemistry (the detection of certain chemical compounds as possible indicators of extraterrestrial life). Early in his career, he developed a method for detecting adenosine triphosphate (ATP, a compound essential to life on Earth), as well as methods for detecting luminescence (light produced by a chemical reaction) in extraterrestrial bacteria. Later, he developed a method for detecting living plant matter by using laser-induced fluorescence from space-borne sensing devices.

Patricia S. Cowings began working at the Ames Research Center in California in 1973 as a research psychologist. After training to become a space shuttle astronaut, she returned to her research. Her major contribution to NASA's mission was the development of the Autogenic Feedback Training Exercise (AFTE) as a treatment for zero-gravity sickness syndrome, popularly known as space sickness. By using AFTE, shuttle astronauts could overcome the symptoms of space sickness without resorting to pharmaceutical drugs that might impair their ability to perform their mission. She also developed exercise programs for astronauts that allow them to maintain muscle strength and tone during extended missions in space.

Irene D. Long, a physician, first went to work at the Kennedy Space Center (KSC) in Florida as a member of the Medical and Environmental Health Office, which is charged with monitoring and maintaining the health of all of the center's employees. In 1994, she was named director of the Biomedical Operations and Research Office at KSC. In this capacity, she was responsible for overseeing all of the center's medical activities, including those for astronauts, and for preparing all biological experiments to be carried aloft on shuttle missions. She also managed the development of the Controlled Ecological Life Support System, a nonsoil environment that not only produces food for humans in space but also recycles its own waste.

Beth A. Brown represents a younger generation of black scientists conducting research at NASA. After receiving a PhD in astronomy in 1998, she went to work for NASA as an astrophysicist at the Goddard Space Flight Center in Greenbelt, Maryland. Assigned to the National Space Science Data Center, she conducted research concerning the environment of elliptical galaxies, many of which contain extremely hot material, and then helped to disseminate that data, as well as astrophysical data concerning our own Milky Way galaxy to interested parties in the scientific community.

Wesley L. Harris was a black NASA administrator whose focus was aeronautics, not space. Harris had made a name for himself as an expert in aeroacoustics, the study of the shock waves resulting from the noise generated by helicopters and other high-speed aircraft, when NASA recruited him in 1993

ASTRONAUT PROGRAM

If the most spectacular development in the history of American science is the U.S. space program, then the most glamorous figures in the history of American science are astronauts. No single figure epitomizes 21st-century science as the astronaut does, and millions of children have grown up dreaming of becoming one. Prior to 1978, the privilege of becoming an astronaut was restricted almost entirely to white males. The missions flown by the National Aeronautics and Space Administration (NASA) called for astronauts with top-notch flying skills, skills that had been difficult for blacks and women to acquire because of the restrictions that prevented them from becoming experienced pilots of fighter jets and experimental aircraft. With the advent of the space shuttle program in 1978, however, NASA found itself in need of scientists, or mission specialists as NASA calls them, as well as pilots who were willing to travel into space and conduct scientific experiments there. That same year, NASA began actively recruiting qualified black scientists and pilots, and since then, more than a dozen African Americans have been chosen to receive training as space shuttle astronauts. Of them, all but three have flown in space. Of the first 114 shuttle missions flown by NASA, black astronauts have participated in 22 of them.

The first African American chosen for the astronaut program, although he never actually became an astronaut, was Edward J. Dwight Jr. At age 10, he witnessed an airplane crash at an airport near his Kansas farm and decided that he could have done better at landing than the pilot, and from then on his primary goal in life was to become a pilot. As soon as he graduated from high school, he applied for the U.S. Air Force pilot training program and continued to apply every time his application was rejected, in the meantime repeatedly taking the battery of sample pilot training tests he had found at the local library. Finally, in 1951, he was permitted to take the real pilot training exam, which he passed with flying colors. Shortly thereafter, he joined the air force, and by 1961, he was a jet fighter pilot and flight instructor with the rank of captain and a BS degree in aeronautical engineering.

That same year, Dwight received a personal invitation from President John F. Kennedy to apply for a position in NASA's astronaut program. Dwight did, and shortly thereafter, he was assigned to the air force's Aerospace Research Pilot School at Edwards Air Force Base (AFB) in California. Before he could complete his training, however, President Kennedy was assassinated. Three days later, Dwight was reassigned to Germany with orders to serve as liaison officer to West Germany's test pilot school and space program, the latter of which did not yet exist.

Clearly, Dwight's position in the astronaut program depended on Kennedy's patronage; so when the president died, Dwight's career as an astronaut died as well, for he never gained readmission to the program.

The next African American chosen for the astronaut program did become an astronaut, but he never flew in space. Robert H. Lawrence Jr. had joined the Air Force Reserve Officers Training Corps (AFROTC) while attending college. After graduation, he was commissioned a second lieutenant in the air force. By 1966, he had become a fighter pilot and a flight instructor with the rank of major and had earned a doctorate in physical chemistry. That same year, he was assigned to the Aerospace Research Pilot School. Upon graduating the following year, he was assigned to the Manned Orbiting Laboratory program at Edwards AFB, in essence the air force's own astronaut training program. Unfortunately, he died during a training mission when the jet fighter he was copiloting crashed while trying to make a complicated, spaceship-like maneuver. A certain amount of controversy surrounds this accident, because Lawrence's parachute failed to open while the parachute of the pilot, who was white, worked perfectly well.

In 1978, NASA chose three more African American astronauts, but this time all three—Guion S. Bluford Jr., Ronald E. McNair, and Frederick D. Gregory—would eventually make it to outer space. The first of them to do so was Bluford. Having developed an interest in flying and science as a boy, as an undergraduate he majored in aerospace engineering and joined the AFROTC. During his career with the Air Force, he flew more than 100 combat missions in Vietnam, received a PhD in aerospace engineering, and served as chief of the Flight Dynamics Laboratory's aerodynamics and airframe branch. As a member of NASA's first class of space shuttle astronauts, he spent his first three and a half years as an astronaut in training to be a mission specialist, which meant receiving specialized training in astronomy, aerodynamics, geology, meteorology, computer science, guidance and navigation, and flight medicine.

Bluford served on the crews of four space shuttle missions. As a mission specialist aboard STS-8 in 1983, he helped conduct a number of experiments on the biophysiological effects of space flight and an advanced technology for detecting potential cancer-causing compounds in biomolecules (the biochemical molecules from which all living things are composed). As a mission specialist aboard STS-61A in 1985, he participated in a number of experiments related to fluid physics, materials processing, life sciences, and navigation aboard Spacelab D-1, a compact manned space laboratory under the direction of the German Aerospace Research Establishment. As payload commander aboard STS-39 in 1991, he oversaw the performance of all of the mission's experiments, including

(continues)

(continued)

the measurement of several forms of electromagnetic radiation from Earth's upper atmosphere, from Saturn and one of its moons, and from several distant stars. As payload commander aboard STS-53 in 1992, he oversaw the performance of a number of classified experiments for the Department of Defense and NASA. He retired from the astronaut program in 1993.

The second African American astronaut to visit space was McNair. Unlike Dwight, Lawrence, and Bluford, McNair had never served in the military, nor was he a trained pilot. Instead, he held a PhD in physics with a specialization in the generation of laser beams (beams of visible light of only one color that have been intensified to the point that they can vaporize heat-resistant materials). At the time of his selection into the astronaut program, he was a recognized expert in the use of lasers to isolate specific chemical compounds and as a tool for studying photochemistry, which deals with the chemical effects of light.

McNair served aboard two shuttle missions. As a mission specialist aboard STS-41B in 1984, he conducted several experiments involving acoustic levitation and chemical separation. He returned to space in 1986 as a mission specialist aboard STS-51L, the last flight of the space shuttle *Challenger*. His primary task during this mission was to deploy a sophisticated telescopic camera that would collect long-term data on Halley's comet, but the *Challenger* blew up shortly after takeoff and he and his crewmates were killed.

The last black member of the first space shuttle class, Frederick Gregory, became the first black astronaut to pilot a space shuttle. After graduating from the U.S. Air Force Academy, he became a helicopter pilot and flew more than 500 rescue missions in Vietnam. He then learned to fly jets and eventually became an experimental test pilot for NASA. Unlike Bluford and McNair, Gregory was trained to be a shuttle pilot instead of a mission specialist. After seven years of training, in 1985, he piloted STS-51B, whose primary mission was to deploy Spacelab–3. He returned to space in 1989 as spacecraft commander of STS-33, a mission dedicated to the Department of Defense (DoD). His third and last mission in space came in 1991 as spacecraft commander of STS-44, another DoD-dedicated mission. Gregory left the astronaut program in 1992, but he continued to work for NASA. By the time he had retired in 2005, he had risen to the post of deputy administrator, the number two position at NASA, and had served for a brief period as acting administrator.

The next black accepted into the astronaut program was Charles F. Bolden Jr. After graduating from the U.S. Naval Academy, he became a fighter pilot in the U.S. Marine Corps and flew more than 100 combat missions in Vietnam. He eventually became a test pilot, and, at the time of his acceptance into the astronaut program in 1980, he was testing experimental aircraft at the Naval Air Test Center. His first trip to space came in 1986, when he served as pilot of STS-61C. During the six-day flight, crew members deployed the SATCOM KU communications satellite and conducted experiments in astrophysics and materials processing. In 1990, he piloted STS-31, the mission during which the Hubble Space Telescope was deployed. Two years later, he served as mission commander of STS-45, the first Spacelab mission designed to collect data concerning Earth's atmosphere as part of NASA's Mission to Planet Earth. His fourth and last trip to space came in 1994, when he served as mission commander of STS-60, the historic first joint U.S.–Russian space shuttle mission involving the participation of a Russian cosmonaut as a mission specialist. Bolden retired from NASA in 1994 to return to active duty in the marine corps.

The first African American woman selected for the astronaut program was Patricia S. Cowings. Cowings held a PhD in psychology and had conducted some groundbreaking work concerning psychophysiological responses to space travel at NASA's Ames Research Center before entering the program. But after completing astronaut training and being selected as a backup mission specialist, she opted to continue her research at Ames. Eventually, she developed treatments for zero-gravity sickness syndrome, better known as space sickness, that did not involve the use of drugs. Thus, Mae C. Jemison, who was accepted into the program in 1987, became the first African American woman to fly in space.

Unlike the previous black astronauts, Jemison was a physician, having received an MD and served extensively as a health care practitioner in southern California and with the Peace Corps in Africa. In 1992, she went aloft aboard STS-47, the first joint mission between NASA and the National Space Development Agency of Japan. As a mission specialist, she took part in about half of the mission's experiments; conducted in the Spacelab-J module, they were designed to investigate the effects of microgravity on various living and human-made substances. She left the program in 1993.

In 1990, Bernard A. Harris became the next black chosen by NASA to serve as a space shuttle astronaut. Like Jemison, Harris was a physician; following his graduation from medical school, he received extensive training as a flight and aerospace surgeon at NASA's Ames Research Center and elsewhere. The focus of his research concerned the effects of space travel on the human body, particularly the skeletal structure, and he continued this research after becoming an astronaut. His first mission in space came in 1993, when he served as a mission specialist aboard

(continues)

(continued)

STS-55, conducting a number of experiments aboard Spacelab D-2, which elaborated on the research begun in 1985 in Spacelab D-1. Two years later, he made his second and final trip into space aboard STS-63, the first mission of the joint Russian-American Space Program. In addition to facilitating a rendezvous and flyby of the Russian space station *Mir,* he oversaw the completion of the biotechnology and other experiments contained in the SPACEHAB-3 payload and participated in a two-man space walk. He resigned from the astronaut program in 1996.

In 1994, NASA chose two new black astronauts, Robert L. Curbeam Jr. and Michael P. Anderson. Curbeam, the first of the two to go into space, studied aerospace engineering at the U.S. Naval Academy. After graduation, he became a fighter pilot and eventually a test pilot. Curbeam made his first trip into space in 1997 as a mission specialist aboard STS-85, which deployed the CRISTA-SPAS payload, a set of experiments for measuring trace gases in the Earth's middle atmosphere, as well as the dynamics of the middle atmosphere. His second space voyage occurred in 2001, when he served as a mission specialist aboard STS-98, which delivered the U.S. laboratory module *Destiny* to the International Space Station (ISS). The process of attaching *Destiny* to the ISS required that Curbeam perform three space walks (called extravehicular activities by NASA) totaling more than 19 hours. In late 2007, he retired from NASA; his final mission was as a mission specialist aboard STS-116, a mission to resupply the ISS in December 2006.

Anderson came from an air force family, and in college, he joined the AFROTC. During his 13-year career in the air force he served as a communication maintenance and computer systems maintenance officer, an instructor pilot and tactics officer, and pilot of one of the Strategic Air Command's airborne command posts. After four years of astronaut training, in 1998, Anderson served as a mission specialist aboard STS-89, which delivered scientific equipment and supplies to the Russian space station *Mir.* In 2003, he returned to space aboard STS-107, the last flight of the space shuttle *Columbia*; as payload commander, he oversaw the completion of many of the mission's 80-plus experiments. Tragically, *Columbia* exploded during reentry, killing Anderson and all of his crewmates.

In 1992, Winston E. Scott joined the growing ranks of black astronauts. Scott studied music in college but, immediately upon graduation, enrolled in the Naval Aviation Officer Candidate School. He eventually learned to fly everything from antisubmarine helicopters to experimental jets and received a graduate degree in aeronautical engineering with a specialty in avionics (the application of electronics to aviation). He concluded his navy career by serving as a test pilot and deputy director of the Naval Air Development Center.

Scott made his first voyage into space in 1996 as a mission specialist aboard STS-72. This mission's primary objective was to retrieve the Space Flyer Unit, a Japanese microgravity research satellite, but he also participated in a two-man space walk to test hardware and tools for completing construction of the ISS. He returned to space the following year as a mission specialist aboard STS-87, whose primary mission was to conduct experiments concerning the effects of microgravity on various physical processes. He also conducted two space walks, one to retrieve a small scientific satellite and the other to test additional hardware and tools for performing maintenance on the ISS. He retired from the astronaut program in 1999.

In 1996, NASA selected two more African American women, Joan E. Higginbotham and Stephanie D. Wilson, to serve as space shuttle astronauts. Upon receiving an undergraduate degree in electrical engineering, Higginbotham went to work for NASA at the Kennedy Space Center as a payload electrical engineer. Over the next nine years, she played increasingly important management roles in preparing the various shuttles and their payloads for launch, and by 1996, she had participated in more than 50 shuttle missions. During her first 10 years as an astronaut, she continued to support shuttle missions. In 2006, she made her first space voyage aboard STS-116, a mission to resupply the ISS; her primary responsibility was to operate the Space Station Remote Manipulator System, a sophisticated robotic system for assembling and maintaining the ISS.

Wilson studied aerospace engineering in college, and after graduation, she went to work for the Martin Marietta Astronautics Group as a loads and dynamics engineer for Titan IV, the primary rocket booster for shuttle launches. Later she worked for the Jet Propulsion Laboratory as a specialist in spacecraft control and communication. Like Higginbotham, she spent her first 10 years in the astronaut program supporting shuttle missions from the ground, continuing her work with boosters and controllers but also in mission control as a prime communicator with shuttle crews in orbit. In 2006, she went into space as a mission specialist aboard STS-121, and in 2007, she returned to space aboard STS-120; both missions were flown in support of the ISS. Benjamin Alvin Drew joined the astronaut program in 2000. A holder of a BS in physics and aeronautical engineering from the U.S. Air Force Academy, Drew flew jet airplanes and helicopters for the air force from 1984 until 2000. Following two years of astronaut training, he was assigned to the Astronaut Office Station Operations Branch. In 2007, he flew aboard STS-118, a support mission for the ISS.

The most recent voyage into space by an African American astronaut came in February 2008, when Leland D. Melvin flew aboard STS-122, yet another mission in support of the ISS. The primary purpose of the

(continues)

(continued)

mission was to deliver and install the European Space Agency's Colum-
bus Laboratory, a facility that makes it possible for the ISS's crew to conduct experiments in weightless conditions related to the life sciences,
materials science, and fluid physics. Melvin, who holds an MS in materials
science engineering, joined the astronaut program in 1998. He spent the
next 10 years training for missions aboard the space shuttle and the ISS,
but he also comanaged the NASA Educator Astronaut Program, which
encourages K–12 students across the country to pursue careers in science,
technology, engineering, and mathematics related to NASA's missions.

See also: Anderson, Michael P.; Astronomy and Astrophysics; Bluford,
Guion S., Jr.; Computer Science; Cowings, Patricia S.; Harris, Bernard A.,
Jr.; Jemison, Mae C.; McNair, Ronald E.; National Aeronautics and Space
Administration; Physics

REFERENCES AND FURTHER READING

Burns, Khephra, and William Miles. *Black Stars in Orbit: NASA's African
American Astronauts.* New York: Harcourt Brace, 1995.
National Aeronautics and Space Administration. "NASA Space Shuttle
Launch Archive." [Online article or information; retrieved January 27,
2006.] http://science.ksc.nasa.gov/shuttle/missions/missions.html.
Spangenburg, Ray, and Kit Moser. *African Americans in Science, Math,
and Invention.* New York: Facts On File, 2003.
Warren, Wini. *Black Women Scientists in the United States.* Bloomington:
Indiana University Press, 1999.

to be its associate administrator of aeronautics. In this capacity, he oversaw
the research efforts of NASA and its subcontractors on projects such as an
advanced supersonic transport, the runway-to-orbit national aerospace plane,
and supercomputers for improving the modeling of aerodynamic forces.

Christine Darden was another black researcher and administrator from
NASA's aeronautics side. After going to work at NASA's Langley Research Center in Hampton, Virginia, in 1967, she was assigned to a number of design projects involving airframe systems (the external coverings of an airplane or rocket).
Eventually, she became a senior program manager in the High Speed Research
Program Office, which was tasked with the responsibility of designing a supersonic transport plane. To this end, she experimented with various airframe
designs that could significantly reduce sonic boom (the destructive effects of
sound waves generated by jets and other supersonic aircraft, such as the Con-
corde, which was banned from flying at supersonic speed over land because of
the sonic boom it generated). She was later named director of the Aeroper-

forming Program Management Office, which conducts extensive research on aviation systems, information technology, high-performance computing, and ultraefficient engine technology for helicopters and fixed-wing aircraft.

To ensure that black scientists and engineers continue to make significant contributions to its overall mission in even greater numbers than before, NASA has established programs to support space-related research by black faculty members and to improve the scientific training that African Americans receive in college. The NASA Astrobiology Institute Minority Institution Research Support (NAI-MIRS) Program supports research by minority faculty members in areas related to astrobiology (the study of the origins, distribution, and future of life in the universe), and it recruits minority faculty members to serve on NAI research teams conducting astrobiological research. The Minority Undergraduate Research and Education Program (MUREP) funds research and development activities at historically black colleges and universities (HBCUs), which contribute substantially to NASA's mission. This approach establishes partnerships and programs that enhance research and educational outcomes in NASA-related fields, as well as pipelines that lead to employment opportunities at NASA for an increasing number of HBCU graduates. In addition to funding individual projects at individual schools, MUREP also supports intercollegiate cooperation among HBCUs with the Minority University–Space Interdisciplinary Network (MU-SPIN). MU-SPIN provides HBCUs with state-of-the-art computers and computer networks, along with the training programs to use the networks competently, thus contributing further to the development of NASA-ready scientists and engineers.

Many NASA initiatives to train and hire the scientists it needs for the future are tailored to the recruitment of African Americans and other minorities by the United Negro College Fund Special Programs (UNCFSP) Corporation. The Motivating Undergraduates in Science and Technology Program awards scholarships and internships to minority undergraduates pursuing degrees in science, technology, engineering, or mathematics. The NASA Science and Technology Institute for Minority Institutions (NSTI-MI) helps minority undergraduate and graduate students gain insight into NASA's research needs and assists them in making the professional contacts that might lead to future employment as NASA researchers. The Curriculum Improvement Partnership Award for the Integration of Research into the Undergraduate Curriculum (CIPAIR) Program helps selected two- and four-year minority institutions to enhance their science curricula and infrastructures so that their students can be trained to conduct research related to NASA's mission. The NASA Administrator's Fellowship Program (NAFP) gives minority faculty the opportunity to conduct research at NASA research centers, but it also gives NASA career employees the opportunity to teach and conduct research at HBCUs, where they can identify and recruit promising researchers for careers with NASA.

See also: Alcorn, George E., Jr., Anderson, Michael P.; Bluford, Guion S., Jr.; Chappelle, Emmett W.; Cowings, Patricia S.; Harris, Bernard A., Jr.; Harris, Wesley L.; Historically Black Colleges and Universities; Howard University College of Medicine; Jemison, Mae C.; King, James Jr.; McNair, Ronald E.; Minority University–Space Interdisciplinary Network; NASA Astrobiology Institute; United Negro College Fund Special Programs Corporation

REFERENCES AND FURTHER READING

Burns, Khephra, and William Miles. *Black Stars in Orbit: NASA's African American Astronauts.* New York: Harcourt Brace, 1995.

National Aeronautics and Space Administration. "National Aeronautics and Space Administration." [Online article or information; retrieved October 29, 2007.] http://www.nasa.gov/.

Spangenburg, Ray, and Kit Moser. *African Americans in Science, Math, and Invention.* New York: Facts On File, 2003.

Warren, Wini. *Black Women Scientists in the United States.* Bloomington: Indiana University Press, 1999.

NASA Astrobiology Institute

The NASA Astrobiology Institute (NAI) promotes, conducts, and leads integrated multidisciplinary research in astrobiology (the study of the origins, evolution, distribution, and future of life in the universe). The institute encourages diversity in this emerging scientific discipline with the NAI Minority Institution Research Support (NAI-MIRS) Program.

NAI is a partnership between the National Aeronautics and Space Administration (NASA) and 16 independent research teams. The members of these teams are drawn from the fields of geology, astronomy, and biology, among others, and they work at various academic institutions, research laboratories, and NASA centers across the country. Each multidisciplinary team is supported by a five-year contract with NASA, and its members form a virtual community that collaborates by using sophisticated communication tools and networks that are established and maintained by NAI. Each team focuses on a specific subject area pertaining to one of three central questions: How did life begin and evolve? Does life exist elsewhere in the universe? What is the future of life on Earth and beyond? The partnership links more than 700 scientists and educators with a director and administrative staff located at the NASA Ames Research Center in Moffett Field, California. NAI also hosts biannual meetings so that the teams can collaborate in person, and it provides financial support for outreach programs to better acquaint the general public with astrobiology and its discoveries, such as the Astrobiology for Secondary Schools curriculum.

NAI-MIRS was established in 2002 to provide opportunities for researchers from historically black colleges and universities (HBCUs) and other minority-serving institutions who are interested in astrobiology to collaborate in the research being done by NAI research teams. The long-range goals of the program are to recruit researchers and students who participate in NAI-MIRS into present and future NAI research teams and to strengthen the visibility and participation of minority-serving institutions in astrobiological research so that they can participate more fully in training the astrobiologists of the future. In 2005, the Tennessee State University Center of Excellence in Information Sciences, which oversees a number of cutting-edge research programs involving astrophysics and astrobiology, and the Minority Institute Astrobiology Collaborative (MIAC), a virtual community for minority-serving institutions modeled after the NAI network, agreed to take the lead role in administering NAI-MIRS.

Each summer, NAI-MIRS funds two fellowships to minority faculty to allow them to spend between 6 and 10 weeks during the summer conducting astrobiological research. The sabbaticals are spent at a world-class facility that conducts astrobiological research, such as the NASA Goddard Space Flight Center (Maryland), the Woods Hole Marine Biological Laboratory (Massachusetts), and the Centro de Astrobiologia in Madrid, Spain, to name three. To be considered for a fellowship, a faculty member must propose a research project that addresses one of the three questions central to astrobiological research and that can be sustained after the completion of the summer sabbatical. Successful applicants are paired with a mentor who is an established researcher in the field. Each fellowship presents the recipient with up to $1,500 per week for up to 10 weeks, up to $5,000 for housing and travel, and $5,000 for supplies to support the research. Fellows also receive funding to cover the expenses incurred by themselves and two students to present their research at a professional conference.

In addition to the summer sabbatical, fellows are eligible to receive funding to support their continued astrobiological research after the completion of the summer sabbatical. Each award provides $5,000 toward the expenses of continuing the professional relationship between the minority fellow and his or her institution and the mentor and his or her institution. As a result of this support, most fellows have accepted invitations to join specific NAI research teams.

See also: Astronomy and Astrophysics; Biology; Historically Black Colleges and Universities; National Aeronautics and Space Administration; Tennessee State University

REFERENCES AND FURTHER READING

NASA Astrobiology Institute. "About the NAI-MIRS Program in Astrobiology." [Online article or information; retrieved June 8, 2007.] http://www. nai-mirs.org/about.php.

NASA Astrobiology Institute. "NASA Astrobiology Institute." [Online article or information; retrieved October 29, 2007.] http://nai.arc.nasa.gov/.

National Association of Black Geologists and Geophysicists

The National Association of Black Geologists and Geophysicists (NABGG) was founded in 1981 in Houston, following several years of informal discussions concerning the establishment of such a group. Although a number of people played important roles in getting the organization off the ground, the driving forces behind NABGG's establishment were Curtis Lucas, Allan Harris, James Briggs, James Davis, Michael Carroll, Ken Yarbrough, Rachel Taylor, Laverne Gentry, John Chance, Zelma Jackson, Millicent McCaskill, Walter Alexander, John Leftwich, Reginald Spiller, and Mack Gipson. Unlike most black professional scientific organizations, the majority of NABGG's members work in private industry, primarily with firms active in oil and gas exploration. Consequently, the group was formed primarily to serve as a vehicle for helping minority geologists and geophysicists establish professional relationships with each other and with the companies they worked for, as well as to develop professional standards and practices for members as employees and as entrepreneurs.

NABGG is a member society of the American Geological Institute and the Geological Society of America. It is also affiliated with the American Association of Petroleum Geologists, the Earth Day Network, and the Digital Library for Earth System Education, and it is represented on the National Petroleum Council, thus making it an advisor to the U.S. Department of Energy. Its permanent staff at its headquarters in Houston coordinates and plans the group's annual convention and monthly technical meetings that are devoted to specific topics of interest.

In addition to its other activities, NABGG seeks to inform minority students of career opportunities that exist in the geosciences, to provide the students with financial aid in the form of scholarships and summer employment, and to assist them in finding jobs as geoscientists upon graduation. As of 2005, the group was providing 10 or more scholarships per year to minority students pursuing undergraduate and graduate degrees in the geosciences; since its inception, NABGG has awarded hundreds of thousands of dollars in scholarships to more than 130 recipients. In 2005, the group formed the Geoscience Education Committee. This committee contributes to the National Science Foundation's Math/Science Nucleus, a nonprofit educational and research organization composed of scientists, educators, and community members that serves as a science resource center for school districts and teachers.

See also: Department of Energy; Gipson, Mack Jr.

REFERENCES AND FURTHER READING

National Association of Black Geologists and Geophysicists. "NABGG: Home of National Association of Black Geologists and Geophysicists." [Online article or information; retrieved May 13, 2006.] http://www.nabgg.com.

National Association for Equal Opportunity in Higher Education

The National Association for Equal Opportunity in Higher Education (NAFEO) is the professional association of the presidents and chancellors of historically black colleges and universities (HBCUs). As part of its effort to increase the number of African American students, faculty, and professionals in the sciences and related fields, NAFEO conducts initiatives such as the Minority-Serving Institutions Cyberinfrastructure Institute, the HBCU/Minority Institution Environmental Technology Consortium (HBCU/MI ETC), and Model Institutions of Excellence. Because HBCU/MI ETC is addressed in a separate article, this article focuses on NAFEO's other science-related initiatives.

NAFEO was founded in 1969 by a group of HBCU presidents as a means of promoting the best interests of African Americans in higher education in general and of HBCUs in particular. As of 2007, NAFEO's members included officials from 118 HBCUs in 25 states, the District of Columbia, the Virgin Islands, and Brazil. The association maintains a permanent headquarters in Washington, D.C., where its professional staff champions the interests of HBCUs before the executive, legislative, judicial, and regulatory branches of federal and state governments and seeks the support, both financial and otherwise, of corporations, foundations, associations, and nongovernmental organizations.

The Minority-Serving Institutions Cyberinfrastructure Institute is a joint venture among NAFEO, the Hispanic Alliance of Colleges and Universities, and the American Indian Higher Education Consortium. The institute provides training and support to HBCUs and other minority-serving institutions that wish to improve their educational offerings by utilizing such technological applications as computational grids for remote processing, data mining and management, Java-based Web service technology, research collaboration using Web portals, and distance learning using video teleconferencing. The institute offers online and classroom training to faculty and students at various schools, who then use their training to develop technology-based learning systems for their own schools.

The Model Institutions of Excellence (MIE) program was created by the National Science Foundation and the National Aeronautics and Space Administration (NASA) to upgrade the quality of science, technology, engineering, and mathematics education for underrepresented minorities. With the support of NAFEO, three of its member schools—Bowie State University (Maryland), Spelman College, and Xavier University of Louisiana—have become MIEs by developing programs designed to recruit, retain, and support African Americans who seek careers in the sciences and related fields. In addition to promoting student preparedness, the MIE program also updates curriculums and teaching methodologies, provides undergraduates with opportunities to conduct meaningful research, and upgrades laboratories and scientific equipment.

See also: Historically Black College and University/Minority Institution Environmental Technology Consortium; Historically Black Colleges and Universities; National Aeronautics and Space Administration; National Science Foundation; Spelman College; Xavier University of Louisiana

REFERENCES AND FURTHER READING

National Association for Equal Opportunity in Higher Education. "National Association for Equal Opportunity in Higher Education." [Online article or information; retrieved October 29, 2007.] http://www.nafeo.org/home.

National Association of Minority Medical Educators

The National Association of Minority Medical Educators (NAMME) is a national organization dedicated to eliminating health disparities that exist for African Americans and other minorities who are underrepresented in the medical profession and therefore underserved by that profession. NAMME seeks to address both problems by increasing the number of underrepresented minorities who graduate from medical and dental colleges and other training programs for the health sciences and who then embark on careers as either medical practitioners or educators, because such graduates are most likely to practice their specialties in communities that are historically underserved by medical practitioners.

NAMME was founded in 1975 at Howard University by a group of educators who were concerned about the shortage of minority health care providers and who wanted to make sure that minorities had ample access to training programs in the health professions. By 2007, the organization had grown to include administrators, practitioners, and students in the disciplines of allied health, allopathic medicine, chiropractic, dentistry, nursing, optometry, osteopathic medicine, pharmacy, podiatry, public health, and veterinary medicine. The organization promotes its agenda in several ways, including the Promoting Health Through Education program, the College Student Development program, and the NAMME Scholarship.

Promoting Health Through Education provides primary and secondary school students an opportunity to participate in a health professions art and essay competition. This annual event is sponsored by NAMME in cooperation with local public schools. Participants advance through several levels of competition, much like a science fair, with finalists participating in a recognition and awards ceremony at NAMME's annual conference. Each winner receives a U.S. savings bond.

The College Student Development program is aimed at undergraduates, and it is presented at college campuses around the country. The program allows undergraduates who may be considering a career in one of the health sciences to meet with a number of recruiters from health professions schools. It also gives students the opportunity to participate in workshops on the admissions and applications procedures for entering postgraduate health-related training programs, preparation for taking standardized examinations, and obtaining financial aid.

The NAMME Scholarship is awarded annually to minority students who have completed the first year of training in a health profession. The number, amount, and duration of each scholarship varies depending on the circumstances of the individual recipient.

See also: Health Disparities; Howard University

REFERENCES AND FURTHER READING

National Association of Minority Medical Educators. "National Association of Minority Medical Educators, Inc." [Online article or information; retrieved October 29, 2007.] http://www.nammenational.org/.

National Cancer Institute

The National Cancer Institute (NCI) is one of the National Institutes of Health (NIH), the federal government's primary agency for supporting and conducting biomedical research. As part of its mission to eliminate disparities in the incidence and treatment of cancer among African Americans and other underserved minorities and to involve more members of those same minorities in the fight against cancer, NCI sponsors the Comprehensive Minority Biomedical Branch.

NCI was established in 1937, and in 1944, it became part of NIH. In 1971, it was given the primary mission of coordinating the National Cancer Program, and over the next 25 years, it conducted or sponsored the research that developed approximately two-thirds of the anticancer drugs approved by the Federal Drug Administration during that period. As of the early 21st century, NCI continued to sponsor cancer research around the country with a number of initiatives, among them the Comprehensive Minority Biomedical Branch (CMBB).

CMBB's ultimate goal is to increase significantly the number of African Americans and other underrepresented minorities participating as competitive NCI/NIH-funded cancer researchers. CMBB seeks to achieve this goal by preparing and recruiting more underrepresented minority individuals to make important contributions to cancer research, by raising the competitive research capacity of historically black colleges and universities (HBCUs) and other minority-serving institutions so that they are better able to produce competent cancer researchers, and by elevating the effectiveness of other programs and organizations that are sincerely interested in increasing the number of competitive underrepresented minority individuals and institutions participating in cancer research. To accomplish the first step, CMBB instituted the Continuing Umbrella of Research Experiences for Underrepresented Minorities (CURE), a series of research and training activities that extend from the high school to the junior investigator levels. To accomplish the second step, CMBB instituted the Minority Institution/Cancer Center Partnership Program (MI/CCP), which establishes research links between HBCUs and other minority-serving institutions and NCI-designated cancer centers.

CURE seeks to develop competent cancer researchers by involving minorities in cancer research as early as high school. A high school student interested in participating in cancer research may enlist a science teacher or guidance counselor to find a principal investigator who has at least two years' funding remaining on an existing NCI research project grant. The principal investigator then applies for a research supplement on the behalf of the student, who is expected to commit to working with the investigator for two full summers. Once the application is approved, the investigator receives $3,000 to cover the expense of employing the high school student as a laboratory assistant for three months each summer for two summers and for purchasing additional research supplies. Should the student work part time for the investigator during the regular school year as well, the investigator receives additional funding to pay the student $6.25 per hour. CURE research supplements for undergraduate students who wish to be involved in cancer research follow the same guidelines, except that undergraduates may be paid up to $8.00 per hour and their investigator may receive up to $200 per month for research supplies.

High school and undergraduate researchers may also be employed en masse by any cancer center already conducting NCI-funded research. In this case, the center receives a research supplement of up to $75,000, plus additional money for research supplies, over a five-year period to cover salaries and other expenses associated with employing student researchers. Students who participate in this program are expected to remain involved for two to five years, and their compensation is based on the practices of the individual cancer center and the minimum wage of the state in which it is located.

CURE supports cancer research by minority graduate or medical students in three ways. Students enrolled in a program leading to an MD, an MS, or a PhD in one of the biomedical, behavioral, clinical, or social sciences, including nursing science and social work, may conduct research under the terms of a research supplement given to a principal investigator or cancer center similar to the ones for high school and undergraduate students. Students working toward an MD or PhD degree in cancer research or cancer prevention are eligible for an Individual Predoctoral Kirschstein–National Research Service Awards (NRSA) Fellowship for Minority Students. This fellowship provides the recipient with a stipend of $19,968 per year, plus funding for tuition, fees, health insurance, supplies, and travel expenses to scientific conferences, while the student conducts cancer research for up to five years.

Minority postdoctoral researchers and junior faculty are funded by similar research supplements, but also by other awards. The Mentored Career Development Award supports basic cancer researchers who have earned a doctorate in medicine (MD), chiropractic medicine (DC), dentistry (DDS), osteopathic medicine (DO), optometry (OD), veterinary medicine (DVM), naturopathic medicine (ND), or pharmacology (PharMD) and who have already been supported by NCI/NIH funding but need additional mentored support in order to become independent researchers. The award consists of a mentored phase of one or more years followed by a transition phase, during which the researcher develops into a principal investigator. Recipients participate in mentored research activities, observe or participate in the NCI/NIH peer review process, and participate annually in workshops on preparing, writing, and submitting NIH grant applications. The Transition Career Development Award is similar to the Mentored Award except that it provides up to three years of support to recipients who have the potential for establishing an independent research program involving cancer biology, etiology, pathogenesis, prevention, diagnosis, or treatment by the end of the three years. The Mentored Clinical Scientist Award and the Mentored Patient-Oriented Research provide five years of support for clinical researchers who hold an MD, DC, DDS, DO, OD, DVM, ND, or PharMD or who are doctorally trained oncology nurses, and who have already been supported by NCI/NIH funding. The former award supports those who need the additional support to become principal investigators, while the latter supports researchers as they gain experience in the advanced methods and experimental approaches needed to conduct independent patient-oriented research related to mechanisms of human disease, therapeutic interventions, clinical trials, and the development of new technologies. All four postdoctoral awards present recipients with up to $75,000 per year plus fringe benefits.

MI/CCP seeks to boost the number of minority cancer researchers by heightening the level of sophistication of the scientific training that is offered at HBCUs and other minority-serving institutions. The rationale behind the establishment of MI/CCP is that minority-serving institutions train the vast majority of minority students who go on to become scientists and medical researchers, but their facilities are insufficiently developed to devote considerable attention to cancer research. Meanwhile, cancer centers possess state-of-the-art research facilities, but the effort they have so far devoted to reducing health disparities in the incidence and treatment of cancer has been disappointing at best. The hope is that, by combining the desire of minority-serving institutions to overcome health disparities with the ability of cancer centers to conduct the proper research, such disparities can be eliminated or greatly reduced. To this end, MI/CCP supports four types of activities: (1) cancer research in any area of basic, clinical, prevention, control, behavioral, or population research; (2) joint research education and career development programs that emphasize the training of minority scientists to appreciate the issues and problems associated with cancer incidence and mortality disparities in minority populations; (3) cancer education programs that sensitize graduate and postdoctoral students in research, medicine, and public health to the need to reduce cancer-related health disparities; and (4) cancer outreach programs that help minority communities develop and manage their own culturally sensitive programs for educating their populations about cancer risk, early detection, screening, prevention, and treatment.

MI/CCP provides three levels of support to minority-serving institutions that wish to collaborate with cancer centers. The Planning Grant for Minority Institution/Cancer Center Collaboration funds the development of pilot programs that either involve a minority investigator in a specific cancer research project, train minority scientists to be cancer researchers, or motivate minority high school or undergraduate students to consider careers in cancer research. The grant awards up to $250,000 per collaboration over the course of three years. The Cooperative Planning Grant for Minority Institution/Cancer Center Partnership helps minority-serving institutions and cancer centers increase the cancer research capabilities at the institutions, increase the number of minority scientists engaged in cancer research, and improve the effectiveness of cancer centers in developing and sustaining activities focused on cancer-related health disparities in the region that the cancer center serves. The grant provides up to $500,000 over the course of three years. The Comprehensive Minority Institution/Cancer Center Partnership brings the work of a cooperative grant to fruition by establishing fully collaborative programs between institutions and centers, and it provides up to $900,000 over the course of three years.

See also: Cancer; Historically Black Colleges and Universities; National Institutes of Health

References and Further Reading

National Cancer Institute, Comprehensive Minority Biomedical Branch. "Opportunities for Minorities in Cancer." [Online article or information; retrieved June 11, 2007.] http://minorityopportunities.nci.nih.gov/index.html.

National Cancer Institute. "National Cancer Institute." [Online article or information; retrieved October 29, 2007.] http://www.cancer.gov/.

National Center for Complementary and Alternative Medicine

The National Center for Complementary and Alternative Medicine (NCCAM) is one of the National Institutes of Health (NIH), the federal government's primary agency for supporting and conducting medical research. As part of its mission to eliminate health disparities among African Americans and other underserved minorities and to increase the number of minority complementary and alternative medicine (CAM) investigators, NCCAM conducts a number of research projects through its Office of Special Populations.

NCCAM was established in 1998 to serve as NIH's lead agency for scientific research on CAM. CAM includes practices that incorporate nonevidence-based practices, non-European medical traditions, or newly developed approaches to healing such as prayer, herbalism, meditation, breathing meditation, chiropractic medicine, yoga, diet-based therapy, progressive relaxation, megavitamin therapy, and visualization. NCCAM explores CAM healing practices in the context of rigorous science, trains CAM researchers, and disseminates authoritative information to the public and professionals about CAM therapies that have been proven to be safe and effective. The Office of Special Populations (OSP) determines to what degree CAM is used in minority communities, establishes the effectiveness of CAM treatments for specific diseases and medical conditions that are prevalent among minority communities, and involves more African Americans and other underrepresented minorities in CAM research.

National surveys taken in the early 21st century showed that a substantial and growing number of Americans use CAM, usually in addition to traditional forms of health care. These same surveys, however, demonstrated little about the use of CAM in minority communities, which is ironic given that such communities have traditionally employed, even invented, a number of alternative forms of health care. Part of OSP's mission, therefore, is to collect data on how traditional beliefs shape the health behaviors of minority communities and whether these beliefs conflict with or complement conventional health care or methods of health promotion and disease prevention. One of the first steps OSP took in this regard was to arrange for the inclusion of a supplemental module concerning CAM use in minority communities as part of the 2002 National Health Interview Survey.

OSP has sponsored a number of research projects designed to test the efficacy and safety of CAM as a means of eliminating health disparities, particularly in regard to four diseases and medical conditions that have considerably higher rates of incidence and mortality among African Americans and other minorities than in the general population: cardiovascular disease, prostate and breast cancer, diabetes, and HIV/AIDS. OSP funded three research projects at the Center for Natural Medicine and Prevention at Maharishi University of Management in Fairfield, Iowa, on the treatment of African Americans with cardiovascular disease, which accounts for more than 25 percent of deaths in all minority populations. These three projects focused on the use of Vedic medicine, a form of traditional medicine developed and practiced on the Indian subcontinent that incorporates herbal formulations and meditation. Specifically, the projects examined the physiologic mechanism of action by which transcendental meditation (TM) might reduce hypertension (high blood pressure), studied the effects of TM on hypertension and carotid artery thickness in older African American women, and evaluated the effects of a traditional Vedic herbal preparation on pathophysiologic markers of cardiovascular disease in high-risk, older African Americans. Three HBCUs—Charles R. Drew University of Medicine and Science, Howard University College of Medicine, and Morehouse School of Medicine—performed as subcontractors on the projects.

African American men suffer disproportionately from prostate cancer—their mortality rate from the disease is twice as high as for the general population—while African American women suffer disproportionately from tumor recurrence resulting from breast cancer. Since the traditional treatments for prostate and breast cancer involve surgery, radiation, and/or chemotherapy, OSP funds the testing of novel approaches and compounds for treating these cancers. One such project at the Center for Cancer Complementary Medicine at Johns Hopkins University studied the efficacy and safety of PC SPES, a Chinese herbal preparation, as a treatment for prostate cancer, while another project at the center investigates the impact of personal and group prayer on immune responses in African American women two months after undergoing surgery and receiving radiation treatment. OSP also funds a study at the National Cancer Institute to determine the chemotherapeutic and cancer-preventive effects of selenium and vitamin E, alone and in combination, on prostate cancer.

Complications arising from diabetes, such as retinopathy and renal disease, are two to four times more likely to occur in minority populations than they are in the general population. OSP funds research on the effect of ginseng as a therapeutic agent for type 2 diabetes, because ginseng is thought to regulate blood glucose levels by modulating the process of glucose metabolism, and on the effect of the herb Ginkgo biloba on glucose metabolism and the mechanism by which it increases pancreatic function. OSP has also funded a study of Reiki (a Japanese form of spiritual healing often compared to faith healing) to determine its ability to reduce pain and improve glycemic control in patients with type 2 diabetes. It is collaborating with the National Institute of Diabetes and Digestive and Kidney Diseases on a study of the effect of chromium supplementation on the symptoms associated with type 2 diabetes and its ability to reduce the need for insulin treatment.

African Americans are nine times more likely to contract HIV/AIDS than Americans of non-Hispanic, European extraction. Moreover, the known treatments for AIDS are expensive and not entirely reliable; so many minorities who contract HIV/AIDS have been using CAM almost exclusively to deal with this devastating disease. OSP is funding a project to identify the various CAM methods used by minorities to treat the symptoms of HIV/AIDS and to determine the efficacy and safety of these many practices.

OSP promotes the expansion of minority participation in CAM research by recruiting minority subjects, supporting minority CAM research training and career development, and disseminating information about CAM to minority communities that may lack access to electronic media. It works with the Health Resources and Services Administration (HRSA) to recruit African American and other minority volunteers for CAM research projects through HRSA's community health centers and migrant health centers. OSP also oversees the NCCAM Institutional Research Training Program for Minority Researchers (IRTPMR), which recruits and trains medical and health profession students and postdoctoral researchers in CAM research at Morgan State University. This program makes use of NIH Research Supplements for Underrepresented Minorities, which encourage principal investigators who are already conducting NCCAM-sponsored research to include minority students, postdoctoral researchers, and junior investigators on their research teams. IRTPMR also provides funding for summer internships at NCCAM facilities for minority students interested in careers as CAM researchers.

In addition to building up the community of individual minority CAM researchers, OSP is involved in building up the minority-serving institutions that produce the majority of minority scientists and medical investigators. To this end, OSP establishes collaborations between minority-serving institutions and CAM research centers, botanical research centers, and NCCAM-funded investigators at other research institutions. These collaborations provide faculty and students at minority-serving institutions with the opportunities and facilities to participate in important CAM research, thus improving the research programs at the minority-serving institutions themselves.

See also: Cancer; Cardiovascular Disease; Charles R. Drew University of Medicine and Science; Diabetes; Health Disparities; HIV/AIDS; Howard University College of Medicine; Morehouse School of Medicine; Morgan State University; National Institutes of Health

References and Further Reading

National Center for Complementary and Alternative Medicine. "National Center for Complementary and Alternative Medicine." [Online article or information; retrieved October 29, 2007.] http://nccam.nih.gov/.

National Center for Complementary and Alternative Medicine. "Office of Special Populations Strategic Plan to Address Racial and Ethnic Health Disparities." [Online article or information; retrieved June 13, 2007.] http://nccam. nih.gov/about/plans/healthdisparities/index.htm.

National Center on Minority Health and Health Disparities

The National Center on Minority Health and Health Disparities (NCMHD) is a branch of the National Institutes of Health (NIH), the federal government's primary agency for supporting and conducting medical research. NCMHD promotes minority health by coordinating the NIH effort to reduce and ultimately eliminate health disparities between African Americans or other underserved minorities and the general public. To this end, NCMHD has established the Centers of Excellence Program for conducting research concerning the diseases and medical conditions most responsible for health disparities. It also sponsors two loan repayment programs for attracting minorities into careers in medical research, particularly in areas in which the health disparities are the greatest.

NCMHD was established in 1990 as the Office of Research on Minority Health. Over the next 10 years, it administered the Minority Health Initiative, a multimillion-dollar biomedical and behavioral research and training program devoted to improving prenatal health, reducing infant mortality, and studying childhood and adolescent lead poisoning, HIV/AIDS, alcohol and drug use, cancer, diabetes, obesity, hypertension, mental disorders, asthma, and visual impairments. The initiative also devoted significant resources to training faculty and students at the high school, undergraduate, graduate, and postdoctoral levels in order to stimulate research related to health disparities in these diseases and medical conditions. In 2000, the office was elevated to the status of a national center of the NIH and took on its present name. It also took on the responsibility of developing and administering the NIH Strategic Research Plan and Budget to Reduce and Ultimately Eliminate Health Disparities, which was put into effect in 2002. As of 2007, NCMHD's mission was to support basic, clinical, social, and behavioral research on health disparities and to promote improvements in research infrastructure and training as they pertain to health disparities.

The Centers of Excellence Program originated in 2002 as the Project EXPORT Program. The program established research centers concerning health disparities within the medical research facilities at colleges, universities, and public and private research centers across the country. Five years later, the program included 75 centers located in 27 states, the District of Columbia, Puerto Rico, and the U.S. Virgin Islands. The centers conduct research independently, and in formal partnerships with other research centers, on the diseases and medical conditions in which health disparities are most pronounced—cardiovascular disease, stroke, cancer, diabetes, HIV/AIDS, infant mortality, mental health, and obesity—as well as lung and liver diseases, psoriasis, scleroderma, and glomerular injury, among others. Research includes not only biomedical investigations but also the nonbiomedical factors that contribute to health disparities, such as individual attitudes toward health care in general, social and physical environments, health care policies as determined by public and private entities, and minority access to health care. Overall, the Centers of Excellence Program seeks to discover new knowledge concerning the interactions of significant biological factors with behavioral and social variables, how they affect each other, and how these interactions influence and contribute to minority health conditions and health disparities.

In addition to conducting research, the Centers of Excellence program also provides training opportunities to researchers and junior faculty from historically black colleges and universities, as well as other minority-serving institutions, disseminates health information to minority communities, encourages minorities to consult health care professionals on a regular basis so as to facilitate early intervention in the course of treating a medical condition, and establishes partnerships with community-based organizations that are also working to eliminate health disparities. Training programs include summer internships for undergraduate and graduate students, research partnerships with postdoctoral researchers and faculty members at minority-serving institutions, and support for research conducted by minority faculty and students at the minority-serving institutions themselves. In terms of community outreach, the centers disseminate health information to minority communities in such a way that builds public trust, engages the community in clinical studies, and contributes to the development of health and science education activities in minority community schools.

One of the best methods for reducing health disparities is to recruit more medical researchers to conduct research related to health disparities. To this end, NCMHD sponsors the Loan Repayment Program for Health Disparities Research (HDR-LRP). This program pays up to $35,000 per year toward a participant's qualified education loan debt; in exchange, the participant conducts two years of basic, clinical, or behavioral research related to a health disparity issue. Individual participants themselves are not required to conduct research as part of an NIH-sponsored program or to come from a minority background; however, at least 50 percent of the program's participants must be African Americans or members of other underserved minorities. NCMHD also sponsors the Extramural Clinical Research Loan Repayment Program for Individuals from Disadvantaged Backgrounds (ECR-LRP). This program is exactly like HDR-LRP except that all participants in ECR-LRP must come from minority backgrounds.

See also: Asthma; Cancer; Cardiovascular Disease; Diabetes; Health Disparities; Historically Black Colleges and Universities; HIV/AIDS; National Institutes of Health; Obesity

REFERENCES AND FURTHER READING

National Center on Minority Health and Health Disparities. "About NCMHD." [Online article or information; retrieved June 15, 2007.] http://ncmhd.nih. gov/about_ncmhd/mission.asp.

National Coalition of Underrepresented Racial and Ethnic Groups in Engineering and Science

The National Coalition of Underrepresented Racial and Ethnic Groups in Engineering and Science (NCOURAGES) is a coalition of professional societies and other organizations that represent the interests of African Americans and other minorities in the sciences and engineering. The coalition's goal is to help increase the number of African Americans and other minorities pursuing careers in fields related to science and technology.

NCOURAGES was founded in 2002 by representatives of its 11 constituent societies. One of the groups, the National Organization for the Professional Advancement of Black Chemists and Chemical Engineers, is particularly concerned with increasing the number of black scientists, while two others—the National Consortium for Graduate Degrees for Minorities in Engineering and Science (GEM) and Mathematics, Engineering, Science Achievement (MESA USA)—are interested in promoting scientific careers among blacks as well as other minorities. Taken together, the interests of the member organizations span the educational pathway from elementary school through graduate school and into the workplace. By forming NCOURAGES, the organizations pooled their efforts to achieve a common goal: an increase in the number of minority scientists and engineers by 450,000 by 2015. The formation of the coalition was motivated by the fact that, in 2001, for example, slightly more than 4 percent of the PhDs in science and engineering that U.S. universities awarded to U.S. citizens went to African Americans, although the percentage of African Americans in the general population is considerably higher.

NCOURAGES's member organizations intend to remedy this situation by helping minority students become aware of their options and then helping them obtain the funding and other support necessary to obtain a doctorate in science or technology. The coalition plans to accomplish its ambitious task by cooperatively using their existing programs involving financial support, research, mentoring, and advocacy, while developing new programs to garner further support, financial and otherwise, from corporations, educational institutions, and government agencies. Although each member of the coalition already devotes a considerable amount of its energy to attracting African Americans and other minorities to careers in science, NCOURAGES allows them to maximize the effectiveness of their efforts and thereby achieve a dramatic increase in minorities with PhDs in science and engineering.

See also: MESA USA; National Consortium for Graduate Degrees for Minorities in Engineering and Science; National Organization for the Professional Advancement of Black Chemists and Chemical Engineers

REFERENCES AND FURTHER READING

National Coalition of Underrepresented Racial and Ethnic Groups in Engineering and Science. "National Coalition of Underrepresented Racial and Ethnic Groups in Engineering and Science." [Online article or information; retrieved October 29, 2007.] http://www.ncourages.org/.

National Consortium for Graduate Degrees for Minorities in Engineering and Science

The National Consortium for Graduate Degrees for Minorities in Engineering and Science, also known as the National GEM Consortium, or simply GEM, provides graduate fellowships in science and engineering to highly qualified African Americans and other minorities who are underrepresented in the scientific community. The consortium's members include a number of corporations, universities, and U.S. government laboratories who provide GEM fellows with financial support and practical experience through advanced-level internships. As of 2007, the consortium had helped more than 200 minorities earn PhDs in the physical sciences, life sciences, and engineering.

GEM resulted from calls in the early 1970s by senior officials with the General Electric Company and the National Academy of Engineering to increase dramatically the number of minorities with graduate degrees in engineering. In 1974, the University of Notre Dame in Indiana hosted a meeting of representatives from 13 research centers, 14 universities, and 5 advocacy organizations to develop methods for answering these requests. Two years later, GEM was officially founded at Notre Dame, but only as a vehicle for providing minorities with financial assistance toward a master's degree in engineering. In 1990, the program was expanded to include fellowships for students pursuing PhDs in science as well. While the focus of GEM continues to be the MS in engineering, as of late, the consortium has devoted an increasing amount of its resources to PhD-in-science fellowships. The consortium maintains a professional staff at its permanent headquarters in Notre Dame, Indiana.

The PhD Science Fellowship Program assists students who wish to earn a doctorate in a number of scientific fields, including anatomy, biochemistry, biology, chemistry, computer science, environmental science, genetics, materials science, pharmacology, physics, and physiology. Applicants are accepted as early as their junior year in college, although many recipients are either graduates of the MS Engineering Program or working professionals. Fellowships may be used at any participating GEM Member University (of which there are 162, including most major public and private universities) to which the recipient of the fellowships had been admitted. A PhD Science Fellowship pays for all of a recipient's tuition and fees for five years, and includes an annual stipend of at least $14,000. During the second through fifth years of the fellowship, the recipient is expected to accept a position at the member university as either a teaching or a research assistant.

Recipients of a PhD Science Fellowship are also expected to complete a 12-week paid internship at a GEM Member Company each summer of their fellowship; as of 2007, there were 66 member companies, including such corporations as Ford Motor Company, Hewlett-Packard, IBM, Intel, Microsoft, and 3M Company. Each intern participates in a research project under the supervision of an experienced scientist, who provides the intern with guidance, support, and assistance. One result of the internship is that many GEM graduates receive employment offers immediately upon graduation from the company with which they interned.

See also: Biochemistry; Biology; Chemistry; Computer Science; Physics

REFERENCES AND FURTHER READING

GEM: The National GEM Consortium. "About GEM." [Online article or information; retrieved February 16, 2007.] http://www.gemfellowship.org/.

National Dental Association

The National Dental Association (NDA) is devoted to serving the needs of black dentists and their patients. To this end, NDA sponsors programs to increase the number of black dentists in private practice, academia, administration, research, health policy, and the armed services, while seeking to improve dental care among underserved minority populations, improve the skills and scientific knowledge of its members, and encourage minority youths to consider careers in dentistry. In addition, the National Dental Association Foundation (NDAF) funds dental research programs at historically black colleges and universities.

NDA was founded in 1932 in Bordentown, New Jersey, as a result of the merger of the Interstate Dental Association (IDA) and the Commonwealth Dental Association of New Jersey. The IDA had begun its existence in 1913 as the Tri-State Dental Association, a group for black dentists in Virginia, Maryland, and the District of Columbia, but by the time of the merger it had chapters in 14 states. Tri-State's principal founder was D. A. Ferguson, a dentist from Richmond, Virginia. In 1901, Ferguson had convinced approximately 200 of his colleagues to form the National Association of Colored Dentists, but for various reasons, this organization ceased to exist after only five years. Undaunted, he continued to push for a national association for African American dentists, and his tireless efforts in this regard contributed to the formation of the present-day NDA. In 2006, the organization boasted a membership of 6,000 black dentists and a national headquarters in Washington, D.C. In addition, NDA served as the parent organization of three auxiliaries—the National Dental Assistants Association, the National Dental Hygienists' Association, and the Student National Dental Organization—and was expanding its membership to include oral health care professionals in Africa, Canada, Central America, Saudi Arabia, and South America.

In 1976, NDA formed the National Dental Association Foundation (NDAF) as a vehicle for raising and dispensing money for scholarships, community outreach, and research projects. NDAF developed the Bright Smiles, Bright Futures program with funds provided by the Colgate-Palmolive Company, a leading manufacturer of toothpaste and tooth brushes. The program is designed to improve the oral health of inner-city schoolchildren, and to this end, NDA dentists from local chapters provide free dental screenings to children in homeless shelters, inner-city schools, churches, day care centers, Boys & Girls Clubs of America, and other community sites. Between 1991 and 1999, the program had been implemented in 20 cities and had screened more than 4 million children. The National Dental Association Foundation/Colgate-Palmolive Scholarship has provided more than $1 million in financial aid to more than 1,000 minority students pursuing careers as dentists, dental hygienists, and dental assistants. NDAF also funds ongoing dental research projects at Howard University, Meharry Medical College, and Morehouse School of Medicine.

See also: Historically Black Colleges and Universities; Howard University; Meharry Medical College; Morehouse School of Medicine

REFERENCES AND FURTHER READING

Dummett, Clifton O., and Lois D. *NDA II: The Story of America's Second National Dental Association.* Washington, DC: National Dental Association Foundation, 2000.

National Dental Association. "National Dental Association." [Online article or information; retrieved May 30, 2006.] http://www.ndaonline.org.

National Eye Institute

The National Eye Institute (NEI) is one of the National Institutes of Health (NIH), the federal government's primary agency for conducting and supporting medical research. As part of its mission to address health disparities concerning diseases and medical conditions related to the eye, NEI implemented a number of initiatives to this effect as part of Vision Research: A National Plan, 1999–2003. NEI also provides ongoing support for eliminating health disparities with the National Eye Health Education Program and Healthy People 2010.

NEI was established in 1968 as NIH's branch in charge of conducting and supporting research and training related to blinding eye diseases, visual disorders, the mechanisms of visual function, the preservation of sight, and the special health problems and requirements of individuals who are visually impaired. Forty years later, the institute supports vision research with approximately 1,600 research grants and training awards to scientists and medical researchers at more than 25 medical centers, hospitals, universities, and other institutions around the country, as well as at its own research facilities in Bethesda, Maryland. As of 2007, NEI-funded research focused on a myriad of diseases and medical conditions such as diabetic retinopathy (damage to the retina caused by complications due to diabetes) and glaucoma (a group of diseases of the optic nerve). One result of NEI-sponsored research has been the development of laser procedures for diagnosing, treating, and correcting a variety of medical conditions related to the eye.

A National Plan for vision research was developed by NEI in 1999 under the auspices of the National Advisory Eye Council. The plan called for NEI to devote a considerable amount of its research to health disparities, particularly as they relate to glaucoma and diabetic retinopathy, both of which affect African Americans disproportionately. Glaucoma is the leading cause of blindness among African Americans. Blacks are three to four times more likely to contract glaucoma than the general population, possibly because of genetic causes, but partly because they often contract glaucoma during middle age while the general population tends to contract it at a later stage in life. In addition, little attention had been devoted to counseling African Americans about the dangers of contracting glaucoma and the need for regular tests for glaucoma beginning at an early age. Glaucoma is easily treated in its early stages; however, many African Americans needlessly go blind from glaucoma, because they are unaware of the seriousness of their condition.

In addition to promoting awareness among middle-aged African Americans about the dangers of glaucoma, Vision Research called for the increased use of laser surgery to correct their glaucoma, a regimen that differs from the surgical procedure usually prescribed for European Americans diagnosed with the condition. The plan also called for studies that investigate the potential link between glaucoma and two medical conditions which African Americans also suffer from disproportionately: hypertension (high blood pressure) and cardiovascular disease (medical conditions that affect the heart and circulatory system).

Diabetes mellitus is one of the leading causes of death in this country, but one of its complications, diabetic retinopathy, is also a major cause of blindness. Diabetes causes the capillaries in the retina to balloon and burst, resulting in the leakage of blood proteins into the retina and the loss of vision. It is estimated that nearly 6 million Americans have undiagnosed diabetes, which puts them at risk to develop diabetic retinopathy as well. Most of these undiagnosed patients are minorities, particularly African Americans, who are more likely than the general population to develop certain forms of diabetes. Consequently, diabetic retinopathy has also been shown to occur more often in blacks than in whites, probably due to a greater susceptibility to the adverse effects of hypertension, which also affects a greater percentage of African Americans than of European Americans. Although currently recommended treatments are over 95 percent effective in preventing further vision loss, about half of those who could benefit from such treatment are not being treated.

Vision Research established two avenues of attack to defeat this problem. One called for greater research into the efficacy of certain drugs, such as vascular endothelial growth factor (VEGE) and PKC 412, that might serve as useful treatments for diabetic retinopathy. The other called for making the African American community more aware of the need to get regular examinations for diabetes. When diabetic retinopathy is caught in its early stages, it is easily treated with laser therapy; however, it has been estimated that up to 50 percent of patients who could benefit from such treatment, a great many of whom are African Americans, are not diagnosed in time to benefit from it. Consequently, part of the NEI study, "Why Preventable Blindness Occurs in Diabetes," attempts to learn why the current health care system is unsuccessful in preventing blindness among African Americans and other minorities from diabetic retinopathy.

Vision Research also called for NEI to further address health disparities in eye care by initiating and supporting programs that recruit minority medical researchers into the field of vision research and that encourage minorities to volunteer for clinical trials. It has been demonstrated that one of the best ways to reduce health disparities is to recruit more minorities into careers as medical researchers, because minority researchers have shown a greater interest than their nonminority counterparts in investigating the medical conditions that contribute to health disparities. To this end, NEI makes use of several programs. One is the NIH Research Supplement for Underrepresented Minorities, which awards additional funding to NIH-sponsored researchers who recruit, supervise, and train minority assistants at the high school, undergraduate, graduate, postdoctoral, and junior investigator levels to conduct research as

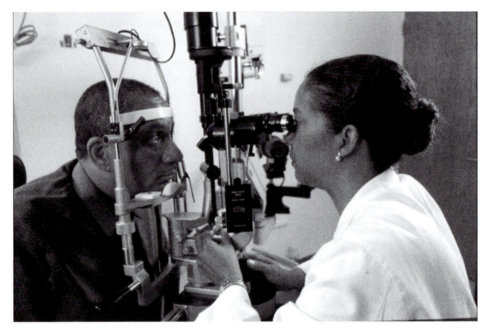

The National Eye Institute works to attract more African Americans to medical careers related to the care and treatment of the eye. (National Eye Institute, National Institutes of Health)

part of their projects. Another is Vision, a school program for grades four through eight that was designed by NEI and the Association for Research in Vision and Ophthalmology. The program includes three lessons that can be taught by vision researchers and eye care professionals while making classroom visits, particularly to minority schools.

Given NEI's interest in developing new pharmaceutical drugs for treating various diseases and medical conditions, Vision Research called for the institute to make a commitment to recruit more African Americans and other minorities to serve as subjects in clinical trials of those and other drugs. As previously noted, it is possible that the genes of African Americans make them more susceptible than the general population to certain eye diseases and medical conditions such as diabetic retinopathy and glaucoma; so it is also possible that minorities will respond to drug treatments for these and other conditions differently than members of the general population. To ensure that minorities receive the best possible treatment, NEI/NIH guidelines now require that clinical trial evidence must be reviewed to show whether clinically important differences concerning race or ethnicity are to be expected in the outcome of the treatment.

The National Eye Health Education Program (NEHEP) was implemented in 1989 with the goal of increasing awareness among health care professionals and the public of the importance of early detection and treatment of eye diseases. As of 2007, NEHEP focused on two diseases, glaucoma and diabetic retinopathy, that contribute the most to health disparities related to eye care. For example, in terms of glaucoma, NEHEP now targets African Americans over the age of 40, whereas the general population is targeted only after age 60. Healthy People 2010 is an initiative of the U.S. Department of Health and Human Services, of which NIH is a part, that provides a statement of national health objectives designed to identify the most significant preventable threats to health and to establish national goals to reduce these threats. Promulgated in 2000, Healthy People 2010 was amended at its midcourse review in 2005 to include a chapter on vision. A major portion of the chapter is devoted to the early detection and treatment of glaucoma and diabetic retinopathy, particularly as they affect minority communities.

See also: Cardiovascular Disease; Diabetes; Health Disparities; National Institutes of Health

REFERENCES AND FURTHER READING

National Center on Minority Health and Health Disparities. "NIH Comprehensive Strategic Plan and Budget to Reduce and Ultimately Eliminate Heath Disparities." [Online article or information; retrieved June 18, 2007.] http://www.ncmhd.nih.gov/strategicmock/our_programs/strategic/pubs/NEI-rev.pdf.

National Eye Institute. "National Eye Institute." [Online article or information; retrieved October 29, 2007.] http://www.nei.nih.gov/.

National Heart, Lung, and Blood Institute

The National Heart, Lung, and Blood Institute (NHLBI) is part of the National Institutes of Health (NIH), the federal government's primary agency for conducting and supporting medical research. In terms of eliminating health disparities, NHLBI conducts extensive research on high blood pressure, cardiovascular disease, obesity and physical inactivity, diabetes, asthma, tuberculosis, sickle cell disease, and Cooley's anemia, which is similar to sickle cell disease. NHLBI programs also seek to increase the number of African Americans and other underrepresented minority scientists pursuing careers in heart, lung, blood, and sleep disorder research, as well as to raise the number of minorities who participate in clinical studies related to NHLBI's mission.

NHLBI was established in 1948 as the National Heart Institute. It became the National Heart and Lung Institute in 1969, and it acquired its present name in 1976. NHLBI is responsible for conducting and supporting research on diseases and medical conditions related to the heart, lungs, blood, blood vessels, and sleep disorders. It is also in charge of ensuring that the nation's blood banks have an adequate and safe supply of blood, and since 1997, it has administered the NIH Women's Health Initiative.

A number of research projects conducted or supported by NHLBI include epidemiological studies of medical conditions that plague African Americans and other minorities disproportionately. These studies seek to identify the genetic and environmental factors that influence the development and progression of diseases that disproportionately affect minorities, determine the mechanisms responsible for the progression of such diseases, and clarify the processes by which environmental, developmental, and psychosocial factors early in life contribute to health disparities later on. These projects often investigate their subject medical conditions from a multiethnic perspective, so as to better understand their prevalence among minorities.

In the early 21st century, cardiovascular disease (CVD) mortality was 20 percent higher in black males than in white males and 31 percent higher in black females than in white females; moreover, the prevalence of stroke was higher in blacks than in whites at all ages. High blood pressure, a risk factor for CVD, tended to be more common, developed at an earlier age, and was more severe for blacks than whites. Lack of physical activity and obesity, which are also risk factors for CVD, plague minority populations much more than they do nonminorities. Consequently, NHLBI has sponsored research to investigate the prevalence and progression of atherosclerosis (hardening of the arteries, a major contributor to hypertension, or high blood pressure), to examine the association between the development of risk factors and the evolution of atherosclerosis and hypertension from childhood to adulthood, to determine the evolution of coronary heart disease and atherosclerosis in young adults, to investigate the association between coronary heart disease and the development of atherosclerosis among adults, to examine the risk factors for coronary heart disease and stroke in the elderly, to identify the environmental and genetic factors influencing the evolution and progression of CVD, to determine the extent to which insulin resistance and the development of certain risk factors related to CVD share common genetic influences, to attempt to identify the major genes associated with high blood pressure, to seek to identify the genetic and other biological factors that increase susceptibility to hypertension-related injury and damage to target organs, and to evaluate the benefits of different therapies to reduce cardiovascular complications in diabetes mellitus.

Whereas these studies were multiethnic, other CVD research projects focused exclusively on African Americans. For example, one study sought to determine the causes and development of hypertension in African Americans in order to improve the diagnosis and treatment of the disease, and another sought to understand, on a pathophysiological basis, why African Americans suffer and die disproportionately from ischemic heart disease, which results from restrictions in the body's blood supply.

In terms of hypertension, NHLBI research projects have compared the effectiveness of lifestyle interventions, such as reduced salt intake, increased physical activity, moderation of alcohol intake, and weight loss, on blood pressure control. Obesity and physical inactivity, which are leading contributors to hypertension, are particularly problematic in African American communities; so NHLBI has brought some of its research resources to bear on these topics. One project studied the effectiveness of weight-control interventions such as diet, physical activity, and psychosocial and familial influences from prepuberty to puberty in black girls at high risk for obesity. Another investigated the effectiveness of a coordinated school and community-based program that provides opportunities to participate in physical activity both in and away from school; effectiveness was measured in terms of the program's ability to prevent the decline in physical activity levels and cardiopulmonary fitness of middle-school-aged girls from a wide range of racial, ethnic, and socioeconomic backgrounds.

NHLBI conducts and supports multiethnic research on asthma and tuberculosis. As of 1998, the death rate from asthma was three times higher for blacks than for whites, and asthma-related hospitalization rates were more than three times higher for blacks than for whites. NHLBI asthma research has sought to identify the genes associated with asthma and to establish their functional role in the development of the disorder; to investigate the mechanistic basis for severe asthma and how it differs from mild to moderate asthma; and to evaluate the long-term effects of two types of anti-inflammatory medications on lung growth and development, physical growth and development, and the severity and frequency of asthma attacks in asthmatic children. NHLBI has also established cooperative centers of research to study asthma disparities in relation to their prevalence, emergency department use, hospitalization rates, and mortality between the general population and minority populations. Tuberculosis (TB) research has used advances in molecular biology and genomics research to investigate its genetic aspects. NHLBI has also initiated efforts to raise health care providers' awareness of the unique ethnic, cultural, and socioeconomic dimensions of TB and to enhance TB education programs in minority medical schools and communities.

NHLBI is a leading sponsor of research on sickle cell disease and a related condition, Cooley's anemia. Sickle cell disease mostly affects people who trace their ancestry to Africa, and about one out of every 500 African American infants are born with it. NHLBI-supported research programs concerning sickle cell disease began in the 1970s; largely as a result, patients with sickle cell anemia now live longer on average and their care is more coordinated, beginning with screening of newborns, the provision of appropriate control of infections, and the prevention of stroke in high-risk children through transfusion therapy. In addition to continuing its efforts to find a cure for sickle cell disease, NHLBI research also seeks to develop new therapies for reducing the deleterious effects of the disease. For example, one study investigates the efficacy of the drug hydroxyurea, which reduces the rate of painful crises in adults with sickle cell disease, as a treatment for children and infants. Other studies examine the efficacy of bone marrow transplantation and chronic transfusions in children with sickle cell disease, identify and characterize the modifier genes responsible for the progression of the disease, and develop more effective pharmaceutical drugs for treating it. Research concerning Cooley's anemia seeks to standardize existing treatments and evaluate new ones, particularly those involving new pharmaceutical drugs, in a network of clinical centers.

Over the years, NHLBI has adhered to the belief that recruiting and retaining more minority medical researchers is the best approach to reducing and eliminating health disparities, because minority researchers are more interested than their nonminority colleagues in devoting their research effort to addressing health disparities. To this end, NHLBI sponsors several initiatives to increase the number of African Americans and members of other underrepresented minorities conducting research on the heart, lungs, blood, sleep disorders, and women's health. One set of programs support faculty and students at historically black colleges and universities (HBCUs) and other minority-serving institutions, which train a disproportionately large number of minority scientists and medical researchers. The HBCU Research Scientist Award offers financial support to HBCUs that offer graduate or professional degrees in the medical sciences so that they can expose their students to cutting-edge developments in biomedical research. The Minority Institution Research Scientist Development Award supports faculty members at HBCUs and other minority-serving institutions who have the interest and potential to conduct high-quality research on cardiovascular, pulmonary, hematological, and sleep disorders; the award also offers additional financial support to the faculty members' institutions and funds research opportunities for the faculty members' students. The Minority Institutional Research Training Program supports the training of graduate and health professional students and individuals in postdoctoral training at HBCUs. The Minority Undergraduate Biomedical Education Program supports the development of pilot programs to encourage HBCUs and other minority-serving institutions to recruit and retain talented undergraduates into careers in the biomedical and behavioral sciences.

Other NHLBI programs support African American faculty and students at institutions other than HBCUs. The Mentored Development Award for Minority Faculty provides financial and mentoring support to minority faculty members who wish to undertake research careers in cardiovascular, pulmonary, hematological, or sleep disorders. The Biomedical Research Training Program for Underrepresented Minorities offers undergraduate, graduate, and health professional students majoring in the life sciences the opportunity to participate in research being conducted at one of NHLBI's laboratories in Bethesda, Maryland. The Short-Term Training for Minority Students Program provides short-term research support to underrepresented minority undergraduate and graduate students and students in health professional schools. NHLBI also participates in three NIH-wide programs: Minority Access to Research Careers (MARC) Summer Research Training, Research Supplements for Underrepresented Minorities, and Minority Biomedical Research Support (MBRS).

NHLBI works to eliminate health disparities among African Americans with several community outreach and education programs. NHLBI supports the National Physicians' Network Project, which provides continuing education and information to health care professionals whose practices cater mainly to blacks. NHLBI provides educational materials to Keeping Hearts Alive, which works with community organizations and leaders to promote cardiovascular health in blacks in Washington, D.C., and Baltimore. The Cardiovascular Disease Enhanced Dissemination and Utilization Centers Program is a partnership between NHLBI and six community-based education centers that seeks to promote community-based cardiovascular health in rural communities with heart disease and stroke death rates far in excess of the national average. The National Asthma Education and Prevention Program awards contracts to local asthma coalitions to improve asthma control in minority communities that are disproportionately affected by the disease.

See also: Asthma; Cardiovascular Disease; Diabetes; Health Disparities; Historically Black Colleges and Universities; Minority Access to Research Careers; Minority Biomedical Research Support; National Institutes of Health; Obesity; Sickle Cell Disease

REFERENCES AND FURTHER READING

National Heart, Lung, and Blood Institute. "National Heart, Lung, and Blood Institute." [Online article or information; retrieved October 29, 2007.] http://www.nhlbi.nih.gov/.

National Heart, Lung, and Blood Institute. "National Heart, Lung, and Blood Institute Strategy for Addressing Health Disparities, FY 2002–2006." [Online article or information; retrieved June 19, 2007.] http://www.nhlbi.nih.gov/resources/docs/plandisp.htm.

National Human Genome Research Institute

The National Human Genome Research Institute (NHGRI) is a part of the National Institutes of Health (NIH), the nation's leading agency for conducting and supporting biomedical research. NHGRI conducts and sponsors a number of research projects related to genetic variations among racial and ethnic groups, and it funds a number of programs to recruit and train more

African Americans and other underrepresented minorities into careers related to genome science.

NHGRI was established in 1989 as the National Center for Human Genome Research. Its mission was to carry out NIH's role in the International Human Genome Research Project, whose goal was to map a complete DNA sequence for one set of human chromosomes. In 1997, the center was elevated to the status of institute, and it acquired its present name. With the successful completion of the Human Genome Project in 2003, NHGRI research since then has focused on studying the genetic components of complex diseases and medical conditions.

Prior to 2001, NHGRI support for minority medical investigators doing research related to the Human Genome Project primarily revolved around two awards. The Genome Scholar Development and Faculty Transition Award enabled promising new minority genome researchers to establish an independent research program in genomic research and analysis and to secure a tenure-track appointment in an academic institution in the United States. The Individual Mentored Research Scientist Award supported highly qualified minority scientists with degrees in bioinformatics, bioengineering, biomathematics, chemistry, computational biology, computer science, engineering, mathematics, physics, or statistics who sought careers in interdisciplinary genomic research and analysis.

In 2001, NHGRI adopted a Minority Action Plan for involving more African Americans and members of other underrepresented minorities in NHGRI's genetic and genomic research. Two major emphases of this research were to investigate how minute variations in DNA sequencing causes racial and ethnic groups to be more susceptible to certain diseases and medical conditions and eventually to develop biomedical remedies for these conditions. The plan includes funding and other support for research training and research collaboration opportunities for minorities interested in pursuing careers related to genome science, as well as for education and outreach activities to educate minority communities about genome science in general and the Human Genome Project in particular.

NHGRI offers a number of research training and career development opportunities for minorities, many of them at its laboratories in Bethesda, Maryland. The Predoctoral Intramural Research Training Award allows medical students or graduate students working toward a degree in biomedical science to perform all or part of their dissertation work under the direction of top NHGRI researchers. The Summer Internship Program in Biomedical Research provides advanced high school students and undergraduates the opportunity to participate in research projects at NHGRI during the summer break. Participants in this program also attend the NIH Summer Seminar Series, which acquaints students with the latest developments in biomedical research and gives them an opportunity to present their summer research findings in a poster presentation. The Undergraduate Scholarship Program for Students from Disadvantaged Backgrounds offers competitive scholarships to students who are committed to careers in biomedical, behavioral, and other health-related research. The program offers $20,000 per year for tuition and other expenses, a 10-week paid summer laboratory experience, scholarship support, and guaranteed employment and continuing training at NHGRI after graduation. Current Topics in Genomic Research is a six-day course taught every summer to faculty at historically black colleges and universities and other minority-serving institutions to update them on the latest developments in genome science. The course focuses on NHGRI's continuing effort to find the genetic basis of various diseases and disorders, as well as current topics concerning the ethical, legal, and social implications of genomic research. Each faculty member who is chosen to attend the short course is invited to bring a promising student from the faculty member's home institution to attend the NIH Genome Scholars Program, which is held concurrently.

In addition to these opportunities, NHGRI supports minority faculty and student research at laboratories other than NHGRI's own. To support research opportunities for minorities at colleges and universities across the country, NHGRI makes use of NIH-wide grant programs, such as the Ruth L. Kirschstein–National Research Service Awards for Individual Postdoctoral and Predoctoral Fellows, the Mentored Quantitative Research Career Development Award, and Research Supplements to Promote Diversity in Health-Related Research. These awards also support minority research at leading independent research facilities such as Cold Spring Harbor Laboratory (New York), The Jackson Laboratory (Maine), and Woods Hole Marine Biology Laboratory (Massachusetts), three of the nation's leading centers for the study of genome science.

As a means of increasing the number of minority researchers and minority institutions that conduct genomic research, recruiting more minorities to participate in study populations concerning genomic research, and studying diseases that disproportionately affect African Americans, NHGRI conducts two special population research program collaborations with Howard University. The African American Type–2 Diabetes Study involves the genetics of type 2 diabetes (diabetes mellitus) in three locations in Nigeria and Ghana. These locations were chosen because they are believed to be the ancestral homelands of most living African Americans and because the populations in these areas have fewer confounding dietary and nutritional variables than in the United States. The African American Hereditary Prostate Cancer Study Network investigates the genes involved in hereditary prostate cancer in black men. The project's goal is to study the genes of 100 families in which at least four men have been diagnosed with prostate cancer at or before the age of

65 and that include at least four other unaffected relatives who are available to be studied. A major portion of both collaborations involves the recruitment and training of six or more young African American scientists to serve as principal investigators in these and related studies in the future.

NHGRI has developed and organized several approaches to help minority communities and the general public understand both the science and the implications of genomic research. "The Human Genome Project: Exploring Our Molecular Selves" and "The Genetic Variation Curriculum Kit" are free, multimedia education kits that can be used by high school teachers to instruct their students about how all humans experience slight variations in their DNA sequencing and how these variations affect them. NHGRI has also sponsored several conferences, meetings, and lectures of interest to minority communities. One such presentation is New Directions for Sickle Cell Therapy in the Genome Era (2003), a consideration of how genome science might be applied both to understand more fully the biology of sickle cell disease and to develop more effective therapeutic and preventive strategies for the disease. Another presentation is The Human Genome Project Conference: The Challenges and Impact of Human Genome Research for Minority Communities (2002). NHGRI also hosts exhibits at the Annual Biomedical Research Conference for Minority Students as a means of educating and recruiting young minority scientists into careers related to genome science.

See also: Cancer; Chemistry; Computer Science; Diabetes; Historically Black Colleges and Universities; Howard University; National Institutes of Health; Physics

REFERENCES AND FURTHER READING

National Human Genome Research Institute. "Initiatives and Resources for Minority and Special Populations." [Online article or information; retrieved June 25, 2007.] http://www.genome.gov/10001192.

National Human Genome Research Institute. "National Human Genome Research Institute." [Online article or information; retrieved October 29, 2007.] http://www.genome.gov/.

National Institute on Aging

The National Institute on Aging (NIA) is part of the National Institutes of Health (NIH), the nation's leading agency for conducting and supporting biomedical research. NIA research focuses on diseases and medical conditions related to the aging process, age-related diseases, and the special problems and needs of the aged. A major focus of NIA research is to determine to what degree race and ethnicity contribute to aging and age-related diseases.

NIA was established in 1974 to provide leadership throughout the health community in matters related to aging research, training, health information dissemination, and other programs relevant to aging and older people. NIA is also the primary federal agency for conducting and supporting research related to Alzheimer's disease. Although NIA supports research at colleges, universities, and independent research facilities across the nation, it also conducts research of its own at its laboratories in Baltimore and Bethesda, Maryland.

With respect to health disparities, NIA has undertaken several studies to determine the effects of race and ethnicity on aging. These studies make clear the fact that race and ethnicity, in the sense of genetically homogeneous human populations, no longer exist in the physiological sense because of extensive intermixing over long periods of time. Instead, race and ethnicity have currency only in the socioeconomic and cultural sense. Consequently, many of the problems that older nonwhite Americans suffer from disproportionately are a function of the facts that they are less likely to have health insurance, less likely to be educated about healthy behaviors and diets, less likely to seek routine medical care, and less likely to have access to preventative medical sciences. Nevertheless, the studies further suggest that race and ethnicity cannot be ignored as determinants in age-related health disparities. For example, it has been demonstrated that racial and ethnic differences in life expectancy and years lived with chronic health problems and disability cannot be explained in terms of socioeconomic or cultural causes alone.

Consequently, NIA-sponsored research on health disparities has focused on understanding how low socioeconomic status may result in poor physical or mental health by operating through various psychosocial mechanisms such as social exclusion, perceived racism, discrimination, prolonged and heightened stress, loss of a sense of control, and low self-esteem, and how these psychosocial mechanisms may lead to physiological changes such as raised levels of cortisol, altered blood pressure response, and decreased immunity that place elderly minority individuals at risk for adverse health and age-related disabilities. These studies have investigated ethnic differences related to menopausal transition; racial differences as contributors to vitamin D insufficiency in the elderly; the role of age-related blood vessel stiffening, diet, and blood clot-dissolving factors in older African Americans; body composition, chemosensory perception, and nutritional status in African Americans; and the relationships between race and visual and cognitive functioning, insomnia, and dementia.

Since 1999, when NIA conducted a review of its policies and practices regarding health disparities related to aging, its clinical research programs have included more minorities in studies that are not directly related to race and ethnicity. NIA also established the Resource Centers for Minority Aging Research (RCMAR) to reduce health disparities related to age by focusing on health promotion, disease prevention, and disability prevention as they relate to health disparities. To this end, the centers recruit members of minority groups to volunteer in epidemiological, psychosocial, and biomedical research dealing with the health of the elderly.

Since 1999, NIA has been more proactive about recruiting minorities into several NIH-wide programs, including Research Supplements for Under-represented Minorities, Intramural Research Training Awards, the annual Technical Assistance Workshop, the Summer Institute on Aging Research, the Minority Dissertation Award, and the Minority Predoctoral Fellowship Program, which offer financial and mentoring support for minority researchers from high school students to junior faculty members. The institute also uses the Claude D. Pepper Older Americans Independence Centers (OAICs), which were established primarily to conduct research on innovative medical devices and treatments that allow the elderly to maintain their independence, as centers for supporting research by minority medical investigators. For example, the Harvard University OAIC has collaborated with minority faculty members at Meharry Medical College and Howard University in several studies related to elderly African Americans.

See also: Health Disparities; Howard University; Meharry Medical College; National Institutes of Health

REFERENCES AND FURTHER READING
National Institute on Aging. "National Institute on Aging." [Online article or information; retrieved October 29, 2007.] http://www.nia.nih.gov/.
National Institute on Aging. "Review of Minority Aging Research at the NIA." [Online article or information; retrieved June 26, 2007.] http://www.nia.nih.gov/AboutNIA/MinorityAgingResearch.htm.

National Institute on Alcohol Abuse and Alcoholism

The National Institute on Alcohol Abuse and Alcoholism (NIAAA) is part of the National Institutes of Health (NIH), the nation's leading agency for conducting and supporting biomedical research. Part of NIAAA's mission is to identify the racial and ethnic factors, if any, that contribute to health disparities concerning alcohol abuse and alcoholism and to develop programs and treatments for reducing and ultimately eliminating health disparities related to the consumption of alcohol.

NIAAA was established in 1970 to serve as NIH's lead institution for research concerning alcohol abuse and alcoholism. As of 2007, NIAAA was conducting and supporting research in a wide range of scientific areas, including epidemiology, genetics, neuroscience, and the health risks and benefits of alcohol consumption, prevention, and treatment. Much of the institute's psychosocial and biomedical research suggests that minority groups, including

African Americans, suffer disproportionately from the effects of alcohol when compared to other segments of the population; at the same time, the research recognizes significant variability among subgroups within minority groups. NIAAA's efforts concerning health disparities focus on developing research programs that explore the causes and consequences of all these differences. The institute also works to increase the number of minority scientists at historically black colleges and universities and other minority-serving institutions conducting alcohol-related research, and it works closely with the National Center on Minority Health and Health Disparities to help minority communities eliminate alcohol-related health disparities.

NIAAA-supported research projects concerning health disparities address a wide range of topics. Epidemiological studies gather information about patterns of alcohol use and alcohol-related problems among racial and ethnic minorities. Biomedical research examines the risk factors that contribute to disparities in the effects of alcohol, such as alcohol metabolism and other cellular and molecular processes involved in alcohol use. Genetics and neuroscience research have led to the development of pharmacological treatments for a variety of problems related to alcohol use. Prevention and intervention research studies whether and how key components of prevention strategies (such as community and family involvement techniques) and sociocultural factors (such as whether drinking is moral, beneficial, or expected of certain people) vary within and among racial and ethnic groups. Research related to treating alcoholism examines the efficacy and effectiveness of standard and innovative treatments for alcohol use disorders among ethnic minorities.

One of the best ways to eliminate alcohol-related health disparities is to recruit and train minority scientists for careers in research related to alcohol abuse and alcoholism. To this end, the institute participates in the NIH Summer Research Fellowship Program, the NIH Summer Internship Program in Biomedical Research, the Clinical Research Training Program, and the Underrepresented Minority Supplement Program, all of which provide financial and mentoring support to qualified minority researchers. These programs give minority faculty members and students, from the high school to the postgraduate levels, the flexibility to conduct research under the auspices of experienced researchers at NIAAA's facilities in Bethesda, Maryland, at another research facility devoted to alcohol research, or at their home institution. The institute also supports several initiatives to strengthen the ability of HBCUs and other minority-serving institutions to contribute to and conduct alcohol research. One program initiates collaborative research projects between minority faculty members at minority-serving institutions and established alcohol researchers, such as the Howard University Collaborative Alcohol Research Center, to enhance the ability of minority researchers eventually to conduct independent projects at their home institutions. Another, the Technical Assistance Workshops program, is conducted at HBCUs, where faculty and students receive instruction concerning how to develop a project, write a grant, and conduct alcohol research. The Alcohol Research Mentoring System recruits minority researchers at HBCUs interested in social or behavioral science research projects and matches them with a senior, NIAAA-funded research mentor, who helps the minority researcher develop a grant application that will result in an independent research project at the minority researcher's home institution.

As part of its efforts to eliminate health disparities related to alcohol, NIAAA provides minority communities with culturally relevant information concerning alcohol abuse and alcoholism. The institute also develops materials for pediatricians and prenatal care professionals so that they can identify children affected by prenatal exposure to alcohol and screen women of childbearing age for at-risk drinking. Outreach programs include efforts to provide health care professionals who serve minority communities with current information regarding alcohol use disorders, interventions, and treatments. To ensure the validity of its research concerning minorities, NIAAA seeks to recruit and involve more minorities in its clinical studies.

See also: Health Disparities; Historically Black Colleges and Universities; Howard University; National Center on Minority Health and Health Disparities; National Institutes of Health

REFERENCES AND FURTHER READING

National Institute on Alcohol Abuse and Alcoholism. "National Institute on Alcohol Abuse and Alcoholism." [Online article or information; retrieved October 29, 2007.] http://www.niaaa.nih.gov/.

National Institute on Alcohol Abuse and Alcoholism. "NIAAA's Strategic Plan to Address Health Disparities." [Online article or information; retrieved June 27, 2007.] http://pubs.niaaa.nih.gov/publications/HealthDisparities/Strategic.html.

National Institute of Allergy and Infectious Diseases

The National Institute of Allergy and Infectious Diseases (NIAID) is part of the National Institutes of Health (NIH), the nation's leading agency for conducting and supporting biomedical research. NIAID conducts and supports research related to understanding, treating, and ultimately eradicating allergic, infectious, and immunologic diseases and medical conditions. With respect to health disparities, NIAID focuses its research projects on HIV/AIDS and other autoimmune and sexually transmitted diseases, organ transplantation, asthma, tuberculosis, and hepatitis C. The institute also supports several programs that recruit more minority scientists into research careers related to the institute's mission, that educate minority populations about the risks and treatments

The National Institute of Allergy and Infectious Diseases works to lower the incidence of HIV/AIDS and other autoimmune diseases among African Americans. (National Institutes of Health)

related to health disparities, and that recruit minorities into clinical trials and other programs that work to eliminate health disparities.

NIAID is the oldest of the institutes and centers that make up NIH. It was established in 1887 as the Laboratory of Hygiene on Staten Island, New York, and it was charged with identifying the causes of cholera and other infectious diseases being brought into this country by immigrants. In 1891, this facility was renamed the Hygienic Laboratory and moved to Washington, D.C., where it began investigating infectious diseases that affected the entire nation. In 1930, it was renamed the National Institute of Health; eight years later, it relocated to Bethesda, Maryland, its current home. In 1948, when the National Institutes of Health was created, the original NIH became known as the National Microbiological Institute, and in 1955, it acquired its present name. Fifty years later, NIAID was conducting and supporting basic and applied research to prevent, diagnose, and treat a wide range of infectious illnesses, including those resulting from bioterrorism.

As of 2001, a disproportionately large number—38 percent—of all Americans who had contracted HIV/AIDS were African Americans. Since the best way to eliminate this particular health disparity is to develop a vaccine for HIV,

NIAID supports a number of programs to develop such a vaccine. In so doing, however, the institute makes sure to include a disproportionately large number—46 percent—of African Americans in its clinical trials investigating the efficacy and side effects of potential HIV vaccines. The inclusion of so many African Americans is necessary, because it is a well-documented fact that certain antiviral agents do not work the same way in African Americans as they do in other subgroups of the American population; therefore, NIAID must strive to make certain that any potential HIV vaccine will work effectively for all members of American society.

Organ transplantation represents another major health problem for African Americans. For example, African Americans comprise approximately 35 percent of the patients on the kidney transplant waiting list, but they are less likely to find a suitable donor, partly because they are less likely than other racial groups to donate organs. Successful transplantation depends on the availability of donated organs and accurate methods to match donor and recipient according to the human leukocyte antigen (HLA) system, which utilizes genetic matching to ensure the compatibility of transplanted organs. This situation is complicated further by the facts that knowledge of the relevant HLA types in African Americans and other minority populations is incomplete and that the immune systems of African Americans tend to be more aggressive about rejecting transplanted organs. Consequently, NIAID supports a national research program to identify HLA genes in African Americans and members of other minority groups and to improve methods for defining gene variants in minority populations that might affect immune response. To date, the program has developed DNA-based technologies that type HLA genes rapidly in minority populations, and it has defined 13 new HLA genes in African Americans. NIAID also conducts clinical trials of innovative therapies that prevent these genes from rejecting a transplanted organ.

Several autoimmune diseases, in which the body's immune system attacks its own cells and organs, disproportionately affect African Americans. For example, African American women are three times more likely than European American women to contract systemic lupus erythematosus, which is particularly destructive of cells and tissue in the cardiovascular and nervous systems, and they are twice as likely to contract scleroderma (hardening of the skin and the abnormal growth of tissue in the muscles, joints, lungs, heart, kidneys, and intestinal tract). Thus, NIAID supports basic research and clinical trials, such as those carried out by the NIH Autoimmunity Centers of Excellence and the Clinical Trials of Stem Cell Transplantation for the Treatment of Autoimmune Diseases, that develop and evaluate therapies for both diseases.

African Americans are three times more likely to be hospitalized for asthma than the general population, and African Americans who live in inner cities are almost six times more likely to die from asthma. To combat this situation, in 1991, NIAID established the National Cooperative Inner-City Asthma Study, which demonstrated the efficacy of a multifaceted asthma educational intervention in reducing asthma severity among inner-city children. Since then, this program has been extended to 23 urban communities nationwide, and it has been expanded to include research to develop immune-based therapies to reduce asthma severity.

In the early 21st century, tuberculosis (TB) reemerged as a major health concern in the United States. Most studies of the modern TB epidemic identify its major causes as urban poverty, household crowding, and high HIV infection rates among African Americans and other minorities. As with HIV/AIDS, the best solution to this problem is to develop a TB vaccine; consequently, NIAID supports research in this area, as well as research to develop better methods for preventing and treating latent TB infection, which is much more likely to be found in minority populations.

Hepatitis C virus (HCV) is a blood-borne disease that causes liver damage. HCV infection normally results from injecting cocaine or other drugs with an infected needle, getting a tattoo or body piercing with an infected instrument, or having sexual intercourse with an infected partner, but it is also prevalent among people who received blood or blood products before 1992, when the federal government took steps to keep it out of the national blood supply. It occurs disproportionately among minority communities and people who live in poverty, but it is particularly dangerous for African Americans, because they tend to respond poorly to standard HCV therapies. In 2001, NIAID initiated the Hepatitis C Framework for Progress as a mechanism for addressing these and other problems related to HCV. Among other things, this plan sponsors research to develop an HCV vaccine and therapeutic strategies that are effective for African Americans.

Sexually transmitted diseases (STDs) also plague African Americans disproportionately. Studies have shown that African Americans account for 60 percent of cases treated in STD clinics, and the reported rates for syphilis and gonorrhea are up to 30 times higher for African Americans than for European Americans. Thus, NIAID supports research to develop new, easy-to-administer treatments for syphilis and gonorrhea, such as a single-dose oral therapy, that promise to increase the number of minorities seeking treatment for STDs. The institute also cooperates with the Centers for Disease Control and Prevention (CDC) in research activities related to the Syphilis Elimination Plan, and it supports research related to the development of vaccines for genital herpes, gonorrhea, and chlamydial infection. In terms of prevention, NIAID supports research that investigates why African Americans and other minorities are more likely to engage in high-risk sexual behavior and evaluates behavioral factors related to STD prevention and control in inner-city high schools.

It is generally believed that the best way to overcome health disparities is to recruit minorities into careers as medical researchers, because minorities have shown historically a disproportionately greater interest in addressing health disparities than nonminority researchers. To this end, NIAID makes use of a number of existing NIH initiatives to train and develop minority scientists. These initiatives include the Research Centers in Minority Institutions and the Minority Biomedical Research Support programs, both of which enhance the ability of historically black colleges and universities and other minority-serving institutions to prepare their students for careers in biomedical research. Other NIH programs, such as Research Supplements for Underrepresented Minorities, support minority individuals, and NIAID makes full use of these programs as well. In 1993, NIAID developed an initiative of its own: Bridging the Career Gap for Underrepresented Minority Students. This two-day seminar invites promising minority students of science or medicine to think seriously about pursuing a research career in an area of interest to NIAID. Every two years, Bridging the Gap brings minority students who are already being supported by an NIH grant to the NIAID campus in Bethesda. The program presents information concerning how to write winning grants and manage a research project, but its emphasis is on what NIAID offers them in terms of research careers.

NIAID also works to eliminate health disparities with a number of education and outreach endeavors. It supports the National HIV Vaccine Communications Outreach, which strives to educate the public about the state of HIV vaccine research. It recruits African Americans and other minorities to serve as volunteers during clinical trials of potential vaccines and therapies for HIV, syphilis, gonorrhea, and TB. It supports projects to increase the number of minority organ donors through such programs as Louisiana's Legacy Donor Registry, and it works with the CDC to disseminate the Asthma Treatment Guidelines, which targets children with asthma living in inner cities.

See also: Asthma; Health Disparities; Historically Black Colleges and Universities; HIV/AIDS; National Institutes of Health

REFERENCES AND FURTHER READING
National Institute of Allergy and Infectious Diseases. "National Institute of Allergy and Infectious Diseases." [Online article or information; retrieved October 29, 2007.] http://www3.niaid.nih.gov/.
National Institute of Allergy and Infectious Diseases. "Office of Special Populations and Research Training." [Online article or information; retrieved June 28, 2007.] http://www3.niaid.nih.gov/about/organization/dea/osprtpage.htm.

National Institute of Arthritis and Musculoskeletal and Skin Diseases

The National Institute of Arthritis and Musculoskeletal and Skin Diseases (NIAMS) is part of the National Institutes of Health (NIH), the nation's leading agency for conducting and sponsoring biomedical research. NIAMS was established in 1986 to conduct and support basic and clinical research programs related to diseases and medical conditions of the joints, muscles, bones, and skin. Twenty years later, the institute was also heavily involved in training basic and clinical scientists to carry out this research and in disseminating information on research progress in these diseases. The institute works to reduce health disparities among African Americans by focusing its research on four diseases and medical conditions that affect African Americans disproportionately: systemic lupus erythematosus, osteoarthritis, vitiligo, and keloids. NIAMS also recruits and trains minority scientists for careers in biomedical research related to these and other medical conditions of interest to the institute, and it educates minority communities about the latest developments in prevention and treatment.

Systemic lupus erythematosus (SLE) is a serious and potentially fatal autoimmune disease that can affect many parts of the body, including the joints and skin. African American women are three times more likely to contract SLE than European American women. They also tend to develop SLE at a younger age and to develop more serious complications over the course of the disease. In 1993, NIAMS implemented an ongoing, multiethnic study of SLE, Lupus in Minority Populations: Nature vs. Nurture (LUMINA), to consider to what degree genetic factors and socioeconomic determinants, such as little education, low income, and poor access to health care, lead to higher rates of incidence and death from SLE in African Americans. To date, the results of the study have revealed limited and often conflicting data on the prevalence, incidence, outcomes, and sociocultural aspects of lupus among ethnic minorities. Nevertheless, NIAMS continues to conduct and support research projects that focus on the genetic aspects of SLE. One project has identified as many as 10 regions in DNA that are linked to SLE, and other projects attempt to understand what, if any, role the genes in these regions play in the progression of SLE to its more serious forms. Other studies have identified genetic factors as important contributors to a higher rate of incidence of lupus-related kidney disease among African American lupus patients. Further studies of the genetics of lupus seek to identify at-risk individuals before they contract SLE and to develop pharmaceutical therapies targeting the genes or gene products that cause or regulate the progression of the disease.

Osteoarthritis, also known as degenerative joint disease, is the most common form of arthritis. This painful and disabling medical condition is characterized by the progressive loss of cartilage in the joints, particularly the knees and hips. Studies have demonstrated that African Americans have a higher risk of contracting osteoarthritis of the hip and knee than do European Americans. The risk is compounded in African Americans who suffer from obesity, another health disparity. By the same token, African Americans are approximately one-half as likely as European Americans to remedy this situation by obtaining a total joint replacement, which is a successful procedure for end-stage arthritis of the knee or hip, even when their insurance coverage will pay for the operation. NIAMS addresses this health disparity in two ways. The first supports research that develops a better understanding of the causes of osteoarthritis, including the role, if any, of genetics. The second investigates the reasons that prevent African Americans from obtaining total joint replacements when they are justified.

Vitiligo is a skin disease that is characterized by the loss of pigment. Although vitiligo remains poorly understood, it is thought to be an autoimmune disease that destroys pigment-producing cells known as melanocytes. Since vitiligo occurs disproportionately among African Americans and among certain families, researchers believe that certain individuals are genetically predisposed to contract the disease. Consequently, NIAMS supports research to identify the gene or genes, if any, that are associated with vitiligo in the familial cases, and then to determine whether the same genes are defective in the sporadic cases. NIAMS also seeks to eliminate vitiligo by supporting basic research concerning the process of melanogenesis (the production of pigment).

Keloids are a special type of scar that results in an overgrowth of tissue at the site of a healed skin injury. They can be firm and rubbery or shiny and fibrous, and they vary in color from pink to dark brown. Keloids are benign and noncontagious, but they are usually accompanied by severe itchiness, sharp pains, and changes in texture. For many, keloids are also a disturbing cosmetic problem, particularly among young patients. The causes of this medical condition, which occurs primarily among African Americans, remain poorly understood. Keloid development is often sporadic, but significant family clustering occurs as well. As with vitiligo, NIAMS supports research to identify the gene or genes responsible for keloids in the familial cases and then to determine to what degree they contribute to the sporadic cases. Since keloids are made from collagen, NIAMS also supports basic research related to collagen synthesis and remodeling.

NIAMS supports several programs for reducing health disparities in its areas of responsibility by increasing the number of minority medical investigators conducting research in those areas. The Collaborative Arthritis and Musculoskeletal and Skin Diseases Award supports research partnerships between senior researchers at major research facilities and minority investigators at historically black colleges and universities and other minority-serving institutions. The NIAMS Small Grants Program provides financial support for research projects that are conducted by minority investigators at HBCUs and other minority-serving institutions. NIAMS also participates in several NIH-wide initiatives to recruit more minority medical investigators such as the Research Supplement for Minorities and the Minority Biomedical Research Support programs.

With respect to community education and outreach, NIAMS has published and distributed thousands of copies of two pamphlets on SLE throughout the African American community: "What Black Women Should Know About Lupus" and "Lupus: A Patient Care Guide for Nurses and Other Health Professionals." The latter was developed and reviewed with the assistance of the National Black Nurses Association. NIAMS has established a community health center in the Adams-Morgan neighborhood of Washington, D.C., so that it can better understand the needs of arthritic African Americans living in an urban environment. The center also gives NIAMS an excellent recruitment center at which to encourage African Americans to serve as volunteers for clinical trials of various therapies for arthritis and other medical conditions within the purview of the institute.

See also: Health Disparities; Historically Black Colleges and Universities; National Institutes of Health

References and Further Reading

National Institute of Arthritis and Musculoskeletal and Skin Diseases. "National Institute of Arthritis and Musculoskeletal and Skin Diseases." [Online article or information; retrieved October 29, 2007.] http://www.niams.nih.gov/.

National Institute of Arthritis and Musculoskeletal and Skin Diseases. "Strategic Plan for Reducing Health Disparities." [Online article or information; retrieved July 2, 2007.] http://www.niams.nih.gov/About_Us/Mission_and_Purpose/strat_plan_hd.asp.

National Institute of Child Health and Human Development

The National Institute of Child Health and Human Development (NICHD) is a part of the National Institutes of Health (NIH), the nation's leading agency for conducting and supporting biomedical research. NICHD was established in 1962 to investigate the physiological aspects of human development, particularly those that occur during pregnancy and those that result in developmental disabilities such as mental retardation. By the early 21st century, its mission had expanded to include research on all stages of human development, including social, cultural, and behavioral, from preconception to adulthood, and to investigate how these factors affect the health of children, adults, families, and communities. Part of NICHD's mission is to reduce and eliminate health disparities within its areas of responsibility, and to this end, it conducts and supports research related to infant and maternal mortality and morbidity, reproductive health, HIV/AIDS in women and teenagers, the early antecedents of disparities in disease and growth, the early antecedents of child well-being and adverse behaviors, school readiness and cognitive and behavioral development, and restoring function and preventing disability. NICHD also recruits and trains minority scientists for careers in medical research relevant to the institute's mission, and it disseminates relevant information about the latest scientific developments in child health and human development to minority communities.

As of the early 21st century, the infant mortality rate in the United States was twice as high for African Americans as it was for European Americans. African American infants were more than twice as likely to suffer from low birth weight, three times as likely to suffer from very low birth weight, and five times as likely to die from low birth weight or premature birth. Studies suggest that this situation stems in large part from the mother's poor health; for example, African American mothers are more than twice as likely to suffer from bacterial vaginosis, the most common form of vaginal infection, than European American mothers. By the same token, an African American woman is four times as likely to die from complications related to childbirth than a European American woman, mostly because of ectopic pregnancy (the fertilized egg is implanted somewhere other than in the uterus) and preeclampsia (hypertension resulting from pregnancy).

NICHD conducts and supports several research initiatives to reduce these disparities. One project studies the efficacy of antibiotic treatment for bacterial vaginosis in African American women. Another develops methods for predicting ectopic pregnancy more definitely and quickly so that preventive measures can be taken. A third supports the Initiative to Reduce Infant Mortality in Minority Populations in the District of Columbia, which collects data and conducts basic and behavioral research related to the problem. NICHD also investigates the medical and behavioral factors related to sudden infant death syndrome (SIDS) and supports the SIDS Back to Sleep campaign, which develops culturally sensitive programs to reduce the prevalence of back-sleeping among African American infants. The Maternal Lifestyles Study examines the development of infants exposed to drugs while in the womb, as well as the effect on maternal mortality of diabetes, hypertension, stress, nutrition, and partner violence.

African American females tend to enter puberty one year earlier than European American females, meaning that their reproductive health needs must be attended to at an earlier age. Perhaps as a result, approximately 10 percent of all African American women of reproductive age get pregnant unintentionally each year. African American women are more than twice as likely to suffer from uterine fibroids, a leading cause of hysterectomy, and, according to some studies, up to 30 times as likely to suffer from gonorrhea. African

American infants are 30 times as likely to suffer from congenital syphilis, a medical condition that often results in physical deformities and mental retardation despite being completely preventable. NICHD works to reduce these disparities by supporting research that studies the risk factors for African American women related to hormone replacement therapy for uterine fibroids, investigates the behavioral factors that contribute to risky sexual behavior among minority teenagers, and develops educational programs and other interventions to help prevent unwanted pregnancies, especially among unwed minority teenagers.

HIV/AIDS is a major contributor to health disparities in the United States. At the turn of the century, almost 60 percent of the teenagers diagnosed with AIDS were African Americans, and almost 60 percent of the women who suffered from AIDS were African Americans. Of American women newly diagnosed with AIDS, more than 80 percent are African Americans. In response to this situation, NICHD has established several programs for preventing and treating AIDS, especially among minority communities. The Pediatric and Maternal HIV Clinical Trials Network, the Adolescent Medicine HIV/AIDS Research Network, and the Adolescent Trials Network develop methods for preventing and treating HIV/AIDS in minority communities. Project ACCESS encourages minority teenagers to take advantage of public health clinics and other forms of health care and to enroll in clinical studies that investigate the efficacy for teenagers of various methods of preventing and treating AIDS. The Women's HIV Pathogenesis Program studies how HIV infection spreads among women in minority communities and how the development of AIDS in minority women differs from its development in minority men. Other institute-supported research seeks to develop microbicides and spermicides that protect women from unwanted pregnancy and HIV infection.

Studies suggest that many health disparities begin before birth as a result of what is known as fetal programming. The early physiological interactions between a fetus, its mother, and the social and physical environment in which she lives may be the root cause for the high incidence among African Americans of such diseases and medical conditions as hypertension, obesity, diabetes, and coronary artery disease. It is believed that these interactions program the fetus in such a way that it is susceptible to certain health disparities, many of which do not manifest themselves until later in life. Consequently, NICHD supports research that investigates fetal programming by studying the factors that disturb or retard fetal development among minorities. Among other factors, these studies examine the effects of smoking and drug abuse on fetal development, as well as the effects of hypertension, diabetes, poor nutrition, and breast-feeding on pregnancy, birth, and health in later life.

At the turn of the century, the majority of African American children lived in female-headed households. As a result, many African American youths grow up in poverty, which contributes directly to heightened exposure to contagious diseases, to developmental delays, to social, emotional, and behavioral problems, to domestic violence, and to accidental and intentional injury and death. Obviously, the root cause of this situation is sociocultural, not biomedical; nevertheless, NICHD supports social and behavioral research projects that demonstrate to policy makers the pressing need to take political and societal action. These projects investigate how socioeconomic status, family structure, and parenting contribute to disparities in child growth and development, and they seek to develop educational programs and other interventions that reduce or eliminate child neglect, child abuse, and unnecessary exposure to injury and disease.

At the turn of the century, African American students in the 4th, 8th, and 12th grades were twice as likely as European American students to perform below basic levels in reading, mathematics, and science. One-half of the 4th and 8th graders and one-third of the 12th graders read so poorly that they were unable to learn by reading alone. Studies also showed that students living in poverty have smaller vocabularies at early ages and that their vocabulary grows much more slowly than that of children living in more advantaged upbringings. These early differences translate into disparities in later vocabulary use and IQ test scores. Consequently, NICHD supports research related to the behavioral, biological, cognitive, cultural, emotional, neurological, and social factors that contribute to language development and disorders, attention deficit disorders, mathematical cognition, problem solving, reading disabilities, and other learning disabilities in minority children. Such research includes an examination of a father's impact on a child's development and how that impact can be strengthened, in addition to the Early Childhood Longitudinal Study, which analyzes the relation between health disparities and school readiness, and the NICHD/District of Columbia Public Schools Early Interventions Reading Project, which seeks to improve the reading ability of minority students with exceptionally poor reading skills.

At the turn of the century, minorities suffered a disproportionate incidence of trauma and illnesses, such as stroke, that lead to permanent disabilities. Such disabilities put a tremendous amount of strain on families that are already under considerable stress; for example, research data suggests that African American couples with young disabled children are twice as likely to divorce as European American couples in the same situation. To remedy these disparities, NICHD supports a number of research programs designed to rehabilitate minorities more quickly and more completely from stroke, spinal cord injury, and pediatric trauma. The institute also supports rehabilitation networks that study how socioeconomic and cultural factors influence the rehabilitation of minorities recovering from pediatric trauma and traumatic brain injury, and it promotes the stability of minority families with disabled children by developing research-based assistance programs based on the special needs of these families.

One of the best ways to overcome health disparities related to child health and human development is to recruit minority scientists to conduct research in these areas. To this end, NICHD participates in a number of NIH-wide initiatives such as Research Supplements for Underrepresented Minorities, the MARC Visiting Professors for Minority Institutions Program, the Minority High School Student Research Apprentice Program, and the Minority Biomedical Research Support Program. The institute also supports the NICHD Institutional Training Programs, which provide financial and mentoring support for historically black colleges and universities and other minority-serving institutions so that they can train students for careers related to NICHD's research interests. In 1991, NICHD partnered with Highland Elementary School in Silver Spring, Maryland, which has a mostly minority student body, as a means of influencing minority students to consider careers in the health sciences. NICHD sponsors activities such as the Scientist Volunteer Program, where institute scientists visit classrooms and help teachers and students with science projects, and Presentation Day, when NICHD scientists and staff members visit and speak on health topics.

In the area of community outreach, NICHD strives to include more African Americans and other minorities in clinical trials of treatments and interventions related to health disparities. Many NICHD clinical trials are conducted at minority-serving hospitals such as Harlem Hospital in New York City and Howard University Hospital in Washington, D.C. These trials include day care and paid transportation, and many include meals for women and children when visits require a full day.

See also: Diabetes; Harlem Hospital; Health Disparities; Historically Black Colleges and Universities; HIV/AIDS; Howard University Hospital; Minority Biomedical Research Support; National Institutes of Health; Obesity

REFERENCES AND FURTHER READING

National Institute of Child Health and Human Development. "Health Disparities: Bridging the Gap." [Online article or information; retrieved July 3, 2007.] http://www.nichd.nih.gov/publications/pubs/upload/health_disparities.pdf.

National Institute of Child Health and Human Development. "National Institute of Child Health and Human Development." [Online article or information; retrieved October 29, 2007.] http://www.nichd.nih.gov/.

National Institute on Deafness and Other Communication Disorders

The National Institute on Deafness and Other Communication Disorders (NIDCD) is one of the National Institutes of Health (NIH), the federal government's primary agency for supporting and conducting medical research. Established in 1988, NIDCD conducts and supports biomedical and behavioral research related to the normal and abnormal processes of hearing, voice, speech, and language, but also of balance, smell, and taste. As part of its mission to eliminate health disparities among African Americans and other underserved minorities, NIDCD researchers seek to detect and diagnose speech-related disorders in speakers of nonstandard English and to establish the prevalence of specific language impairment in African American children.

The increased usage of nonstandard English by many U.S. residents over the years has made it increasingly difficult to diagnose communication disorders in those speakers, because most tests for such disorders assume that the person being tested speaks standard English. The result is that many people, particularly children, who have a communication disorder go undiagnosed, and many who have no problem are misdiagnosed. Consequently, NIDCD researchers developed the Diagnostic Evaluation of Language Variation (DELV) test for assessing language skills among speakers of so-called Black English. Current research involves fine-tuning DELV so that it can differentiate between language impairment and normal language development in African American children between the ages of 4 and 6.

Specific language impairment (SLI) is a condition whereby the development of a child's ability to use a language to speak, read, and write is delayed. As of 2004, no data existed concerning the prevalence of SLI among African American children, even though approximately 8 percent of white kindergartners are known to suffer from it. This situation further contributes to the misdiagnosis or nondiagnosis of language disorders among children who speak Black English. Consequently, NIDCD researchers seek to develop diagnostic tools for identifying SLI in children who speak nonstandard English.

NIDCD works to increase the number of African Americans and other underserved minorities pursuing careers as communication disorder researchers. To this end, NIDCD partners with the Atlanta University Complex of historically black colleges and universities and with Howard University to maintain a student research trainee program whereby black college students are recruited to conduct research at NIDCD laboratories. The program includes components related to the use of biotechnology to solve communication disorders and getting one's research published. Each student in the program has access to a scientific mentor who is currently conducting an NIDCD research project.

See also: Health Disparities; Historically Black Colleges and Universities; Howard University; National Institutes of Health

REFERENCES AND FURTHER READING

National Institute on Deafness and Other Communication Disorders. "National Institute on Deafness and Other Communication Disorders." [Online article or information; retrieved October 29, 2007.] http://www.nidcd.nih.gov/.

National Institute on Deafness and Other Communication Disorders. "National Institute on Deafness and Other Communication Disorders Health Disparities Strategic Plan Fiscal Years 2004–2008." [Online article or information; retrieved October 17, 2007.] http://www.nidcd.nih.gov/about/plans/strategic/health_disp.asp.

National Institute of Dental and Craniofacial Research

The National Institute of Dental and Craniofacial Research (NIDCR) is part of the National Institutes of Health (NIH), the nation's leading agency for conducting and supporting biomedical research. Established in 1948, NIDCR conducts and supports research and research training to understand, treat, and prevent infectious and inherited diseases of the teeth, mouth, head, neck, face, and jaw, as well as procedures and medical conditions related to plastic surgery. As part of its effort to eliminate health disparities, NIDCR supports research at its Centers for Research to Reduce Oral Health Disparities. The institute also supports programs to recruit and train minority scientists for careers as oral health researchers, and it disseminates information related to oral health to minority communities.

Oral health problems have little, if anything, to do with race or ethnicity per se. Socioeconomic status, however, is a powerful determinant of one's ability to afford and obtain quality oral health care. Since minorities are more likely to live in poverty and suffer from other deleterious manifestations of low socioeconomic status, they are more likely to suffer from poor oral health. In 1992, NIDCR opened the first of four Regional Research Centers on Minority Oral Health (RRCs). Each RRC established a partnership between a minority dental school or an academic institution serving a large minority population and an institution with proven expertise in the design and conduct of oral health research. The RRCs conducted basic and clinical research related to oral health problems that are prevalent among African American and other minority populations, such as orofacial injury from violence, dental caries (cavities), oral manifestations of HIV infection, oral cancer, periodontal diseases (which affect the gums and supporting bone structures) in adults, oral microbiology, genetic studies of salivary proteins, and clinical studies of the oral microbiology of elderly African Americans.

Beginning in 2001, NIDCR began replacing the RRCs with five Centers for Research to Reduce Oral Health Disparities, located at Boston University, the University of Michigan, the University of California at San Francisco, the

The National Institute of Dental and Craniofacial Research studies how diseases of the teeth, mouth, head, neck, face, and jaw affect African Americans. (National Institutes of Health)

University of Washington, and New York University. While the RRCs focused on the oral health of all minorities, the centers focus their research on the oral health of minority children, particularly in terms of developing methods and techniques for eliminating oral health disparities. As of 2007, the research being conducted at the centers was aimed at reducing the prevalence of two infectious diseases that particularly plague minority children: dental caries, and periodontal disease, such as gingivitis and other disorders of the gums and supporting bone structures. One project's findings suggest that mothers who give birth to low-birth-weight infants have an unusually high incidence of periodontal disease, whereas other studies have suggested that minorities who suffer from periodontal disease are also more likely to suffer from other diseases and medical conditions associated with health disparities such as stroke, diabetes, and atherosclerosis (hardening of the arteries). These findings have given rise to other studies of oral health that investigate potential minute genetic differences that might contribute to oral health disparities, as well as to projects to develop, for dental caries and periodontal disease, vaccines and nonantibiotic treatments that are particularly accessible to minorities.

At the turn of the century, African Americans who contract oral or pharyngeal cancers tended to do so 10 years earlier, on average, than European Americans. Moreover, the mortality rate from oral and pharyngeal cancers was twice as high for African Americans as for European Americans. Consequently, NIDCR supports research to understand the causes for this particular health disparity at its Comprehensive Oral Health Center for Discovery at the University of Pittsburgh. Recent studies suggest that alcohol and tobacco use greatly increases the risk of contracting an oral or pharyngeal cancer, especially when they are used in great quantities and in conjunction with one another; so other studies have been undertaken to investigate this relationship and the degree to which it might result from minute genetic differences.

NIDCR works to overcome oral health disparities by recruiting and training minority faculty and students to conduct research related to oral health disparities. Most of this effort is focused on the Centers for Research to Reduce Oral Health Disparities, which provide training and career opportunities for minority scientists and health care professionals interested in careers related to improving oral health in minority populations. The institute also makes use of a number of NIH-wide initiatives to increase the number of minority medical investigators, such as the Minority Research Scientist Development Award in Health Disparities. NIDCR seeks to make its research more efficacious for minorities by recruiting minorities to volunteer as subjects for clinical trials.

See also: Diabetes; Health Disparities; National Institutes of Health

REFERENCES AND FURTHER READING

National Institute of Dental and Craniofacial Research. "Health Disparities Program." [Online article or information; retrieved July 4, 2007.] http://www.nidcr.nih.gov/Research/Extramural/ClinicalResearch/HealthDisparitiesProgram.htm.

National Institute of Dental and Craniofacial Research. "National Institute of Dental and Craniofacial Research." [Online article or information; retrieved October 29, 2007.] http://www.nidcr.nih.gov/.

National Institute of Diabetes and Digestive and Kidney Diseases

The National Institute of Diabetes and Digestive and Kidney Diseases (NIDDK) is part of the National Institutes of Health (NIH), the nation's leading agency for conducting and supporting biomedical research. As part of its mission to help eliminate health disparities, NIDDK conducts and supports research on diabetes mellitus, obesity, end-stage renal disease, hepatitis C virus (HCV) and liver disease, and diseases of the prostate gland. The institute also recruits and trains African Americans and other minorities for careers in research related to its overall mission, and it disseminates to physicians, health care professionals, and community centers that serve minorities information regarding the latest developments for preventing and treating the diseases and medical conditions that fall within its purview.

NIDDK's mission has changed somewhat over the years, as indicated by its changing name. It was established in 1950 as the National Institute of Arthritis and Metabolic Diseases. In 1972, it was renamed the National Institute of Arthritis, Metabolism and Digestive Diseases, and in 1981, it became the National Institute of Arthritis, Diabetes and Digestive and Kidney Diseases; it acquired its present name and mission in 1986. Since its inception, NIDDK has conducted and supported much of the research related to internal medicine undertaken in the United States, focusing on such diseases and medical conditions as diabetes, obesity, inborn errors of metabolism, endocrine disorders, mineral metabolism, digestive and liver diseases, nutrition, urology and kidney disease, and diseases of the blood and blood-producing organs.

Diabetes mellitus, also known as type 2 diabetes, is one of the leading contributors to health disparities. African American adults are almost twice as likely to suffer from diabetes mellitus as European American adults; moreover, African American children are more than four times as likely to contract diabetes mellitus as European American children. African Americans with diabetes mellitus are almost three times as likely as European Americans who suffer from the disease to suffer from coronary heart disease and certain other complications affecting the small blood vessels. The reasons for these disparities remain unclear; however, some studies have suggested that a genetic component, as well as cultural and behavioral factors, influences the development of certain cardiovascular complications in patients with diabetes mellitus. Consequently, NIDDK conducts and supports research to determine the behavioral, socioeconomic, cultural, metabolic, and physiological reasons for disparities in the incidence of diabetes mellitus in African Americans and other minority populations, particularly the role played by genetics in the development of diabetes-related cardiovascular complications. NIDDK also conducts and supports research to ascertain why diabetes mellitus, which used to be considered an adult disease because of its prevalence among the aged, the obese, and the physically inactive, now affects so many minority children as well.

As of the early 21st century, obesity was the most common nutritional disorder in the United States. Since 1980, Americans in general have been eating more but engaging in less physical work and play. The result is an epidemic of obesity, with approximately 50 percent of the American population being considered overweight or obese. This epidemic seems to be affecting African Americans and other minorities more than European Americans. For example, 65 percent of African American women are considered to be overweight, and more than 10 percent are considered to be obese. Although genetic factors are believed to have contributed to this situation, it is also believed that an even larger role is played by environmental factors such as the ready availability of inexpensive, tasty foods with high contents of sugar and fat. In addition to

The National Institute of Diabetes and Digestive and Kidney Diseases conducts a number of outreach programs, such as this one at Ketcham Elementary School in Washington, D.C., to interest more African American children in careers in medical research. (National Institutes of Health)

conducting and supporting research related to the genetic and physiological aspects of obesity, NIDDK also conducts and supports research related to obesity's environmental aspects as well. This research includes projects that develop effective educational programs to induce all Americans, not just minorities, to eat less and exercise more.

End-stage renal disease is a form of chronic kidney failure that requires some form of replacement therapy such as dialysis or transplant. As of the early 21st century, African Americans were four times as likely to suffer from end-stage renal failure as European Americans. This disparity is partly explained by the fact that African Americans are also more likely to suffer from diabetes mellitus and hypertension, two of the major causes of end-stage renal disease. Moreover, African Americans tend to develop end-stage renal failure seven years earlier, on average, than European Americans. To better understand the mechanisms that contribute to health disparities in terms of this disease, NIDDK established the Family Investigation of Nephropathy and

Diabetes (FIND) study. FIND seeks to identify which genes, if any, are responsible for making certain racial and ethnic subgroups more susceptible to kidney failure, particularly end-stage renal disease. Since African Americans suffer disproportionately from this disease, FIND has included a disproportionately large number of African Americans in its clinical trials. A related project is the African American Study of Kidney Disease and Hypertension (AASK), which investigates to what degree many of the biomedical agents used to treat hypertension—such as beta-adrenergic blockers, calcium channel blockers, and angiotensin-converting enzyme inhibitors—influence the progression of kidney disease caused by hypertension in African Americans. A large portion of the research related to AASK has been performed by African American faculty members and their graduate students at the four historically black medical colleges.

Kidney transplant is the preferred method of treating end-stage renal disease. It is much more difficult, however, for African Americans to receive a donated kidney, in large part because African Americans are much less likely than the general public to donate organs for transplant purposes. Consequently, NIDDK supports the Minority Organ Tissue Transplant Education Program as a means of increasing the number of African Americans and other minorities who donate kidneys and other organs for transplant purposes.

Hepatitis C virus is a major cause of liver disease and a major source of health disparities. African Americans are three times as likely to contract HCV as European Americans but only about one-third as likely to respond positively to the standard antiviral treatments used against HCV. They are also much less likely to receive a donated liver, the only sure cure for end-stage liver disease caused by HCV. NIDDK conducts and supports research to discover why African Americans infected with HCV tend not to respond to treatment with alpha interferon and ribavirin, the standard therapy for HCV. The study looks for answers in differences in viral strain or genotype, immunological factors, and genetic differences in interferon signaling and response pathways. Because most antiviral therapy clinical studies have included too few African Americans as test subjects, this project recruits a disproportionately large number of African Americans so as to test the efficacy of various antiviral agents in African Americans, as well as in other subgroups of the American population.

Benign prostatic hypertrophy (BPH) and chronic prostatitis (CP) are the most common forms of nonmalignant diseases of the prostate. It is known that African American men are much more likely to contract cancer of the prostate than European American men, and it is suspected that the same holds true for BPH and CP, which are commonly found in men with cancer of the prostate. However, it remains to be proven that BPH and CP constitute a health disparity, and so NIDDK conducts and supports research to confirm or deny the suspicion as part of its Chronic Prostatitis Collaborative Research Network. The network's research also studies disparities in the effectiveness of screening programs that test for BPH and CP and the efficacy of various therapies on these diseases in African Americans.

NIDDK also works to eliminate health disparities by recruiting and training minorities to pursue careers in research related to the institute's overall mission. To this end, NIDDK's Office of Minority Health Research Coordination provides financial support to historically black colleges and universities and other minority-serving institutions to help them improve their infrastructure, including classrooms, laboratories, course offerings, faculty, and technology, for teaching students how to conduct basic and clinical research. NIDDK also supports various NIH-wide initiatives to increase the diversity of biomedical research such as Small Grants for Underrepresented Investigators, the Medical Student Research Scholars Program, the National High School Student Summer Research Program, and the Short-Term Education Program for Minority Students.

NIDDK also works to eliminate health disparities with several education and outreach activities. The National Diabetes Education Program and the National Kidney Disease Education Program disseminate culturally sensitive information about how to reduce one's risk of contracting diabetes and kidney disease through churches and community centers that serve African Americans and other minorities. NIDDK also established the Sisters Together: Move More, Eat Better program as an outreach program for African American women to help them reduce their risk of contracting any of the diseases and medical conditions associated with obesity.

See also: Diabetes; Health Disparities; National Institutes of Health; Obesity

REFERENCES AND FURTHER READING

National Institute of Diabetes and Digestive and Kidney Diseases. "National Institute of Diabetes and Digestive and Kidney Diseases." [Online article or information; retrieved October 29, 2007.] http://www2.niddk.nih.gov/.

National Institute of Diabetes and Digestive and Kidney Diseases. "Strategic Plan on Minority Health Disparities." [Online article or information; retrieved July 5, 2007.] http://www.niddk.nih.gov/federal/planning/mstrathealthplan.htm.

National Institute on Drug Abuse

The National Institute on Drug Abuse (NIDA) is part of the National Institutes of Health (NIH), the nation's leading agency for conducting and supporting biomedical research. Established in 1973, NIDA conducts and supports research and research training related to drug abuse, drug addiction, and the prevention and treatment of both. The drugs that fall within NIDA's purview include alcohol and club drugs [Rohypnol and ketamine, cocaine, heroin, inhalants, LSD (acid), marijuana, MDMA (Ecstasy), methamphetamine, PCP/phencyclidine, prescription medications, smoking and nicotine, and anabolic steroids]. With respect to health disparities, NIDA seeks to better understand and address the physiological and behavioral aspects of drug abuse and addiction as they pertain to African Americans and other minorities and to develop culturally specific prevention and treatment methods.

Conventional wisdom holds that African Americans and other racial and ethnic minorities are more likely to use and abuse drugs than European Americans and that drug abuse and addiction are more prevalent in urban rather than in rural environments. Little scientific evidence exists, however, to either confirm or deny these beliefs. In fact, what little evidence there is suggests that European Americans begin using drugs at an earlier age than African Americans or other minorities, that minorities tend to progress to addiction at a faster rate, and that drug abuse and addiction are rapidly becoming as pervasive in rural areas as in big cities. Moreover, although many clinical trials have been conducted to learn more about the physiological effects of drug abuse and addiction, relatively few of these trials have included African Americans or other minorities as test subjects. Consequently, much remains to be known about how drug abuse and addiction affect minorities physiologically and about how those effects differ, if at all, between minorities and European Americans.

In 1993, NIDA established the Special Populations Office to encourage increased research on drug abuse in minority populations and to increase the participation by minorities in drug abuse research, both as researchers and as research subjects. Since then, the office has been instrumental in establishing a number of projects that investigate the incidence and causes of drug abuse and addiction and its consequences in minority populations. For example, the Epidemiological Research on Drug Abuse Program includes, among other things, projects to identify to what degree minority drug users are at risk to contract such diseases and medical conditions as HIV/AIDS and other sexually transmitted diseases, tuberculosis, hepatitis C virus (HCV), difficult or abortive pregnancies, and mental disorders. Other projects seek to develop methods and interventions for preventing drug abuse and addiction among minorities. For example, evidence suggests that African American youths, on average, do not begin to use drugs until their high school years, so the office encourages the development of antidrug educational programs and other drug abuse prevention strategies aimed specifically at African American youths just entering this age group.

The office also encourages the inclusion of a significant number of African Americans and other minorities, especially those from rural areas, in the National Drug Abuse Treatment Clinical Trials Network. Pharmacological stud-

The National Institute on Drug Abuse seeks to know whether or not one's ethnicity makes one more or less susceptible to drug addiction. (National Institutes of Health)

ies indicate that differences exist in the ability of some ethnic populations to metabolize pharmaceutical drugs; so it is important to know whether a particular pharmaceutical-based intervention plan will benefit minorities as well as it would the general population. To this end, the office seeks to increase the number of neuroscience and basic behavioral science studies that examine how specific pharmaceutical-based treatment programs affect the underlying neural and behavioral processes of racial and ethnic minorities.

NIDA also works to eliminate health disparities by recruiting and training more minorities for careers in biomedical research related to the institute's mission. The Historically Black Colleges and Universities (HBCU) Initiative and the Minority Institutions Drug Abuse Research Program provide financial support for HBCUs and other minority-serving institutions that wish to participate in research related to drug abuse and addiction. As part of these programs, NIDA has established centers on drug abuse research at Howard University and Hampton University. It has also made formal arrangements with Howard, North Carolina Central University, and Morgan State University, whereby NIDA scientists and HBCU faculty members and students collaborate in research projects conducted at the HBCUs. The Visiting Scholars Program encourages minority faculty members at HBCUs and other minority-serving institutions to participate in ongoing research at NIDA's campus in Bethesda, Maryland, so that they can learn state-of-the-art research techniques. Summer Research with NIDA provides opportunities for qualified minority high school students and college undergraduates to participate in NIDA-supported research projects at laboratories across the country, and the Minority Recruitment and Training Program provides the same sort of opportunities at NIDA facilities. NIDA also makes use of several NIH-wide initiatives such as the Underrepresented Minority Supplement Program, which provides additional funding to researchers who are already conducting NIDA-supported research so that they can recruit minority researchers to participate.

As part of its overall mission to disseminate information to the general public, NIDA develops and distributes culturally sensitive material to the African American community and other minority communities regarding drug abuse and addiction and how to prevent and treat it. For example, NIDA has created a radio public service announcement campaign on marijuana abuse aimed at African American youths between the ages of 13 and 25, the ages at which they are most likely to begin experimenting with drugs. The institute also develops material for distribution throughout the African American community, such as culturally specific versions of *Preventing Drug Abuse Among Children and Adolescents: A Research-Based Guide*, 2nd ed. (Washington, DC: National Institute on Drug Abuse, no date), *Principles of Drug Addiction Treatment: A Research-Based Guide* (Washington, DC: National Institute on Drug Abuse, 2000), and *NIDA Clinical Toolbox: Science-Based Materials for Drug Abuse Treatment Providers*. (http://www.nida.nih.gov/tb/clinical/clinicaltoolbox.html). The latter publication provides health care providers who cater to minority populations with the latest information on drug treatment.

See also: Hampton University; Historically Black Colleges and Universities; HIV/AIDS; Howard University; Morgan State University; National Institutes of Health; North Carolina Central University

REFERENCES AND FURTHER READING

National Institute on Drug Abuse. "National Institute on Drug Abuse." [Online article or information; retrieved October 29, 2007]. http://www.nida.nih.gov/.

National Institute on Drug Abuse. "Strategic Plan on Reducing Health Disparities." [Online article or information; retrieved July 9, 2007.] http://www.drugabuse.gov/StrategicPlan/HealthStratPlan.html.

National Institute of Environmental Health Sciences

The National Institute of Environmental Health Sciences (NIEHS) is part of the National Institutes of Health (NIH), the nation's leading agency for conduct-

The National Institute of Environmental Health Sciences studies how environmental pollution affects the health of people living in our nation's inner cities. (Steven R. McCaw/National Institutes of Health)

ing and supporting biomedical research. Founded in 1969, NIEHS conducts and supports research and research training related to how the environment influences the development and progression of human disease. In terms of health disparities, NIEHS investigates the interrelationships among poverty, environmental pollution, and health. It also recruits and trains minority scientists for careers in research related to the institute's areas of interest, and it works for environmental justice in minority communities.

The use of agricultural chemicals, especially pesticides, has increased greatly over the last several decades, but their effect on human health is still poorly understood. NIEHS conducts an Agricultural Health Study of farmers, pesticide applicators, and their families to determine the health consequences of long-term exposure to agricultural chemicals. Because many of these agricultural workers are blacks, the study includes a significant sampling of African Americans. The study investigates how agricultural chemicals affect pregnancy, childhood development, and the autoimmune system, as well as how they contribute to the development and progression of asthma and other respiratory conditions, degenerative retinal disease, and neurological diseases. Of particular interest to the study's researchers is the pesticide dieldrin, which has been linked with abnormally high incidences of breast cancer in African American women.

NIEHS supports a number of studies related to the development of asthma and other respiratory ailments in African Americans and other minorities living in the nation's big cities. The Five Cities Study assesses the danger posed to respiratory function of inner-city minority children by ozone, acid aerosols, and particulate air pollution. The Inner-City Asthma Study seeks to develop methods for reducing the incidence of asthma in inner-city minority youth caused by allergens and environmental tobacco smoke. Developing a Geographic Framework for Studying Respiratory Health in Harlem investigates two African American communities in New York City in terms of the health dangers posed by long-term exposure to diesel exhaust from trucks and buses and to soot from smokestack emissions. The Community-Based Prevention/ Intervention Research (CBPIR) Program studies the contribution to asthma made by exposure to cockroaches and dust allergens. The National Allergen Study investigates the levels of major allergens found in the homes of minorities across the nation and determines to what degree these allergens contribute to respiratory ailments.

Lead is a common contaminant of inner-city environments; so NIEHS supports a number of projects to eliminate lead's deleterious effect on the health of urban minorities. The Treatment of Lead-Exposed Children Clinical Trial tests the effectiveness of a drug known as succimer on reversing the long-term neurobehavioral consequences of too much lead in the blood. One NIEHS study identified a correlation between low birth weight, a problem common among inner-city minorities, and high levels of lead in the mother's bones, and others seek methods for reducing such lead levels. Other NIEHS studies have demonstrated a correlation between high levels of lead in the bones or blood with hypertension and kidney disease, two major contributors to health disparities. The CBPIR Program also funds two projects for reducing lead levels in minority children.

Recent evidence suggests that African Americans and other minorities are disproportionately vulnerable to hazardous air pollutants such as polycyclic aromatic hydrocarbons and environmental tobacco smoke, both of which are known to cause lung cancer. NIEHS's Environmental Genome Project addresses this issue by investigating whether the minute genetic differences in African Americans and other minorities are different enough to make them more susceptible to environmental disease.

Many rural minority communities rely heavily on fishing as a major source of their dietary needs. Unfortunately, many rural waters and hence the fish that live in them are tainted with polychlorinated biphenyls (PCBs) and other toxic contaminants. NIEHS studies have demonstrated that fetuses in mothers with a high blood level of PCBs suffer from several developmental problems later in life, such as poor short-term memory during the preschool years and poor long-term memory up to the age of 11.

Systemic lupus erythematosus (SLE) is an autoimmune disease that causes severe damage to the kidneys, joints, and other tissues. Although SLE can affect anyone, the majority of those who suffer from SLE are African American women. The causes of SLE are unknown, but it has been suggested that environmental factors play a role in its development. To further investigate this theory, NIEHS supports the Carolina Lupus Study. The study considers the role played by such environmental factors as silica dust, ultraviolet light, solvents, heavy metals, and pesticides on the development of SLE in black and white women in North and South Carolina.

Recent evidence has suggested that exposure to endocrine disruptors (environmental compounds that can interfere with natural hormonal processes) increases a woman's risk of developing breast cancer, especially if she is an African American. Endocrine disruptors include the organochlorine pesticides such as DDT and dieldrin, certain plasticizers such as phthalates, and various industrial compounds such as cadmium, lead, styrene, dioxin, and PCBs. NIEHS's Long Island Breast Cancer Study investigates the possible link between high incidences of breast cancer and high levels of exposure to organochlorine pesticides and air pollutants among minority women living in the urban environment of New York's Long Island. Similar studies of the connections between endocrine disruptors and breast cancer, as well as other forms of cancer and reproduction-related disorders, are being conducted among African American women living in rural North Carolina and in the inner city of Los Angeles.

NIEHS also seeks to eliminate health disparities by recruiting and training more African Americans and other underrepresented minorities for careers as environmental health science researchers. To this end, NIEHS supports the Advanced Research Cooperation in Environmental Health (ARCH) program. ARCH provides assistance to historically black colleges and universities (HBCUs) and other minority-serving institutions that want to upgrade their capability to conduct high-level environmental health science research. It does so by arranging partnerships between HBCUs and major research institutions. As of 2007, Xavier University of Louisiana and Southern University had entered into such partnerships with Tulane University and the University of Texas Medical Branch at Galveston, respectively. The institute supports the Meyerhoff Scholars Program at the University of Maryland Baltimore County, a major producer of African American scientists. NIEHS also collaborates with a group of faculty researchers at the Morehouse School of Medicine and provides special training opportunities for students at Morehouse College and Durham Technical Community College (North Carolina), the latter being near the NIEHS campus in North Carolina's Research Triangle Park. The Minority Worker Training Program trains young people living near hazardous waste sites or contaminated properties for careers in remediation and environmental health. The K–12 Environmental Health Science Education Program provides a better understanding of environmental principles to students in elementary and secondary schools whose student bodies are predominantly minorities, with the hope of instilling in these students an interest in pursuing a career in environmental health science. NIEHS also supports a number of NIH-wide initiatives to increase the number of minority scientists, such as the National Research Service Award for Predoctoral Fellowships for Minority Students and Research Supplements for Underrepresented Minorities.

Many minority communities have been victimized over the years by environmental polluters, and yet these communities often lack the resources to properly address the resultant issues. NIEHS supports the Environmental Justice: Partnership for Communication Program as a way to redress this problem. The program brings together research scientists, health care providers, and community leaders in partnerships that can use scientific evidence and political clout to elicit action from local governments and, in some cases, the polluters themselves. NIEHS's Mississippi Delta Project attempts to bring environmental justice to minority communities along the lower Mississippi River, which for decades has served as a major dumping ground for petroleum refineries and other industrial polluters.

See also: Asthma; Cancer; Health Disparities; Historically Black Colleges and Universities; Meyerhoff Scholars Program; Morehouse School of Medicine; National Institutes of Health; Southern University and A&M College System; Xavier University of Louisiana

REFERENCES AND FURTHER READING

National Institute of Environmental Health Sciences. "Environmental Health Topics." [Online article or information; retrieved October 29, 2007.] http://www.niehs.nih.gov/health/topics/index.cfm.

National Institute of Environmental Health Sciences. "National Institute of Environmental Health Sciences." [Online article or information; retrieved October 29, 2007.] http://www.niehs.nih.gov/.

National Institute of General Medical Sciences

The National Institute of General Medical Sciences (NIGMS) is part of the National Institutes of Health (NIH), the nation's leading agency for conducting and supporting biomedical research. Founded in 1962, NIGMS does not conduct biomedical research projects of its own; rather, it supports the development of new methods, techniques, and equipment for conducting cutting-edge research in the areas of biochemistry, bioinformatics, biophysics, cell biology, computational biology, developmental biology, genetics, pharmacology, and physiology. In terms of health disparities, the institute's Division of Minority Opportunities in Research (MORE) supports research and research training programs that increase the number of minority scientists conducting research in these areas. These programs include the Minority Access to Research Careers (MARC) Program, the Minority Biomedical Research Support (MBRS) Program, the Bridges to the Future Programs, and several career development and research fellowships and awards.

MARC programs allow historically black colleges and universities (HBCUs) and other minority-serving institutions to enhance their ability to train students for careers in biomedical research. Undergraduate Student Training in Academic Research (U*STAR) Awards support undergraduate biomedical programs at institutions that offer bachelor's degrees in the biomedical sciences. Individual National Research Service Awards (NRSA) support outstanding U*STAR graduates who wish to pursue a graduate degree in the biomedical sciences. Post-Baccalaureate Research Education Program Awards and Individual Predoctoral Kirschstein-NRSA Fellowships enable minority students with bachelor's degrees in the biomedical sciences to pursue a doctorate in a related field. Faculty Predoctoral Fellowships support junior faculty members at HBCUs and other minority-serving institutions who wish to obtain a research doctorate in a biomedical science, thus making themselves better prepared to train their students for research careers, and Faculty Senior Fellowships allow senior faculty to update their research skills and/or move into new areas of research through a year-long period of intensive research in a state-of-the-art research environment.

MBRS programs support faculty members at HBCUs and other minority-serving institutions who wish to conduct cutting-edge biomedical or behavioral research. The Pilot Project Award supports junior faculty researchers who wish to change the focus of their research. Support of Competitive Research (SCORE) and the Research Advancement Award assist faculty researchers who have published their results in peer-reviewed publications but who have yet to obtain funding from non-NIH sources. Research Continuance Awards aids senior faculty researchers who are published but who now wish to conduct research on a part-time basis. Institutional Development Awards allow institutions to provide state-of-the-art laboratories and other facilities to their faculty researchers who conduct biomedical and behavioral research. The Research Initiative for Scientific Enhancement and Initiative for Maximizing Student Diversity programs enhance the ability of minority faculty to conduct research by supporting the training and research activities of their graduate students, thus making these students ready and able to participate in their mentors' research projects.

The Bridges to the Future Programs includes the Bridges to the Baccalaureate Degree and the Bridges to the Doctoral Degree initiatives. The Baccalaureate program helps minority students make the transition from two-year junior or community colleges to four-year colleges and universities offering undergraduate degrees related to the biomedical or behavioral sciences. The

Doctoral program helps minority students make the transition from universities offering the MS degree as the terminal degree in the biomedical sciences to universities offering the PhD degree.

In addition to MARC, MBRS, and Bridges to the Future, MORE provides fellowships and supplemental awards to institutions with substantial minority enrollments to permit them to enhance their research and research training capabilities. The Faculty Development Award funds faculty members with a PhD degree in a biomedical science who seek to conduct biomedical research at a research-intensive laboratory. Fellowship Awards for Minority Students support highly qualified minority students working toward a PhD degree in the biomedical or behavioral sciences and who intend to embark on careers in biomedical research. Institutional Research and Academic Career Development Awards help postdoctoral researchers at research-intensive institutions who also teach at an HBCU or other minority-serving institution so as to enhance the opportunity to establish collaborations between the two types of institutions. Research Supplements to Promote Diversity in Health-Related Research provide additional funding to researchers who already hold grants from NIGMS to encourage them to include minority students and researchers on their research teams.

See also: Biochemistry; Health Disparities; Historically Black Colleges and Universities; Minority Access to Research Careers; Minority Biomedical Research Support; National Institutes of Health

REFERENCES AND FURTHER READING

National Institute of General Medical Sciences. "Minority Programs." [Online article or information; retrieved July 9, 2007.] http://www.nigms.nih.gov/Minority/.

National Institute of General Medical Sciences. "National Institute of General Medical Sciences." [Online article or information; retrieved October 29, 2007.] http://www.nigms.nih.gov/.

National Institute of Mental Health

The National Institute of Mental Health (NIMH) is part of the National Institutes of Health (NIH), the nation's leading agency for conducting and supporting biomedical research. Established in 1946, NIMH seeks to reduce the burden of mental illness and behavioral disorders by conducting and supporting research related to the mind, brain, and behavior. In terms of health disparities, the institute conducts research concerning how African Americans respond to stress and other traumatic situations, how African Americans respond to various pharmaceutical therapies for mental illnesses and related conditions, and how to make mental health services more accessible to African Americans and more responsive to their needs.

At the turn of the century, mental disorders and drug abuse disorders were on the rise among the general population in the United States. At the time, no data existed to suggest whether African Americans and other minorities are particularly susceptible to mental and behavioral disorders; however, studies showed conclusively that minorities were much less likely to seek treatment for such disorders. Consequently, NIMH undertook a survey to determine the socioeconomic factors, such as cost, language, stigma, fear, distance to treatment, and misperceptions by clinicians, that prevent minorities from seeking mental health treatment. The institute also supports research to develop effective prevention and treatment programs that take into account these and other socioeconomic factors.

Behavioral studies have demonstrated that African Americans and other minorities often cope with stress in ways that differ from the majority population. NIMH conducts research that studies the basic psychological processes related to stress, trauma, and coping to better understand how these differences affect mental health in minority as well as majority populations. The institute also works to develop culturally sensitive interventions to reduce the stigma of mental illness among minorities so as to encourage them to take advantage of the appropriate mental health services as early as possible.

One of the leading causes of death among African American women is AIDS. Moreover, women who are infected with HIV/AIDS are likely to have children or spouses who are also infected and for whom the women are often the primary caregivers. The stress of experiencing one's own slow death while witnessing the slow deaths of loved ones is extraordinarily stressful, and yet few African American women who have HIV/AIDS seek mental health services. NIMH conducts research to better understand not only how the social and cultural context in which minorities live affect decision making, impulsivity, and substance abuse, all of which contribute to risky behaviors that are likely to result in HIV infection, but also how best to develop methods that prevent HIV infection by taking these factors into account.

Minute genetic differences owing to race and ethnicity are known as single nucleotide polymorphisms (SNPs). SNPs in the enzymes that metabolize pharmaceutical drugs create major problems for the physicians and other health care professionals who prescribe such drugs as treatment for mental and behavioral disorders. Often, SNPs are responsible for rendering certain drug therapies useless, if not dangerous, for certain individuals. NIMH supports pharmacogenetic research to identify the SNPs responsible for these responses and to develop methods for neutralizing them so as to make drug therapies effective for all patients regardless of race or ethnicity. As part of this effort, the institute works to increase the number of African Americans and other minorities who volunteer to serve as subjects during clinical trials of new pharmaceutical drugs for treating mental and behavioral disorders.

NIMH also addresses health disparities by recruiting and training more African Americans and other minorities for research careers in areas of interest to the institute. Not only do minorities represent an underutilized source of potential medical researchers, but also minority researchers have demonstrated a particularly strong interest in addressing health disparities. NIMH seeks to help historically black colleges and universities and other minority-serving institutions that offer degrees in the biomedical sciences establish research partnerships with majority research and academic institutions that conduct significant amounts of biomedical research. Such partnerships provide minority-serving institutions with access to research expertise and mentors who are able to help minority faculty members become better researchers, as well as better teachers of research methods. The NIMH Minority Research Infrastructure Support Program provides funding for minority-serving institutions to improve their laboratories and other research facilities so as to enhance their ability to teach students how to conduct biomedical research, while the NIMH Career Opportunities in Research Education Program provides training for qualified high school students and college undergraduates in areas relevant to mental health. The institute also supports a number of NIH-wide initiatives to increase the number of minority medical investigators, such as the Research Supplements to Promote Diversity in Health-Related Research, which provide additional funding to researchers who already hold grants from NIMH to encourage them to include minority students and researchers on their research teams.

See also: Health Disparities; Historically Black Colleges and Universities; HIV/AIDS; National Institutes of Health

REFERENCES AND FURTHER READING

National Institute of Mental Health. "Five-Year Strategic Plan for Reducing Health Disparities." [Online article or information; retrieved July 12, 2007.] http://www.nimh.nih.gov/about/strategic-planning-reports/nimh-five-year-strategic-plan-for-reducing-health-disparities.pdf.

National Institute of Mental Health. "National Institute of Mental Health." [Online article or information; retrieved October 29, 2007.] http://www.nimh.nih.gov/.

National Institute of Neurological Disorders and Stroke

The National Institute of Neurological Disorders and Stroke (NINDS) is part of the National Institutes of Health (NIH), the nation's leading agency for conducting and supporting biomedical research. NINDS conducts and supports basic and clinical research related to the brain, spinal cord, and peripheral nerves, as well as to their development, degeneration and regeneration, and disorders and diseases. In terms of health disparities, NINDS focuses its research on stroke, the neurological complications associated with HIV/AIDS and diabetes, the treatment and management of chronic pain disorders, the cognitive and emotional health of children, and epilepsy. NINDS also works to reduce health disparities by recruiting and training more African Americans and other minorities for careers in research related to the institute's areas of interest and by including more minorities in clinical trials related to neurological disorders.

NINDS was established in 1950 as the National Institute of Neurological Diseases and Blindness. In 1968, its blindness-related research became the nucleus of the newly formed National Eye Institute, and it acquired its present name. As of 2007, research activity at NINDS focused on the entire range of neurological disorders; in addition to the diseases and medical conditions already mentioned, NINDS investigates Alzheimer's disease and other dementias, amyotrophic lateral sclerosis, head and spinal cord injuries, Huntington's disease, Parkinson's disease, multiple sclerosis, muscular dystrophy, and neurofibromatosis, among others.

Stroke (the loss of brain function due to an interruption of the blood supply to all or part of the brain) occurs at a higher incidence among African Americans than in the general population. Moreover, stroke tends to occur in African Americans at an earlier age, on average, and is 80 percent more likely to result in death. To learn more about this health disparity, NINDS conducted stroke surveillance studies among multiethnic communities in New York City and the Baltimore-Washington metropolis that investigated stroke incidence and risk factors for strokes resulting from hemorrhaging and ischemia (a restriction of the blood supply owing to a defect in the blood vessels). It also conducted the African American Antiplatelet Stroke Prevention Study, a community network for recruiting African Americans to volunteer for clinical trials related to stroke. The institute supports the Stroke and Cerebrovascular Disease Prevention–Intervention Research Program at the Morehouse School of Medicine, which focuses on stroke as it relates to African Americans.

At the turn of the twenty-first century, almost 70 percent of all AIDS patients were minorities. Moreover, although the rate of incidence seemed to be dropping among certain populations, it was on the rise among African Americans, particularly women. To make matters worse, AIDS patients often suffer from dementia and other neurological complications that apparently are brought on by the disease's progression; these complications are known collectively as neuroAIDS. NINDS supports research by the Collaborative Neurological Sciences (CNS) HIV Antiretroviral Therapy Effects Research project, which studies the rate of incidence of neuroAIDS among minorities, as well as research by the Neurological AIDS Research Consortium, which attempts to identify genetic polymorphisms that might predispose certain racial or ethnic minorities to contracting neuroAIDS. The institute also supports the Manhattan HIV Brain Bank, the California NeuroAIDS Tissue Network, and the National NeuroAIDS Tissue Consortium, which ensure that researchers have access to ample supplies of racially and ethnically diverse tissue and fluids from the brain and spinal cord.

At the turn of the century, the rate of incidence of diabetes among African Americans was 70 percent higher than for European Americans. Moreover, studies suggested that leg amputations resulting from diabetic complications, which are normally an indicator of neurological problems brought on by the progression of diabetes, occur more frequently among diabetics who are minorities. NINDS supports research to determine whether the prevalence of lower extremity amputation among minorities is related to the development of neurological problems such as sensory-motor neuropathy or to other considerations. Such research includes Specialized Center Grant Cooperative Agreements, which support research conducted by minority faculty members and students at historically black colleges and universities (HBCUs) and other minority-serving institutions concerning the neurological complications of diabetes in minority populations.

Studies suggest that chronic pain disorders such as migraine headaches may be more prevalent in minority populations. Other studies suggest that minorities have different definitions of unacceptable levels of pain and that these definitions induce minorities not to seek medical care for pain resulting from neurological causes. To answer these and related questions, NINDS supports research at the Pain Research Consortium at NIH; part of the consortium's mission is to assess ethnic differences in response to pain and to identify treatments and strategies for managing chronic pain that are culturally sensitive and appropriate.

The normal cognitive and emotional development of urban minority children is challenged by a number of factors. These factors include exposure to environmental toxins such as lead, high rates of premature labor resulting in low-birth-weight babies, neglect, and domestic and community violence. Studies have demonstrated that children growing up in these conditions often develop some of the symptoms of anxiety and stress associated with post-traumatic stress disorder such as nightmares, emotional detachment, and clinical depression. NINDS supports research that investigates the linkages between environment, including prenatal and postnatal experiences, and normal and dysfunctional behavioral and neural development, especially as they relate to the lifelong health problems to which minorities are particularly susceptible.

At the turn of the century, studies suggested that African Americans of all ages were about 25 percent more likely than the general population to experience one or more epileptic seizures and to first experience an epileptic seizure at an earlier age. Elderly African Americans are four times more likely to suffer from status epilepticus, which is characterized by continuous or repetitive seizures, than the general population. Although some studies have suggested that this health disparity might be caused by socioeconomic differences and other factors such as nutrition and exposure to violence, other studies suggest that genetics might play a more important role. Consequently, NINDS supports research to learn more about genetic and other factors that result in an individual's increased susceptibility to epilepsy. This research includes the Epilepsy Clinical Research Program, which studies the pharmacological effect of antiepileptic drugs in older minorities, and the Multi-center Study of Idiopathic Generalized Epilepsy, which tests for differences in susceptibility between African Americans and European Americans. NINDS also supports the Medical College of Virginia Epilepsy Research Center, which studies status epilepticus in the African American community of Richmond, Virginia, as well as studies that look for connections between epilepsy and other medical conditions that contribute to health disparities, such as alcoholism, cardiovascular disease, and sickle cell disease.

One of the best ways to reduce health disparities is to recruit and train more African Americans and other minorities into careers as medical researchers, because minority researchers have demonstrated a greater interest in working to solve health disparities. To this end, NINDS supports a number of programs to enhance the ability of HBCUs and other minority-serving institutions to train their students for careers in biomedical research. The Developmental Neuroscience Research Program has established an exploratory neuroscience research center at the Morehouse School of Medicine, and the Specialized Neuroscience Research Program has contributed to significant improvements in the laboratory facilities and other research infrastructure related to neuroscience research at Howard University and Meharry Medical College. NINDS also supports programs that help individual minorities receive the education and training they need to begin or sustain a research career in neuroscience. The Society for Neuroscience Travel Fellowship, which is funded by NINDS, provides predoctoral and postdoctoral minority researchers with the opportunity to attend various seminars and enrichment activities and to be mentored by a senior neuroscience researcher. CNS Awards support minority faculty at minority-serving institutions as they develop independent research programs at their schools. The Training Program for Physicians provides minority physicians with subspecialty training in clinical and basic research in neuroscience. The Mini-Sabbaticals Program allows minority scientists to participate in ongoing research projects at NINDS facilities in Rockville, Maryland, as a way to enhance their scientific and research skills. Internships in Brain and Nervous System Research is a summer program at NINDS for qualified minority high school, undergraduate, graduate, and medical students. NINDS supports the establishment of education programs for minority neuroscience scholars programs through national scientific societies, such as the Society for Neuroscience, as a means of including such societies in efforts to diversify the pool of neuroscience researchers. Finally, NINDS makes use of a number of NIH-wide initiatives to recruit and train minority researchers, such as the NIH Research Supplements for Underrepresented Minorities Program.

See also: Cardiovascular Disease; Diabetes; Health Disparities; Historically Black Colleges and Universities; HIV/AIDS; Howard University; Meharry Medical College; Morehouse School of Medicine; National Eye Institute; National Institutes of Health; Sickle Cell Disease; Society for Neuroscience

REFERENCES AND FURTHER READING

National Institute of Neurological Disorders and Stroke. "Five-Year Strategic Plan on Health Disparities." [Online article or information; retrieved July 12, 2007.] http://www.ninds.nih.gov/about_ninds/plans/disparities.htm.
National Institute of Neurological Disorders and Stroke. "National Institute of Neurological Disorders and Stroke." [Online article or information; retrieved October 29, 2007.] http://www.ninds.nih.gov/.

National Institutes of Health

The National Institutes of Health (NIH) is the nation's leading agency for conducting and supporting research and research training in the biomedical sciences. NIH conducts and supports a number of research and research training programs that are designed to reduce and ultimately eliminate health disparities in the United States.

NIH was established in 1887 on Staten Island, New York, as the Laboratory of Hygiene. Its primary duty was to check immigrants from Europe for infectious diseases. Four years later, the laboratory was moved to Washington, D.C., renamed the Hygienic Laboratory, and charged with investigating infections and contagious diseases across the nation. In 1930, the laboratory became known as the National Institute of Health, and it moved its facilities to Bethesda, Maryland, where it remains today. By 1948, a number of other institutes devoted to medical research had been established, and that same year, they were placed under the aegis of NIH, now known as the National Institutes of Health. As of 2007, NIH consisted of more than two dozen institutes and centers that conduct and support cutting-edge research related to aging, alcohol abuse and alcoholism, allergies, arthritis, bioengineering, the blood, cancer, child health, complementary and alternative medicine, deafness and other communications disorders, dental and craniofacial diseases, diabetes, digestive and kidney diseases, drug abuse, environmental health sci-

The National Institutes of Health conducts or sponsors the majority of medical research related to minority health disparities. (National Institutes of Health)

ence, the eyes, the heart, human development, infectious and contagious diseases, the lungs, general medical sciences, genetics, mental health, minority health and health disparities, musculoskeletal and skin diseases, neurological disorders and stroke, and nursing.

The Minority Health and Health Disparities Research and Education Act of 2000 established the National Center on Minority Health and Health Disparities (NCMHD) at NIH. Passage of the act was prompted by the fact that, over the previous 20 years, the health of Americans in general had improved significantly, but the health of minorities in general was not improving at the same rate. Moreover, certain diseases and medical conditions such as asthma, cancer, cardiovascular disease, diabetes, hypertension, infant mortality, mental illness, obesity, sexually transmitted diseases, and stroke were plaguing minority communities at significantly higher rates than the general public, and yet medical experts were at a loss to explain why. NCMHD was tasked with developing a plan and a budget whereby NIH might begin investigating health disparities with the intention of reducing them and eventually getting rid of them altogether.

In 2002, NCMHD issued the NIH Strategic Research Plan and Budget to Reduce and Ultimately Eliminate Health Disparities. The plan included provisions to address health disparities in three ways: (1) conduct research into the diseases and medical conditions that contribute the most to health disparities, (2) develop research training programs for African Americans and other minorities underrepresented in the field of medical research so that they could conduct research concerning health disparities, and (3) implement outreach and education programs to disseminate the results of NIH research to minority communities and to inspire minority youths to consider careers as medical researchers. The plan called on each NIH institute and center to develop a plan of its own, whereby it would work to reduce health disparities within its areas of interest and cooperate with other institutes and centers concerning diseases and medical conditions that cut across institutional boundaries.

As of 2007, all of NIH's institutes and centers were well on the way to implementing their plans for reducing health disparities. In addition to conducting biomedical research regarding health disparities, the various institutes were also examining the effects of socioeconomic status, education level, access to and the quality of health care, racial and ethnic discrimination, and cultural issues as factors that contribute to health disparities. For the most part, health disparities research was conducted by the individual institutes but with participation by NCMHD in areas related to funding and interinstitute coordination. Budgetary amounts varied from one institute to another, depending on the degree to which their areas of interest included health disparities, but the initial annual budget (fiscal year 2002) for addressing health disparities for NIH as a whole was more than $2.5 billion.

See also: Asthma; Cancer; Cardiovascular Disease; Diabetes; Health Disparities; Medical Research; National Center on Minority Health and Health Disparities; Obesity

REFERENCES AND FURTHER READING

National Center on Minority Health and Health Disparities. "National Institutes of Health Strategic Research Plan and Budget to Reduce and Ultimately Eliminate Health Disparities, Volume I." [Online article or information; retrieved July 11, 2007.] http://ncmhd.nih.gov/our_programs/strategic/pubs/VolumeI_031003EDrev.pdf

National Institutes of Health. "National Institutes of Health." [Online article or information; retrieved October 29, 2007.] http://www.nih.gov/

National Medical Association

The National Medical Association (NMA) is the foremost national professional organization for black physicians. Calling itself The Conscience of American Medicine, the NMA works to increase the number of blacks practicing medicine and to improve health care for minorities and underserved populations. In terms of scientific research, it funds and operates the W. Montague Cobb/NMA Health Policy Institute (Cobb Institute), which focuses on the conditions affecting health that are more prevalent among African Americans than among the general U.S. population, such as cancer, cardiovascular disease, diabetes, environmental health, HIV/AIDS, and violence.

The NMA was founded in 1895 in Chicago, by a number of black physicians, chief among them the noted surgeon Daniel Hale Williams, who had been denied admission to the American Medical Association because of their race. Throughout its history, the NMA has worked to ensure that black Americans receive equitable health care; for example, the NMA was a driving force behind the establishment of the federal Medicare and Medicaid programs, which help pay for medical treatment and prescription drugs for low-income patients who otherwise would have to do without. As of 2006, the group's membership had risen to more than 30,000, enough to sustain a permanent staff, a national headquarters in Washington, D.C., a professional journal devoted to medical education and research, and the Cobb Institute.

One way the NMA delivers better health care to black Americans is by sponsoring a strenuous program of continuing medical education for its member physicians. Presented annually at the national convention and various regional conventions, as well as at meetings of the state and local societies, these programs keep physicians up-to-date on the latest developments in 23 medical specialties from aerospace medicine to urology. In addition, the organization publishes the *Journal of the National Medical Association*, which, since 1909, has featured articles addressing medical news, opinions, case reports, studies, book reviews, and guest editorials. For example, the May 2006 issue included articles about the association between race and breast cancer stages and the challenges that medical professionals face in dealing with the aftermath of Hurricane Katrina, which devastated the lives of many African Americans living along the Gulf Coast. Since its inception, the journal has provided African American medical scientists with a venue for publishing the results of their cutting-edge research.

Another way the NMA advances its organizational goal is to advocate national health care policies that improve the quality and availability of health care for blacks and other minority and underserved populations. To this end, the NMA conducts the National Colloquium on African American Health as a vehicle for influencing the national health agenda in favor of minorities. Yet another way is to conduct public education programs to prevent health problems and to promote healthy lifestyles among those same populations. For example, the NMA has conducted consumer awareness programs in cancer, infant immunizations, radon, secondhand smoke, smoking cessation, and women's health. It also conducts a program, known as Project IMPACT, to

THE MEDICAL AND SURGICAL OBSERVER

The Medical and Surgical Observer (1892) was the first medical journal devoted exclusively to the professional needs of African American physicians and surgeons. Although it remained in publication for only 18 months, it paved the way for the publication of other, more successful medical journals for black doctors. It also played an important role in the establishment of the National Medical Association, the nation's premier professional organization for African American physicians and surgeons.

The Medical and Surgical Observer was founded in 1892 by Miles V. Lynk, an African American doctor who practiced medicine in the black community of Jackson, Tennessee. Lynk was concerned that the leading medical journals of the day ignored the health concerns of African Americans and the professional needs of the African American doctors who served them. Lynk perceived that a journal devoted to the medical issues pertaining to African Americans would do much to improve the education of the physicians who read it, thus resulting in better treatment for their patients. Serving as the journal's editor, publisher, chief contributor, and advertising manager, Lynk published articles pertaining to black patients' case reports, new treatments for medical conditions that were particularly prevalent in black communities, the personal chronicles of black physicians, and professional ethics. He also reprinted articles of professional interest from the nation's leading medical journals. The journal did not focus on the issue of racism that had led to its founding, but its pages discussed various aspects of racism, particularly the fact that many a black surgeon had to turn over some of his more difficult cases to white surgeons, because the racist policies of the local hospital prevented black surgeons from entering the operating room. Perhaps most important, the journal served as a means for African American physicians across the South, many of whom were the only black doctors practicing in their town or county, to learn about one another and to establish an informal professional network.

The Medical and Surgical Observer focused on two issues: medical education as it pertained to African Americans and the professional development of African American doctors. At the time, six medical colleges admitted black students, and Lynk published frequent updates on what those colleges were doing in terms of their admissions standards and the quality of the physicians and surgeons they turned out. He also called on all of the six colleges to maintain rigor in their curriculums, because to do otherwise would only compromise the health of the black doctors' patients. Lynk also called repeatedly for the establishment of a national medical association that would admit African Americans, especially since the nation's largest association for physicians and surgeons, the American Medical Association, refused to admit blacks no matter what their qualifications were. In 1895, such an organization, the National Medical Association, was formed in Chicago.

Despite its service to the African American medical community, *The Medical and Surgical Observer* did not survive for long. It failed to attract enough advertisers and subscribers to stay in business, and it ceased publication in 1894.

See also: American Medical Association; National Medical Association

REFERENCES AND FURTHER READING

Tennessee Online, "Tennessee History Classroom: Dr. Miles V. Lynk." [Online article or information; retrieved July 23, 2007.] http://www.tennesseehistory.com/class/Lynk.htm.

increase the awareness, knowledge, and participation of African American physicians and patients in all aspects of biomedical research and clinical trials. Recent pharmacological research, for example, has demonstrated significant genetic differences among racial and ethnic groups concerning metabolism, clinical effectiveness, and side effects as they relate to many clinically important drugs. Therefore, Project IMPACT aims to bring such differences to light during clinical trials, not afterward, so that the health concerns of minorities can be better addressed.

The NMA's most serious commitment to medical research is the Cobb Institute. Founded in 2004 after five years of planning and named after the noted black physical anthropologist W. Montague Cobb, the institute's mission is to address the long-standing problems of health disparities among ethnically diverse populations in the United States and to explore solutions to improve the health status of all Americans through policy development, education, and research. To this end, the institute focuses on medical conditions such as asthma, cancer, cardiovascular disease, diabetes, HIV/AIDS, and obesity, all of which are more prevalent or more likely to result in death among the African American population than among the U.S. population at large. The institute's activities are conducted by four major centers: the Multicultural Health Center; the Research, Surveillance and Professional Education Center; the Community/Public Media Information Center; and the Mobilization and Advocacy Center.

See also: American Medical Association; Asthma; Cancer; Cardiovascular Disease; Cobb, W. Montague; Diabetes; Health Disparities; HIV/AIDS; Obesity; Williams, Daniel H.

References and Further Reading

National Medical Association. "The National Medical Association: The Conscience of American Medicine." [Online article or information; retrieved May 30, 2006.] http://www.nmanet.org.

Wright, Charles H. *The National Medical Association Demands Equal Opportunity: Nothing More, Nothing Less.* Southfield, MI: Charro Book Co., 1995.

National Organization for the Professional Advancement of Black Chemists and Chemical Engineers

The National Organization for the Professional Advancement of Black Chemists and Chemical Engineers (NOBCChE) is devoted to increasing the number of African American chemists in both academia and private industry. To this end, NOBCChE (pronounced No-be-shay) provides support for professional black chemists and chemical engineers looking to enter or advance in the fields of chemistry and chemical engineering. It recruits minority students into both fields and provides financial assistance to minority students seeking degrees in chemistry or chemical engineering.

In 1972, five chemists and two chemical engineers—Joseph Cannon, Lloyd N. Ferguson, William M. Jackson, William Guillory, Henry C. McBay, Charles Merideth, and James Porter—formed an ad hoc committee to establish a professional organization for African Americans working in the fields of academic and industrial chemistry. Following an enthusiastic response from their black colleagues, the group formed an executive board in 1973 and convened the organization's first annual meeting the following year in New Orleans; at this meeting, Guillory was elected NOBCChE's first president. As of 2006, the organization boasted 32 chapters at colleges and universities, another 20 chapters for chemists and chemical engineers working in private industry, and a national headquarters on the campus of Howard University in Washington, D.C.

NOBCChE's major vehicle for promoting chemical research has been the annual meeting. Held every year since the first one in 1974, annual meetings have included the presentation of more than 100 technical papers covering virtually every aspect of chemistry. One important aspect of the annual meeting's commitment to research is a health symposium concerning a particular topic related to biochemistry. The purposes of the health symposium are to increase awareness of certain medical conditions among the African American community, to encourage more blacks to participate in clinical tests of potential pharmaceutical treatments for those conditions, and to encourage black chemists just entering the profession to take up the challenges presented by a particular condition. The health symposium at the 2006 annual meeting addressed clinical depression in the African American community; in addition to discussing why clinical depression often goes undiagnosed in the black community, the expert panel also discussed the science behind some of the commonly prescribed antidepressant pharmaceuticals. Previous health symposiums had addressed breast and prostate cancer, coronary heart disease, and diabetes, to name a few.

NOBCChE conducts several programs at its annual meeting as part of its outreach to minority students who might be considering careers as chemists. The NOBCChE Teachers Workshop presents K–12 science teachers with teaching strategies and techniques designed to improve the test scores of minority and underrepresented students, thus encouraging them to pursue careers in science and technology. The National Science Competition, which consists of the Science Fair and the Science Bowl, is for students in middle school or high school. The Science Fair is a poster competition in which students compete individually, and the Science Bowl features teams of four players who compete against each other in a quiz bowl format. Twenty percent of the Science Bowl's questions are about African American inventors, scientists, and engineers.

To recognize and encourage outstanding performances by professionals in the field of chemistry, NOBCChE presents several annual awards, all of them named after prominent black chemists. The Percy L. Julian Award recognizes outstanding achievements in pure and applied research, the Henry C. McBay Award recognizes science educators who have demonstrated a commitment to the mentoring of future chemists or chemical engineers, and the Lloyd Ferguson Award recognizes outstanding young scientists (professionals in the first 10 years of their scientific careers). NOBCChE also presents scholarships and fellowships (funded wholly or in part by Dow Chemical, Dupont, Eastman Kodak, GlaxoSmithKline, Procter & Gamble, and Rohm and Haas) to outstanding black graduate and undergraduate students pursuing degrees in either chemistry or chemical engineering.

See also: Biochemistry; Cancer; Chemistry; Diabetes; Ferguson, Lloyd N.; Julian, Percy L.; McBay, Henry C.

REFERENCES AND FURTHER READING

National Organization for the Professional Advancement of Black Chemists and Chemical Engineers. "NOBCChE: National Organization for the Professional Advancement of Black Chemists and Chemical Engineers." [Online article or information; retrieved June 13, 2006.] http://www.nobcche.org/.

National Science Foundation

The National Science Foundation (NSF) is an independent federal agency. Its mission is to support basic, cutting-edge research in the STEM disciplines (science, technology, engineering, and mathematics). Established in 1950, NSF funds approximately 20 percent of federally supported basic scientific research conducted by the nation's colleges and universities. Each year, it issues more than 10,000 awards and grants to fund the most promising research projects, but it also supports proposals for developing innovative education and training programs. In terms of diversity, NSF works to increase the number of African Americans and other underrepresented minorities pursuing careers in scientific research via a number of programs. Although the majority of these programs support the training of minority scientists at historically black colleges and universities (HBCUs) and other minority-serving institutions, many of them support the training of minority scientists at other institutions as well.

NSF funds three programs that seek to increase the number of African Americans and other minority students receiving degrees in the sciences and related disciplines: Alliances for Broadening Participation in STEM (ABP), the HBCU Undergraduate Program (HBCU-UP), and Centers of Research Excellence in Science and Technology (CREST). ABP creates alliances of national research laboratories and universities, HBCUs, community colleges, public school systems, industry, professional STEM organizations, and federal, state, and local agencies, which then provide innovative academic and enrichment activities for minority students at HBCUs and other minority-serving institutions. ABP facilitates three types of alliances: Louis Stokes Alliances for Minority Participation (LSAMP) enhance undergraduate education, Bridge to the Doctorate (BD) provides support for the first two years of graduate school, and Alliances for Graduate Education and the Professoriate (AGEP) recruit, train, and support graduate students through the completion of the doctoral dissertation. LSAMP and AGEP awards furnish the recipient institution with up to $1 million over five years, and BD provides the same amount over two years.

HBCU-UP funds enhancements to the teaching of science and related subjects at HBCUs. These enhancements include new course and multidisciplinary degree program offerings; the integration of student research, technology, and cyberinfrastructure resources into the STEM curriculum; the development of tutoring and mentoring programs; and the establishment of paid research internships and summer enrichment programs. HBCU-UP also funds various professional development programs for faculty members, such as teaching and mentoring training and sabbaticals and faculty exchange programs, to make it easier for faculty to conduct research.

CREST enhances the research capabilities of HBCUs and other minority-serving institutions by establishing centers that integrate STEM education and research at such institutions. Colleges and universities that wish to become CREST centers must be willing to begin offering doctoral degrees in one or more of the STEM disciplines. They must also be willing to serve as resource centers in one or more research fields for other minority-serving institutions

Student participants between sessions at the National Science Foundation Historically Black Colleges and Universities–Undergraduate Program (HBCU-UP) National Research Conference, 2007. (Photo by Colellaphoto.com)

in their region, thus enabling those institutions to enhance their ability to train minority scientists. Each CREST award presents the receiving institution with up to $5 million over a period of five years to improve or upgrade its science and technology infrastructure. Universities that already offer doctorates in one or more of the STEM disciplines may participate in the CREST program through its subsidiary program, HBCU Research Infrastructure for Science and Engineering (HBCU-RISE). These awards provide up to $1 million over three years. Institutions that are willing to form alliances with small businesses to facilitate the transfer of technology from their laboratories to the marketplace are eligible for additional funding through the CREST Small Business Innovation Research and Small Business Technology Transfer Diversity Collaboration Supplements. These awards provide the alliance with a one-time payment of up to $150,000.

NSF supports a number of other programs to increase the number of minority scientists in particular STEM disciplines. Opportunities for Enhancing Diversity in the Geosciences supports institutions that develop programs for recruiting and training more minorities for careers in the geosciences, which include earth science, geography, geology, and meteorology. Such programs include formal and informal precollege geoscience education programs, as well as programs that encourage minorities to pursue and obtain undergraduate and graduate degrees in the geosciences. The Partnerships for Research in Education and Materials (PREM) program recruits and trains minorities for research careers in materials science, an interdisciplinary field that includes applied physics and chemistry, as well as chemical, civil, electrical, and mechanical engineering. PREM supports the establishment of long-term, collaborative education and research partnerships between HBCUs and other minority-serving institutions and the various centers and facilities supported by the NSF Division of Materials Research so as to enhance the ability of the institutions to prepare their students for careers in materials science. PREM programs train high school, undergraduate, and graduate students with innovative course offerings and exchanges and professional development programs for minority faculty. Research Initiation Grants (RIG) and Career Advancement Awards (CAA) to Broaden Participation in the Biological Sciences seek to increase the number of minority scientists who submit to NSF grant proposals related to the biological sciences. RIGs support researchers who are just beginning their careers while they gather preliminary data or establish collaborations that will lead to formal, competitive grant applications. CAAs support established researchers who seek to further develop their research skills or to pursue a different line of inquiry than they have pursued previously. Undergraduate Research and Mentoring in the Biological Sciences supports colleges and universities that develop innovative, year-round research and mentoring activities to recruit and train minorities for research careers in the biological sciences. The Undergraduate Research Collaboratives in Chemistry initiative supports the development of programs that introduce more hands-on research into chemistry courses for first- and second-year minority undergraduates.

See also: Historically Black Colleges and Universities

REFERENCES AND FURTHER READING

National Science Foundation. "National Science Foundation." [Online article or information; retrieved October 29, 2007.] http://www.nsf.gov/.

National Science Foundation. "Sampling of Active Programs by Target Audience or Activity." [Online article or information; retrieved July 16, 2007.] http://www.nsf.gov/od/sampling_activeprograms/sampling.jsp.

National Society of Black Physicists

The National Society of Black Physicists (NSBP) is the preeminent professional organization for African Americans in the field of physics. The organization's primary goals are to increase the number of black physicists in the United States, to support their efforts to conduct physical research, and to increase the nation's appreciation for their contributions to physics.

NSBP grew out of a 1973 meeting of more than 40 black physicists who had gathered at Fisk University in Nashville, Tennessee, to honor Donald Edwards, John McNeil Hunter, and Halson V. Eagleson, three of the most prominent black physicists of the day. Over the next four years, a number of conversations were held regarding the establishment of a permanent organization to promote and celebrate the work of African American physicists. In 1977, NSBP was formally established at another mass meeting of black physicists, this time at Morgan State University in Baltimore, who elected Walter E. Massey and James Davenport as cochairs of the organization. In the early 1990s, the group established its permanent headquarters in the Department of Physics at North Carolina A&T State University in Greensboro, but by 2005, the headquarters had been relocated to more spacious quarters in Arlington, Virginia.

Much of the NSBP's work is done at the level of the scientific section, of which there are 15. These sections help plan presentations for the annual conference as well as other meetings, workshops, and minicourses. They also help keep the general membership aware of funding sources for research and training in their respective areas of specialization, while serving as forums for networking, information exchanges, and research collaboration. The 15 sections are astronomy and astrophysics; atomic and molecular physics; chemical and biological physics; condensed matter and materials physics; cosmology, gravitation, and relativity; fluid and plasma physics; geophysics, atmospheric physics, ocean physics, space physics and environmental physics; health physics; history of physics, physics and society, and public policy; mathematical and computational physics; medical physics; nuclear and particle physics; photonics and optical physics; physics education research; and technology transfer, business development, and entrepreneurism.

NSBP's most important vehicle for networking and exchanging information is the annual meeting. To heighten awareness of the contributions of physicists of color, for several years (2004–2006) NSBP held its annual meeting in conjunction with the National Society of Hispanic Physicists. At the meeting, one or two physicists are annually inducted into the NSBP Society of Fellows for outstanding contributions to NSBP, physics research, and/or physics education, and other awards are presented to African American physicists for their contributions to the field. One of the most important results of the annual meeting has been the development of an informal network whereby minority students working toward degrees in physics are supported and encouraged.

As further support for prospective minority physicists, NSBP awards a number of college scholarships. The most prestigious is a scholarship provided jointly by NSBP and the University of California-Lawrence Livermore National Laboratory. This $5,000 renewable scholarship includes the opportunity to complete an internship at Lawrence Livermore, one of the nation's foremost research facilities devoted to nuclear research. *Black Enterprise* magazine cosponsors three scholarships, named after the notable black physicists Willie Hobbs Moore, Harry L. Morrison, and Arthur B. C. Walker, to encourage more African Americans to pursue advanced degrees in physics. The American Astronomical Society cosponsors the Harvey W. Banks Scholarship in Astronomy, the Walter S. McAfee Scholarship in Space Physics, the Ronald E. McNair Scholarship in Space and Optical Physics, and the Michael P. Anderson Scholarship in Space Science to commemorate the achievements of the four black scientists. The American Physical Society cosponsors the Corporate-Sponsored Scholarship for Minority Undergraduate Students Who Major in Physics. Other NSBP scholarships honor Elmer S. Imes and Robert A. Ellis and are funded by Walter and Shirley Massey and Ellis's former colleagues at the Princeton Plasma Physics Laboratory, respectively. The Morehouse Physics Prize recognizes a graduate of a historically black college or university who has shown considerable promise as a physics researcher or teacher.

NSBP actively supports and encourages students at the K–12 level as well. A number of NSBP members serve as Science Ambassadors, that is, they give lectures to elementary, middle, and high school students encouraging them to pursue careers in science and technology, especially physics. NSBP also sponsors several fall career planning meetings, which are designed to encourage and support minorities considering a career in the physical sciences, and a number of summer intern programs. Perhaps the most innovative of these summer programs is the Herman R. Branson Summer Course in Biophysics, which NSBP organizes in conjunction with the Biophysical Society. This 10-week summer program includes a formal introductory course in biophysics at a major research university, more often than not Florida A&M University, and a placement in the university's biophysics research lab. Enrollment in the course is limited to 12 students, all of whom are rising juniors or seniors majoring in biology, chemistry, mathematics, or physics. Students who successfully complete the course receive academic credit and a stipend for participating in research.

See also: Anderson, Michael P.; Astronomy and Astrophysics; Biology; Branson, Herman R.; Chemistry; Fisk University; Florida A&M University; Historically Black Colleges and Universities; Imes, Elmer S.; Massey, Walter E.; McAfee, Walter S.; McNair, Ronald E.; Morgan State University; North Carolina A&T State University; Physics; Walker, Arthur II

References and Further Reading

National Society of Black Physicists. "National Society of Black Physicists." [Online article or information; retrieved October 29, 2007.] http://nsbp.org/.

Network of Minority Research Investigators

The Network of Minority Research Investigators (NMRI) is a group of senior biomedical researchers, most of them either black or Hispanic, who are associated with the National Institute of Diabetes and Digestive and Kidney Diseases (NIDDK), one of the National Institutes of Health (NIH). As of 2005, NMRI's membership stood at approximately 100. The network encourages junior medical investigators (who have just received their MD or PhD degrees) and who are members of minorities or other underrepresented groups to consider careers as biomedical researchers. The network also assists junior investigators to obtain NIH grant money for conducting research in the fields of clinical trials, diabetes, digestive diseases, endocrinology, epidemiology, genetic metabolic diseases, genetics and gene therapy, hematology, HIV/AIDS and immunology, kidney diseases, metabolism, minority health, obesity and nutrition, pancreatic diseases, and urology. In addition, NMRI serves as a source of feedback to NIDDK from the minority and underrepresented biomedical research community; NIH encourages such feedback as part of its ongoing effort to eliminate racial and ethnic health disparities. The network pursues its goals through two principal vehicles: the NMRI Workshop and the NMRI Oversight Committee.

The NMRI Workshop has been held annually in Bethesda, Maryland, the location of NIDDK and NIH, since the first meeting in 2002. One of the workshop's purposes is to acquaint junior medical investigators with NIH procedures regarding the submission and assignment of research grants. Participants are instructed as to the number and type of grants NIH offers each year, how to apply for each type, and how to put together a winning grant application. The workshop permits attendees to participate in mock study sessions, which demonstrate the workings of NIH study sessions, the committees that review applications and make recommendations as to whether they should be approved. The mock studies provide guidance to junior investigators on what makes favorable impressions on reviewers. For example, attendees are advised to narrow the focus of their proposed study, because this reduces the possibility that the grant application will be criticized for being ambiguous or overambitious. Such information is crucial to the success of a given grant application; in a typical year, fewer than 10 percent of all applications receive NIH funding. Workshop participants also get advice on how to manage the transition of their research careers from student to postdoctoral researcher to full-time faculty member at a research institution, how to develop an independent research program, and how to manage funds, resources, and people.

The NMRI Oversight Committee consists of 10 members of NMRI, as well as various representatives from NIH. The committee oversees many of the activities that are essential to the successful maintenance of the network. These activities include recruiting new NMRI members, facilitating the development of mentoring relationships between NMRI members and junior investigators, coordinating the activities of NMRI with professional societies whose interests intersect or overlap with those of NIDDK, and exploring mechanisms for evaluating the effectiveness of the network in terms of helping junior investigators obtain grant funding, promotions, and tenure.

See also: Diabetes; Health Disparities; HIV/AIDS; National Institute of Diabetes and Digestive and Kidney Diseases; National Institutes of Health; Obesity

REFERENCES AND FURTHER READING

Network of Minority Research Investigators. "Network of Minority Research Investigators (NMRI)." [Online article or information; retrieved October 29, 2007.] http://nmri.niddk.nih.gov/.

NIH Black Scientists Association

The NIH Black Scientists Association (NIH BSA) is a group of scientists, physicians, technologists, students, and science administrators, most of whom are African Americans, who work at the National Institutes of Health (NIH) in Bethesda, Maryland. NIH BSA is not an official branch of NIH, but rather an autonomous association recognized by NIH. The purposes of the association are to promote the individual and collective professional advancement of black scientists at NIH and to advocate various health and scientific issues of importance to underrepresented minority communities in general and to the African American community in particular. Membership is open to anyone who shares the association's goals.

The NIH BSA serves the interests of its members in a variety of ways. Most important, it functions as a sounding board on issues concerning the recruitment, development, recognition, and promotion of black scientists and clinicians at NIH, as well as the selection and care of NIH's black patients and research subjects. It also provides members with information about issues of common interest, helps them develop important personal and professional contacts, offers career support and enhancement, and sponsors social events throughout the year. The association accomplishes much of its work through its standing committees, which include a Speakers Bureau, Career Development, Finance, and Communications and Membership, and general meetings, which take place bimonthly.

As part of its commitment to professional development, NIH BSA sponsors the seminar series called Science Working for Us, three annual seminars that highlight the research accomplishments of black medical researchers. The largest event is the Annual John Diggs Lecture, which has taken place every July since 1995. The lecture covers topics such as the impact of HIV/AIDS on African Americans and Hispanics, issues related to organ donation and transplantation as they apply to minorities, and asthma in minority populations. Other seminars are given in the fall and during February, Black History Month, and they cover topics such as the systemic treatment of ovarian cancer. The association also sponsors job fairs and workshops in conjunction with private and public research institutions as a way to foster research collaborations and to help members find appropriate post-NIH employment. The association also maintains BSCINET, an e-mail network that disseminates information regarding opportunities for black biomedical researchers at research facilities and institutions around the world.

NIH BSA also plays an important role in advancing the mission of NIH. NIH officials are acutely aware that serious health disparities exist between minority and underserved populations and the U.S. population in general, and they are actively working to eliminate those disparities. NIH BSA provides NIH officials with solutions and feedback regarding potential solutions to the problem of providing minorities and underserved populations with appropriate access to health care. The association also advises NIH on which health problems of particular interest to minorities should become the focus of future study.

See also: Asthma; Cancer; Health Disparities; HIV/AIDS; National Institutes of Health

REFERENCES AND FURTHER READING

NIH Black Scientists Association. "NIH Black Scientists Association." [Online article or information; retrieved June 22, 2006.] http://bsa.od.nih.gov.

Norfolk State University

Norfolk State University (NSU) is one of Virginia's several state-supported historically black colleges and universities (HBCUs). In terms of scientific research, it is best known for its work in biotechnology, the biomedical sciences, and materials science.

Located in Norfolk, Virginia, NSU was founded in 1935 as the Norfolk Unit of Virginia Union College (today University), another of Virginia's state-supported HBCUs. Seven years later, it became an independent college and changed its name to Norfolk Polytechnic College. Two years after that, it was made a part of Virginia State College (today University), yet another of Virginia's state-supported HBCUs, and changed its name to Norfolk State College. In 1956, it began offering bachelor's degrees on its own, and in 1969, it became, once again, an independent college. In 1979, it attained university status and took on its present name. Today, it offers MS degrees in computer science and materials science.

NSU's scientific research concerning biotechnology is conducted under the auspices of the university's Center for Biotechnology and Biomedical Sciences

(CBBS). A major current project involves the development of a male birth control pill capable of inhibiting some or all of the stages of the fertilization process. Many past and present attempts to develop an effective, safe, and reliable male contraceptive involve chemical or hormonal manipulation of testicular function, that is, shutting down the production of sperm cells. These attempts have failed because of severe negative side effects such as a subsequent hormonal imbalance or the production of chemically induced, genetically altered sperm cells. NSU researchers were the first to develop a nonhormonal approach toward male contraception by demonstrating that the transition-state analogues of certain amino sugars are potent competitive inhibitors of the fertilization process. Current efforts are focused on improving the efficacy of these compounds, as well as discovering new compounds that could serve as potential male contraceptives.

CBBS researchers also investigate the chemistry of biomedicine. One project studies the important role played by surfaces in biomedicine, as most biochemical reactions occur along the surfaces of cells. The goal is to develop a better understanding of the biochemistry of cell surfaces so that surface planes can be manipulated to ease complex reactions and enhance reaction turnover rates. Another project studies the chemistry of molybdenum. Molybdenum is an essential element in the enzymes that catalyze the uptake of inorganic nitrogen by bacteria, plants, and fungi, as well as the enzymes that play important roles in the metabolism of guanine and adenine, two of the components of DNA (deoxyribonucleic acid) and RNA (ribonucleic acid). A third project investigates eye lens protein in an effort to understand what brings about cataracts (an abnormality of the eye whereby the lens becomes less transparent, making it almost impossible to see). So far, researchers have discovered that lens transparency depends on the specific packing of proteins, that the protein alpha-crystallin plays an important role in ordering this process, and that certain ions of sodium and calcium, when combined with overexposure to ultraviolet radiation, may inhibit the role played by alpha-crystallin.

Yet another project examines the genetics of human cytomegalovirus (HCMV), a genus of herpes viruses including the viruses that cause chicken pox and mononucleosis. Like many viruses, HCMV lies dormant in the DNA of its host cell, sometimes for life, until some biochemical factor causes it to begin expressing itself; when this happens, the virus reproduces itself and the host organism becomes infected. Like all viruses, HCMV expresses its gene products in sequence; first, it produces proteins that assist in the synthesis of DNA and RNA, and then it synthesizes the proteins that aid in the packaging of the virus. To better understand this process, NSU researchers study how the sequence of HCMV gene expression is regulated, with the eventual goal of developing methods for interrupting this sequence as a way to prevent HCMV infections.

Researchers at Norfolk State University conduct cutting-edge research at the school's Center for Biotechnology and Biomedical Sciences. (Norfolk State University)

The other major focal point for scientific research at NSU is the university's Center for Materials Research (CMR). Founded in 1992, CMR fosters cutting-edge research in the development of innovative, high-tech materials. For example, sophisticated solid-state lasers require state-of-the-art crystals to focus and intensify light; so NSU researchers have designed and grown (the process by which synthetic crystals are developed from inorganic materials) more than 20 customized crystals for specific uses. Current work in this vein focuses on the use of nanotechnology (the fabrication of materials at dimensions that can be measured in nanometers, or billionths of a meter) as the preferred method for processing materials into crystals. Of particular interest are nanopowders (powders with an average particle diameter of less than 200 nanometers). Nanopowders have a very high surface-area-to-volume ratio, which accounts for much of their unique behavior.

Another CMR project involves the development of lightweight, flexible, and inexpensive polymer thin films for use in photovoltaic devices. Such devices are used in applications that convert light into energy, such as solar panels for space flight missions and high-speed signal processing devices for the information superhighway. A related project involves the development of organic thin films for use in high-speed optical computers, which use light instead of electricity to perform computations.

These and other projects are facilitated by CMR's Electron Spin Resonance (ESR) and Nuclear Magnetic Resonance (NMR) laboratories. ESR is used to examine the magnetic properties of the materials developed at CMR as well as to facilitate the development of materials with improved mechanical durability, thermal and radiation resistance, and conductivity. NMR is used to study the structural and magnetic properties of new materials developed for use in applications related to spintronics (an emergent technology that exploits an electron's spin as well as its electromagnetic charge). Two notable spintronic devices are mass storage devices for computer hard drives and spin valves (devices capable of detecting the extremely weak magnetic field originating from a tiny magnetic bit on a computer disk).

See also: Biochemistry; Biotechnology; Computer Science; Historically Black Colleges and Universities; Virginia State University

REFERENCES AND FURTHER READING

Norfolk State University. "Norfolk State University." [Online article or information; retrieved October 29, 2007.] http://www.nsu.edu/.

Norfolk State University. "Research@NSU." [Online article or information; retrieved December 5, 2006.] http://www.nsu.edu/researchatnsu/index.html.

North Carolina A&T State University

North Carolina A&T State University (A&T) is the largest historically black college or university in North Carolina. As of 2004, A&T was the nation's top producer of minorities with degrees in one or more of the STEM disciplines (science, technology, engineering, and mathematics). In keeping with its vision to remain a high-activity research institution, A&T's Division of Research and Economic Development maintains a number of research centers and research clusters devoted to exploring the cutting edges of science.

A&T was established in 1891, when the North Carolina general assembly empowered the state's agricultural and mechanical college in Raleigh to begin instructing blacks. For two years, such instruction was provided at Raleigh's Shaw College, but in 1893, the A. and M. College for the Colored Race, as legislature called the school, was moved to Greensboro, where it remains today. A&T conferred its first bachelor's degrees in 1898. In 1915, the name of the college was changed to the Negro Agricultural and Technical College of North Carolina. In 1941, the school began conferring graduate degrees; in 1957, the word "Negro" was dropped from the name; and in 1967, the school was officially designated North Carolina Agricultural and Technical State University. In 1972, A&T became a part of the University of North Carolina system. By 2006, A&T had established four research centers (the Center for Advanced Materials and Smart Structures, the Center for Composite Materials Research, the Center for Cooperative Systems, and the Center for Energy Research and Technology) and two research clusters (biotechnology/biosciences and advanced materials/

nanotechnology) that are engaged in scientific research. In addition, A&T oversees the operations of two research institutes for outside agencies: the North Carolina Agromedicine Institute and the National Institute of Aerospace.

The Center for Advanced Materials and Smart Structures conducts research with advanced ceramic materials and their composites. The center's projects involving advanced materials include basic research in advanced ceramics, advanced composites, electronic ceramic devices, and III-V nitrides (the newest generation of semiconductor materials). The center also investigates smart structures, systems containing multifunctional parts that can perform sensing, control, and actuation duties and that are made from smart materials (materials with one or more properties that can be significantly altered in a controlled fashion by external stimuli, such as stress, temperature, moisture, and electric or magnetic fields). The Center for Composite Materials Research conducts similar research, except that its activities focus on composites made from polymers rather than ceramics.

The Center for Cooperative Systems performs high-impact research in aerospace, space exploration, and biomimetics; also known as bionics, biomimetics is the application of methods and systems found in nature to the study and design of engineering systems and modern technology. The center analyzes, designs, and simulates advanced cooperative systems technologies for making current and future aerospace transportation more affordable, more efficient, and more reliable. Current research projects address the development of electronic system technologies for enhancing space vehicle mission planning; improvements in various aspects of flight dynamics such as guidance, navigation, and control; and better ways to monitor the health of a vehicle's crew.

The Center for Energy Research and Technology seeks to improve economic competitiveness while reducing the environmental impact that results from excessive energy consumption. Its research focuses on developing ways to use energy more efficiently in buildings and industrial processes. The North Carolina Agromedicine Institute seeks to promote the health and safety of the state's agricultural workers, including those who labor in forests or fisheries, through research, education, and outreach. The National Institute of Aerospace conducts research related to the aerospace and atmospheric sciences. It develops innovative techniques in the areas of aeroacoustics, aerodynamics, aerospace structures and materials, aerothermodynamics, atmospheric and vehicle sensor system technology, and atmospheric chemistry and radiation science.

The Biotechnology & Bio Sciences Research Cluster is a collaboration among the School of Agriculture and Environmental Sciences, the School of Technology, and the Colleges of Arts & Sciences and Engineering. The cluster's interdisciplinary research teams study microbial, plant, and animal systems with an eye toward developing new biotechnologies capable of enhancing human health. Specific projects involve bioinformatics, biopharmaceuticals, bioremediation (any process that uses microorganisms, fungi, green plants, or their enzymes to return the environment altered by contaminants to its original condition), biosensing (the use of biosensors, or sensors that combine a biological receptor and a physical or chemical transducer, a device that converts one type of energy to another for the purpose of measurement or information transfer), E-bio supported systems, which integrate electronic and biological systems, fermentation, food safety, genomics (the study of an organism's genome and the use of its genes), neutriceuticals (high-tech nutrients), phytoremediation (bioremediation through the use of plants only), plant tissue culture and transformation, and utilization of agricultural and food industry by-products. The cluster's teams collaborate with teams from a number of other institutions, including the North Carolina Agromedicine Institute.

The Advanced Materials and Nanotechnology Research Cluster develops new smart, multifunctional, and other advanced materials. Unlike the Center for Advanced Materials and Smart Structures, this cluster focuses on materials that are constructed in nanoscale (i.e., their dimensions do not exceed 100 nanometers, or 100 billionths of a meter).

As part of its commitment to scientific research, A&T also supports original undergraduate research. The results of this research are presented publicly at the annual Ronald E. McNair Commemorative Celebration and Research Symposium. Named in honor of the NASA astronaut and A&T alumnus, the symposium provides undergraduate scholars the opportunity to present research findings, hear scholarly presentations, hear about and view cutting-edge research, engage in meaningful scientific dialogues, and network with other scholars and graduate school representatives while celebrating McNair's life and achievements.

See also: Historically Black Colleges and Universities; McNair, Ronald E.

REFERENCES AND FURTHER READING

North Carolina A&T State University. "North Carolina A&T State University." [Online article or information; retrieved October 29, 2007.] http://www.ncat.edu/.

North Carolina A&T State University, Division of Research and Economic Development. "Centers & Institutes." [Online article or information; retrieved August 15, 2006.] http://www.ncat.edu/~divofres/centers.

North Carolina Central University

North Carolina Central University (NCCU) is one of several historically black colleges and universities in North Carolina. In terms of scientific research, the school is best known for its work in biomedicine and quantum dots.

NCCU was founded in 1909 in Durham, North Carolina, as the National Religious Training School and Chautauqua for the purpose of preparing African Americans for the ministry. In 1915, the name was shortened to National Training School. Eight years later, it was purchased by the state of North Carolina, christened the Durham State Normal School, and transformed into an institution for training blacks to teach in elementary and secondary schools. In 1925, it was renamed the North Carolina College for Negroes, and shortly thereafter it began offering bachelor's degrees in the liberal arts. Graduate courses in the sciences were first offered in 1939, and in 1947, the name was changed to North Carolina College at Durham. In 1969, NCCU acquired university status and took on its present name, and in 1972, it became part of the University of North Carolina system.

Most of NCCU's research in biomedicine is conducted under the auspices of the Julius L. Chambers Biomedical/Biotechnology Research Institute (BBRI). Dedicated in 1999, BBRI conducts research concerning cancer, cardiovascular disease, developmental biology, and the neuroscience of drug abuse and addiction. It also conducts research for the National Aeronautics and Space Administration (NASA).

BBRI's cardiovasulcar researchers investigate the cellular, environmental, genetic, and molecular aspects of cardiovascular function under both healthy and diseased conditions. Specifically, they study a broad range of mechanisms affecting the heart, lungs, kidneys, and blood vessels that offer insight into the basis of cardiovascular disease and how the various components of the cardiovascular system respond to disease and treatment. A current project examines how calcium regulates the amounts of the various biochemical compounds found throughout the cardiovascular system. Another project studies how certain second messengers (biochemical compounds that relay signals within a cell to guide its functions) contribute to complications arising from the treatment of cardiovascular disease. A third project studies the function of nitric oxide as a second messenger of the processes that lead to hypertension and kidney disease. Yet another studies how the bacterium *Chlamydophila pneumoniae* contributes to the development of atherosclerosis (hardening of the arteries) and the stability of plaque (the fatty deposits that line arterial walls). A fifth studies how the intercellular messengers known as endocannabinoids regulate the functions of the blood vessels, and a sixth examines the influence of stress on normal and diseased blood vessels.

BBRI's cancer researchers study how cancer is triggered by a variety of biological, physical, and chemical agents. Most of BBRI focuses its current toxicology/carcinogenesis research on how toxic agents cause cancer by stimulating the functions of genes, particularly those that regulate the growth and proliferation of cells, whose makeup has been altered, usually as a result of a viral infection. Current projects attempt to define the critical steps in carcinogenesis and to understand the interplay between genes and the environment. Of particular interest is the role played in carcinogenesis by single nucleotide polymorphisms (minute variations in the DNA sequences between members of the same race, gender, or ethnic group).

BBRI's developmental biology researchers focus on the extracellular matrix (the part of any tissue that is not part of a cell). The extracellular matrix serves to connect and separate different tissues, but it also provides support and anchorage for cells, serves as a storage depot for cellular growth factors, and regulates intercellular communication. Current projects examine the role played by extracellular matrix proteins such as agrin and olfactomedin–2 in the development of the nervous system and as contributors to such neurological disorders as Alzheimer's disease and Parkinson's disease.

BBRI's research concerning the neuroscience of drug abuse focuses on how additive drugs work at the cellular and molecular levels. A current project studies how THC, the active compound in *Cannabis sativa*, better known as marijuana, affects the ability of neurons and glial cells (the supporting tissue of the brain and spinal cord) to transmit signals throughout the nervous system. A related project studies how THC affects communications along the signal pathways in immune and cardiovascular cells. A third project studies how certain opium-like substances, such as enkephalins, endorphins, and dynorphins, are synthesized by the body and released in the brain and adrenal cells. The goal of this project is to understand how opioid and cannabinoid compounds produce therapeutically beneficial effects such as pain relief, at the same time avoiding the unwanted side effects associated with drugs of abuse.

BBRI's NASA Center of Excellence was established in 2003. Current projects study the effects of simulated microgravity on the cardiovascular system. Future plans for the center include a broad range of research consistent with NASA's mission to explore outer space in both manned and unmanned missions.

NCCU's department of physics specializes in research involving the use of electron beams, such as the one designed and installed by NCCU personnel at the Free Electron Laser Laboratory at nearby Duke University. The bulk of this research focuses on studying and designing quantum dots, semiconductor nanostructures (structures whose dimensions can be measured in nanometers) that confine the motion of electrons in all three spatial directions. Quantum dots have superior optical properties that make them suitable for use as light sources in photovoltaic cells and diode lasers. Because of their brightness and stability, quantum dots are superior to the traditional organic dyes used in biological analysis. Quantum dots are also being investigated for use in quantum computation, whereby precise measurements of the spin and other properties of electrons can be made.

The department's researchers also play an active role in the activities of the Continuous Electron Beam Accelerator Facility (CEBAF) at the Thomas

Jefferson National Accelerator Facility in Newport News, Virginia. Funded by the Department of Energy, the Jefferson Lab explores the nature of matter by conducting basic research on the role played by gluons (the subatomic particles that theoretically glue together quarks, the basic building blocks of all matter, by acting as carriers of the strong nuclear force, the force that binds quarks into proton and neutrons). In conjunction with Zagreb University in Croatia and CEBAF, the department cosponsors international conferences concerning CEBAF's past, present, and future research.

See also: Cancer; Cardiovascular Disease; Department of Energy; Historically Black Colleges and Universities; National Aeronautics and Space Administration

REFERENCES AND FURTHER READING

North Carolina Central University. "North Carolina Central University." [Online article or information; retrieved October 29, 2007.] http://www.nccu.edu/.

North Carolina Central University. "Research at NCCU." [Online article or information; retrieved December 11, 2006.] http://www.nccu.edu/research/.

Oak Ridge Associated Universities

Oak Ridge Associated Universities (ORAU) is a consortium of doctoral-granting academic institutions, most of which are located in the southern United States. The consortium advances scientific research and education by collaborating in the research conducted at the Oak Ridge National Laboratory (ORNL), a major research facility of the Department of Energy. In terms of diversity, ORAU sponsors a number of research and education programs dedicated to involving African Americans and other underrepresented minorities in the cutting-edge work being performed at ORNL.

ORNL was established in 1943 in a remote corner of Tennessee that became known as Oak Ridge. Originally known as Clinton Laboratories, it was part of the Manhattan Project, the nation's effort to build an atomic bomb, and its mission was to convert uranium into plutonium for use in Fat Man, the atomic bomb that was dropped on Nagasaki, Japan. After the war, the laboratory, which became known as ORNL in 1948, shifted the focus of its research to the search for useful applications of atomic energy, and eventually it became one of the nation's most important research centers for energy, environmental, and basic scientific research and technology development. In the early 21st century, ORNL's research ranged from studies of nuclear chemistry and physics to inquiries into global warming, energy conservation, high-temperature superconductivity, and the development of new materials.

ORAU was established in 1946 as the Oak Ridge Institute of Nuclear Studies (ORINS) to be a vehicle for involving Southern universities, particularly the University of Tennessee at nearby Knoxville, in the high-tech research being conducted at ORNL. ORINS began as a consortium of 14 colleges and universities, which used the facilities, programs, and research expertise at ORNL and the faculty at the University of Tennessee to improve and expand their graduate programs in physics and chemistry and to augment the facilities available to their own faculty for conducting advanced research in physics, chemistry, and nuclear medicine. At the same time, the consortium contributed significantly to the quality of research being conducted by ORNL researchers. In 1966, ORINS changed its name to ORAU to reflect the expansion of ORNL's basic research to include topics not related to nuclear energy. By 2007, the number of institutions in the consortium had grown to 111 full and associate members from across the nation, including 13 historically black colleges and universities (HBCUs): Alabama A&M University, Clark Atlanta University, Fisk University, Howard University, Jackson State University, Johnson C. Smith University, Meharry Medical College, Morehouse College, Morgan State University, North Carolina A&T State University, Tennessee State University, Tuskegee University, and Virginia State University.

As part of its mission to conduct science education programs related to its research, in 1992, ORNL established the Oak Ridge Institute of Science and Education (ORISE). The institute is managed by ORAU, it conducts science education programs for K–12 students and teachers, and it offers research scholarships and fellowships to undergraduates, postgraduates, postdoctoral researchers, and professors. As part of its commitment to increasing the diversity of the nation's scientific workforce, ORISE administers a number of initiatives by various federal agencies, not just DOE, at ORNL and at other locations to involve more African Americans and other underrepresented minorities who attend HBCUs or other minority education institutions (MEIs) in ORNL's research. These initiatives include the HBCU/MEI Council, the DOE Faculty and Student Team Program at ORNL, the Minority Institutions Biological and Environmental Student Research Participation Program, the National Oceanic and Atmospheric Administration (NOAA) Education Partnership Program with Minority Serving Institutions Graduate Sciences Program, the NOAA Educational Partnership Program with Minority Serving Institutions Undergraduate Scholarship Program, the Nuclear Regulatory Commission (NRC) HBCU Faculty Research Participation Program, the NRC HBCU Student Research Participation Program, the ORNL/OARU HBCU/MEI Faculty Summer Research Program, the Office of Civilian Waste Management Minority Service Institution Undergraduate Scholarship Program, the U.S. Department of Homeland Security Summer Faculty and Student Research Team Program, and the Postdoctoral Research Participation at the Joint POW/MIA Accounting Command/Central Identification Laboratory Program.

The HBCU/MEI Council seeks to build scientific research and education relationships between ORAU's 18 HBCU/MEI members and the large research universities that belong to ORAU. The council also assists HBCU/MEIs to develop cutting-edge technology and then transfer it to private industry.

The DOE Faculty and Student Team Program at ORNL brings teams from HBCU/MEIs to ORNL to conduct research concerning energy, the environment, and the basic sciences for 10 weeks during the summer. Teams consist of a faculty member and two or three students, all from the same school, whose discipline or major is related to biomedicine, biology, computer science, earth science, environmental science, or physics, among others. Support includes stipends for faculty and students and partial reimbursement for travel and housing.

The Minority Institutions Biological and Environmental Student Research Participation Program is a DOE-sponsored, 10-week summer program for students interested in conducting research related to health and the environment. The program is open to graduate students whose research is related to atmospheric science, biochemistry, biology, biophysics, bioremediation, biostatistics, chemistry, earth sciences, ecology, genetics, genomics, marine science, measurement science, molecular and cellular biology, molecular nuclear medicine, nuclear medicine, pathology, physics, physiology, radiation biology, structural biology, or toxicology, among others. The sponsored research may take place at any DOE national laboratory, not just at ORNL; financial support includes a stipend of $650 per week and partial reimbursement of travel expenses.

The National Oceanic and Atmospheric Administration (NOAA) Educational Partnership Program with Minority Serving Institutions Graduate Sciences Program provides graduate students the opportunity to conduct research related to the atmospheric, environmental, and oceanic sciences. Students who successfully complete the two-year program are offered entry-level employment with NOAA. Financial support includes tuition, book expenses, fees, and housing allotments for two years as well as 16 weeks' salary per summer for working as an NOAA intern. The NOAA Educational Partnership Program with Minority Serving Institutions Undergraduate Scholarship Program provides 10 scholarships and internships annually to undergraduates at HBCU/MEIs whose studies relate to NOAA's research interests. Juniors and seniors majoring in atmospheric science, biology, cartography, chemistry, computer science, engineering, environmental science, geodesy, geography, marine science, mathematics, meteorology, photogrammetry, physical science, physics, or remote sensing are eligible for the program. Recipients receive a one-year scholarship not to exceed $4,000, a two-year summer internship at a NOAA research installation (not necessarily ORNL) with a stipend of $650 per week, and a weekly housing allowance during the internship.

The Nuclear Regulatory Commission (NRC) HBCU Faculty Research Participation Program funds research opportunities for faculty members whose work relates to NRC's research interests. Professors at HBCUs who teach or conduct research in the computer science, engineering, the geosciences, health physics, materials science, mathematics, molecular/radiation biology, physical sciences, or statistics-related nuclear material control are eligible. Although most sponsored research is conducted at NRC facilities (not necessarily ORNL) over 10 to 12 weeks during the summer, some research may be conducted during 9- to 12-month appointments on the campuses of certain host universities under the guidance of principal investigators who have experience conducting NRC-sponsored research. The NRC HBCU Student Research Participation Program offers graduates and undergraduates studying or majoring in computer science, engineering, the geosciences, health physics, materials science, mathematics, molecular/radiation biology, or the physical sciences the opportunity to conduct research for 10 to 12 weeks during the summer. Financial support includes a stipend ($500 per week for undergraduates and $600 for graduate students) and a travel allowance.

The ORNL/OARU HBCU/MEI Faculty Summer Research Program seeks to establish research relationships with professors at minority-serving institutions by involving them in long-term research projects at ORNL. Professors who conduct research in computer science; engineering; the geosciences; the life, health, or medical sciences; marine science; mathematics; or the physical sciences are eligible for the program, which runs for 10 weeks every summer. Financial support includes a monthly stipend based on annual salary and a travel and housing allowance.

The DOE Office of Civilian Radioactive Waste Management (OCRWM) Minority Service Institution Undergraduate Scholarship Program offers scholarships to undergraduates pursuing careers of interest to the OCRWM. Juniors and seniors majoring in engineering, engineering technology, mathematics, or science are eligible for one of 12 two-year scholarships, which pay up to $8,000 per year for tuition and fees and a monthly stipend of $700.

The U.S. Department of Homeland Security (DHS) Summer Faculty and Student Research Team Program provides professors and undergraduates the opportunity to conduct research of interest to DHS. Teams consisting of one professor and one or two students from the same school and whose discipline/ major is either biology, computer science, engineering, mathematics, or physics, among others, are eligible to conduct research at one of the DHS Centers of Excellence, which are located in California, Maryland, Minnesota, and Texas. Research takes place during 12 weeks in the summer; financial support includes stipends of $1,200 per week for professors, $600 per week for graduate students, and $500 for undergraduates, plus allowances for travel and relocation.

The Postdoctoral Research Participation at the Joint POW/MIA Accounting Command/Central Identification Laboratory Program offers recent graduates of doctoral programs the opportunity to participate in research related to locating, exhuming, and identifying the remains of U.S. military personnel lost during past military service. Anyone who has earned a PhD within the last five years from an HBCU/MEI that is related to DNA analysis; forensic dentistry; osteology; physical, biological, or forensic anthropology; or related scientific disciplines is eligible. Research is funded by the U.S. Navy and takes place at the Joint POW/MIA Accounting Command/Central Identification Laboratory at Hickam Air Force Base in Hawaii. Appointments are from 10 weeks to one year, and they are renewable.

See also: Alabama A&M University; Biochemistry; Biology; Chemistry; Clark Atlanta University; Computer Science; Department of Energy; Fisk University; Historically Black Colleges and Universities; Howard University; Jackson State University; Meharry Medical College; Morgan State University; North Carolina A&T State University; Physics; Tennessee State University; Tuskegee University; Virginia State University

REFERENCES AND FURTHER READING

Oak Ridge Associated Universities. "About ORAU: Diversity in Action." [Online article or information; retrieved June 4, 2007.] http://www.orau.org/diversity/.

Oak Ridge Associated Universities. "Oak Ridge Associated Universities." [Online article or information; retrieved October 29, 2007.] http://www.orau.org/.

Oak Ridge Institute for Nuclear Studies. "Our Commitment to Diversity." [Online article or information; retrieved June 4, 2007.] http://see.orau.org/Diversity.aspx.

Partnership for Minority Advancement in the Biomolecular Sciences

The Partnership for Minority Advancement in the Biomolecular Sciences (PMABS) links six historically black colleges and universities (HBCUs) in North Carolina for the purpose of expanding the teaching of the biomolecular sciences in North Carolina's public colleges and secondary schools serving African Americans. PMABS originated in 1989, when several of North Carolina's minority-serving institutions joined forces with the University of North Carolina at Chapel Hill (UNC-CH) to introduce biomolecular science into high school and college classrooms. As of 2007, PMABS members included six HBCUs (Elizabeth City State University, Fayetteville State University, Johnson C. Smith University, North Carolina A&T State University, North Carolina Central University, and Shaw University). The other members are the University of North Carolina at Pembroke, which originated as a school for the state's Native Americans, and UNC-CH, which serves as the partnership's headquarters.

PMABS focused its early efforts on bolstering the expertise of high school science teachers as well as providing them with more instructional tools. To this end, the Secondary Science Educator Program helps participating teachers implement the PMABS curriculum in their classrooms, and it organizes field trips to the laboratories of the partnership's institutions of higher learning. Destiny, the Traveling Laboratory, is an innovative outreach program for public school student bodies that are primarily made up of minorities. This laboratory on wheels presents innovative science modules that offer students the opportunity for a hands-on, inquiry-based learning experience. In collaboration with Boston University Medical School's CityLab, PMABS universities host two-week summer workshops for high school teachers, where participants learn laboratory projects that they can take back to their classrooms.

In 1994, PMABS received a grant from the Howard Hughes Medical Institute that enabled it to expand the college aspects of its programming. PMABS now offers research internships and teaching assistantships so that undergraduates can develop research skills, provides professional development workshops on grant writing and Internet use, develops undergraduate courses that not only improve students' knowledge but also boost their ability to write and use a computer, and equips undergraduate instructional laboratories for use in PMABS-supported courses.

PMABS programming also provides college educators with the Collaborative Electronic Learning Laboratory (CELL) and a postdoctoral training program known as SPIRE (Seeding Postdoctoral Innovators in Research and Education). As part of the CELL program, each of the partnership's biology departments was provided with state-of-the-art computer hardware and software and given the training to use the equipment for classroom instruction. SPIRE is an innovative postdoctoral program that combines traditional research at UNC-CH with teaching at one of the partnership's other institutions.

See also: Historically Black Colleges and Universities; North Carolina A&T State University; North Carolina Central University

REFERENCES AND FURTHER READING

Partnership for Minority Advancement in the Biomolecular Sciences. "Who We Are." [Online article or information; retrieved February 23, 2007.] http://www.unc.edu/pmabs/whoweare.html.

Pfizer Medical Humanities Initiative

The Pfizer Medical Humanities Initiative (PMHI) seeks to enhance the patient–physician relationship by fostering a balance between humane care and scientific expertise in the health care field. Part of its mission includes supporting programs that make medical education more affordable, and to this end, it funds several fellowships and scholarships that help African Americans and other underrepresented minorities become physicians and medical researchers.

PMHI was founded in 1997 by Pfizer, Inc., a leading manufacturer of pharmaceutical drugs, out of concern that changes in health care were threatening the patient–physician relationship. Since then, PMHI has focused on promoting a strong health care system by honoring physicians, medical students, and medical programs whose community involvement, service, compassion, mentoring, leadership, and integrity improve the system. To this end, Pfizer sponsors awards, fellowships, and scholarships to highlight the awardees' contributions, to further improve the health care system, and to promote medical excellence through education. As a means of improving the system by increasing the diversity of the medical profession, PMHI sponsors the Pfizer Minority Medical School Scholarship, the Pfizer/UNC Minority Medical Journalism Scholarship, and the Pfizer Minority Science Scholarship.

The Minority Medical School Scholarship was established by Pfizer in 1984 to recognize deserving minority medical students. The program provides full tuition scholarships to eight students per year at the four historically black U.S. medical schools: Charles R. Drew University of Medicine and Science, Howard University College of Medicine, Meharry Medical College, and Morehouse School of Medicine. Two students from each school are selected annually to receive the award. As of 2007, the program had supported more than 135 students.

The Minority Medical Journalism Scholarship helps eligible students complete a two-year master's program in medical journalism at the University of North Carolina at Chapel Hill's School of Journalism and Mass Communication. PMHI intends these scholarships to improve the quantity and quality of reporting about health and medical issues in minority communities, so that minorities will be able to make more informed choices about their health care issues. The award also seeks to promote careers as physicians and medical researchers to minorities, thus further diversifying the medical profession. The award provides a $4,000 stipend and full tuition for the program's first three semesters. The Minority Science Scholarship was established in 2003 at St. Thomas Aquinas College in Sparkill, New York, as a way to increase the number of minority undergraduates pursuing a bachelor's degree in one of the sciences. Two full-tuition scholarships are awarded each year to minority students majoring in a science who are entering their junior or senior year.

In addition to the scholarships that it awards directly, PMHI funds a number of scholarships awarded by other organizations, including two that promote diversity in the medical profession. The American Medical Association Foundation offers ten $10,000 Minority Scholars Awards annually to minority medical students in their first or second year of medical school. The Student

National Medical Association offers five $5,000 David E. Satcher, M.D. Research Fellowships annually to researchers studying obesity prevention and intervention. Both awards are fully funded by PMHI.

See also: American Medical Association; Charles R. Drew University of Medicine and Science; Howard University College of Medicine; Meharry Medical College; Morehouse School of Medicine; Satcher, David; Student National Medical Association

REFERENCES AND FURTHER READING

PositiveProfiles.com., "About PMHI." [Online article or information; retrieved May 25, 2007.] http://www.positiveprofiles.com/content/about/tier_2/about_landing.asp#mission.

Prairie View A&M University

Prairie View A&M University is one of several historically black colleges and universities in Texas. Prairie View sponsors scientific experimentation in several research centers, most notably the Center for Applied Radiation Research, the Center of Excellence for Communication Systems Technology Research, the Future Aerospace Science and Technology Center, the Texas Gulfcoast Environmental Data Center, the Thermal Science Research Center, and the Cooperative Agriculture Research Center. Also, the departments of physics and engineering administer I2I (Invention To Innovation), which oversees cutting-edge research conducted outside the purview of these other centers. The school also operates the Prairie View Solar Observatory, which is discussed in a separate article.

Prairie View grew out of two schools, both founded by the state of Texas. The first, Alta Vista Agricultural and Mechanical College of Texas for Colored Youth, was founded in 1876 in Prairie View, and the second, Prairie View State Normal School, was founded three years later. In 1887, the A&M college was made a department of the normal school, and in 1889, the combined schools were renamed Prairie View State Normal and Industrial College. The school began offering a four-year senior college curriculum in 1919 and selected graduate courses in 1939. In 1945, Prairie View attained university status, and in 1973, it acquired its present name.

The Center for Applied Radiation Research (CARR) is sponsored by the National Aeronautics and Space Administration (NASA), and the vast majority of its work addresses the need to shield the occupants and instruments in spacecraft from harmful radiation. Much of this work involves the design and testing of new structures and materials for use in outer space. To determine the amount of radiation that people and structures must be able to withstand, researchers have outfitted the International Space Station and each mission of the space shuttle with various types of radiation counters to monitor the radiation field inside the spacecraft. The data from these counters is then exploited by CARR researchers in the making of 3-D computer models by which structures and materials can be tested for their ability to withstand radiation. A current project evaluates the ability of bucky papers (paper-like materials made from single-walled nanotubes, which are extremely strong but lightweight carbon nanoscale structures) to offer enhanced protection from radiation. Another project evaluates the ability of a variety of commercial off-the-shelf electronics apparatus, which NASA is using increasingly in both human and robotic space flights, to operate in an environment containing known levels of space radiation.

The Center of Excellence for Communication Systems Technology Research (CECSTR) investigates various aspects of modern communications systems such as analog-to-digital (mixed signal) systems, digital signal processing (DSP), high-speed (broadband) communications, and image processing. The center also supports NASA's Exo-atmospheric Trans-solar Wind Aircraft program, an effort to develop an aircraft that can travel through the outermost reaches of the atmosphere where the air is too thin to support traditional aircraft. To this end, CECSTR developed a novel technique for detecting vibrations in the wing of the Pathfinder Plus, one of the prototypes for this aircraft. This technique models the physics of the wing as it vibrates, then detects the vibration signal of the wing using its frequency content.

The Future Aerospace Science and Technology Center conducts research on high-tech materials that promise to have applications in space science. Typical projects examine the effects of extreme heat and humidity on glass/vinyl ester composites, the uses of regolith material (such as soil or dust) and LTM45 composite (made from a certain type of epoxy resin) for space radiation shielding applications, and the short-term aging effects on thermal and mechanical properties of IM7/5250-4 composites (made from toughened bismaleimide resin).

The primary research interest of the Texas Gulfcoast Environmental Data Center involves exploring the capability of hyperspectral imaging (a passive remote sensing technique that observes the electromagnetic radiation emitted by the target in hundreds of spectral bands) to detect stress in agricultural crops. Other research interests include image analysis of the Gulf Coast sea surface temperature, and ecological studies of crayfish in the River Nile in Egypt.

The Thermal Science Research Center conducts research on topics related to thermodynamics, fluid mechanics, and heat transfer such as nucleate boiling, subcooled flow boiling, local heat transfer, natural convection in enclosures, mixed convection in internal and external geometries, optical interferometry, thermal transport problems, environmental flows, and microconvection.

The Cooperative Agricultural Research Center (CARC) conducts research in four areas of the food and agricultural sciences: animal systems, food systems, plant and environmental systems, and socioeconomic and family systems. However, the emphasis of its research concerns dairy goats and meat goats, which are studied at the center's International Goat Research Center (IGRC). IGRC was developed in 1983 through grants from the Science and Education Administration and the U.S. Department of Agriculture, and it is considered to be a world leader in goat research. The center focuses its research on improving goat management and care in the areas of reproduction and reproductive efficiency; health, disease, and toxicology; and value-added processing. The center also collects and studies genetic material from all breeds of goats in an effort to preserve their future genetic diversity.

I2I (Invention To Innovation) oversees a number of projects in an effort to help cutting-edge research make the transition to invention and then to widespread application. A typical project involves the development of computational fluid dynamics (CFD) technology for use in supersonic ramjet/scramjet combustion. The work involves detailed analysis using CFD technology of a rocket-based combined cycle propulsion system for a single-stage-to-orbit (SSTO) space vehicle. Another project involves the conversion of the General Motors Corporation's Electrical Vehicle 1 (EV1) into an automobile powered by a fuel cell (an electrochemical energy conversion device that is designed to continuously replenish the reactants consumed). It is hoped that the project will contribute to the design of a fuel cell power system that could play an important role in fuel cell development.

See also: Historically Black Colleges and Universities; National Aeronautics and Space Administration; Prairie View Solar Observatory

REFERENCES AND FURTHER READING

Prairie View A&M University. "Prairie View A&M University." [Online article or information; retrieved October 29, 2007.] http://www.pvamu.edu/pages/1.asp.

Prairie View A&M University. "Research Centers." [Online article or information; retrieved December 18, 2006.] http://www.pvamu.edu/pages/634.asp.

Prairie View Solar Observatory

Prairie View Solar Observatory (PVSO) is the only observatory in the country that is operated by a historically black college or university. A division of the Prairie View A&M University in Prairie View, Texas, PVSO conducts cutting-edge research in solar astronomy. It also sponsors research in other areas, most notably those related to atmospheric plasma.

PVSO's primary interest is solar flares (violent explosions in the sun's atmosphere), particularly the preflare stage and the processes by which energy builds up prior to eruption. Current research is focused on searching for structures in the sun's chromosphere and photosphere that outline the sun's magnetic field configuration and might serve as precursors of solar flares. The observatory participates in the Max Millennium Project for Flare Research, and since 2002, it has supported the mission of the Reuven Ramaty High Energy Solar Spectroscopic Imager (RHESSI), a NASA mission to explore the basic physics of particle acceleration and explosive energy release in solar flares.

Another PVSO research project studies the sun's long-term variations. It has been known since 1978 that the distribution of solar radiation is anything but constant, and a number of researchers have questioned the effects of such variation on terrestrial phenomena such as climate and weather. For example, certain evidence suggests that solar magnetic flux has doubled in the last 50 years and that this phenomenon is responsible for global warming, whereas other evidence refutes the doubling of solar flux. Consequently, PVSO researchers are working to develop new indices to quantify solar variations so that their effects on earthly phenomena can be better understood.

PVSO also supports a number of research projects related to the physics of plasma (the extremely hot, soupy-like mix of ions and electrons that is neither solid, liquid, nor gas) in planetary atmospheres. It is estimated that 99 percent of the universe's matter exists in the plasma state; so PVSO researchers are conducting several projects for a better understanding of phenomena related to the behavior of plasma in planetary atmospheres. One project involves the production of plasma by means of a machine called the Rotamak. This device creates plasma by heating matter to extremely high temperatures in a Pyrex(R) chamber and then generating current in the plasma with a rotating magnetic field. By observing the behavior of the plasma thus created, PVSO researchers have been able to develop the Guiding Field Line Motion Approach. This model allows scientists to approximate certain dynamics of plasma such as current and flow velocity, which gives them greater insight into the behavior of plasma as it swirls about in planetary atmospheres.

Other plasma-related projects include the development of a numerical method to build and define new magnetic coordinates in Earth's ionosphere as well as the Prairie View Dynamo Code. Because the behavior of atmospheric plasma is heavily influenced by planetary magnetic fields, so too are the behaviors of plasma-related phenomena in the ionosphere. Consequently, PVSO researchers have defined magnetic field coordinates for Earth, Jupiter, Uranus, and Neptune as a tool for developing a more accurate interpretation of planetary data acquired by various space exploration missions. They have also developed a computer model for using these coordinates to model the ionospheric dynamo (how the movement of plasma throughout Earth's iono-sphere is affected by Earth's magnetic field and by thermospheric winds, which are the result of heating caused by solar radiation). Previous models used a dipole field aligned with the Earth's rotation axis, but this procedure results in unacceptably large distortions of electromagnetic activity in the parts of the ionosphere directly above the equator, the points most distant from the Earth's magnetic poles. Consequently, PVSO researchers developed the Prairie View Dynamo Code (PVDC), which replaces the dipole model with a more sophisticated model of the International Geomagnetic Reference Field, the Earth's main magnetic field.

See also: Astronomy and Astrophysics; Historically Black Colleges and Universities; Physics; Prairie View A&M University

REFERENCES AND FURTHER READING

Prairie View Solar Observatory. "Prairie View Solar Observatory." [Online article or information; retrieved December 18, 2006.] http://www.pvamu.edu/cps/.

Provident Hospital and Training School

Chicago's Provident Hospital and Training School was one of the six major training institutions for providing black physicians with postgraduate medical instruction prior to the Civil Rights Movement. It was founded, however, as a place where black women could further their careers as nurses, and its course of training included nursing as well as the medical specialties.

The idea to establish Provident came in the late 1880s, when a Chicago minister, L. H. Reynolds, approached Daniel Hale Williams, the eminent black physician, about his sister, Emma. Emma Reynolds wished to work as a nurse, but she could not find a hospital in Chicago that would provide her with the necessary training. At Reverend Reynolds's instigation, Williams organized a group of local leaders to raise money for a hospital where black men as well as women could study and practice medicine, and in 1891, their efforts resulted in the opening of the Provident Hospital and Training School. At first, Provident's patients were mostly white, as was its staff, but by 1915, the vast majority of the physicians, nurses, and patients were black.

Although Provident provided quality training for nurses and surgical interns from the beginning, it was not until 1917 that the first organized effort was made to provide quality postgraduate instruction as well. That same year, the Laboratory of Surgical Research of Chicago began offering short, intensive courses in surgical specialties to Provident interns. These courses were discontinued in 1920, and for the next nine years, no further postgraduate instructions was offered. Then, in 1929, Provident became affiliated with the

University of Chicago. Under the guidance of the university, Provident acquired the larger Chicago Lying-In Hospital, to which it moved its entire operation in 1933. Meanwhile, in 1932, the university had opened a residency program in general and orthopedic surgery at Provident, which attracted many black graduates of Midwestern medical schools. Part of the program included advanced training at hospitals in other parts of the country and in Europe, making a Provident residency a highly sought-after position. Ironically, the program became less desirable as a result of the successes of the Civil Rights Movement, which opened up residencies for blacks at larger, more prestigious hospitals; unable to compete with these hospitals, in 1965, Provident discontinued its surgical training program.

Provident also provided black physicians with the opportunity to perform research. Typical of the type of research conducted at Provident was a 10-year study (1942–1951) of gall bladder surgery. At the time, it was incorrectly believed that African Americans suffered rarely if ever from biliary tract disease (the development of gallstones), but the study demonstrated conclusively that African Americans were just as susceptible to gallstones as anyone else. Another typical project was the development of different techniques for performing a vagectomy (the surgical removal of a segment of the vagus nerve, which runs from the brain through the face to the abdomen) as a remedy for peptic ulcer.

As was the case for most predominantly black hospitals, the Civil Rights Movement brought on a financial crisis for Provident. As black Americans won the right to be treated in formerly all-white hospitals, they used the facilities of hospitals like Provident less and less. Provident struggled to survive until 1987, when it finally shut its doors. Shortly thereafter, however, an outcry from the community it had served won its reopening in 1993, this time as part of the Cook County Hospital system. In 1994, Provident resumed its teaching mission, this time as an affiliate of Loyola University's medical school.

While no longer considered a black-run hospital, Provident continues to serve the health needs of the community, including a variety of health outreach efforts. For example, beginning in 2005, some 15 faculty members at Provident's department of family medicine volunteered to serve as mentors to the Future Doctors of America Club. This club involves African American students in the 7th through 12th grades who attend Chicago's Daniel Hale Williams Preparatory School of Medicine in activities designed to encourage and support them on their way to medical careers.

See also: Daniel Hale Williams Preparatory School of Medicine; Williams, Daniel H.

REFERENCES AND FURTHER READING

Organ, Claude H., and Margaret Kosiba, eds. *A Century of Black Surgeons: The U.S.A. Experience.* Norman, OK: Transcript Press, 1987: 265–310.

The Provident Foundation. "History: Provident Hospital." [Online article or information; retrieved November 17, 2005.] http://www.provident foundation.org/history.

Quality Education for Minorities Network

The Quality Education for Minorities (QEM) Network is a nonprofit organization dedicated to improving the education of African Americans and other minorities. Among its many endeavors are a number of initiatives that support the efforts of the National Science Foundation (NSF) to increase the number of minorities in the sciences while enhancing the quality of science education received by minority students from kindergarten through graduate school. The network boasts a professional staff and permanent headquarters in Washington, D.C. Its motto is, "Quality education for minorities improves the quality of education for all."

The QEM Network grew out of the QEM Project, which was based at the Massachusetts Institute of Technology and funded by the Carnegie Corporation of New York. In 1990, the QEM Project issued a report, *Education That Works: An Action Plan for the Education of Minorities*. Cambridge, Mass. (MIT Room 26–153, Cambridge 02139): Quality Education for Minorities Project, Massachusetts Institute of Technology, [1990]

That same year, the QEM Network was established to carry out the plan set out in *Education That Works* (no longer in print). Toward that end, the network seeks to help communities build state and local support for enhanced minority education, to monitor state and national legislation and other educational policies that affect the quality of minority education, to evaluate programs and projects for enhancing minority education and then promote those that hold the most promise for success, to develop model approaches for improving minority education, and to serve as a clearinghouse for information related to minority education.

One of the QEM Network's first initiatives was to help increase the number of minority scientists and engineers. To this end, in 1991, the QEM/MSE (mathematics, science, and education) Network was established. QEM/MSE is a coalition of institutions of higher education, public school districts, and federal and private agencies and organizations whose primary focus is on mathematics, science, and education (MSE). These latter entities include the Carnegie Corporation, NSF, the National Aeronautics and Space Administration (NASA), the Department of Energy, the Department of Health and Human Services, and the National Institutes of Health. As of 2007, the QEM/MSE Network's institutional membership included the following historically black colleges and universities (HBCUs): Delaware State University, Dillard University, Elizabeth City State University, Grambling State University, Hampton University, Jackson State University, Jarvis Christian College, Johnson C. Smith University, Morgan State University, North Carolina A&T State University, Philander Smith College, and Spelman College.

The coalition's original goal was to meet the numerical goals established in *Education That Works* and in its own 1992 publication, *Together We Can Make It Work: A National Agenda to Provide Quality Education for Minorities in Mathematics, Science, and Engineering.* (QEM Network: Washington, DC, 1992). Thus, the QEM/MSE Network set out to quadruple the number of minority students receiving MSE undergraduate degrees annually, triple the number of minority students receiving MSE doctorates annually, and quintuple the number of minority college students newly qualified to teach MSE annually, all by the year 2000. To this end, QEM/MSE sought to spur institutions at the national, state, and local levels to participate more fully in attaining these goals while conducting national and statewide conferences and holding proposal development and evaluation workshops to promote student and faculty development. Specifically, these conferences and workshops focused on identifying the barriers to attaining QEM/MSE's goals and developing innovative methods for removing them.

QEM/MSE also supports such NSF graduate and undergraduate initiatives as Science and Technology Centers (STC) and the Historically Black Colleges and Universities-Undergraduate Program (HBCU-UP) Technical Assistance Project. STC offers doctoral students the opportunity to conduct research at NSF-supported research institutions. QEM/MSE supports the project with the Integrative Partnerships Program (IPP), which helps minority students participate in STC. Specifically, IPP recruits and places minority doctoral students in paid summer and academic year research internships within the STC network. As of 2007, summer internships came with a stipend of up to $6,600, and academic year internships came with a stipend of up to $40,500. IPP also promotes the development of research relationships between STC centers and faculty members with PhDs who teach at HBCUs offering graduate degrees in science and related disciplines by offering stipends of $9,000 plus travel and housing allowances to qualified faculty members so that they can conduct research at STC institutions. HBCU-UP seeks to enhance the quality of undergraduate education in science and related disciplines at HBCUs through curriculum reform and enhancement, faculty professional development, student support, research experiences for undergraduates, and scientific instrumentation to improve instruction. QEM/MSE supports HBCU-UP by conducting workshops for representatives of HBCUs to help them improve the quality of their grant proposals, evaluate unsuccessful proposals, manage and evaluate projects resulting from successful proposals, and find alternative sources of funding so that the projects can be continued after the cessation of HBCU-UP funding.

The QEM Network specifically works to increase the number of black biologists with the QEM/BIO Project. This project provides technical assistance to professors of HBCUs and other minority-serving institutions so that they can participate more fully in the research sponsored by NSF's Directorate of Biological Sciences. The project was initiated in 2004 with a three-year grant from NSF, and it teaches participants, who must be actively engaged in biological research, how to apply successfully for research grants and how to manage NSF-funded research once a proposal has been approved. The project also alerts participants to potential funding opportunities within the directorate (which supports research related to biological infrastructure, integrative organismal biology, environmental biology, and the molecular and cellular biosciences) and offers them opportunities to serve as members of review panels to increase their awareness of the grant proposal review process.

In terms of K–12 science education, the QEM Network supports two NSF initiatives: the Discovery Research K–12 (DR-K12) Program and the Math and Science Partners (MSP) Program. DR-K12 was formed from three former NSF elementary and secondary education programs: Teacher Professional Continuum, Instructional Materials Development, and Centers for Learning and Teaching. It funds research, development, and evaluation activities concerning the generation and application of knowledge as it applies to the learning and teaching of science at the K–12 levels. To make sure that educators at HBCUs and other minority-serving institutions that focus on teacher preparation are aware of this program and can take full advantage of it, the network sponsors the annual QEM DR-K12 Workshop in Washington, D.C. MSP seeks to improve K–12 student achievement in science and mathematics by ensuring that all students have access to and are prepared for challenging and advanced science courses. It also seeks to enhance the quality and diversity of the teachers who instruct those courses. In this regard, the network conducts workshops for HBCUs to help them become so-called teacher institutes, as defined by MSP guidelines.

The QEM Network Internship Program provides opportunities for minority students, particularly undergraduates attending HBCUs, to interact with individuals involved in policy making as it relates to science education. As of 2007, the network was offering two types of internships. Science Student Internships at NSF provide rising juniors and seniors with opportunities to increase their awareness and knowledge of the circumstances that prevent most undergraduate minority students from receiving a quality education and to become familiar with the programs and strategies being used to address these circumstances. Health-focused Internships are available to HBCU undergraduates majoring in an allied health field, any of the biomedical or life sciences, biomedical research, pharmacy, physical or occupational therapy, predentistry, premedicine, or public health. These internships are supported by the U.S. Department of Health and Human Services' Office of Minority Health. They provide students with opportunities to increase their knowledge and understanding of health disparities, particularly HIV/AIDS, that disproportionately affect underrepresented minority groups. Internships also help students learn the ability to design, develop, and lead outreach activities aimed at reducing such disparities.

NSF's Major Research Instrumentation (MRI) Program seeks to make scientific equipment for research and research training more accessible to colleges, universities, and research organizations whose missions address scientific education. The QEM Network supports MRI by conducting workshops across the country to help faculty at minority-serving institutions prepare successful proposals for obtaining the scientific equipment their institutions require.

See also: Biology; Delaware State University; Department of Energy; Hampton University; Historically Black Colleges and Universities; HIV/AIDS; Jackson State University; Morgan State University; National Aeronautics and Space Administration; National Institutes of Health; National Science Foundation; North Carolina A&T State University; Spelman College

REFERENCES AND FURTHER READING

Quality Education for Minorities Network. "Quality Education for Minorities." [Online article or information; retrieved April 11, 2007.] http://qemnet work.qem.org/.

Research Infrastructure in Minority Institutions

The Research Infrastructure in Minority Institutions (RIMI) Program seeks to enhance the ability of historically black colleges and universities (HBCUs) and other minority-serving institutions to prepare their students to conduct top-quality research in the medical sciences. RIMI is funded and administered by the National Center on Minority Health and Health Disparities (NCMHD). In 2007, NCMHD set aside slightly more than $5 million for that year's expenditures on the RIMI Program.

Part of NCMHD's mission is to eliminate the health disparities that affect specific population groups such as African Americans, Native Americans, and Hispanic Americans. It is known that many diseases and adverse medical conditions affect these and other groups to a much greater degree than they do the general population. To this end, NCMHD seeks to develop a cadre of clinical, biomedical, and behavioral research scientists with the skills, knowledge, and abilities to engage in innovative research and research training that will contribute to reducing and eliminating health disparities in the United States. To reach this goal, in 1992, NCMHD implemented the RIMI Program as a means of maximizing the number of blacks and other minorities capable of joining this cadre.

RIMI's purpose is to bolster the research infrastructure (which includes people and management systems as well as buildings and equipment) of institutions of higher learning that have demonstrated the ability to produce highly qualified minority research scientists, a disproportionally large number of whom devote their professional careers to addressing issues of health disparities among minorities. Specifically, RIMI offers grant money to HBCUs as a means by which they can build institutional research infrastructure, strengthen faculty research, enhance faculty capacity for research training, and prepare students for careers in research. RIMI aims to improve the research infrastructure not only at institutions with graduate programs that conduct basic research, but also at institutions with undergraduate programs that play an important role in the early training of a majority of minority researchers.

In the first 15 years of its existence, RIMI contributed significantly to the development of the biomedical research programs at HBCUs such as Alabama State University, Southern University, Winston-Salem State University, and Spelman College. RIMI funds a number of different initiatives at HBCUs. As of 2007, the program granted up to $200,000 per year to a four-year institution and up to $100,000 per year to a two-year institution for purposes of hiring faculty and buying research equipment and supplies. RIMI also provides a one-time grant for renovations and alterations to laboratory and administrative facilities of up to $150,000 for a four-year institution and up to $125,000 for a two-year institution. As a means of encouraging faculty at HBCUs to develop independent research projects related to NCMHD's goals, RIMI contributes to the salaries of up to three faculty members per school; expenses include up to 40 percent of a faculty member's salary during the regular school year and up to 100 percent during the summer session. This funding allows the school to hire additional faculty to cover for the ones who are conducting NCMHD-related research. Of equal importance is that faculty engaging in research can involve their students as well, thus giving them a solid grounding in the basics of conducting scientific research.

See also: Alabama State University; Health Disparities; Historically Black Colleges and Universities; National Center on Minority Health and Health Disparities; Southern University and A&M College System; Spelman College; Winston-Salem State University

REFERENCES AND FURTHER READING

Grants.gov. "Research Infrastructure in Minority Institutions (RIMI)[P20]." [Online article or information; retrieved April 17, 2007.] http://www.grants.gov/search/search.do?oppId=12637&mode=VIEW.

Roman-Barnes Society

The Roman-Barnes Society originated as a professional organization for black ophthalmologists (specialists in the anatomy, functions, and diseases of the eye) and otolaryngologists (who specialize in the anatomy, functions, and diseases of the ears, nose, and throat). For the last 30 or more years, however, it has included only black ophthalmologists, after its otolaryngologists formed a separate group.

The Roman-Barnes Society came into existence as a result of racial discrimination on the part of the American Academy of Ophthalmology and Otolaryngology (AAOO). Each year at its annual meeting, the AAOO held a social function that was open to whites only, the academy's black members being uninvited. Consequently, at the AAOO's 1967 meeting, Axel Hansen, H. Philip Venable, Claude L. Cowen Sr., Andrew H. Jackson, Chester C. Pryor, and Joseph B. Forrester made plans to form a new scientific-social organization for the academy's black members. This new society was named after Charles V. Roman, the first African American physician to receive training in both ophthalmology and otolaryngology, and W. Harry Barnes, the noted black otolaryngologist.

From 1968 to 1978, the Roman-Barnes Society met at each AAOO annual meeting. The program included a scientific talk followed by a social program. When, in 1978, the AAOO separated into two organizations, one devoted to ophthalmology and the other devoted to otolaryngology, the Roman-Barnes Society split in two as well. The ophthalmologists retained the name Roman-Barnes Society; however, the otolaryngologists named their new organization in honor of Barnes only.

See also: Barnes, W. Harry; Roman, Charles V.

REFERENCES AND FURTHER READING

The John Q. Adams Center for the History of Otolaryngology. "The Roman-Barnes Society." [Online article or information; retrieved November 17, 2005.] http://www.wntnet.org/museum/exhibits/africanamerican_roman barnes.cfm.

Savannah River Environmental Sciences Field Station

The Savannah River Environmental Sciences Field Station is the first field station in the United States devoted entirely to minority graduate and undergraduate research in the biological sciences. Located in South Carolina on the Department of Energy's (DOE) Savannah River Site, it is administered by South Carolina State University, but its member institutions include two dozen historically black colleges and universities (HBCUs) in Alabama, Florida, Georgia, North Carolina, South Carolina, and Tennessee.

The concept of a biological field station devoted to minority research was first proposed in 1995 by Ambrose Anoruo, at the time a professor of biology at South Carolina State. Anoruo's vision called for one-day activities, designed for hands-on experience, in which minority undergraduates would visit the field station with their instructors to collect specimens to study and analyze later at their own institutions. He also called for extended semester and summer courses in agriculture, engineering, environmental science, and natural resource management to be taught at the field station by faculty from the member institutions. DOE quickly granted its approval to use the Savannah River Site, and the following year, South Carolina State organized a consortium of HBCUs in the Southeast to found and operate the field station. Since its inception, the field station has hosted more than 1,500 undergraduates from the member institutions. The first multiweek courses were offered in 1998, and the first summer courses were added in 2000.

In 2001, the field station's original concept was broadened by the addition of graduate courses and internships leading to a certificate in environmental monitoring and restoration. Holders of the certificate are qualified to assist DOE and its contractors in the completion of environmental restoration projects at DOE national laboratories and operational sites. They are also qualified to hold professional positions with the Environmental Protection Agency, equivalent state and federal agencies, and private conservation organizations. Coursework includes learning about patterns and processes in environmental pollution and remediation, environmental policy and law, groundwater monitoring and remediation, environmental restoration technology, and report writing.

See also: Department of Energy; Historically Black Colleges and Universities; South Carolina State University

REFERENCES AND FURTHER READING
South Carolina State University. "Savannah River Environmental Sciences Field Station." [Online article or information; retrieved December 20, 2006.] http://www.cnrt.scsu.edu/fieldstation/.

Sickle Cell Disease Association of America

The Sickle Cell Disease Association of America (SCDAA) is a national voluntary organization that seeks to heighten awareness about sickle cell disease, a medical condition that primarily affects people of African descent, and to work toward discovering more effective treatments and ultimately a cure. The association grants scholarships to students suffering from sickle cell disease, awards fellowships to medical researchers working with the disease, and maintains an online forum to serve as a clearinghouse for information about the illness.

SCDAA was founded in 1971 in Racine, Wisconsin, at a conference of 15 community organizations that wished to coordinate a national approach to finding a universal cure for sickle cell disease and improving the quality of life for individuals and families who suffer from it. Originally known as the National Association for Sickle Cell Disease, SCDAA acquired its present name in 1994. At the national level, SCDAA seeks to raise the nation's consciousness about the seriousness of sickle cell disease by preparing and disseminating educational materials, participating in national and regional educational conferences, developing and promoting service programs that serve the interests of those who suffer from sickle cell disease, and encouraging adequate support for research activities leading to improved treatment and an eventual cure. As of 2007, the association was made up of state and local chapters in 30 states, and it maintained a professional staff at its permanent headquarters in Baltimore.

SCDAA promotes research concerning sickle cell disease with the SCDAA Post-Doctoral Fellowship. This fellowship supports medical researchers just beginning their professional careers who wish to conduct research related to the disease. Recipients must conduct original research at a nonprofit institution of higher learning or research facility under the mentorship of a medical investigator with experience in sickle cell disease research. The award presents the recipient with $25,000 per year for two years to cover salary and supplies.

Much of SCDAA's educational and promotional work is done by the Medical and Research Advisory Committee (MARAC). Under the direction of SCDAA's chief medical officer, MARAC develops the content of educational materials, plans the educational program for the national conference, develops guidelines and protocols for a national counselor certification program, and reviews and approves research breakthroughs for publication by the association. MARAC members answer questions that are posted on the association's Sickle Cell Disease Forum bulletin board and oversee the Forum's content, which includes hundreds of articles relating to sickle cell disease for parents, teenagers, and young people.

One of the ways SCDAA heightens awareness of sickle cell disease is by awarding the Kermit B. Nash Academic Scholarship. Named after a professor of social work whose research studied the psychosocial aspects of sickle cell anemia, the scholarship recognizes the academic achievements of individuals with sickle cell disease while supporting the continuance of their education. The scholarship awards $5,000 per year for four years to a graduating high school senior who plans to attend a four-year college. In addition to the cash award, the recipient is invited to attend the national convention, all expenses paid, and make a presentation.

See also: Sickle Cell Disease

REFERENCES AND FURTHER READING

Sickle Cell Disease Association of America. "About SCDAA." [Online article or information; retrieved May 30, 2007.] http://www.sicklecelldisease.org/info/index.phtml.

Significant Opportunities in Atmospheric Research and Science

Significant Opportunities in Atmospheric Research and Science (SOARS) is a four-year paid summer internship program that encourages and supports African American and other minority undergraduates who are pursuing careers in the atmospheric sciences. SOARS is conducted each summer at the University of Colorado at Boulder. It is administered by the University Corporation for Atmospheric Research (UCAR) and funded by UCAR, the National Science Foundation, the National Oceanic and Atmospheric Administration, the National Center for Atmospheric Research, the Center for Multi-scale Modeling of Atmospheric Processes, and the UCAR Office of Programs (UOP).

SOARS's mission is to broaden participation in the atmospheric sciences and related disciplines by engaging students from groups historically underrepresented in science and preparing them to succeed in graduate school. In addition to providing interns, known as protégés, with meaningful research experiences, the program also immerses them in a learning community and provides them with professional mentors to guide their research and encourage their professional development. Protégés receive direct instruction from skilled practitioners of the atmospheric sciences and participate in meaningful ways in ongoing research projects of their own choosing. Typical projects include studying how a rapidly changing climate affects planet Earth and its human inhabitants, how the chemical composition of the atmosphere is changing, and what causes severe weather events like hurricanes, tornadoes, and floods. Protégés also take part in a three-day leadership training workshop, a weekly scientific writing and communication workshop, and multiple professional development seminars, and returning protégés also serve as mentors to new protégés.

SOARS is conducted each summer for 10 weeks, beginning in late May and ending in early August. Each protégé is matched with a science research mentor, who guides the protégé's original research over the course of a summer and a writing mentor who helps the protégé improve scientific writing and public presentation skills. New protégés are also matched with a community mentor and a peer mentor (a returning protégé). Protégés are expected to conclude each summer by writing a paper about their research and by making a formal presentation at a colloquium sponsored jointly by UCAR, NCAR, and UOP. Protégés work 40 hours a week, receive a biweekly paycheck and a free furnished apartment, as well as paid travel to and from Boulder. In addition, protégés receive funds to attend national scientific conferences to present their research, and successful protégés qualify for tuition grants toward their undergraduate or graduate education.

Protégés spend their initial summer at NCAR or UOP in Boulder. If a returning protégé wants to pursue a research topic that cannot be supported by one of the partnering laboratories in Boulder, then SOARS assists the protégé in identifying alternative laboratories, usually one of the national laboratories of the Department of Energy, the National Aeronautics and Space Administration (NASA), or NOAA, where the project can be pursued. In such cases, protégés are still paired with mentors, and they come to Boulder for the leadership workshop in May and the Protégé Colloquium in August.

SOARS is open to college juniors and seniors who are majoring in atmospheric science or a related field such as biology, chemistry, computer science, earth science, engineering, environmental science, the geosciences, mathematics, meteorology, oceanography, physics, or one of the social sciences and who plan to pursue a career in a field related to atmospheric science. A typical protégé class contains between 25 to 30 protégés, of whom approximately one-third are African Americans. Applicants typically have experienced, and worked to overcome, educational or economic disadvantage and/or have personal or family circumstances that may complicate their continued progress in research careers.

See also: Biology; Chemistry; Computer Science; Department of Energy; National Aeronautics and Space Administration; National Science Foundation; Physics

REFERENCES AND FURTHER READING
Significant Opportunities in Atmospheric Research and Science, "About SOARS." [Online article or information; retrieved April 18, 2007.] http://www.soars.ucar.edu/.

Society of Black Academic Surgeons

The Society of Black Academic Surgeons (SBAS) was founded in 1989 to serve as a support network for African American surgeons who teach as well as practice. Additionally, SBAS seeks to stimulate, mentor, and inspire young surgeons and medical students to pursue careers as teachers of surgery. Membership is not restricted by race; to become an SBAS fellow, one must be a reputable surgeon or surgical investigator who occupies a faculty position in a university department of surgery, one of its affiliated hospitals, or a freestanding surgical residency program; who is an investigator or teacher in a nonuniversity academic department of surgery or an approved surgery program; or who is a qualified practitioner of a surgical specialty such as neurosurgery, orthopedics, otorhinolaryngology, urology, or plastic and reconstructive surgery. Surgical residents are invited to join as associate fellows. As of 2006, more than 200 teaching surgeons belonged to SBAS.

The primary vehicles by which SBAS enhances the proficiency of its members are the annual meeting and scholarly publications. Held in collaboration with some of the leading departments of surgery in the United States, the annual meeting provides outstanding programs in both the science and practice of surgery. Participants at these programs disseminate knowledge of recent advances in basic science and clinical research in surgery, and they present and discuss new information relevant to the treatment of surgical patients. For example, the 2006 annual meeting, hosted by the University of Cincinnati Department of Surgery, featured scientific sessions on clinical trials and education, oncology, trauma and critical care, and cardiothoracic and vascular surgery. The first annual meeting was hosted by Duke University in 1989; since then, the annual meeting has been hosted by Charles R. Drew University of Medicine and Science, Harvard University, Howard University College of Medicine, and Morehouse School of Medicine, to name but four. In terms of scholarly publications, SBAS publishes *American Journal of Surgery* and supports *Current Surgery,* both of which are devoted to disseminating information about advances in surgery.

As part of its commitment to recruiting bright young medical students into the ranks of academic surgeons, SBAS gives Honorary Fellowships to outstanding surgeons who have mentored minority surgeons. It also presents the Dr. Claude H. Organ, Jr. Resident Award, named after one of SBAS's founders, to one or more outstanding surgical residents each year.

See also: Charles R. Drew University of Medicine and Science; Howard University College of Medicine; Morehouse School of Medicine

REFERENCES AND FURTHER READING

Society of Black Academic Surgeons. "Welcome to the Society of Black Academic Surgeons." [Online article or information; retrieved June 23, 2006.] http://www.sbas.net.

Society for Neuroscience

The Society for Neuroscience (SfN) is the nation's largest professional organization of scientists and physicians devoted to studying the brain and nervous system. The society promotes diversity in its field via the activities of its Committee on Diversity in Neuroscience.

SfN was founded in 1969 to promote the exchange of information among physicians and researchers who specialized in the relatively new field of neuroscience. Over the course of the next 40 years, its goals expanded to include support for increased funding for neurological education and research and to publicizing information about the latest developments in neurological research. Meanwhile, the society's membership grew from approximately 500 in 1969 to roughly 37,000 in 2007, and it now maintains a professional staff at its permanent headquarters in Washington, D.C. As part of its commitment to diversifying the ranks of neuroscientists, the Committee on Diversity in Neuroscience conducts the Neuroscience Scholars Program. The committee also oversees the completion and closeout of the Minority Neuroscience Fellowship Program (MNFP).

Funded by a grant from the National Institute of Neurological Disorders and Stroke (NINDS), the Neuroscience Scholars Program enhances the career development of African Americans and other underrepresented minorities in neuroscience. In addition to receiving funding to cover the expense of attending the society's annual meeting and special program activities, recipients of one of the program's three-year fellowships have access to mentoring and networking opportunities that enhance their ability to develop fruitful research collaborations in the future and otherwise advance their professional careers. Fellowships are awarded to both predoctoral and postdoctoral applicants, and they are not renewable.

MNFP was a training program, funded by NINDS and the National Institute of Mental Health, to attract more underrepresented minorities to research and teaching programs related to the neurological aspects of mental health. MNFP Fellows received funding for predoctoral and postdoctoral education and for training programs, as well as a paid membership in SfN, thus increasing their opportunities to develop mentoring and networking relationships. After more than 10 years of continuous funding, in 2007, the NIMH/NINDS grant that funded MNFP was closed out, thus canceling the program.

See also: National Institute of Mental Health; National Institute of Neurological Disorders and Stroke

REFERENCES AND FURTHER READING
Society for Neuroscience. "Diversity in Neuroscience." [Online article or information; retrieved May 10, 2007.] http://www.sfn.org/index.cfm?page name=DiversityInNeuroscience.
Society for Neuroscience. "Society for Neuroscience." [Online article or information; retrieved October 29, 2007.] http://www.sfn.org/.

South Carolina State University
South Carolina State University (SCSU) is the historically black land-grant university of South Carolina. In terms of scientific research, SCSU is best known for its involvement in the Savannah River Environmental Sciences Field Station,

the Minority University–Space Interdisciplinary Network (MU-SPIN), and the Association of Research Directors, 1890 Land Grant Universities.

SCSU was founded in 1896 in Orangeburg as the Colored Normal, Industrial, Agricultural, and Mechanical College of South Carolina. Its mission was to prepare the state's blacks for careers as teachers, mechanics, and farmers and to do so by working in conjunction with nearby Claflin College (today Claflin University). In 1920, SCSU and Claflin parted company, and in 1954, its name was changed to South Carolina State College. In 1992, it attained university status and took on its present name. Its alumni include the physical chemist Gloria L. Anderson, the chemist Linneaus C. Dorman, and the biologist Ernest E. Just.

SCSU established and administers the Savannah River Environmental Sciences Field Station, the first field station in the United States devoted entirely to minority graduate and undergraduate research in the biological sciences. Located on the Department of Energy's (DOE) Savannah River Site, it serves as a home for environmental researchers from SCSU as well as two dozen other historically black colleges and universities in Alabama, Florida, Georgia, North Carolina, South Carolina, and Tennessee. The field station offers one-day, hands-on activities whereby undergraduates and their professors can collect specimens for later study in their classrooms. The field station also offers graduate and summer courses that cover a number of aspects related to environmental science.

SCSU is one of five historically black colleges or universities (HBCUs) chosen to be an Expert Institute by the MU-SPIN Network Resources and Training Sites (NRTS) program. As an Expert Institute, SCSU develops its technological expertise in several research areas of interest to the National Aeronautics and Space Administration (NASA) and uploads that expertise to the so-called NRTS virtual university, where it can be accessed by more than 80 other colleges and universities. SCSU also serves as headquarters for the Association of Research Directors, 1890 Land Grant Universities, which coordinates most of the agricultural research that is conducted at land-grant HBCUs and that is funded by the U.S. Department of Agriculture.

See also: Anderson, Gloria L.; Association of Research Directors, 1890 Land Grant Universities; Department of Energy; Dorman, Linneaus C.; Just, Ernest E.; Minority University–Space Interdisciplinary Network; Savannah River Environmental Sciences Field Station

REFERENCES AND FURTHER READING

South Carolina State University. "Research & Outreach." [Online article or information; retrieved August 30, 2007.] http://www.scsu.edu/research outreach.aspx.

South Carolina State University. "South Carolina State University." [Online article or information; retrieved October 29, 2007.] http://www.scsu.edu/.

Southern Regional Education Board

The Southern Regional Education Board (SREB) is a nonprofit, nonpartisan organization that coordinates the efforts of leaders in government and education in its 16 member states to improve educational programs from prekindergarten through graduate school. As part of its commitment to increasing the number of African American and other minority professors teaching science and related disciplines in Southern colleges and universities, the organization sponsors the SREB-State Doctoral Scholars Program (DSP).

SREB was founded in 1948 as a means by which the Southern states could improve their education systems, which at the time were the worst in the nation, by pooling their resources and working together for common solutions. As of 2007, SREB's member states included Alabama, Arkansas, Delaware, Florida, Georgia, Kentucky, Louisiana, Maryland, Mississippi, North Carolina, Oklahoma, South Carolina, Tennessee, Texas, Virginia, and West Virginia. In addition to DSP, its most innovative programs included two school improvement networks known as High Schools That Work and Making Middle Grades Work, a fully integrated Web site for e-learners and adult learners, the nation's largest educational technology collaboration of state K–12 and postsecondary agencies, and the nation's only regional council on collegiate nursing education. SREB is funded by appropriations from the member states and by funds from charitable foundations and federal agencies. The organization maintains a professional staff at its permanent headquarters in Atlanta.

DSP was initiated in 1993 as a vehicle to increase the number of minority students who earn doctoral degrees, particularly in science and related disciplines, and then seek to teach at Southern colleges and universities. The program was begun with funding from The Pew Charitable Trusts and the Ford Foundation, and today it is part of the Compact for Faculty Diversity, which does across the nation what DSP does in the South. During the first 14 years of its existence, the program produced more than 300 graduates and was providing or had provided assistance to more than 400 more. As of 2007, more than 200 of its graduates were teaching in institutions of higher learning, and approximately 135 of them were teaching in the SREB states.

DSP offers two awards packages to doctoral students who intend to become college faculty upon graduation. The Five-Year Package provides three years of direct program support and two more years of institutional support. This award is for doctoral students who are just beginning or who are still within the first year of their programs. Recipients receive tuition and fees, an annual stipend of $15,000, and access to professional development programs. The One-Year Package supports doctoral students who have completed all course work but are still in the process of completing their dissertation. This award includes one year of tuition and fees, a $15,000 stipend, and a $500 research allowance. Recipients of the One-Year Package are also eligible for support from the Professional Development Fund to cover the expenses of presenting their research at a national or regional conference or scientific meeting. To be eligible for either package, an applicant must hold a bachelor's or master's degree from a regionally accredited college or university. Although both packages are awarded regardless of field of study, preference is given to students pursuing PhDs in science, technology, engineering, or mathematics, because the shortage of minority faculty in these disciplines is particularly acute. However, the program does not support students working toward a medical degree, such as the MD or DVM, whether or not they intend to teach at the postsecondary level. Because part of the funding for DSP comes from the states themselves and their universities, some of SREB's member states have chosen not to participate in the program. Nevertheless, as of 2007, 40 institutions in Alabama, Arkansas, Georgia, Kentucky, Louisiana, Maryland, Mississippi, South Carolina, Tennessee, Virginia, and West Virginia were DSP participants, as were Howard University in the District of Columbia and five institutions of higher learning in New Jersey.

In addition to receiving financial assistance for the expenses of their doctoral studies, DSP scholars also receive an allowance to cover the expenses incurred by attending the annual Institute on Teaching and Mentoring. The institute is an annual, four-day conference of minority doctoral scholars. Hosted by SREB and sponsored by the Compact for Faculty Diversity, the institute helps attendees perfect the skills necessary to succeed in graduate school and as teaching professors. It also provides them with opportunities to share their knowledge about research with their peers and to create networks with scholars and faculty from around the country.

See also: Howard University

REFERENCES AND FURTHER READING

Southern Regional Education Board. "Southern Regional Education Board." [Online article or information; retrieved October 29, 2007.] http://www.sreb.org/.

Southern Regional Education Board Doctoral Scholars Program. "About the Program." [Online article or information; retrieved May 31, 2007.] http://www.sreb.org/programs/dsp/process/about_the_program.asp.

Southern University and A&M College System

Southern University and A&M College System is the nation's only historically black university system. Today, Southern encompasses five institutions offering four-year graduate, professional, and doctorate degrees: universities in Baton Rouge, New Orleans, and Shreveport, a law center in Baton Rouge, and the Southern University Agricultural Research and Extension Center (SUAREC) in Baton Rouge. Although scientific research is conducted at all campuses except the law center, in terms of science Southern is best known for SUAREC's research on urban forestry.

In 1880, the Louisiana state legislature chartered a school "for the education of persons of color" in New Orleans, and this school eventually became Southern University. In 1890, an agricultural and mechanical (A&M) division was added, and in 1914, the school was relocated to Baton Rouge. The law center was added in 1947, the New Orleans campus in 1956, and the Shreveport campus in 1964. In 1974, these four institutions were formally organized as the Southern University and A&M College System. In 2001, SUAREC was added to the system.

Agricultural research at Southern goes back to 1890, when cooperative extension and agricultural programs for farmers were initiated. The Center for Small Farm Research, which was established in 1983, conducts research related to sustainable agricultural production systems, human nutrition, and diet and health. All of these programs were transferred to SUAREC from Southern's College of Agricultural, Family and Consumer Sciences. Currently, SUAREC focuses its research activities on value-added product development, alternative small farm enterprise development, innovative uses for agricultural by-products, issues related to nutrition and consumer sciences, and urban forestry.

Of all of SUAREC's research activities, the work regarding urban forestry is perhaps the most interesting. Current research concerns the ability of trees to absorb large amounts of carbon dioxide from an urban atmosphere and convert it into water, absorb as much as 90 percent of the harmful ultraviolet-B radiation in sunlight, reduce water pollution and soil erosion by absorbing excessive runoff from rainstorms (a mature tree absorbs approximately 2,500 gallons of storm water runoff per year), and reduce heating and cooling costs experienced by homes and businesses by 10 to 30 percent. Much of the research in these areas is conducted in SUAREC's urban tree farm. In essence, the farm serves as an experimental forest for determining a species' ability to survive and thrive in an urban environment. The farm contains thousands of trees of 40 different species, including several varieties of maple, hickory, dogwood, mulberry, gum, pine, oak, and elm, as well as a host of other species. It also produces large bare-root seedlings of the most adaptable species for urban and community forestry projects throughout the state, and it maintains an outreach service to educate the public as to the many benefits of planting and preserving trees in urban areas.

REFERENCES AND FURTHER READING

Southern University and A&M College System. "Agricultural Research and Extension Center." [Online article or information; retrieved August 20, 2006.] http://www.suagcenter.com.

Southern University and A&M College. "Southern University and A&M College." [Online article or information; retrieved October 29, 2007.] http://web.subr.edu/.

Spelman College

Spelman College is a historically black women's college in Atlanta. Despite its nonuniversity status, Spelman's faculty and students conduct cutting-edge scientific research in a number of areas, particularly in biology and the life sciences.

Spelman was founded in 1881 as the Atlanta Baptist Female Seminary. Three years later it took on the name Spelman Seminary, and in 1924, it acquired its present name. The college is part of the Atlanta University Center academic consortium, thus affording its faculty and students opportunities to collaborate with scientists at Clark Atlanta University, Morehouse College, and Morehouse School of Medicine, which also belong to the center. Spelman researchers also maintain important ties with researchers at two other Atlanta research institutions: Emory University and the Georgia Institute of Technology. Spelman operates several centers devoted to scientific research, including the Center for Biomedical and Behavioral Research, the Amgen Center for Molecular Biology, the Center for Environmental Sciences Education and Research, and the MacVicar Health Center for Education and Research. The college also serves as a model institution in terms of developing science curriculums for historically black colleges and universities (HBCUs) and other minority-serving institutions.

The Center for Biomedical and Behavioral Research (CB^2R) was established in 1996 with a grant from a National Institutes of Health program, Research Infrastructure in Minority Institutions. As of 2007, CB^2R supported 12 principal investigators conducting research in biology, chemistry, computer science, information sciences, physics, and psychology. Their research covered a broad range of subjects, including the interactions of various neurochemical systems in the neural control of social/reproductive behavior, cell movements during sexual reproduction and early embryonic development, pollination and plant reproduction, the genetics of complex human diseases, the development of reagents suitable for use in vaccine development in primates, behavioral ecology and host–parasite evolution, cognitive robotics and bioinformatics, the physics of laser interactions with biomaterials, and the effects of early life stress on behavioral and psychological outcomes in nonhuman primates.

The Amgen Center for Molecular Biology, which is funded by the Amgen Corporation, conducts research on molecular biology and biotechnology. The center also provides research opportunities during the regular school year and during the summer for biology majors.

*Spelman College, a historically black women's college in Atlanta, Georgia, is an impor-
tant center for research related to molecular biology and the environmental sciences.*
(Spelman College)

The Center for Environmental Sciences Education and Research is funded
by the Department of Energy (DOE). It pairs Spelman faculty members with
DOE researchers to involve them in environmental research projects being
conducted at DOE national laboratories.

The MacVicar Health Center for Education and Research conducts research
related to the health of African American women. To this end, its researchers
study medical conditions such as diabetes and stroke, which are becoming
increasingly prevalent in African American women.

Spelman serves as one of six institutions of higher learning in the National
Aeronautics and Space Administration's (NASA) Model Institutions for Excellence (MIE) Program. MIE resulted from a joint project by NASA and the
National Science Foundation to develop a model curriculum for teaching science at HBCUs and other minority-serving institutions, which traditionally
have lagged behind other institutions in terms of possessing the necessary
equipment and facilities for encouraging and supporting undergraduate
research in the sciences. In essence, Spelman serves as a testing ground for
the MIE curriculum; if it proves successful, then Spelman will participate in
exporting this curriculum to other HBCUs and minority-serving institutions.

See also: Biology; Chemistry; Clark Atlanta University; Computer Science; Department of Energy; Historically Black Colleges and Universities; Morehouse School of Medicine; National Aeronautics and Space Administration; National Institutes of Health; National Science Foundation; Physics; Research Infrastructure in Minority Institutions

REFERENCES AND FURTHER READING

Spelman College. "Center for Biomedical and Behavioral Research (RIMI)." [Online article or information; retrieved May 17, 2007.] http://www.spelman.edu/academics/research/rimi/.

Spelman College. "Spelman College." [Online article or information; retrieved October 29, 2007.] http://www.spelman.edu/.

Star Schools Program

The Star Schools Program is an initiative of the U.S. Department of Education to improve, by means of distance learning, the instruction received by K–12 students in science and related subjects. Although the program is open to any student regardless of background, it originally focused on African Americans and other underserved minorities who attend school in relatively underfunded school districts.

Star Schools was implemented in 1988 as a means of improving student learning in science, mathematics, foreign languages, and English as a second language. The program enables partnerships consisting of state departments of education, local school districts, and private telecommunications providers to establish distance learning programs. Funds granted by Star Schools to the partnerships are used to obtain telecommunications facilities and equipment, develop and acquire instructional programming for students, provide preservice and in-service staff development for teachers and staff, provide educational programming for parents and community members, obtain technical assistance for teachers and staff in the use of the facilities and programming, and improve instruction in science and mathematics through the use of video games and computer simulations. In terms of dollar amounts, the program allocated more than $55 million to partnerships in fiscal years 2004 through 2006 alone.

Star Schools was originally intended to enhance the education of students from underfunded school districts. Such students tend disproportionately to be underserved minorities, including African Americans, and such districts often lack the money to hire teachers to teach subjects like chemistry, physics, and calculus. Televising programs about these and other subjects, it was believed, would make students more inclined to learn these subjects, in large part because of the glamour associated with the state-of-the-art telecommunications systems that brought them the programming. In time, however, it was demonstrated that all schoolchildren, regardless of ethnic or socioeconomic background, benefit from distance learning, provided that the programming is well done and the telecommunications systems are of high enough quality.

It is estimated that, in the first eight years of the program, Star Schools programming reached more than 10 million learners, and it instilled in many elementary and middle school students an interest in science that teachers had never witnessed before. The program also instilled in teachers a renewed interest in teaching science because they now had custom-designed tools to make their instruction more innovative and appealing to students. For example, one interactive program taught elementary students about outer space by allowing them to talk to an astronaut, even though the astronaut was in Houston and the students were in their classrooms. An unexpected bonus of the program is that it increased the awareness in school districts that many elementary school teachers have not been trained to provide quality science instruction to their students and that now Star Schools projects provide programming for elementary students in science to address this issue.

Originally, the program was designed to provide access to students, primarily in rural areas, unable to receive science and mathematics courses, especially advanced placement courses for high school students. As the Star Schools Program progressed, however, it became clear that the science and mathematics programming for elementary and middle school students was much more effective than it was for high school students, who had the ability to opt out of such courses if they so desired. Consequently, during the first decade of the 21st century, Star Schools programming in science and mathematics increased for grades K–8 and decreased for grades 9–12. Nevertheless, the program allowed school districts without the resources to teach advanced placement courses in science and mathematics to provide such courses to their high school students, thus improving students' overall performance and boosting their interest in learning about, and considering careers in, science, technology, engineering, and mathematics.

See also: Chemistry; Physics

REFERENCES AND FURTHER READING

The Education Coalition. "Reflections on the Star Schools Program After Eight Years." [Online article or information; retrieved June 6, 2007.] http://www.tecweb.org/vault/stars/reflect.html.

U.S. Department of Education. "Star Schools Program." [Online article or information; retrieved June 6, 2007.] http://www.ed.gov/programs/starschools/index.html.

Student National Medical Association

The Student National Medical Association (SNMA) is an independent, student-run organization for African American medical students and other medical students of color. Its primary purposes are to transform medical education so that it suits the needs of African Americans and other underrepresented minorities, increase the quantity and quality of careers in medicine available to minority medical students upon completion of their educations, help prepare minority medical students to excel in such careers, involve its members in community service programs, and recruit minorities to careers in medicine and medical research.

The SNMA was founded in 1964 as a subdivision of the National Medical Association (NMA), the nation's leading organization for African American physicians and surgeons, as a way to bring black medical practitioners into the NMA at an early stage in their careers. Its two charter chapters were established at Meharry Medical College and Howard University College of Medicine. Seven years later, the organization separated from the NMA so that it could focus all of its efforts on representing the needs of medical students. Today, the association includes hundreds of chapters across the country, and its membership of more than 6,000 includes medical students, premedical students, residents, and interns. The SNMA maintains a professional staff at its permanent headquarters in Washington, D.C.

As part of its commitment to enhancing medical education as it pertains to minority medical students, SNMA holds an Annual Medical Education Conference. The 2007 conference focused on academic medicine, and its program included workshops and forums emphasizing the importance of research as a factor in a medical student's education and professional development. In addition to stressing to medical students the need to involve themselves in some form of medical research, these meetings also investigated ways to make opportunities to conduct medical research more readily available to medical students. The workshops and forums also invited attendees to consider careers in academic medicine as a means of increasing the number of African American and other underrepresented minority faculty in medical colleges. To increase the number of minority faculty members at medical education programs across the country, SNMA conducts the Physician-Researcher Initiative. This program encourages SNMA members to consider careers as medical professors and academic researchers by providing them with the types of research experiences most likely to further a career in academic medicine and by establishing a mentoring program for students interested in academic medicine.

To help minority medical students stay in school and excel at their studies, SNMA conducts the Academic and Clinical Excellence in Training (ACE-IT) Program. This program helps students improve their skills as they relate to leadership, test taking, communications, and information and time management. To help minority medical students obtain a position in their chosen specialty after completing their educations and to help them decide on a specialty in the first place, SNMA operates the MedConnect online forum. MedConnect gives students information about the specialties they are considering, puts them in touch with minority physicians already engaged in those specialties, and guides them toward the appropriate residency program.

SNMA also supports its members by offering them scholarships. The SNMA David E. Satcher, M.D. Research Fellowship allows its recipients to conduct research related to obesity prevention and obesity intervention. Every year, five Satcher Fellows are chosen, each of whom receives $5,000. The award is funded by the Pfizer Medical Humanities Initiative. The SNMA offers three other types of scholarships, one for premedical students who are preparing for medical school, one for medical students in their first or second year who are studying basic medical science, and one for medical students in their third or fourth year who are studying clinical science. To be eligible for one of these scholarships, an applicant must be an active SNMA member, be involved in a non-SNMA community service, and demonstrate leadership capabilities and superior scholastic aptitude.

As a means of increasing the number of minority students in premedical programs throughout the country, SNMA conducts the Pipeline Program. This program includes four initiatives: Premedical Minority Enrichment and Development (PMED), the Minority Association of Premedical Students (MAPS), Health Professions Recruitment Exposure Programs (HPREP), and the Youth Science Enrichment Program (YSEP). PMED provides SNMA members with opportunities to serve as mentors to premedical undergraduates and recent graduates holding bachelor's degrees as a means of encouraging them to apply for medical school. Mentors also guide their charges through the process of applying to medical school and help them get ready for medical school after they are accepted. MAPS encourages premedical students to join SNMA as associate members and to form their own SNMA chapters. As of 2007, approximately one in three SNMA members was a premedical student. HPREP exposes high school students to science-related activities as a means to getting them interested in medical careers, and YSEP stimulates an interest in science and health among elementary and middle school students.

In terms of community service, SNMA regions and chapters conduct a number of local projects that are tailored to the specific needs of their communities. One national project, however, is the HIV Intervention and Prevention HIP Corps Project. This project involves SNMA members in HIV/AIDS intervention and prevention training under a contract with the Centers for Disease Control and Prevention. SNMA members are responsible not only for educating their communities about the realities of HIV/AIDS, but also for training their fellow members and otherwise administering the entire project.

See also: HIV/AIDS; Howard University College of Medicine; Meharry Medical College; National Medical Association; Pfizer Medical Humanities Initiative; Satcher, David

REFERENCES AND FURTHER READING
Student National Medical Association. "Welcome to SNMA." [Online article or information; retrieved April 25, 2007.] http://www.snma.org/.

Sullivan Commission on Diversity in the Healthcare Workforce

The Sullivan Commission on Diversity in the Healthcare Workforce was convened to identify the problems that prevent African Americans and other minorities from pursuing careers as doctors, dentists, or nurses. Among other things, its final report called for sweeping changes in how minorities are educated at the K–12 level, how health care schools select students, and how the nation finances health care education for the individual.

The Sullivan Commission was established in 2003 in response to the growing discrepancy between the number of African Americans and other minorities in the American population (25 percent) and the percentage of minorities working as nurses (9 percent), physicians (6 percent), and dentists (5 percent). The commission grew out of a grant made by the W. K. Kellogg Foundation to the Duke University School of Medicine for the purpose of doing something to increase the number of minorities working in the health care professions. The commission was chaired by Louis W. Sullivan, former secretary of Health and Human Services and former president of the Morehouse School of Medicine; former U.S. senator and presidential candidate Bob Dole was an honorary cochair. Serving with Sullivan on the commission were 15 commissioners, including former U.S. congressman Louis Stokes. The commission held hearings and gathered information for almost 18 months before issuing its final report. That report, "Missing Persons: Minorities in the Health Professions" (2004), summarized the commission's findings and made recommendations for increasing the number of minorities working as health care professionals.

The commission operated on the rationale that increasing the number of minority health care professionals is the best way to reduce and ultimately eliminate health disparities, because minority health care professionals are almost always more motivated to do something, in terms of primary care or research, about the medical problems affecting their communities. Toward this end, the commission made 37 recommendations to rectify the situation.

One set of recommendations dealt with so-called pipeline issues, that is, making sure that enough qualified minority students come out of the nation's K–12 school programs to succeed in medical school and become health care professionals. One recommendation called on health care (medical, dental, and nursing) schools, hospitals, businesses, and community interest groups to partner with public schools to provide minority students with classroom and other learning opportunities to increase their appreciation for and their aptitude in the basic sciences. Another called on the U.S. Public Health Service, state health organizations, colleges, and health care schools to provide public awareness campaigns to encourage minority youths to consider careers in the health care professions. A third calls on four-year colleges and health care schools to establish so-called bridging programs that facilitate the transition of minority students from two-year schools (that have demonstrated an impressive ability and willingness to educate minorities) to four-year programs in premedical, predental, or nursing. A fourth calls on health care schools to develop innovative programs for minorities who wish to change careers and become health care professionals. A fifth calls on health care schools to reduce their reliance on standardized test scores and other traditional methods for evaluating applicants and to focus more on developing tutoring and mentoring programs to assist otherwise qualified minority applicants to become successful doctors, dentists, and nurses.

Another set of recommendations dealt with financing a career as a health care professional, because most minorities come from families who are unable to pay the high cost of medical, dental, or nursing school without substantial assistance. Generally speaking, these recommendations call on a wide range of public and private entities to replace the traditional education loan with a variety of scholarships, loan forgiveness and repayment programs, and tuition reimbursement strategies to students and institutions. Perhaps most important, the commission called on all of the public and private entities involved in the nation's health care system to accept responsibility for implementing the commission's recommendations by establishing specific goals, standards, policies, and accountability mechanisms to increase the diversity of the health care workforce.

See also: Health Disparities; Morehouse School of Medicine

REFERENCES AND FURTHER READING

Sullivan Commission. "Missing Persons: Minorities in the Healthcare Workforce: A Report of the Sullivan Commission on Diversity in the Healthcare Workforce." [Online article or information; retrieved July 23, 2007.] http://www.jointcenter.org/healthpolicy/docs/SullivanExecutiveSummary.pdf.

Tennessee State University

Tennessee State University (TSU) is one of the largest historically black institutions of higher learning in the United States. In terms of science, the school is best known for its contributions to astronomy and astrophysics.

TSU was founded in 1909 in Nashville, Tennessee, as the Agricultural and Industrial State Normal School. It began accepting students three years later, and in 1922, it was made a four-year teachers' college. In 1958, it was designated the state's land-grant university for black students, and in 1972, it became part of Tennessee's state university system.

TSU faculty and students conduct research in a number of fields, but its most impressive research is being done under the auspices of the Center of Excellence in Information Sciences. The center was founded in 1986 as part of the state's Centers of Excellence program, which was designed to increase the amount of research being done at Tennessee's state universities. The center's name is a bit misleading; today, it is actually a center for research centers that conduct research ranging far afield from just the information sciences. For example, the Center for Space Science conducts research in astronomy and astrophysics for the National Aeronautics and Space Administration (NASA), and the Center for Systems Science Research conducts similar research for the National Science Foundation. Research projects in astrophysics, for example, concentrate on the photometry and spectroscopy of cool giants, chromospherically active stars, solar-type stars, planetary–candidate host stars, binary and multiple stars, and pulsating variables.

At present, TSU astronomers are building and managing robotic telescopes and applying automation to astronomy to conduct long-term research projects. These projects include measuring the brightness changes in sun-like stars, searching for planets around other stars, studying magnetic activity in aging stars, and measuring the fundamental properties of double and multiple stars. The astronomers make use of seven automatic photoelectric telescopes in the Patagonia Mountains of southern Arizona that are maintained for TSU by the Fairborn Observatory but that are controlled from the TSU campus.

Perhaps the most exciting discovery in which astronomers from the TSU Automated Astronomy Group have participated is the discovery of the first solid-core planet found outside our solar system. Many other extrasolar planets had been discovered, but all of them are gaseous, suggesting that planets are formed mostly by one method, the collapse of a dense cloud of gases and dust. But in 2005, a team of astronomers from the United States, Japan, and Chile, known as the N2K Consortium, discovered a solid-core planet orbiting the star known as HD 149026 in the Hercules constellation, about 260 light years from Earth. Automated telescopes in Hawaii had made the initial discovery of the planet, known as HD 149026 B, but TSU's astronomers used the Fairborn telescopes to confirm it. Further study of HD 149026 B by the TSU Automated Astronomy Group has revealed that it is about three-quarters the size of Jupiter, its atmosphere is about 2000°C, and it takes almost three days to orbit HD 149026. The planet's discovery lends credence to a competing theory about how planets are formed, that is, that they come into being when two smaller bodies of rocks and other space debris collide.

See also: Astronomy and Astrophysics; National Aeronautics and Space Administration; National Science Foundation

REFERENCES AND FURTHER READING

Tennessee State University. "Research at TSU." [Online article or information; retrieved August 21, 2006.] http://www.tnstate.edu/interior.asp?mid=77.

Tennessee State University. "Tennessee State University." [Online article or information; retrieved October 29, 2007.] http://www.tnstate.edu/.

Texas Southern University

Texas Southern University (TSU) is one of several state-supported, historically black colleges and universities in Texas. In terms of scientific research, it is best known for the work being done in its Research Center for Biotechnology and Environmental Health.

TSU was founded in 1935 as the Houston College for Negroes by the Houston Independent School District. In 1947, the school was purchased by the state of Texas and renamed the Texas State University for Negroes; it acquired its present name four years later. In 1973, the state legislature designated TSU as a special-purpose institution for urban programming, and ever since its curriculum has been focused on critical areas of urban concern such as business, city planning, education, environment, health, justice, law enforcement, and public works. However, the school also conducts research in support of the National Aeronautics and Space Administration's (NASA) Lyndon B. Johnson Space Center, NASA's headquarters for human space flight that is located in Houston. Most NASA-related research is conducted under the auspices of the Research Center for Biotechnology and Environmental Health (RCBEH).

RCBEH's research focuses on the toxic effects of the space environment on humans. For example, crew members living and working in a microgravity environment lose bone and muscle mass, and their immune systems do not work as well as they do under G1 (normal gravity) conditions. Other problems include exposure to infectious microorganisms, the toxic waste by-products of life support systems, and low doses of space radiation. As humans spend more and more time in space on prolonged missions or on the International Space Station, finding solutions to these problems becomes increasingly important. Toward this end, RCBEH researchers focus their efforts on two areas: the control of microorganisms in the space environment and the effects of space travel on the human genome.

RCBEH researchers conduct a number of experiments related to controlling, if not eliminating, harmful microorganisms from the space environment. One project investigates the feasibility of embedding natural antimicrobial chemicals into materials and fabrics, including membrane and filter materials for water purification, to prevent the growth of microorganisms in space life support systems. Another project seeks to assess the environment of space microbes by using the tools and techniques of genomics and nanobiotechnology. Part of this project involves studying how fungi and the products of their metabolisms interact with human cells in laboratory cultures incubated under simulated microgravity conditions.

RCBEH researchers also conduct a number of experiments related to the effects of the space experience on human genes. One project attempts to identify the genes and cellular pathways (pathways by which biochemical compounds are transported and utilized by the body) that are altered by microgravity. Since the various types of organs and tissues may be affected differently by microgravity, cells from a variety of organs and tissues are studied to see how microgravity affects their activities. The results of this study will be used to develop therapeutic intervention aimed at managing more effectively the adverse health effects of space flight. Another project investigates whether cells in simulated microgravity environments are more susceptible to genotoxic compounds such as natural antimicrobial chemicals. A third project studies whether acute and chronic exposure to space radiation reduces the stability of the human genome by decreasing the DNA repair capacity of target cells, especially lymphocytes (the cells that fight infection) and, if this destabilization occurs, whether it is amplified by exposure to microgravity. A fourth investigates how microgravity affects the immune system by altering certain physiological functions in a way that induces an inflammatory response for the immune system to deal with. Specifically, this project seeks to understand how microgravity affects the behavior of the stress-activated transcription factor NF-kB, because it is known that abnormal activation of NF-kB results in inflammation. A fifth project studies the effect of the antioxidant alpha-tocopherol on microgravity-induced oxidative stress.

See also: Historically Black Colleges and Universities; National Aeronautics and Space Administration

REFERENCES AND FURTHER READING

Texas Southern University. "Research Center for Biotechnology and Environmental Health." [Online article or information; retrieved December 21, 2006.] http://www.tsu.edu/academics/science/research/nasa.asp.

Texas Southern University. "Welcome to Texas Southern University." [Online article or information; retrieved October 30, 2007.] http://www.tsu.edu/.

Thurgood Marshall College Fund

The Thurgood Marshall College Fund (TMCF) provides scholarship money to historically black colleges and universities (HBCUs) for the purpose of help-

The Thurgood Marshall College Fund, named in honor of U.S. supreme court justice Thurgood Marshall, supports black college students majoring in the sciences. (Joseph Lavenburg, National Geographic Society, Collection of the Supreme Court of the United States)

ing students complete their education. In terms of science, the fund administers scholarships funded by Philip Morris USA to support students pursuing degrees in science.

TMCF was established in 1987 as the Thurgood Marshall Scholarship Fund for the purpose of providing financial assistance to students at HBCUs. It is named in honor of Thurgood Marshall, the lead attorney for Oliver Brown in *Brown v. Board of Education* [347 U.S. 483 (1954)], the landmark U.S. Supreme Court case that eventually led to the legal desegregation of public schools; Marshall later became the first African American to serve as a Supreme Court associate justice. In 2007, TMCF acquired its present name. The fund maintains a professional staff at its permanent headquarters in New York City.

Since its inception, TMCF has awarded more than $50 million to HBCUs for individual scholarships and institutional support. The fund does not grant money directly to students, but rather to its member schools, which in turn award scholarships based on merit and financial need. As of 2007, 47 HBCUs in 22 states, the District of Columbia, and the Virgin Islands received scholarship money and other financial support from TMCF.

TMCF is funded by a number of sources, but mainly by corporations around the country. One of those corporations is Philip Morris USA, the nation's largest manufacturer of cigarettes, which provides the financial support for the PM USA Scholarship Fund. Administered by TMCF, this scholarship is available to any junior or senior pursuing a bachelor's degree in biology, chemistry, computer science, engineering, or physics, as well as a few nonscience disciplines, at Florida A&M University, Howard University, Norfolk State University, North Carolina A&T State University, Virginia State University, or Winston-Salem State University. All awards are made on the basis of a student's demonstrated financial need and the potential for completing the degree program. During the 2006 school year, the PM USA Scholarship Fund awarded 17 one-year scholarships of up to $5,000 each, depending on tuition at the recipients' schools. In addition, recipients who are juniors are encouraged to apply for paid summer internships with Philip Morris, whose headquarters are in Richmond, Virginia, and whose major manufacturing and research facilities are in Virginia and North Carolina.

See also: Biology; Chemistry; Computer Science; Florida A&M University; Historically Black Colleges and Universities; Howard University; Norfolk State University; North Carolina A&T State University; Physics; Virginia State University; Winston-Salem State University

REFERENCES AND FURTHER READING

Thurgood Marshall College Fund. "Philip Morris USA/Thurgood Marshall Scholarship Fund." [Online article or information; retrieved June 1, 2007.] http://www.thurgoodmarshallfund.org/scholarships/pm.htm.

Tougaloo College

Tougaloo College is a historically black private college in Madison County, Mississippi, near Jackson, the state capital. With respect to science, Tougaloo is best known for its commitment to undergraduate research in the Tougaloo Center for Undergraduate Research and the Tougaloo College & Mississippi College Undergraduate Research Symposium.

Tougaloo was founded in 1869 by the American Missionary Association of New York as a church related, but not church controlled, teacher training school for freedpeople. Two years later, the state of Mississippi chartered the school as Tougaloo University, although it did not offer college courses until 1897, and from 1871 to 1892, the state funded Tougaloo's teacher training program. Tougaloo began granting the bachelor of arts degree in 1901, and in 1916, it acquired its present name. In 1954, Tougaloo merged with Southern Christian Institute in nearby Edwards; the new institution was known as Tougaloo Southern Christian College until 1962, when it became known once again as Tougaloo College.

Despite its lack of university status, Tougaloo has long focused on producing graduates well equipped for careers in the sciences. Almost two-thirds of Tougaloo's graduates go on to graduate or professional school immediately after graduation, and approximately 40 percent of the physicians and dentists practicing in Mississippi in the early 21st century were Tougaloo alumni. As part of its commitment to providing undergraduates with a firm grounding in scientific research, the college operates the Tougaloo Center for Undergraduate Research (TCUR). Under the auspices of TCUR, which procures funding for the necessary laboratory facilities and equipment, faculty and students work together on original research projects that cover a wide range of interests. Since 2003, TCUR has sponsored an annual symposium whereby Tougaloo students can present the results of this research. In 2006, student presentations addressed, among other topics, the effect of curcumin (a component of the Indian curry spice turmeric that has known medicinal properties) on the epidermal growth factor receptor in human lung cancer cells, how the polymorphisms (various physical forms) of a certain blood platelet receptor contribute to cardiovascular disease, the effects of complementary and alternative medicine on patients with breast cancer, the relationship between spirituality and hypertension and diabetes, and an assessment of the effects of environmental changes on mice with Fragile X syndrome, the most common cause of inherited mental impairment.

In addition to the TCUR symposium, Tougaloo cosponsors the Tougaloo College & Mississippi College Annual Undergraduate Research Symposium. This symposium seeks to integrate research and technology across disciplines and to build local and regional research programs so that students and faculty have opportunities to engage in integrated research projects. At the third annual symposium in 2006, students from the two sponsoring schools plus Jackson State University, Millsaps College, Rust College, and the University of Southern Mississippi made oral and poster presentations regarding their research. At that symposium, presentations by Tougaloo students addressed, among other topics, the psychological, social, and ethical ramifications of Nazi experimentation on Jewish concentration camp prisoners and other unethical human experimentation; the chemistry of weight loss; a study of body mass index as a predictor of cardiovascular risk factors within Mexican American, Caucasian American, and African American adults; and the antiviral effect of Arbidol (an antiviral agent that has been used successfully against avian flu) on H3N2 (a subtype of the influenza A virus), which had shown increased resistance to standard antiviral drugs between 1994 and 2005.

See also: Cancer; Chemistry; Diabetes; Jackson State University

REFERENCES AND FURTHER READING

Tougaloo College. "The Tougaloo Center for Undergraduate Research." [Online article or information; retrieved May 18, 2007.] http://www.tougaloo.edu/content/academics/programs/undresearch.htm.

Tougaloo College. "Tougaloo College." [Online article or information; retrieved October 30, 2007.] http://www.tougaloo.edu/.

Tuskegee School of Veterinary Medicine

The Tuskegee School of Veterinary Medicine (SVM) is the foremost school in the United States for training African Americans for the doctor of veterinary medicine (DVM) degree. It was founded at Tuskegee Institute (today Tuskegee University) in 1944; at the time, it was one of only 11 schools of veterinary medicine in the country and the only one that admitted African Americans on a regular basis. Today, the school is an integral but autonomous unit of Tuskegee's College of Veterinary Medicine, Nursing and Allied Health. To date, SVM has trained more than 75 percent of the black veterinarians who have been educated in this country, as well as more than 90 percent of the veterinarians who have studied in the United States for the DVM degree. The school's veterinary training includes hands-on experience in the Veterinary Teaching Hospital, which focuses on large and small animal medicine and surgery; in addition, veterinary students are trained in pathology, parasitology, and microbiology.

In terms of scientific research, SVM is best known for the work being done in its Center for the Study of Human–Animal Interdependent Relationships. The center uses a multidisciplinary approach to study, strengthen, and promote the health benefits that people and animals derive from one another. Research projects seek to acquire more scientific knowledge about human–animal relationships and develop techniques to assure that people and animals receive the maximum benefit from their relationships. The center arose from a 1976 symposium that SVM cosponsored with the Tuskegee Veterans Administration Hospital (today Tuskegee Medical Center) that focused on these benefits, but it did not become fully established until 1997, when it received a grant from the U.S. Public Health Service. Past and current research involves human and animal communication, grief and bereavement from pet loss, animal abuse, the human–animal bond and self-psychology, the contribution of pet attachment to dissociation and self-absorption, persistent myths regarding immunosuppression and safe pet ownership, and the veterinarian's role in the HIV/AIDS epidemic. The center has also developed the Tuskegee Behavior Test for Selecting Therapy Dogs to minimize risks to patients and pets, and it conducts the Pets Uplifting People's Spirit (PUPS) program, an animal-assisted therapy program at the Tuskegee Veterans Administration Hospital.

See also: HIV/AIDS; Tuskegee University; Tuskegee Veterans Administration Hospital

REFERENCES AND FURTHER READING

Tuskegee University. "School of Veterinary Medicine." [Online article or information; retrieved December 30, 2006.] http://www.tuskegee.edu/Global/category.asp?C=41703.

Tuskegee University

Tuskegee University is perhaps the foremost historically black college or university (HBCU) in the United States in terms of its commitment to scientific research. It was the first HBCU to offer PhD programs in integrative biosciences and materials science and engineering, and it is the only HBCU to offer the PhD degree in aerospace engineering. At one time, it oversaw most of the scientific research conducted at the Tuskegee Veterans Administration Hospital (today Tuskegee Medical Center), the first (and for years, the only) Veterans Administration (VA) facility to be staffed by African American doctors. Its school of veterinary medicine, the only one at an HBCU, trains approximately 75 percent of the African American veterinarians educated in this country.

Tuskegee was founded in 1881 by the state of Alabama as the Negro Normal School in Tuskegee. It opened for business in a building provided by Tuskegee's Butler Chapel AME Zion Church, and its first principal (president) was the renowned educator Booker T. Washington. Shortly thereafter, the school relocated to a nearby abandoned 100-acre plantation, which became the nucleus of the present site. In 1892, the school was renamed the Tuskegee Normal and Industrial Institute. The VA Hospital was established in 1923 on land donated by the institute, and the School of Veterinary Medicine was founded in 1944. In 1985, Tuskegee attained university status and acquired its present name.

As its early names imply, Tuskegee was intended to train African Americans to teach or to earn a living in one of the industrial trades. It also provided training to black farmers throughout the South, particularly after the arrival in 1896 of renowned botanist George Washington Carver. Carver's groundbreaking research on peanuts and sweet potatoes transformed the family farm in much of the South, but it also served as a springboard for the establishment of other research programs, including ones that had little or nothing to do with agriculture. Much of this research was funded and/or conducted under the auspices of the Carver Research Foundation, which was established by Carver and managed by Tuskegee. As of the early 21st century, Tuskegee researchers were conducting scientific research in a number of centers of excellence. These centers include the Center for Advanced Materials, the Center for Computational Epidemiology and Risk Analysis, the Center for the Integrated Study of Food, Animal and Plant Systems, the Center for Food and Environmental Systems for Human Exploration and Development of Space, and the George Washington Carver Agricultural Experiment Station. This entry outlines the research conducted by these centers, and the Tuskegee VA Medical Center, the Tuskegee School of Veterinary Medicine, and the Carver Research Foundation are addressed in separate articles.

The Tuskegee Center for Advanced Materials (T-CAM) was started in 1987 with a grant from the National Science Foundation to study surface integrity in the machining of high-strength steels and superalloys (alloys able to withstand extreme temperatures). Today, it studies and develops a wide range of advanced composites (materials made from several different substances), particularly those of interest to the nation's military and health care industries. T-CAM also spearheads the university's PhD program in materials science and engineering, a multidisciplinary program that includes advanced training in chemistry, computer science, mathematics, and physics, as well as aerospace, chemical, electrical, and mechanical engineering. T-CAM also serves as the home and lead institution for the Alabama Center for Nanostructured Materials (materials whose dimensions are so small they are measured in nanometers, each of which equals one billionth of a meter). T-CAM's recently completed or ongoing projects have involved such materials as graphite/epoxy composite laminates and thermoset/clay nanocomposites made from aerospace-grade resins and organically modified clays for use in extremely high and low temperatures, composite isogrid structures (sheets of material, usually metal, with integral metal stiffeners in a triangular pattern on one side) and relatively inexpensive polyimide-based nanocomposites for use in space exploration, polymer-based composites capable of withstanding short-term but rapid high-temperature excursions for use in supersonic missiles, a family of polystyrenes in which the phenyl ring has been modified to yield polymers that are amorphous and semicrystalline, silicon-carbon-nitrogen composites and silicon-carbon-coated carbon/carbon composites for use in a variety of high-temperature applications, and shear thickening fluid/fabric composites for use in flexible body armor. T-CAM also works closely with the Tuskegee Center for Innovative Manufacturing of High Performance Materials, which focuses on the development of new methods for processing structured nanocomposites, and with the Center for Integrative Graduate Education and Research in Nanomaterials, which specializes in training African Americans for high-tech jobs in nanotechnology.

The Center for Computational Epidemiology and Risk Analysis (CCERA) employs the techniques developed by the emerging field known as computational science to develop computer models for solving problems related to the spread and development of diseases affecting humans and animals. Some of the models developed to date by CCERA researchers address trypanosomiasis in cattle and human populations, schistosomiasis among humans, anaplasmosis in cattle populations, HIV/AIDS among humans, and massive fish deaths caused by the parasite *Amyloodinium ocellatum.*

The Center for the Integrated Study of Food, Animal and Plant Systems (CISFAPS) studies the full dimension of animal and plant food systems from production to consumption. The center focuses on aspects of food safety that affect small farmers, especially those in economically disadvantaged communities of the Southern states, where a majority of small farmers raise cattle and poultry that they process themselves. Such aspects include animal and plant production and health, the slaughter and processing of food animals, food preparation and consumption, and public health surveillance and monitoring. CISFAPS demonstration programs help small farmers produce food that is safe to eat, and its research programs help federal and state regulatory agencies make science-based decisions concerning the standardization of techniques that prevent the spread of food-borne illnesses. CISFAPS draws on the expertise of Tuskegee's School of Veterinary Medicine and its College of Agricultural, Environmental, and Natural Sciences to conduct research in the areas of agricultural economics, agronomy, anthropology, epidemiology, human nutrition, immunology, microbiology, pathology, plant pathology, risk analysis, and virology.

Established in 1986, the Center for Food and Environmental Systems for Human Exploration and Development of Space (CFESH) supports the efforts of the National Aeronautics and Space Administration (NASA) to develop advanced life support systems for long-duration space missions. Specifically, CFESH focuses on peanuts and sweet potatoes, two crops whose foliage, roots, and nuts can be processed into a variety of foods. CFESH researchers are developing the technology and systems for growing, processing, and recycling the waste by-products of peanuts and sweet potatoes during NASA missions related to exploring and settling the solar system.

Established in 1897, the George Washington Carver Agricultural Experiment Station (GWCAES) conducts research related to plant biotechnology, pest management, food safety, food technology and product development, food chemistry, agricultural and environmental engineering, waste management, and environmental quality. Research in plant biotechnology continues the investigations begun by George Washington Carver in the early 20th century on peanuts and sweet potatoes. Current projects focus on genetically engineering sweet potatoes that are resistant to viruses and herbicides and that can be grown under hydroponic conditions, but GWCAES biotechnology researchers also collaborate in the work being done by CFESH. Pest management researchers have developed methods, such as soil solarization, drip irrigation, and the application of plastic mulch, that kill pests without using pesticides. They have also developed methods for using ultraviolet radiation to control diseases in fruits and vegetables after they have been harvested. Food safety researchers focus on controlling food-borne diseases; current research explores the efficacy of an edible biofilm containing natural antimicrobials as a defense against the harmful bacteria sometimes found in postharvest fruits and vegetables. Food technology and product development research is focused on finding new ways to convert sweet potatoes into consumer-acceptable food products. Current projects involve supplementing white bread flour with sweet potato flour and developing a ready-to-eat breakfast cereal and a beverage made from sweet potatoes. Food chemistry research studies the chemical components in food, including nutrients, toxic compounds, and health-promoting phytochemicals. Current projects involve increasing in diets the levels of beneficial food components such as antioxidants and Omega–3, –6, and –9 fatty acids while decreasing the levels of health-risk components like saturated and transfatty acids, salt, cholesterol, and total energy content. Agricultural and environmental engineering researchers seek to develop a better understanding of the dynamics of mitigation wetlands (wetlands set aside or created from farmland to compensate for the loss of natural wetlands). For example, recent studies have demonstrated that pollutants such as sediments, nitrogen, phosphorus, organic compounds, metals, and pesticides can be removed from the water passing through a mitigation wetland by means of the wetland's natural physical, chemical, and biological activities. Waste management research investigates how the use of poultry litter as fertilizer, a common practice on small farms throughout the South, affects the food chain. Recent research has demonstrated that trace elements of certain potentially hazardous chemicals are alarmingly high in Fuquay and Madison soils, both of which are found throughout Alabama, that have been treated with poultry litter for more than 20 years. Environmental quality research is focused on the end state and effect of environmental contaminants, such as pesticides and pharmaceutical residues, in soil and water, particularly how such contaminants are broken down by microbes in the soil and how they affect the quality of water found in private wells.

See also: Carver, George Washington; Carver Research Foundation; Historically Black Colleges and Universities; HIV/AIDS; National Aeronautics and Space Administration; National Science Foundation; Tuskegee Veterans Administration Hospital

REFERENCES AND FURTHER READING

Tuskegee University. "Research." [Online article or information; retrieved December 22, 2006.] http://www.tuskegee.edu/Global/category.asp?C= 34615&nav=menu200_15.

Tuskegee University. "Tuskegee University." [Online article or information; retrieved October 30, 2007.] http://www.tuskegee.edu/.

Tuskegee Veterans Administration Hospital

Tuskegee Veterans Administration Hospital was the first veterans hospital for African Americans in the United States. As such, it became an important institution for training black physicians as well as for conducting research related to the medical conditions that predominate among African Americans, veterans as well as nonveterans.

The establishment of a veterans hospital for blacks became a real necessity after World War I, during which a number of African Americans served and were wounded. While hospital care for veterans was provided by the Veterans Bureau, such care was so strictly segregated that many black veterans, especially in the South, could not gain admission to a veterans hospital. Consequently, the Treasury Department Hospitalization Committee recommended that a veterans hospital for blacks be constructed somewhere in the South. The idea gained the approval of President Warren G. Harding, whose administration contacted officials at Tuskegee Institute (today Tuskegee University) in Alabama for advice concerning the location of such a hospital, to be known officially as Veterans Hospital 91. In 1921, Tuskegee Institute agreed to donate 300 acres of its land to the hospital, and by 1923, the 600-bed Tuskegee Veterans Administration Hospital (TVAH) was open for business.

The logic of segregation demanded that TVAH be operated by blacks, meaning that its medical staff be composed mostly of black physicians and nurses. However, various persons in Alabama, from the governor to the Ku Klux Klan, demanded that whites receive the prestigious positions at the hospital. At the same time, black Americans made it clear that they expected their hospital to employ black administrators, physicians, and nurses, and by 1924, their wishes had prevailed.

In its early days, TVAH specialized in neuropsychiatry and tuberculosis, the two medical conditions from which the most veterans suffered. By 1942, the number of beds had grown from 600 to 1,100, more than 1,000 of them devoted to neuropsychiatry, and the rest were devoted to medical-surgical patients. By 1954, the total number of beds had doubled to slightly more than 2,200, of which 1,600 were devoted to neuropsychiatry.

In 1949, TVAH began a surgical residency program for black medical school graduates, the first of its kind in the South. Initially, the program provided certification in general surgery as well as ophthalmology, which deals with the anatomy, functions, and diseases of the eye. Regular instruction was provided by teams of medical professors from Emory University in Atlanta and the University of Alabama, with occasional visits by faculty members from Meharry Medical School and Howard University College of Medicine. By 1973, when the program was phased out, it had grown to include training in dentistry, gynecology, internal medicine, pediatrics, physical medicine/rehabilitation, and psychiatry.

Not surprisingly, medical research at TVAH focused on neuropsychiatry. TVAH researchers were particularly interested in the neurological effects of syphilis, a sexually transmitted disease that results from an infection by the bacterium *Treponema pallidum*. Certain forms of syphilis, such as neurosyphilis and syphilitic meningoencephalitis (paresis), are crippling if not fatal because they eat away at the brain. TVAH researchers sought to develop

TUSKEGEE SYPHILIS EXPERIMENT (TUSKEGEE SYPHILIS STUDY)

The Tuskegee Syphilis Experiment is perhaps the most notorious medical experiment in the history of the United States. Conducted in Tuskegee, Alabama, between 1932 and 1972, it tracked the progress of untreated syphilis in 400 unsuspecting black adult males who participated in the study because they believed they were receiving appropriate medical treatment. As a result of the experiment, the guidelines regarding what test subjects must be told before they can give informed consent to participate in a clinical study were made more stringent, and institutional review boards were established to ensure that the guidelines are adhered to. Another result was the reluctance of African Americans to participate in clinical studies, to seek preventative medical care such as regular check-ups and mammograms, and to trust public health officials in general. In 1997, President Bill Clinton publicly apologized to the remaining survivors of the study group and their families for the federal government's shameful involvement in the experiment.

The Tuskegee Syphilis Experiment was inspired by the so-called Oslo Study, a study of untreated syphilis in several hundred white males that was conducted in Oslo, Norway, between 1909 and 1928. Syphilis is a painful and fatal disease, and at the time of the Oslo Study, the only effective treatment for it called for the administration of arsenic and mercury, two highly toxic chemicals that had to be administered with the greatest of care. Because the cure was almost as painful and as potentially fatal as the disease, the Oslo Study hoped to find out exactly how untreated syphilis progressed so that other, safer cures might be devised. Meanwhile, officials with the U.S. Public Health Service (USPHS) were concerned about the spread of syphilis in the United States, especially among the black population. The Oslo Study raised the question as to whether untreated syphilis progressed in black males the same way it did in white males; so the USPHS decided to undertake a study of its own to find out.

A survey of the rate of occurrence of syphilis in black males showed that Southern blacks were particularly susceptible to the disease. For example, in Macon County, Alabama, the principal community of which is Tuskegee, it was estimated that 36 percent, or more than one-third, of black adult males suffered from untreated syphilis. Tuskegee was also the home of Tuskegee Institute (today Tuskegee University), a major institution of higher learning for blacks. Its teaching hospital, the John A. Andrew Hospital, was a major treatment center for blacks in Alabama and neighboring states, and its facilities were more than adequate for supporting a study. Thus, when the time came to pick a locale for the USPHS study, Tuskegee seemed to be the ideal choice.

The original plan for the experiment, as it was developed in 1928, called for the USPHS to track the progress of untreated syphilis in black males for only six to eight months, then to provide the test subjects with treatment for the disease. Payment for the treatment was to be provided by the Julius Rosenwald Fund, a private philanthropy that actively sought ways to improve the African American lifestyle. However, the stock market crash of 1929 forced the Rosenwald Fund to cancel its monetary support of the study, and as a result, the treatment portion of the experiment fell by the wayside. Nevertheless, planning for the experiment continued, and in 1932, the USPHS had established a testing facility, staffed mostly with its own personnel, at the John A. Andrew Hospital. Although some hospital staff members participated in the study to a limited degree, most never knew that the experiment did not involve treatment.

The experiment recruited 600 black adult males from Macon County and surrounding counties, 400 who suffered from syphilis and 200 who served as a control group. For the most part, the test subjects were illiterates who did not even know they suffered from syphilis. Most were told that they had "bad blood" and that the diagnostic spinal taps, administered periodically to monitor the progress of syphilis, were "special free treatments" that would make them better. Further inducements to remain in the program until "autopsy" included free medical treatment for minor conditions unrelated to syphilis; free, regular checkups performed by government doctors, which was something of a status symbol in rural black Alabama; and a special 25-year certificate from the government that was suitable for framing. Meanwhile, the experiment was allowed to run on and on, and eventually it was decided to let it continue until all the participants were dead. By the time the experiment was halted in 1972, all but 74 of the test subjects had died. Twenty-eight had died directly from syphilis, and another 100 had died from related complications. Meanwhile, 40 wives had been infected with the disease, and they bore 19 children who were born with congenital syphilis.

Although they were never told by the USPHS, approximately 250 of the subjects almost found out they had syphilis when they registered for the draft during World War II. The U.S. military ordered these men to obtain treatment for their condition, but the USPHS arranged for them to be exempted from the draft so that they could continue in the program— without treatment. The experiment became even more sinister after 1947, when penicillin became available as a safe, effective treatment for syphilis. Despite this advancement, the USPHS refused to administer penicillin to the test subjects, instead permitting them to die from their disease.

Although the USPHS made every effort to keep the test subjects ignorant of the true nature of the experiment, it never made any attempt to

(continues)

(continued)

keep it a secret from the general medical community. A number of reports were published in major medical journals and presented at major medical conferences, including at least one meeting of the American Medical Association. In fact, the experiment was common knowledge among syphilis experts around the world. Yet, amazingly, word of the nature of the experiment seems never to have reached the black community in Tuskegee, much less any of the test subjects.

The beginning of the end of the experiment came in 1966, when Peter Buxton, a USPHS venereal disease investigator in San Francisco, found out about it. After he wrote to the director of the USPHS Division of Venereal Diseases questioning the morality of the experiment, he was contacted by the Centers for Disease Control and Prevention, which reaffirmed the experiment's necessity. Undeterred, Buxton continued to question the experiment's morality through the appropriate channels, but when he realized he would never change the minds of his superiors, he contacted the press. In 1972, both *The Washington Post* and *The New York Times* published long accounts of the experiment, which made it clear that the experiment had continued with the blessing of both the U.S. surgeon general and the secretary of the Department of Health, Education and Welfare (today Health and Human Services). Shortly thereafter, the Tuskegee Syphilis Experiment came to an end.

Shortly after the news appeared in the media, Charlie Pollard, a longtime member of the study group, filed suit in federal court on the grounds that his civil rights had been violated. The suit eventually became a class action lawsuit, *Pollard et al. v. United States et al.*, which was settled when the federal government agreed to compensate the surviving subjects and the families of those who had died in the amount of $9 million and to assure all study survivors access to appropriate health care.

The outrage caused by the revelation of the role played by top-level government officials in the Tuskegee Syphilis Experiment led directly to the passage of the National Research Act of 1974. This act created the National Commission for the Protection of Human Subjects of Biomedical and Behavioral Research and mandated the establishment of institutional review boards. After meeting off and on for four years, in 1979, the commission issued the Belmont Report, so called because it had been written at the Smithsonian Institution's Belmont Conference Center in Washington, D.C. The report identifies the basic ethical principles that should underlie the conduct of biomedical and behavioral research involving human subjects, and it presents guidelines that should be followed to ensure that research is conducted in accordance with those principles. It also called for special care to be exercised when the research involves human subjects who belong to vulnerable groups such as racial minorities, the economically disadvantaged, the very sick, and the institutionalized, and it cautioned against involving members of such groups in research solely for administrative convenience or because they are easy to manipulate as a result of their illness or socioeconomic condition.

In compliance with the National Research Act, virtually every entity conducting research on human subjects moved quickly to establish an institutional review board. These bodies oversee the conduct of research involving human subjects to ensure compliance with the guidelines of the Belmont Report and the federal regulations passed in its wake governing human subject protections.

See also: American Medical Association; Julius Rosenwald Fund; Tuskegee University

REFERENCES AND FURTHER READING

Gray, Fred D. *The Tuskegee Syphilis Study*. Montgomery, AL: Black Belt Press, 1998.

Jones, James H. *Bad Blood: The Tuskegee Syphilis Experiment*, exp. ed. New York: Free Press, 1993.

Reverby, Susan M., ed. *Tuskegee's Truths: Rethinking the Tuskegee Syphilis Study*. Chapel Hill: University of North Carolina Press, 2000.

a treatment for neurosyphilis from blood containing the tertian strain (the third stage through which *T. pallidum* progresses in the course of destroying its victim). When African Americans proved to be relatively immune to the tertian strain, researchers developed a superior treatment from quartan blood (containing the fourth stage of *T. pallidum*).

Unfortunately, an infamous research project concerning syphilis was conducted at TVAH. Known both as the Tuskegee Syphilis Study and the Tuskegee Syphilis Experiment, this project studied the effects of syphilis on untreated patients from 1932 to 1972. In other words, the project's administrators refused to treat their patients with penicillin, even after it became available for therapeutic use in the early 1940s. In all fairness to TVAH researchers, the project was carried out by medical personnel assigned to the U.S. Public Health Service's Venereal Disease Program, and the only involvement TVAH personnel had was to perform autopsies on the deceased subjects. Nevertheless, because all of the project's 400 or so subjects were black, the project has become symbolic of the racist treatment of blacks, and TVAH continues to be embarrassed by its involvement, however minor.

Since much useful medical research is performed on animals before it is performed on humans, TVAH researchers benefited greatly from their proximity to the Tuskegee School of Veterinary Medicine. A typical collaboration between researchers from both institutions was the modification of the Swenson technique for treating congenital megacolon. Also known as Hirschsprung's disease, congenital megacolon is a condition whereby the colon becomes enlarged, leading to chronic constipation and an enlarged abdomen. Veterinary researchers at Tuskegee Institute had developed the Swenson technique for use on dogs, whereby the enlarged part of the colon is surgically removed and the remaining colon is connected directly to the anus, and in 1952, TVAH researchers modified the Swenson technique for use on humans.

In 1997, TVAH, now known as the Tuskegee VA Medical Center, was merged with the VA medical center in Montgomery, Alabama, to form the Central Alabama Veterans Health Care System (CAVHCS), with TVAH being designated CAVHCS East Campus. Under the new arrangement, the Tuskegee facility provides veterans with the whole gamut of health care services, but it continues to focus on conditions related to mental health.

See also: Howard University College of Medicine; Meharry Medical College; Tuskegee School of Veterinary Medicine; Tuskegee University

REFERENCES AND FURTHER READING

Organ, Claude H., and Margaret Kosiba, eds. *A Century of Black Surgeons: The U.S.A. Experience.* Norman, OK: Transcript Press, 1987: 335–376.

U.S. Department of Veterans Affairs. "Central Alabama Veterans Health Care System, East Campus." [Online article or information; retrieved November 17, 2005.] http://www1.va.gov/directory/guide/facility.asp?ID=141&dnum=ALL.

United Negro College Fund Special Programs Corporation

The United Negro College Fund Special Programs Corporation (UNCFSP) is an independent nonprofit organization that supports historically black colleges and universities (HBCUs) and other minority-serving institutions. UNCFSP's Division of Science and Technology works to link academia, government, and private industry in an extensive partnership network to further the study and practice of science and technology in such institutions.

The United Negro College Fund was founded in 1944 as a vehicle for raising funds for the nation's HBCUs. UNCFSP was formed in 2000 by the United Negro College Fund with the broad mandate of supporting all colleges and universities, domestic and international, that serve African Americans and other minorities as their primary mission. Its work in this regard concerning science is overseen by the Division of Science and Technology, which seeks to equip the minority higher education community by means of infrastructure building, workforce development, and knowledge building. To this end, the division works to obtain fellowships, internships, and research awards for faculty and students at HBCUs. It also helps HBCUs obtain grants for building their science infrastructure, which includes hiring professors and staff, developing courses, obtaining research equipment, and constructing laboratories. UNCFSP maintains a professional staff at its permanent headquarters in Fairfax, Virginia.

Of all its governmental and corporate partners, none is more important to the success of the UNCFSP mission than the National Aeronautics and Space Administration (NASA). NASA funds a number of initiatives that UNCFSP is able to employ for the benefit of the minority institutions it serves. These initiatives include the Motivating Undergraduates in Science and Technology (MUST) Project, the NASA Science and Technology Institute for Minority Institutions (NSTI-MI), the Curriculum Improvement Partnership Award for the Integration of Research into the Undergraduate Curriculum (CIPAIR) Program, and the NASA Administrator's Fellowship Program (NAFP).

The MUST Program is a joint partnership among UNCFSP, the Hispanic College Fund, and the Society for Hispanic Professional Engineers. MUST awards scholarships and internships to minority undergraduates pursuing degrees in science, technology, engineering, or mathematics. Each year, MUST awards approximately 100 scholarships of up to $10,000 each to minority students who also receive special tutoring and mentoring as part of the scholarship. Recipients who maintain a B average are eligible for a paid internship in their chosen field at a NASA research center or other research facility. MUST scholarships are renewable for up to three years.

NSTI-MI is held annually at the NASA Ames Research Center in Moffett Field, California. The institute gives minority graduates and undergraduates access not only to the scientists and facilities at the Ames Center, but also to the Silicon Valley's many research and development companies that conduct cutting-edge research for NASA. This access gives attendees the ability to develop ideas for and to have contact with research projects consistent with the NASA mission that they might be interested in pursuing after graduation. The inaugural meeting of the institute in 2006 included undergraduate students from six HBCUs: Alcorn State University, Clark Atlanta University, Delaware State University, Morehouse College, Morgan State University, and Rust College.

While MUST and NSTI-MI apply mostly to the large HBCUs, CIPAIR is a UNCFSP initiative for preparing small HBCUs and two-year colleges that serve minorities to conduct research related to NASA's mission. CIPAIR was established in 2007 by combining two previous UNCFSP programs: the Curriculum Improvement Partnership Award and the Partnership Award for the Integration of Research. CIPAIR's goal is to strengthen the science curriculum and infrastructure at selected two- and four-year minority institutions so that they can train students to conduct NASA-related research. Like NSTI-MI, the program also promotes contact between small minority institutions and NASA researchers. CIPAIR offers selected institutions a one-time grant of between $400,000 and $600,000; if selected, a two-year college must establish a partnership with a NASA research center, and a four-year college must establish a partnership with a two-year college.

NAFP was originally designed to enhance the professional development of NASA career employees, but UNCFSP is able to utilize it to further the professional development of minority faculty who teach science and related disciplines. Under the STEM Faculty of Minority Institutions Program, recipients conduct research for 12 months at a NASA center or other research facility, after which they return to their home institutions. This program has led to the development or enhancement of dozens of science courses at HBCUs, as well as the establishment of research laboratories and the increased involvement of undergraduates in NASA-related research. As part of the NASA Career Employees Fellowship, which is also part of NAFP, fellowship recipients spend nine months teaching and/or conducting research at an HBCU or other minority-serving institution.

Another of UNCFSP's important government partners is the U.S. Department of Energy (DOE). The Mentorship for Environmental Scholars (MES) and Workforce Development Initiatives (WDI) programs are conducted by UNCFSP and sponsored by DOE. MES provides paid summer internships in laboratory research in biotechnology, computer science, and the environmental sciences to undergraduates from groups that are underrepresented in those fields, and WDI trains and recruits undergraduates from those same groups for DOE careers in research and management.

See also: Clark Atlanta University; Delaware State University; Department of Energy; Historically Black Colleges and Universities; Morgan State University; National Aeronautics and Space Administration

REFERENCES AND FURTHER READING

United Negro College Fund Special Programs Corporation. "United Negro College Fund Special Programs Corporation." [Online article or information; retrieved October 30, 2007.] http://www.uncfsp.org/spknowledge/default.aspx?page=home.default.

University of Arkansas at Pine Bluff

The University of Arkansas at Pine Bluff (UAPB) is the foremost historically black institution of higher learning in Arkansas. With respect to scientific research, it is best known for the work being done at its Aquaculture/Fisheries Center of Excellence.

The university was founded in 1873 in Pine Bluff as Branch Normal College. As a branch of the Normal Department of the Arkansas Industrial Uni-

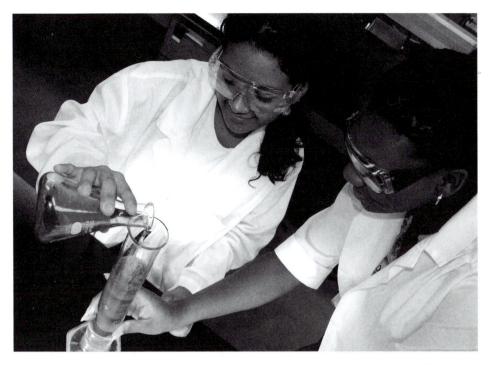

Students at the University of Arkansas at Pine Bluff prepare for careers as biologists.
(University of Arkansas at Pine Bluff)

versity (today the University of Arkansas), its mission was to train black teachers. The name and the mission changed in 1927, when the school became known as the Arkansas Agricultural, Mechanical and Normal College (Arkansas AM&N), and its mission was expanded to provide African Americans with an education in the agricultural and industrial arts. In 1972, the school attained university status and acquired its present name.

Aquaculture research began at UAPB in 1974 with the discovery that tilapia, African freshwater fish resembling American sunfish, are able to reduce what is known as off-flavor in pond-raised catfish, a serious problem that had threatened the very existence of the state's commercial catfish industry. Further research showed that tilapia, when used as forage in channel catfish ponds, can significantly increase the spawning success of the catfish. These and other discoveries by UAPB researchers led to the establishment of the Aquaculture/Fisheries Center of Excellence in 1988.

In addition to offering the MS degree in aquaculture and fisheries, the center serves Arkansas's multimillion-dollar freshwater fisheries industry, which specializes in catfish, baitfish, and recreational fishing in the Mississippi Delta. The center's researchers seek to provide research-based solutions to the problems faced by the state's and region's commercial fisheries. To this end, the center conducts research in the areas of fish health, fish nutrition, pond and hatchery management, water quality, productions systems, economics and marketing, engineering, food technology, small impoundments, fisheries management, and larval fish ecology.

Research efforts concerning catfish have focused on pond management strategies related to stocking densities and sizes, production economics, diseases, new dietary ingredients, intensifying production to increase yields, catfish marketing, new equipment development for catfish production, and value-added products from catfish. Recent research on baitfish has focused on the development of hatchery techniques for the major bait species raised (golden shiners, goldfish, and fathead minnows), nutritional requirements and diets for various life stages, stocking and feeding rates, and diseases. In terms of recreational fishing, the center's research has studied largemouth bass populations and stocking programs in the Arkansas River, fisheries populations in the White River, and the crappie fishery in Lake Chicot. Other projects examine the early life stages of hybrid striped bass and their potential use to correct stunted prey populations in farm ponds, the development of recommendations for successful community and urban fishing programs in the state, the nutritional requirements of pacu (a South American freshwater fish that is closely related to the piranha), the economics of effluent treatment, the ion requirements of marine shrimp raised in freshwater, and the effect of pesticides and herbicides on fish and plankton blooms.

REFERENCES AND FURTHER READING

University of Arkansas at Pine Bluff, Aquaculture and Fisheries. "Aquaculture/ Fisheries–Center of Excellence." [Online article or information; retrieved January 2, 2007.] http://www.uaex.edu/aqfi/.
University of Arkansas at Pine Bluff. "University of Arkansas at Pine Bluff." [Online article or information; retrieved October 30, 2007.] http:// www.uapb.edu/.

University of the District of Columbia

The University of the District of Columbia (UDC) is the nation's only historically black, urban land-grant institution of higher learning. In the area of scientific research, it is best known for the work being done by its Center of Excellence for Renewable Energy.

UDC was formed in 1977 by the merger of Federal City College, Washington Technical Institute, and District of Columbia Teachers College, which was itself formed from the 1955 merger of the all-black Miner Teachers College and the all-white Wilson Teachers College. Because several of these schools had been historically black, and because UDC is a member of the Thurgood

Marshall College Fund (which supports HBCUs only), UDC is considered to be an HBCU.

The Center of Excellence for Renewable Energy (CERE) was established in 2006 on the last day of the International Conference on Renewable Energy for Developing Countries 06, which was hosted by the UDC School of Engineering and Applied Science in Washington, D.C. The center's mission is to provide a national and international center for innovation in the rapidly growing area of renewable energy resources, such as wind, solar, and fuel cells. The center also seeks ways to apply renewable energy resources in the remote areas of Third World countries as a means of powering water distribution systems and satisfying base electrical demand. Current projects include the Zero Energy Visitors' Center on the UDC campus and the use of renewable energy to power a water project in Ethiopia.

The Zero Energy Visitors' Center demonstrates the viability of using renewable energy technologies as a means of satisfying base electrical demand. The center receives half of its power from an array of photovoltaic solar modules and the other half from a wind turbine generator. This hybrid system powers a 600-square-foot mobile visitors' center with a self-maintained heating and cooling system, a big screen television, and soda and coffee machines. The electricity from the hybrid system is also used to light part of the UDC campus and to power an electric submersible pump in a large, transparent water tank, where the pumped water is continuously recycled for demonstration purposes.

The water project involves the development of a low-cost, low-maintenance water distribution system in the Tole and Sadden Sado districts of southwestern Ethiopia. This area was chosen for the demonstration project because of the scarcity of water and the lack of funds for building and maintaining a more traditional, diesel-driven system. The project pumps more than 20 cubic meters of water per day, enough to provide several villages with plenty of water for drinking and sanitation purposes, and it is powered entirely by a hybrid solar/wind system that costs virtually nothing to operate or maintain.

See also: Thurgood Marshall College Fund

REFERENCES AND FURTHER READING

University of the District of Columbia. "Center of Excellence for Renewable Energy." [Online article or information; retrieved January 3, 2007.] http://www.udc.edu/cere/index.htm.

University of the District of Columbia. "University of the District of Columbia." [Online article or information; retrieved October 30, 2007.] http://www.udc.edu/.

University of Maryland Eastern Shore

The University of Maryland Eastern Shore (UMES) is Maryland's historically black, land-grant college. The school's best-known scientific research is for the work being done at the Agricultural Experiment Station at UMES and the Living Marine Resources Cooperative Science Center.

UMES was established in 1886 in Princess Anne by the Delaware Conference of the Methodist Episcopal Church. Originally known as the Delaware Conference Academy, its purpose was to train African Americans for careers as teachers and ministers. The name was changed to the Industrial Branch of Morgan State College and later to Princess Anne Academy, and with the new names came an expanded mission: to provide African Americans with training in the agricultural and mechanical trades. In 1919, the state of Maryland assumed control of the school, transformed it into its land-grant college for African Americans, and renamed it the Eastern Shore Branch of the Maryland Agricultural College. The school was popularly (but not officially) known as Princess Anne College until 1948, when it became a division of the University of Maryland and took on the name Maryland State College. In 1970, the school attained university status and acquired its present name. Today, UMES offers graduate degrees in a number of scientific areas, including the PhD degree in food science and technology, marine-estuarine-environmental sciences, and toxicology.

The Agricultural Experiment Station at UMES conducts research in environmental quality, sustainable agriculture, human health and safety, and food science. Virtually all of its research focuses on the agricultural conditions of the Delmarva Peninsula, where UMES is located. Environmental quality research projects study such things as the use of superabsorbent polymers as a way to control ammonia buildup in poultry litter, the use of aerial imaging and remote sensing to prevent the under- and overapplication of fertilizers, the efficacy of gel technology and self-planting plugs as methods for replanting eelgrass and other submerged aquatic vegetation in the coastal inlets of the Chesapeake Bay, and the development of alternative practices for minimizing the movement of nitrogen, phosphorus, and trace elements from and through soils. Sustainable agriculture research projects include the use of native microorganisms to enhance the growth and nutritional quality of soybeans and other legumes, the use of bacteriophages (bacteria that attack other bacteria) as a way to prevent certain soil bacteria from damaging crops, the identification of the strains of soybeans and other crops that possess an enhanced ability to absorb phosphorus, the identification of drought-resistant strains of cowpeas that are suitable for cultivation in the Delmarva Peninsula, and the use of natural substances, rather than manufactured pesticides, to eliminate parasites in sheep and goats bred for their meat. Human health and safety researchers are focused on assessing the drinking water quality of underserved farms and families in the Mid-Atlantic region, but they also test

The University of Maryland Eastern Shore houses the Living Marine Resources Cooperative Science Center, which studies the ecosystems of the Chesapeake Bay. (University of Maryland Eastern Shore)

a variety of fabrics and materials for use in protective clothing for pesticide applicators. Food science research seeks to gain greater knowledge about the nature and behavior of the pathogens that infect seafood, crabmeat, and poultry, such as *Vibrio parahaemolyticus*, *Listeria monocytogenes*, and the antibiotic-resistant strains of *Salmonella*, respectively.

The Living Marine Resources Cooperative Science Center (LMRCSC) is a joint effort among UMES (the lead institution), Delaware State University, Hampton University, Savannah State University (Georgia), the University of Miami School of Marine and Atmospheric Science (Florida), and the University of Maryland Biotechnology Institute Center of Marine Biotechnology, with funding provided by the National Oceanic and Atmospheric Administration. The center studies the aquatic organisms that inhabit the coastal and estuarine waters of the Chesapeake Bay, as well as the animals that inhabit adjacent marshlands, but it also devotes considerable attention to the socioeconomics of fisheries and aquaculture as part of the effort to protect, restore, and enhance coastal and marine fish habitats and fish stocks. The research interests of LMRCSC faculty include the microbial diversity of coastal bays, the influence of variations in climatic factors on water quality, zooplankton ecology, the morphology of mollusk shells, habitat contamination and the early life history of fish, identifying molecular biomarkers that measure susceptibility to carcinogens, the effects of nonessential metals on ecosystems, using physiological biomarkers to assess the health of fish, the application of fish health management techniques as a means of improving the yields from wild stocks, the factors impacting eelgrass decline in coastal bays and the resultant changes emanating from that decline in the fisheries habitat, the effect of heavy metal on aquatic organisms, developing methods for detecting heavy metals in plants and sediments, and developing methods for analyzing trace element organic pollutants such as herbicides and pesticides in aqueous solutions.

See also: Delaware State University; Hampton University

REFERENCES AND FURTHER READING
University of Maryland Eastern Shore. "Academics and Research." [Online article or information; retrieved January 3, 2007.] http://www.umes.edu/ Academic/index.aspx.
University of Maryland Eastern Shore. "University of Maryland Eastern Shore." [Online article or information; retrieved October 30, 2007.] http://www. umes.edu/.

University of the Virgin Islands

The University of the Virgin Islands (UVI) is the only historically black institution of higher learning in the U.S. Virgin Islands. In the area of scientific research, it is best known for the work being done at the UVI Agriculture Experiment Station, the Water Resources Research Institute, and the Center for Marine and Environmental Studies.

UVI was founded in 1962 as the College of the Virgin Islands. In 1986, it attained university status, acquired its present name, and was declared an official HBCU. Today, it has campuses on the islands of St. Croix and St. Thomas.

The UVI Agriculture Experiment Station is located on St. Croix. Its researchers focus on the semiarid, subtropical conditions that prevail among the islands of the Caribbean Sea's Lesser Antilles, where easterly trade winds provide a nearly constant breeze and alternating periods of drought and heavy rain. To help the local agricultural community increase production, improve efficiency, and develop new enterprises by preserving and propagating native species, the station's research focuses on animal science, aquaculture, biotechnology, forage agronomy, fruit and ornamental crops, and vegetable crops. Specific projects include crossing St. Croix White sheep ewes with Dorper rams to produce lambs that grow more wool over their lifetimes; combining drip irrigation techniques with the use of plastic mulch to reduce water consumption while increasing the yield of tomato, cucumber, pepper, and culinary herb crops; developing techniques for growing and producing increased amounts of the ornamental plant known as *Euphorbia leucocephala*, or Christmas snowflake; identifying the varieties of papaya that are most resistant to papaya ringspot virus; developing an aquaponic system that produces both tilapia and leaf lettuce; and the development of sheep grazing management techniques for maintaining the productivity and stability of Guinea grass pastures.

Established in 1973, the Water Resources Research Institute (WRRI) focuses on the quality, quantity, and management aspects of using rainwater cistern systems as a major part of the domestic water supply. Other research considers the water economy of a low-flush toilet in a water-deficient region, the effects of rainfall on the islands' undeveloped tropical bays, and the effects of runoff from undeveloped and lightly developed watersheds on the tropical ecosystems of plankton. WRRI also maintains a weather station on St. Croix that records historical meteorological data for the Virgin Islands.

Established in 1999, the Center for Marine and Environmental Studies (CMES) conducts research, outreach, and education programs across the Virgin Islands. Most of its research is conducted under the auspices of the center's MacLean Marine Science Center, located on the St. Thomas campus. Research projects include assessing the impact of sedimentation from land development on coral reefs, evaluating the effectiveness of protected marine areas as habitats for sustainable fisheries, determining the importance of mangrove and seagrass beds as nursery habitats for fisheries production, and establishing monitoring programs to track the condition of coral reefs within the U.S. Virgin Islands. CMES also operates the Virgin Islands Marine Advisory Service and the Virgin Islands Environmental Resource Station as a means of increasing the awareness of marine resources and coastal environments.

REFERENCES AND FURTHER READING

University of the Virgin Islands. "Research and Public Service." [Online article or information; retrieved January 6, 2007.] http://www.uvi.edu/pub-relations/uvi/home.html.

University of the Virgin Islands. "University of the Virgin Islands." [Online article or information; retrieved October 30, 2007.] http://www.uvi.edu/.

Ventures Scholars Program

The Ventures Scholars Program (VSP) is a national membership program that provides useful information and advice to African Americans and other underrepresented minorities and to first-generation college-bound students; both categories of students must be interested in pursuing careers related to science. The program's database permits students to get in touch with schools and programs that interest them, and it permits schools to contact students they are interested in recruiting.

VSP grew out of the Minorities in Medicine (MIM) Program, which was established to increase the number of minority college graduates who were well prepared for the rigors of medical school. Although MIM was not formally created until 1990, earlier versions of the program had existed since the mid-1960s. In 1999, MIM became VSP, and the scope of the program broadened to include students interested in careers in any of the sciences, not just medicine, as well as careers related to allied health professions, engineering, mathematics, or technology. VSP is operated by Ventures in Education, Inc., which maintains a professional staff at its permanent headquarters in New York City.

Membership in VSP is open to any high-achieving student who belongs to an underrepresented minority or whose parents or guardians never attended college. High school students who score above a certain minimum on various standardized tests like the SAT or ACT, who maintain a solid B average, who identify themselves as being from one or both of the preceding backgrounds, and who express an interest in a science-related career are invited to join, free of charge. Undergraduates with an appropriate background and interest and who maintain a grade-point average of at least 3.0 are extended the same privilege. Once a student has joined VSP, the student's name and information are entered into VSP's database, where it can be retrieved by colleges and universities looking to diversify their departments and programs related to science. High school students can also access the database to learn about colleges and universities that are interested in recruiting minorities into their science-based programs, find out what resources and opportunities those schools offer, and then contact them directly, and undergraduates enjoy the same opportunities concerning graduate programs and professional schools. In 2007, more than 20,000 high school students and almost 5,000 undergraduates signed up to be Ventures Scholars; almost half of the high school scholars and slightly more than half of the undergraduate scholars identified themselves as being African American or black.

As part of its service to students, VSP maintains a national consortium of colleges, universities, professional schools, professional associations, and national organizations with a particular interest in science and related disciplines. By joining VSP, these entities can use the VSP database of students as a recruiting tool. Just as VSP student members are encouraged to contact the schools and programs that interest them, VSP institutional members are encouraged to contact students they are interested in. As of 2007, more than 200 institutions and organizations were participating in the VSP national consortium.

REFERENCES AND FURTHER READING
Ventures Scholars Program. "Welcome to the Ventures Scholars Program." [Online article or information; retrieved June 1, 2007.] http://www. venturescholar.org/.

Virginia State University
Virginia State University (VSU) is Virginia's historically black, land-grant university. Its best-known scientific research is the work being done in its M. T.

Carter Agricultural Research Center, but VSU conducts research in a number of other areas as well.

Virginia State University was founded in 1882 in Ettrick as the Virginia Normal and Collegiate Institute. In 1902, the name was changed to Virginia Normal and Industrial Institute, and the school was given the mission of training African Americans to pursue careers in teaching and the industrial arts. In 1920, it was made Virginia's land-grant institution for African Americans, and three years later the curriculum again offered undergraduate courses. The school became known as Virginia State College for Negroes in 1930 and as Virginia State College in 1946. In 1979, it attained university status and acquired its present name.

The Carter Center conducts agricultural research in a number of areas, including aquaculture, environmental issues, food safety, pest management, plant science, and small ruminants (sheep and goats). Aquaculture research focuses on the production of channel catfish and rainbow trout as a means of providing small farmers with an alternative source of income. To this end, researchers help farmers optimize production by developing the management systems and establishing the parameters for water quality, feeding regimes, and the optimum sizes of stocked fish. Environmental researchers develop efficient and economical management practices for applying agricultural chemicals, evaluate the impact of wetlands and riparian zones on water quality, investigate the end result of agricultural chemicals in soil and sediment, and study the effectiveness of conservation grasses as a means of abating the transport of nutrients and pesticides from and through soil. Food safety research evaluates methods and approaches for verifying and preventing the transfer of food-borne pathogens, such as certain soil bacteria, from the farm to the dinner table. Pest management researchers look for biologically based solutions, rather than ones that involve agrichemicals, for eliminating the pests most common to the Mid-Atlantic region. For example, one approach involves the regulation of light, temperature, and humidity in unheated plastic shelters known as high tunnels. Plant science research seeks to diversify cropping systems to enhance agricultural income and profitability, protect water quality from runoff containing nitrogen through reduced fertilizer use, and support the production of protein-rich grains for food and feed uses. Plant researchers also experiment with nonnative species such as castor bean, kenaf, sunn hemp, mung bean, tepary bean, faba bean, meadowfoam, and vernonia to determine their potential as crop plants in the Mid-Atlantic region, as well as the on-farm production of biodiesel fuels made from canola. Small ruminant research focuses on the feasibility of producing goats for meat and sheep for wool as a viable alternative to growing tobacco.

VSU researchers also conduct a number of programs sponsored by various agencies of the federal government in a wide number of fields. Such projects include measuring the thermal-optical properties of solid state laser materials

Virginia State University's M. T. Carter Agricultural Research Center conducts research related to aquaculture and plant science, among other areas. (Virginia State University)

for the National Aeronautics and Space Administration (NASA), characterizing superconducting materials with muon spin rotation for the Department of Energy, investigating the anticancer potential of laser-induced indoles for the National Institutes of Health, studying mechanically milled iron alloys for high-temperature and magnetic applications, and using laser radiation to study selected properties of materials for the Department of Defense.

See also: Department of Energy; National Aeronautics and Space Administration; National Institutes of Health

REFERENCES AND FURTHER READING
Virginia State University. "Research." [Online article or information; retrieved January 8, 2007.] http://www.vsu.edu/pages/152.asp.

Virginia State University. "Virginia State University." [Online article or information; retrieved October 30, 2007.] http://www.vsu.edu/pages/1.asp.

Wayne State University

Wayne State University is one of Michigan's major public universities and one of the nation's major research universities. Its School of Medicine operates the Center for Urban and African American Health.

Located in downtown Detroit, Wayne State grew out of the Detroit Medical College, which was established in 1868, the Detroit Normal Training School, which was founded in 1881, and Detroit Junior College, which was established in 1917. In 1934, these three institutions were combined to form Wayne University. The school acquired its present name in 1956, and three years later it became a constitutionally chartered university of the state of Michigan.

In the early 21st century, Detroit had the third-largest African American population of any U.S. city and the highest percentage of African Americans (81.6 percent) of all U.S. cities. Consequently, for a number of years, the Wayne State School of Medicine (SOM) had taken a particular interest in the health of African Americans living in an urban environment. When the National Institutes of Health (NIH) began looking to fund an intensive study of the effects of urban living on people of various ethnic and racial backgrounds, SOM seemed like the ideal venue for the study. In 2003, SOM opened the Center for Urban and African American Health (CUAAH) with the funding of a five-year grant from NIH.

CUAAH's research is conducted by 34 investigators from Wayne State's departments, centers, and programs whose primary interests are related to anthropology, bioinformatics, biostatistics, demography, epidemiology, exercise physiology, family medicine, genomics, gerontology, hypertension, internal medicine, nursing, obstetrics and gynecology, oncology, psychology, and sociology. All projects are thematically related in that they deal with the effects of obesity, diet, and related lifestyle factors on such disparate medical conditions as cardiovascular disease and breast cancer. In general, the center's research seeks to understand how and to what degree environmental exposures, socioeconomic status, and psychosocial factors interact with biological and genetic characteristics to affect the health of urban-dwelling African Americans, as well as how these same factors contribute to the success or failure of multifaceted care plans that promote the adoption of healthy lifestyles.

One of the center's major projects is focused on the relationships among obesity, oxidative stress (an abnormal reaction to the normal processes of aerobic metabolism), and salt sensitivity (a jump in blood pressure whenever salt is consumed). The study seeks to understand how the regulation of sodium in the diet affects blood pressure, how obesity and weight loss contribute to salt sensitivity, how salt sensitivity is affected by environmental stressors, psychobehavioral attributes, and genetic factors, and to what degree oxidative stress is caused by weight loss and salt sensitivity. A related project is focused on obesity and weight loss in obese African American breast cancer survivors, because oxidative stress has been implicated as a possible cause of the recurrence of breast cancer.

CUAAH's third major project studies the efficacy of dyadic intervention for obese patients who are recovering at home from a cardiovascular disease or a medical condition like hypertension, heart failure, diabetes mellitus, and coronary heart disease. In the past, care plans for cardiac rehabilitation patients have been focused on the patient alone. Recent research, however, suggests that dyads (the patient and the caregiver, such as a spouse or other relative) benefit from a care plan that increases the patient's active participation in the treatment, develops positive communications between patient and caregiver about executing the care plan (for example, the need to change certain lifestyle habits like smoking or eating certain foods), helps the patient make the psychological adjustments necessary for successful lifestyle changes, increases the dyad's knowledge and understanding about available services, and assists the dyad through the difficult process of cardiac rehabilitation. To further test the hypotheses implicit in such research, the center will compare the success of traditional care plans with those involving dyadic intervention.

See also: Cancer; Cardiovascular Disease; Diabetes; National Institutes of Health; Obesity

REFERENCES AND FURTHER READING

Wayne State University. "Center for Urban and African American Health." [Online article or information; retrieved May 22, 2007.] http://www.med.wayne.edu/intmed/CUAAH/cuaah.htm.

Wayne State University. "Wayne State University." [Online article or information; retrieved October 30, 2007.] http://www.wayne.edu/.

West Virginia State University

West Virginia State University (WVSU) is West Virginia's historically black, land-grant institution. In the area of scientific research, it is best known for the work being done by its Bioplex Project on anaerobic digestion (a process for treating and recycling farm waste).

Located in the town of Institute, WVSU was founded in 1891 as the West Virginia Colored Institute. Although it was established as the state's land-grant college for African Americans, its early curriculum focused on training blacks to be teachers and vocational workers. In 1915, it became West Virginia Collegiate Institute and began offering undergraduate degrees as well. In 1929, the name was changed to West Virginia State College, and in 2004, it attained university status and acquired its present name.

The Bioplex Project is a multidisciplinary research project that seeks to recycle agricultural by-products through anaerobic digestion. An anaerobic digester makes use of anaerobic decomposition, a natural process whereby a range of many different species of naturally occurring bacteria, all doing a different job at a different step in the digestion process, cause organic material such as waste paper, grass clippings, leftover food, and sewage to decompose under hot, humid conditions. This process is speeded up in the digester, which is a large, airtight, mechanical mixer. Anaerobic digestion has been used for years to process organic waste as an alternative to dumping it in a landfill, but the Bioplex Project takes the process a step further by focusing on converting the by-products of animal waste, particularly poultry litter from West Virginia poultry farms, into usable products such as biogas and fertilizer.

The project maintains a 10,000-gallon pilot digester on the WVSU campus, and the material from the digester is used in the project's experiments. Although one aspect of the research is the conversion of poultry litter into methane gas, the main focus is on the conversion of the nitrogen in poultry litter into ammonium so that it can be reused as fertilizer. Part of this effort involves the elimination of pathogens, such as the bacteria *Escherichia coli* and *Salmonella* and the protozoan *Cryptosporidium muris*, from the solid effluent that remains after the decomposition process is completed. Another important focus is on the use of the liquid effluent in hydroponic systems for growing lettuce, tomatoes, and vegetables.

REFERENCES AND FURTHER READING

The Bioplex Project at West Virginia State University. "Welcome to the Bioplex Project." [Online article or information; retrieved January 9, 2007.] http://bioplexproject.wvstateu.edu.

West Virginia State University. "West Virginia State University." [Online article or information; retrieved October 30, 2007.] http://www.wvstateu.edu/.

Winston-Salem State University

Winston-Salem State University (WSSU) is one of several historically black institutions of higher learning operated by the state of North Carolina. With respect to scientific research, it is best known for the work being done at its Biomedical Research Infrastructure Center.

WSSU was founded in 1892 in Winston-Salem as Slater Industrial and State Normal School, and its mission was to prepare African Americans for teaching and various industrial occupations. In 1925, it became known as Winston-Salem State Teachers College, and in 1969, it attained university status and acquired its present name. Founded in 1996, the Biomedical Research Infrastructure Center (BRIC) is funded by grants from the Research Infrastructure in Minority Institutions Program. As of 2007, BRIC focused its research on four areas: electrophysiology, medicinal chemistry, neuroscience, and microbial physiology. Much of this research is conducted in collaboration with researchers from nearby Wake Forest University School of Medicine.

BRIC's electrophysiology and neuroscience researchers seek to understand how and why hypertension (high blood pressure) alters the efficiency of the autonomic nervous system (ANS), which governs the cardiovascular, respiratory, and digestive systems. Preliminary work on this project has demonstrated that hypertension brings on dramatic changes in the behavior of the ANS's ganglion neurons and that these changes most likely take place because the biochemical synapses that link the neurons are interfered with by the action of angiotensin II, a biochemical that constricts the blood vessels and contributes to high blood pressure. Researchers now hope to verify this connection and, once it is verified, to develop methods for eliminating or reducing the influence on angiotensin on the ANS.

Research in microbial physiology focuses on how microorganisms adapt and grow at low temperatures. To date, work in this regard suggests that the cold shock response (an organism's tendency to produce certain proteins whenever it is exposed to low temperature) occurs so that the organism's cells can continue to function normally. BRIC researchers are pursuing this line of inquiry by studying cold shock dead protein A (CsdA), one of the proteins produced by the bacterium *Escherichia coli* in response to cold shock. Since CsdA is also found in the cells of other organisms, including humans, researchers hope that their discoveries concerning CsdA will shed light on how other organisms thrive in cold temperatures.

Medicinal chemistry researchers synthesize and test drugs to be used to eradicate cocaine and methamphetamine addiction. Current work focuses on developing certain cocaine-like substances known as piperidines into pharmaceuticals that can satisfy the addict's craving for cocaine or methamphetamine without themselves being addictive.

See also: Chemistry

REFERENCES AND FURTHER READING

Winston-Salem State University. "Biomedical Research Infrastructure Center." [Online article or information; retrieved January 10, 2007.] http://www.wssu.edu/WSSU/UndergraduateStudies/College+of+Arts+and+Sciences/Biomedical+Research+Infrastructure+Center.

Winston-Salem State University. "Winston-Salem State University." [Online article or information; retrieved October 30, 2007.] http://www.wssu.edu/wssu.

Xavier University of Louisiana

Xavier University of Louisiana is the nation's only historically black, Roman Catholic university. In the field of science, it is best known for the work being done by its College of Pharmacy and its Center for Undergraduate Research. Xavier is one of two historically black colleges and universities (HBCUs) that have been designated Minority Institutions of Excellence by the National Aeronautics and Space Administration (NASA).

Xavier was founded in 1915 in New Orleans, by Saint Katherine Drexel and the Sisters of the Blessed Sacrament as a high school for African Americans.

Two years later, the school began a program for training black teachers, and in 1925, the school became a college, offering courses in liberal arts and the sciences. The College of Pharmacy was added in 1927, and the Graduate School was established in 1932. As of 2007, Xavier was one of the top producers of African American graduates with undergraduate degrees in either biology or physics and of African American graduates who go on to medical school. That same year, the American Association of Colleges of Pharmacy estimated that almost 25 percent of the black pharmacists practicing in the United States in 2007 had received their degrees from Xavier and that more African Americans earn the doctorate in pharmacy degree (PharMD) at Xavier than anywhere else.

The College of Pharmacy conducts cutting-edge research concerning pharmaceutical drugs in its Clinical Trials Unit (CTU). Since its establishment in 1997, CTU has conducted clinical studies of drugs for the treatment of asthma, congestive heart failure, diabetes, dyslipidemia, erectile dysfunction, hypertension, irritable bowel syndrome, and pneumonia. Most of CTU's clinical trials are Phase III studies, which are randomized controlled trials on large patient groups (300–3,000 or more, depending on the condition) that are aimed at being the definitive assessment of a drug's efficacy. Phase III trials are the most expensive, time-consuming, and difficult trials to design and run, especially when they involve therapies for chronic conditions such as the preceding ones.

The College's Division of Basic Pharmaceutical Sciences conducts basic research on a wide range of biochemical compounds. One set of projects studies the effect of certain environmental conditions on the behavior of biochemical compounds. These projects have included, among others, studies of the effect of xenobiotics (such as pharmaceutical drugs) on binding interactions of the estrogen receptor, the influence of environmental agents on the recombination of DNA strands known as Alu sequences, the role of metallothionein in oxidatve stress in the heart, the development of a general method to clone and characterize steroid receptors, the effects of manganese and nickel in rural and urban environments of New Orleans, the neurotoxicity of manganese, and methods for measuring mobile forms of uranium. Another set of projects works to develop novel drug delivery systems for treating alcohol and drug abuse and HIV/AIDS.

With funding from the U.S. Department of Health and Human Services, the College of Pharmacy operates a Centers of Excellence Scholars Program. This three-year program gives African American students who are working toward their PharMD an opportunity to participate in basic and clinical biomedical research with a faculty mentor. Participants work with their mentors part time during the academic year and full time during the summer; in return, they perfect their basic research skills, are paid $7 per hour, receive $1,000 per year to cover the expenses of attending workshops and scientific conferences, and get another $2,500 to cover the cost of supplies.

The Center for Undergraduate Research obtains funding for programs in virtually all of the university's departments that stimulate original research by undergraduates. To showcase the results of this research, the center has presented, since 2004, an annual Festival of Scholars, at which students make oral and poster presentations. Some of the scientific research presented at the 2007 festival included studies of seafood shells as a natural bisorbent filter to remove metal pollutants from water, of the antidiabetic agents in streptozotocin-induced diabetes in rats, of chloroethoxyethane purines as potential anticancer agents, of novel approaches to the construction of spirocyclic amines and spirocyclic ethers, of sugar production by the enzymatic hydrolysis of cellulose, of the unique genome differences in chimpanzees and humans, of concerted evolution in unisexual lizards, of the synthesis of benzoate esters with potential biological activities, of DNA reconstruction and replication, and of the effects of temperature, medium, and pH on the production of *Sclerotium* (the genus of fungi that causes the plant disease known as southern blight).

Given its excellence in science education, Xavier was chosen as one of six institutions of higher learning to participate in NASA's Model Institutions for Excellence (MIE) Program. NASA and the National Science Foundation have developed the MIE curriculum, a model series of courses for teaching science at HBCUs and other minority-serving institutions, which traditionally have lagged behind other institutions in terms of possessing the necessary equipment and facilities for encouraging and supporting undergraduate research in the sciences. In essence, Xavier serves as a testing ground for the MIE curriculum; if the curriculum proves to be effective, then Xavier will participate in exporting it to other HBCUs and minority-serving institutions.

See also: Asthma; Biology; Diabetes; Historically Black Colleges and Universities; HIV/AIDS; National Aeronautics and Space Administration; National Science Foundation; Physics

REFERENCES AND FURTHER READING

Xavier University of Louisiana. "Center for Undergraduate Research." [Online article or information; retrieved May 19, 2007.] http://www.xula.edu/CUR/.

Xavier University of Louisiana. "Division of Clinical and Administrative Sciences: About the Clinical Trials Unit." [Online article or information; retrieved May 19, 2007.] http://newsite.xula.edu/cop/clinicaltrials.php.

Xavier University of Louisiana. "Xavier University of Louisiana." [Online article or information; retrieved October 30, 2007.] http://www.xula.edu/.

Bibliography

AAAS Experts & Speakers Service. "Shirley M. Malcom, Ph.D." 2008. http://www.aaas.org/ScienceTalk/malcom.shtml.

Abramson, Charles I., ed. *Selected Papers and Biography of Charles Henry Turner (1867–1923), Pioneer of Comparative Animal Behavior Studies*. Assisted by Latasha D. Jackson and Camille L. Fuller. Lewiston, NY: Edwin Mellen Press, 2003.

Alabama A&M University, School of Agricultural and Environmental Sciences. "Agricultural Research Centers." n.d. http://saes.aamu.edu/Research/AgResearchProgram.html.

Alabama A&M University. "Welcome to Alabama A&M University." 2006. http://www.aamu.edu/.

Alabama State University. "Research Infrastructure in Minority Institutions at Alabama State University." 2008. http://www.alasu.edu/RIMI.

Alabama State University. "Welcome to Alabama State University." 2008. http://www.alasu.edu/.

Alfred P. Sloan Foundation. "Programs: Education and Careers in Science and Technology." n.d. http://www.sloan.org/programs/pg_education.shtml.

Alfred P. Sloan Foundation. "Welcome." n.d. http://www.sloan.org/main.shtml.

American Academy of Otolaryngology. "Early African Americans in Otolaryngology." n.d. http://www.entnet.org/HealthInformation/earlyAfricanAmericans.cfm

American Association for the Advancement of Science. "AAAS: Advancing Science, Serving Society." 2008. http://www.aaas.org.

American Association for Cancer Research. "American Association for Cancer Research." 2001–2008. http://www.aacr.org/default.aspx.

American Association for Cancer Research. "Minorities in Cancer Research." n.d. http://www.aacr.org/home/membership-/association-groups/minorities-in-cancer-research.aspx.

American Chemical Society. "ACS Department of Diversity Programs." n.d. http://portal.acs.org/portal/acs/corg/content?_nfpb=true&_pageLabel=PP_TRANSITIONMAIN&node_id=1166&use_sec=false&sec_url_var=region1.

American Chemical Society. "American Chemical Society." 2008. https://portal.acs.org/portal/acs/corg/memberapp.

American College of Veterinary Pathologists. "American College of Veterinary Pathologists." 2007. http://www.acvp.org/.

American College of Veterinary Pathologists. "Minority Fellowship." 2007. http://www.acvp.org/training/pfizer.php.

American Dental Education Association. "American Dental Education Association." 2007. http://www.adea.org/.

American Dental Education Association. "Center for Equity and Diversity." n.d. http://www.adea.org/ced/default.htm.

American Dental Education Association. *Opportunities for Minority Students in U.S. Dental Schools,* 5th ed., 2006–2008. Washington, DC: American Dental Education Association.

American Geological Institute. "American Geological Institute." 2008. http://www.agiweb.org/index.html.

American Heart Association, "Cardiovascular Disease Statistics." March 25, 2008. http://www.americanheart.org/presenter.jhtml?identifier=4478.

American Institute of Biological Sciences. "American Institute of Biological Sciences." April 5, 2008. http://www.aibs.org/core/index.html.

American Institute of Biological Sciences. "Diversity Programs and Resources." 2008. http://www.aibs.org/diversity.

American Medical Association. "AMA—Helping Doctors Help Patients." 1995–2008. http://www.ama-assn.org/.

American Medical Association. "Minority Affairs Consortium." 1995–2008. http://www.ama-assn.org/ama/pub/category/20.html.

American Medical Student Association. "Achieving Diversity in Dentistry and Medicine." 2008. http://www.amsa.org/addm/index.cfm.

American Medical Student Association. "American Medical Student Association." 2008. http://www.amsa.org/.

American Museum of Natural History. "Neil deGrasse Tyson, Astrophysicist." 2006–2007. http://research.amnh.org/users/tyson/.

American Physical Society. "Committee on Minorities in Physics Annual Report for January 2006—December 2006." January 2006. http://www.aps.org/about/governance/committees/commin/upload/COM_AnnualReport_2006.pdf.

American Physical Society. "APS Physics." 2008. http://www.aps.org/.

American Psychological Association. "American Psychological Association." 2008. http://www.apa.org/.

American Society for Cell Biology. "The American Society for Cell Biology." 2008. http://www.ascb.org/.

American Society for Cell Biology. "The Minority Affairs Committee." 2008. http://www.ascb.org/index.cfm?navid=90.

American Society for Microbiology. "American Society for Microbiology." 2008. http://www.asm.org/.

American Society for Microbiology. "Underrepresented Minority Groups in the Life Sciences." n.d. http://www.asm.org/general.asp?bid=16715.

Answers.com. "Theodore K. Lawless." 2006. http://www.answers.com/topic/theodore-k-lawless.

APA Online. "Ethnic Minority Affairs Office." 2008. http://www.apa.org/pi/oema/aboutus.html.

Association of American Medical Colleges. "Diversity." 1995–2008. http://www.aamc.org/diversity/start.htm.

Association of American Medical Colleges. "Minorities in Medical Education: Facts & Figures 2005." Spring 2005. https://services.aamc.org/Publications/index.cfm?fuseaction=Product.displayForm&prd_id=133&prv_id=154.

Association of American Medical Colleges. *Minority Student Opportunities in United States Medical Schools*. Washington, DC: AAMC, 2005.

Association of Black Anthropologists. "Association of Black Anthropologists." May 1999. http://www.indiana.edu/~wanthro/candice1.htm.

Association of Black Cardiologists. "Association of Black Cardiologists, Inc." n.d. http://www.abcardio.org/.

Association of Black Psychologists. "The Association of Black Psychologists." n.d. http://www.abpsi.org/index.htm.

Astronomers of the African Diaspora. May 27, 1997. http://www.math.buffalo.edu/mad/physics/index.html.

Astronomy Department, the University of California at Berkeley. "Gibor Basri, Professor of Astronomy." July 22, 2007. http://astro.berkeley.edu/~basri/.

Bailey, Eric J. *Food Choice and Obesity in Black America: Creating a New Cultural Diet*. Westport, CT: Greenwood Publishing, 2006.

Baltrip, Kimetris N. "Samuel Nabrit, 98, Scientist and a Pioneer in Education, Dies." NYTimes.com. January 6, 2004. http://www.nytimes.com/2004/01/06/education/06NABR.html?ex=1388725200&en=0e78b968bd56fde6&ei=5007&partner=USERLAND.

Bedini, Silvio A. *The Life of Benjamin Banneker: The First African-American Man of Science*, 2nd ed. Baltimore: Maryland Historical Society, 1999.

Berry, Leonidas H. *Gastrointestinal Pan-Endoscopy*. Springfield, IL: Charles C. Thomas, 1974.

Berry, Leonidas H. *The Clinical Significance of Gastrointestinal Endoscopy*. Nutley, NJ: Roche Laboratories, 1976.

Berry, Leonidas H. *I Wouldn't Take Nothin' for My Journey: Two Centuries of an Afro-American Minister's Family*. Chicago: Johnson Publishing, 1981.

BEST: Building Engineering and Science Talent. "The BEST Initiative." 2007. http://www.bestworkforce.org.

Beta Kappa Chi. "Beta Kappa Chi (BKX) National Scientific Honor Society." n.d. http://www.betakappachi.org.

Bigelow, Barbara C., ed. *Contemporary Black Biography*, vol. 7. Detroit, MI: Gale Research, 1994.

Biophysical Society. "Biophysical Society." n.d. http://www.biophysics.org/.

Biophysical Society. "Minority Resource Center." n.d. http://www.biophysics.org/minority/.

The Bioplex Project at West Virginia State University. "Welcome to the Bioplex Project." 2005. http://bioplexproject.wvstateu.edu.

Black Entomologists. "Black Entomologists." n.d. http://www.blackentomologists.org/.

Blackman, Dionne J., and Christopher M. Masi. "Racial and Ethnic Disparities in Breast Cancer Mortality: Are We Doing Enough to Address the Root Causes?" *Journal of Clinical Oncology* 24, 14 (May 10, 2006): 2170–2178.

The Body: The Complete HIV/AIDS Resource. "HIV/AIDS Among the African American Community." June 2007. http://www.thebody.com/index/whatis/africanam.html.

Bowser, Rene. "Medical Civil Rights: The Exclusion of Physicians of Color from Managed Care—Business or Bias?" (September 2005). U of St. Thomas Legal Studies Research Paper No. 05–14. http://ssrn.com/abstract=834284.

Brown, Valerie J. "Kenneth Olden, Master Fencer." *American Journal of Public Health* 94, 11 (November 2004): 1905–1907.

Burns, Khephra, and William Miles. *Black Stars in Orbit: NASA's African American Astronauts.* New York: Harcourt Brace, 1995.

Camille and Henry Dreyfus Foundation. "The Camille & Henry Dreyfus Foundation, Inc." n.d. http://www.dreyfus.org/.

Carey, Charles W. Jr. *American Scientists.* New York: Facts On File, 2005.

Carson, Ben, and Cecil B. Murphey. *Gifted Hands: The Ben Carson Story.* Grand Rapids, MI: Zondervan, 1990.

Carson, Ben. "Mini-Biography." n.d. http://www.drbencarson.com/snapshot.html.

Central State University. "Central State University." n.d. http://www.centralstate.edu/.

Central State University. "Water Resources Management." n.d. http://www.centralstate.edu/academics/bus_ind/water_res/wrm/index.html.

Cerami, Charles A. *Benjamin Banneker: Surveyor, Astronomer, Publisher, Patriot.* New York: Wiley, 2002.

Charles R. Drew University of Medicine and Science. "Welcome to Drew." n.d. http://www.cdrewu.edu/_022/_html/.

Chen, Adrian. "In the Shadow of Science: Blacks Scientists and Inventors Struggle for Visibility from One Generation to the Next." *The Michigan Daily* (February 22, 2005). http://media.www.michigandaily.com/media/storage/paper851/news/2005/02/22/News/In.The.Shadow.Of.Science-1429030.shtml.

CIRTL Diversity Institute. "Mission, Goals & Strategy." 2004. http://cirtl.wceruw.org/DiversityResources/about/mission/.

Clark Atlanta University. "Clark Atlanta University." n.d. http://www.cau.edu/.

Clark Atlanta University. "Research Programs: Research Centers." n.d. http://www.cau.edu/acad_prog/default.html.

Climate Change Research Section, National Center for Atmospheric Research. "Warren M. Washington." January 3, 2008. http://www.cgd.ucar.edu/ccr/warren/.

Cobb, W. Montague. "Race and Runners." *Journal of Health and Physical Education* 3, 56 (1936).

Cobb, W. Montague. "The First Hundred Years of the Howard University College of Medicine." *Journal of the National Medical Association* 57 (1967): 408–420.

Cobb, W. Montague. "Harold Dadford West, Ph.D., LL.D.: A Good Man and True." *Journal of the National Medical Association* 68, 4 (July 1976): 269–275.

Collins, Daniel. *Your Teeth: A Handbook of Dental Care for the Whole Family.* Garden City, NY: Doubleday, 1968.

Computer Scientists of the African Diaspora. May 25, 1997. http://www.math. buffalo.edu/mad/computer-science/.

Consortium for Plant Biotechnology Research. "HBCU Program." n.d. http://cpbr.org/hbcu.html.

Contemporary Black Biography. (Multivolume series) Detroit, MI: Gale Cengage.

Cooke, Lloyd M. *Cleaning Our Environment—The Chemical Basis for Action.* Washington, DC: American Chemical Society, 1969.

Council for Chemical Research. "CCR Diversity Award." n.d. http://www.ccrhq.org/about/Diversityaward.htm.

Council for Chemical Research. "The Council for Chemical Research." n.d. http://www.ccrhq.org/.

Cowings, Patricia S., and William Toscano. "Motion and Space Sickness." In *Motion and Space Sickness,* edited by George H. Crampton. Boca Raton, FL: CRC Publishing, 1990: 354–372.

Daniel Hale Williams Preparatory School of Medicine. "Welcome to Our School!" 2002. http://www.wpsm.cps.k12.il.us/.

Delaware State University. "Delaware State University." 2008. http://www.desu.edu/.

Delaware State University, Office of the Associate Provost for Research. "Research Administration and Centers." 2008. http://www.desu.edu/research.

Delta Sigma Theta. "Delta Sigma Theta Sorority, Inc." 2005–2007. http://www.deltasigmatheta.org/cms/.

Dental Pipeline, "About Us." 2006. http://www.dentalpipeline.org/au_aboutus.html.

Development Fund for Black Students in Science and Technology. "Development Fund for Black Students in Science and Technology." April 2, 2007. http://dfbsst.dlhjr.com/.

"Doctoral Degree Awards to African Americans Reach Another All-Time High." *The Journal of Blacks in Higher Education.* 2006. http://www.jbhe.com/news_views/50_black_doctoraldegrees.html.

Dummett, Clifton O., and Lois D. *NDA II: The Story of America's Second National Dental Association.* Washington, DC: National Dental Association Foundation, 2000.

Dustan, H. P. "Obesity and Hypertension in Blacks." *Cardiovascular Drugs and Therapy* 4, 2 (March 1990): 395–402.

The Education Coalition. "Reflections on the Star Schools Program After Eight Years." n.d. http://www.tecweb.org/vault/stars/reflect.html.

Edwards, Cecile Hoover, et al. *Human Ecology: Interactions of Man with His Environment; an Introduction to the Academic Discipline of Human Ecology.* Dubuque, IA: Kendall/Hunt, 1991.

Elders, Joycelyn, and David Charnoff. *Joycelyn Elders, M.D.: From Sharecropper's Daughter to Surgeon General of the United States of America.* Waterville, ME: Thorndike Press, 1997.

Embree, Edwin R., and Julia Waxman, *Investment in People: The Story of the Julius Rosenwald Fund.* New York: Harper, 1949.

Endocrine Society. "The Endocrine Society." n.d. http://www.endo-society.org/

Endocrine Society. "Minority Activities." n.d. http://www.endo-society.org/minorityactivities/.

Environmental Careers Organization. *Beyond the Green: Redefining and Diversifying the Environmental Movement*. Boston: Environmental Careers Organization, 1992.

Environmental Careers Organization. "Diversity Initiative." n.d. http://www.eco.org/site/c.dnJLKPNnFkG/b.942795/k.122B/Diversity_Initiative.htm.

Environmental Careers Organization. "Welcome to ECO!" n.d. http://www.eco.org/site/c.dnJLKPNnFkG/b.795025/k.AA86/The_Environmental_Careers_Organization.htm.

"The Epidemiology of Cardiovascular Disease in Black Americans." *New England Journal of Medicine* 335, 21 (November 21, 1996): 1597–1599.

Erich Jarvis Lab. "General Information." n.d. http://www.jarvislab.net/GenInfo.html.

The Faces of Science: African Americans in the Sciences. "St. Elmo Brady." n.d. https://webfiles.uci.edu/mcbrown/display/brady.html.

FAMU College of Pharmacy and Pharmaceutical Sciences. "Research Centers and Programs." 2003. http://pharmacy.famu.edu/Research.asp.

Federation of American Societies for Experimental Biology. "Federation of American Societies for Experimental Biology." n.d. http://www.faseb.org/.

Federation of American Societies for Experimental Biology. "Minority Access to Research Careers." n.d. http://marc.faseb.org/.

Ferguson, Lloyd. *Electron Structures of Organic Molecules*. Upper Saddle River, NJ: Prentice Hall, 1952.

Ferguson, Lloyd. *The Modern Structural Theory of Organic Chemistry*. Upper Saddle River, NJ: Prentice Hall, 1963.

Ferguson, Lloyd. *Textbook of Organic Chemistry*, 2nd ed. New York: Van Nostrand, 1965.

Ferguson, Lloyd. *Organic Chemistry: A Science and an Art*. Bel Air, CA: Willard Grant Press, 1972.

Ferguson, Lloyd. *Highlights of Alicyclic Chemistry*. Danbury, CT: Franklin Books, 1973.

Ferguson, Lloyd. *Organic Molecular Structure: A Gateway to Advanced Organic Chemistry*. Bel Air, CA: Willard Grant Press, 1975.

Ferguson, Lloyd N., with Gabrielle S. Morris. *Increasing Opportunities in Chemistry, 1936–1986*. Berkeley, CA: Regional Oral History Office, The Bancroft Library, University of California, 1992.

Fikes, Robert Jr. "Careers of African Americans in Academic Astronomy." *Journal of Blacks in Higher Education* 29 (Autumn 2000): 132–134.

First Science Ph.D.s Awarded to African Americans. "The Faces of Science: African Americans in the Sciences." November 25, 2007. https://webfiles.uci.edu/mcbrown/display/first_phds.html.

Fisk University. "Fisk University." 2007. http://www.fisk.edu/.

Fisk University. "Natural Sciences and Mathematics." 2007. http://www.fisk.edu/page.asp?id=185.

Florida A&M University. "Florida A&M University." 2008. http://www.famu. edu/.

Fort Valley State University. "College of Agriculture, Home Economics and Allied Programs." 2007. http://www.ag.fvsu.edu/.

Fort Valley State University. "Fort Valley State University." 2008. http://www.fvsu. edu/.

Gates, Henry L., and Cornel West. *The African-American Century: How Black Americans Have Shaped Our Country*. New York: Free Press, 2000.

The Gates Millennium Scholars. "About GMS." n.d. http://www.gmsp.org/ publicweb/aboutus.aspx.

Gates, Sylvester. *Superspace or 1001 Lessons in Supersymmetry*. San Francisco: Benjamin/Cummings Publishing, 1983.

Gates, Sylvester. "Taking the Particle Out of Particle Physics." *Quotient* 12, 4 (1986).

GEM: The National GEM Consortium. "About GEM." 2008. http://www. gemfellowship.org/.

Gordon Research Conferences. "Gordon Research Conferences." 2008. http://www.grc.org/.

Gordon Research Conferences. "The GRC Underrepresented Minority (URM) Diversity Initiative." 2008. http://www.grc.org/diversity.aspx.

Granat, Diane. "America's 'Give While You Live' Philanthropist." *APF Reporter*, 21, 1 (2003). http://www.aliciapatterson.org/APF2101/Granat/Granat.html.

Grant, R. W. "Invited Commentary: Untangling the Web of Diabetes Causality in African Americans." *American Journal of Epidemiology* 166, 4 (August 15, 2007): 388–390.

Grants.gov. "Research Infrastructure in Minority Institutions (RIMI)[P20]." February 16, 2007. http://www.grants.gov/search/search.do?oppId=12637&mode=VIEW.

Graves, Joseph. *The Emperor's New Clothes: Biological Theories of Race at the Millennium*. New Brunswick, NJ: Rutgers University Press, 2001.

Graves, Joseph. *The Race Myth: Why We Pretend Race Exists in America*. New York: Plume Books, 2005.

Griffith, Ezra E. H. *Race and Excellence: My Dialogue with Chester Pierce*. Iowa City: University of Iowa Press, 1998.

Haas Center for Public Service. "Mickey Leland Energy Fellowship: A Summer Internship Program Providing Energy Opportunities for Minority Students." n.d. http://haas.stanford.edu/external_fellowships/fellowship.php?ef_id=142&.

Hall, W. Dallas, Neil B. Shulman, and Elijah Saunders. *Hypertension in Blacks: Epidemiology, Pathophysiology and Treatment*. Chicago: Year Book Medical Publishers, 1985.

Handbook of Texas Online. "Roman, Charles Victor." n.d. http://www.tsha.utexas. edu/handbook/online/articles/RR/frost.html.

Harris, Wesley L., *Defense Manufacturing in 2010 and Beyond: Meeting the Changing Needs of National Defense*. Washington, DC: National Academies Press, 1999.

Harris, Wesley L. *Incentive Strategies for Defense Acquisitions*. 2001. Fort Belvoir, Va.: Defense Acquisition University Press.

Harrison, Ira E., and Faye V. Harrison, eds. *African-American Pioneers in Anthropology*. Urbana: University of Illinois Press, 1999.

Hayden, Robert C. *Eleven African American Doctors*, rev. ed. New York: Twenty-First Century Books, 1992.

Hayden, Robert C. *Seven African American Scientists*. New York: Twenty-First Century Books, 1992.

The HBCU Network, "The History of HBCUs." 2008. http://www.hbcunetwork.com/The_History_Of_HBCUs_Timeline.cfm.

Health Policy Institute of Ohio. "Understanding Health Disparities." November 2004. http://www.healthpolicyohio.org/publications/healthdisparities.html.

Health Professionals for Diversity Coalition. "About Health Professionals for Diversity." 2007. http://www.hpd-coalition.org/about.htm.

Henry, Warren E. *Elementary Qualitative Chemical Analysis*. Tuskegee, AL: Tuskegee University Press, 1937.

HHC-Harlem Hospital Center. "Harlem Hospital Center." 2008. http://www.ci.nyc.ny.us/html/hhc/html/facilities/harlem.shtml.

Howard University. "Howard University." n.d. http://www.howard.edu/.

Howard University College of Medicine. "Howard University College of Medicine." n.d. http://www.med.howard.edu.

Howard University Office of Research Administration. "Research Centers and Institutes." 2003. http://ora.howard.edu/centers/int.htm\#top.

Institute of Medicine. *The Right Thing to Do, the Smart Thing to Do: Enhancing Diversity in Health Professions: Summary of the Symposium on Diversity in Health Professions in Honor of Herbert W. Nickens, MD*. Washington, DC: National Academies Press, 2001.

Institute of Medicine. *In the Nation's Compelling Interest: Ensuring Diversity in the Health Care Workforce*. Washington, DC: National Academies Press, 2004.

Institute of Medicine of the National Academies. "About." February 15, 2008. http://www.iom.edu/CMS/AboutIOM.aspx.

International Society on Hypertension in Blacks. "About ISHIB." 2005. http://www.ishib.org/AI_index.asp.

Iowa Commission on the Status of African Americans. "Scientists and Inventors." n.d. http://www.state.ia.us/dhr/saa/AA_culture/scientists_inventors.html.

Jackson State University. "Jackson State University." 2007. http://www.jsums.edu/.

Jackson State University, Office of Vice President for Research Development & Federal Relations. "Centers & Institutes." 2005. http://www.jsums.edu/~ordsfr/centers.htm.

Jefferson, Roland M. "The Japanese Flowering Cherry Trees of Washington, D.C.: A Living Symbol of Friendship." *National Arboretum Contribution* 4 (1977).

Jemison, Mae. *Find Where the Wind Goes: Moments from My Life*. New York: Scholastic Press, 2001.

Johns Hopkins Medicine "Hopkins Neurosurgeon Separates Zambian Siamese Twins, Practiced with 3-D 'Workbench.'" January 15, 1998. http://www.hopkinsmedicine.org/press/1998/JANUARY/980115.HTM

Just, Ernest E., Robert Chambers, Warren H. Lewis, Edwin G. Conklin, Frank R. Lillie, Merle H. Jacobs, Clarence E. McClung, Albert P. Mathews, Margaret R. Lewis, Thomas H. Morgan, Edmund B. Wilson, Edmund V. Cowdry, and Ralph S. Lillie. *General Cytology: A Textbook of Cellular Structure and Function for Students of Biology and Medicine.* Chicago: University of Chicago Press, 1924.

Just, Ernest E. *Biology of the Cell Surface.* Philadelphia, PA: P. Blakiston's Son & Co., 1939.

Just, Ernest E. *Basic Methods for Experiments on Eggs of Marine Animals.* Philadelphia, PA: P. Blakiston's Son & Co., 1939.

JustGarciaHill.org, "Biographies." 2007. http://justgarciahill.org/jghdocs/ webbiography.asp.

Karter, Andrew J. "Race and Ethnicity: Vital Constructs for Diabetes Research." *Diabetes Care* 26, 7 (2003): 2189–2193.

Kentucky State University. "Kentucky State University." 2004. n.d. http://www.kysu.edu/.

Kentucky State University Aquaculture. "KSU's Program of Distinction." http://www.ksuaquaculture.org/.

Kessler, James H., J. S. Kidd, Renee A. Kidd, and Katherine A. Morin, eds. *Distinguished African American Scientists of the 20th Century.* Phoenix, AZ: Oryx Press, 1996.

Kinnon, Joy Bennett. "Is Our Air Killing Us? The Asthma Attack on Black America— The Prevalence of Asthma in the African American Community." *Ebony* (July 2001). http://findarticles.com/p/articles/mi_m1077/is_9_56/ai_76285233.

Krapp, Kristine, ed. *Notable Black American Scientists.* Detroit, MI: Gale Research, 1999.

Lamb, Yvonne S. "Prof. Samuel Massie Dies; Broke Naval Academy's Race Barrier." *Washington Post*, April 15, 2005: B06.

Langston University. "Research & Extension." 2000. http://www.luresext.edu/ index.htm.

Langston University. "Langston University." 2007. http://www.lunet.edu/.

Lawrence, Margaret Morgan. *The Mental Health Team in the Schools.* New York: Behavioral Publications, 1971.

Lawrence, Margaret Morgan. *Young Inner City Families: Development of Ego Strength under Stress.* New York: Human Sciences Press, 1975.

Leadership Alliance. "The Leadership Alliance." 2008. http://www.theleadershipalliance.org/matriarch/default.asp.

Leevy, Carroll M. *Practical Diagnosis and Treatment of Liver Disease.* New York: Medical Book Department of Harper & Brothers, 1957.

Leevy, Carroll M. *Evaluation of Liver Function in Clinical Practice.* Indianapolis, IN: Lilly Research Laboratories, 1965, 1974.

Leevy, Carroll M. *The Hepatic Circulation and Portal Hypertension.* New York: New York Academy of Sciences, 1970.

Leevy, Carroll M. *Liver Regeneration in Man.* Springfield, IL: Charles C. Thomas, 1973.

Leevy, Carroll M. *Diseases of the Liver and Biliary Tract: Standardization of Nomenclature, Diagnosis Criteria, and Prognosis*. Washington, DC: U.S. Department of Health, Education and Welfare, 1976.

Leevy, Carroll M. *Guidelines for Detection of Hepatoxicity Due to Drugs and Chemicals*. Washington, DC: National Institutes of Health, 1979.

Leffall, LaSalle D. *No Boundaries: A Cancer Surgeon's Odyssey*. Washington, DC: Howard University Press, 2005.

Lewis, Julian H. *The Biology of the Negro*. Chicago: University of Chicago Press, 1942.

Lightfoot, Sarah Lawrence. *Balm in Gilead: Journey of a Healer*. Reading, MA: Addison-Wesley, 1989.

Lincoln University of Missouri. "Cooperative Research." 2008. http://www.lincolnu.edu/pages/375.asp

Lincoln University of Missouri. "Lincoln University of Missouri." 2008. http://www.lincolnu.edu/pages/1.asp.

Love, Spencie. *One Blood: The Death and Resurrection of Charles R. Drew*. Chapel Hill: University of North Carolina Press, 1996.

Maclin, A. P., et al., eds. *Magnetic Phenomena: The Warren E. Henry Symposium on Magnetism, in Commemoration of His 89th Birthday and His Work in Magnetism*. New York: Springer-Verlag, 1989.

Maloney, Arnold H. *Some Essentials of Race Leadership*. Xenia, OH: Aldine Publishing, 1924.

Maloney, Arnold H. *Pathways to Democracy*. Boston: Meador Publishing, 1945.

Maloney, Arnold H. *Amber Gold; an Adventure in Autobiography*. Boston: Meador Publishing, 1946.

Maloney, Arnold H. *After England—We; Nationhood for Caribbea*. Boston: Meador, 1949.

Manning, Kenneth R. *Black Apollo of Science: The Life of Ernest Everett Just*. New York: Oxford University Press, 1983.

Massie, Samuel P. "The Chemistry of Phenothiazine." Chemical Reviews, 54, 697 (1954).

Massie, Samuel P., with Robert C. Hayden. *Catalyst: The Autobiography of an American Chemist*. Laurel, MD: S.P. Massie, 2005.

Mathematicians of the African Diaspora. "J. Ernest Wilkins, Jr." 2005. http://www.math.buffalo.edu/mad/PEEPS/.

Mayberry, B. D. *The History of the Carver Research Foundation of Tuskegee University, 1940–1990*. Tuskegee, AL: Tuskegee University Press, 2003.

McMurray, Emily, ed. *Notable Twentieth-Century Scientists*. Detroit, MI: Gale Research, 1995.

McMurry, Linda O. *George Washington Carver: Scientist and Symbol*. Norwalk, CT: Easton Press, 1994.

Medical Makers. "Dr. Daniel Collins." n.d. http://www.thehistorymakers.com/biography/biography.asp?bioindex=1080&category=medicalMakers.

Meharry Medical College. "Meharry Medical College." n.d. http://www.mmc.edu/.

Merrill, Ray M., and Otis W. Brawley. "Prostate Cancer Incidence and Rates of Mortality Among White and Black Men." *Epidemiology* 8, 2 (March 1997): 126–131.

Minority Environmental Leadership Development Initiative. "Minority Environmental Leadership Development Initiative." January 30, 2003. http://www.umich.edu/~meldi/index.html.

Minority Environmental Leadership Development Initiative. *The Paths We Tread: Profiles of the Careers of Minority Environmental Professionals, MELDI Career Resource Guide to Environmental Jobs*, and *MELDI Guide to Negotiating the Job Market*. Ann Arbor: University of Michigan, School of Natural Resources and Environment, 2005. http://www.umich.edu/~meldi/PDF/ProfilesBook_0605.pdf.

Minton, R. F. "The History of Mercy-Douglass Hospital." *Journal of the National Medical Association* 43, 3 (May 1951): 153–159.

MIT Aero|Astro. "Wesley L. Harris." n.d. http://web.mit.edu/aeroastro/people/harris/.

Morehouse School of Medicine. "About MSM." 2007. http://www.msm.edu/aboutmsm/index.htm.

Morgan State University Estuarine Research Center. "Research Programs." n.d. http://www.morgan.edu/erc/research.html.

Morgan State University. "Morgan State University." n.d. http://www.morgan.edu/.

Nabrit, Samuel N. "Regeneration in the Tail-Fins of Fishes." *Biological Bulletin* 56: 235–266.

NASA Astrobiology Institute. "About the NAI-MIRS Program in Astrobiology." n.d. http://www.nai-mirs.org/about.php.

NASA Astrobiology Institute. "NASA Astrobiology Institute." April 8, 2008. http://nai.arc.nasa.gov/.

The National Academies. "Welcome to the Ford Foundation Diversity Fellowships Home Page." 2008. http://www7.nationalacademies.org/fordfellowships/.

National Aeronautics and Space Administration. "Biographical Data: Bernard A. Harris, Jr. (M.D.)." January 1999. http://www.jsc.nasa.gov/Bios/htmlbios/harris.html.

National Aeronautics and Space Administration. "Biographical Data: Ronald E. McNair." December 2003. http://www.jsc.nasa.gov/Bios/htmlbios/mcnair.html.

National Aeronautics and Space Administration. "Astronaut Bio: Michael P. Anderson." May 2004. http://www.jsc.nasa.gov/Bios/htmlbios/anderson.html pp. 132–135.

National Aeronautics and Space Administration. "Astronaut Bio: Guion S. Bluford, Jr." February 2007. http://www.jsc.nasa.gov/Bios/htmlbios/bluford-gs.html.

National Aeronautics and Space Administration. "National Aeronautics and Space Administration." April 18, 2008. http://www.nasa.gov/.

National Aeronautics and Space Administration, Goddard Space Flight Center. "Minority University—Space Interdisciplinary Network." October 17, 2006. http://muspin.gsfc.nasa.gov/.

National Agricultural Library. "NAL Collections: Jefferson, Roland Maurice, Collection." June 13, 2007. http://www.nal.usda.gov/speccoll/collectionsguide/collection.php?find=J.

National Association of Black Geologists and Geophysicists. "NABGG: Home of National Association of Black Geologists and Geophysicists." n.d. http://www.nabgg.com.

National Association for Equal Opportunity in Higher Education. "HBCU/MI Environmental Technology Consortium." 2005. http://www.nafeo.org/etc/index.html.

National Association for Equal Opportunity in Higher Education. "National Association for Equal Opportunity in Higher Education." 2007. http://www.nafeo.org/home

National Association of Minority Medical Educators. "National Association of Minority Medical Educators, Inc." 2008. http://www.nammenational.org/.

National Cancer Institute. "National Cancer Institute." n.d. http://www.cancer.gov/.

National Cancer Institute, Comprehensive Minority Biomedical Branch. "Opportunities for Minorities in Cancer." n.d. http://minorityopportunities.nci.nih.gov/index.html.

National Center for Complementary and Alternative Medicine. "National Center for Complementary and Alternative Medicine." n.d. http://nccam.nih.gov/.

National Center for Complementary and Alternative Medicine. "Office of Special Populations Strategic Plan to Address Racial and Ethnic Health Disparities." October 24, 2007. http://nccam.nih.gov/about/plans/healthdisparities/index.htm.

National Center on Minority Health and Health Disparities. "About NCMHD." n.d. http://ncmhd.nih.gov/about_ncmhd/mission.asp.

National Center on Minority Health and Health Disparities. "National Institutes of Health Strategic Research Plan and Budget to Reduce and Ultimately Eliminate Health Disparities, Volume I." 2002. http://ncmhd.nih.gov/our_programs/strategic/pubs/VolumeI_031003EDrev.pdf.

National Center on Minority Health and Health Disparities. "NIH Comprehensive Strategic Plan and Budget to Reduce and Ultimately Eliminate Heath Disparities." n.d. http://www.ncmhd.nih.gov/strategicmock/our_programs/strategic/pubs/NEI-rev.pdf.

National Coalition of Underrepresented Racial and Ethnic Groups in Engineering and Science. "National Coalition of Underrepresented Racial and Ethnic Groups in Engineering and Science." n.d. http://www.ncourages.org/.

National Dental Association. "National Dental Association." 2004. http://www.ndaonline.org.

National Energy Technology Laboratory. "Advanced Research: Historically Black Colleges and Universities and Other Minority Institutions (HBCU/OMI) Program." n.d. http://www.netl.doe.gov/technologies/coalpower/advresearch/hbcu.html.

National Eye Institute. "National Eye Institute." n.d. http://www.nei.nih.gov/.

National Geographic's Strange Days on Planet Earth, "Tyrone Hayes, PhD, Biologist." 2008. http://www.pbs.org/strangedays/episodes/troubledwaters/experts/bio_hayes_tyrone.html.

National Heart, Lung, and Blood Institute. "National Heart, Lung, and Blood Institute." n.d. http://www.nhlbi.nih.gov/.

National Heart, Lung, and Blood Institute. "National Heart, Lung, and Blood Institute Strategy for Addressing Health Disparities, FY 2002–2006." http://www.nhlbi.nih.gov/resources/docs/plandisp.htm.

National Human Genome Research Institute. "Initiatives and Resources for Minority and Special Populations." September 10, 2007. http://www.genome.gov/10001192.

National Human Genome Research Institute. "National Human Genome Research Institute." n.d. http://www.genome.gov/.

National Institute on Aging. "National Institute on Aging." n.d. http://www.nia.nih.gov/.

National Institute on Aging. "Review of Minority Aging Research at the NIA." February 16, 2008. http://www.nia.nih.gov/AboutNIA/MinorityAgingResearch.htm.

National Institute on Alcohol Abuse and Alcoholism. "National Institute on Alcohol Abuse and Alcoholism." n.d. http://www.niaaa.nih.gov/.

National Institute on Alcohol Abuse and Alcoholism. "NIAAA's Strategic Plan to Address Health Disparities." n.d. http://pubs.niaaa.nih.gov/publications/HealthDisparities/Strategic.html.

National Institute of Allergy and Infectious Diseases. "Office of Special Populations and Research Training." March 10, 2008. http://www3.niaid.nih.gov/about/organization/dea/osprtpage.htm.

National Institute of Allergy and Infectious Diseases. "National Institute of Allergy and Infectious Diseases." March 25, 2008. http://www3.niaid.nih.gov/.

National Institute of Arthritis and Musculoskeletal and Skin Diseases. "National Institute of Arthritis and Musculoskeletal and Skin Diseases." n.d. http://www.niams.nih.gov/.

National Institute of Arthritis and Musculoskeletal and Skin Diseases. "Strategic Plan for Reducing Health Disparities." n.d. http://www.niams.nih.gov/About_Us/Mission_and_Purpose/strat_plan_hd.asp.

National Institute of Child Health and Human Development. "Health Disparities: Bridging the Gap." n.d. http://www.nichd.nih.gov/publications/pubs/upload/health_disparities.pdf.

National Institute of Child Health and Human Development. "National Institute of Child Health and Human Development." April 9, 2008. http://www.nichd.nih.gov/.

National Institute on Deafness and Other Communication Disorders. "National Institute on Deafness and Other Communication Disorders." April 1, 2008. http://www.nidcd.nih.gov./

National Institute on Deafness and Other Communication Disorders. "National Institute on Deafness and Other Communication Disorders Health Disparities Strategic Plan Fiscal Years 2004–2008." April 1, 2008. http://www.nidcd.nih.gov/about/plans/strategic/health_disp.asp.

National Institute of Dental and Craniofacial Research, "Health Disparities Program." January 28, 2008. http://www.nidcr.nih.gov/Research/Extramural/ClinicalResearch/HealthDisparitiesProgram.htm.

National Institute of Dental and Craniofacial Research. "National Institute of Dental and Craniofacial Research." n.d. http://www.nidcr.nih.gov/.

National Institute of Diabetes and Digestive and Kidney Diseases. "Strategic Plan on Minority Health Disparities." November 1, 2007. http://www.niddk.nih.gov/federal/planning/mstrathealthplan.htm.

National Institute of Diabetes and Digestive and Kidney Diseases. "National Institute of Diabetes and Digestive and Kidney Diseases." April 9, 2008. http://www2.niddk.nih.gov/.

National Institute on Drug Abuse. *Preventing Drug Abuse Among Children and Adolescents: A Research-Based Guide*, 2nd ed. Washington, DC: National Institute on Drug Abuse, 2003.

National Institute on Drug Abuse. *Principles of Drug Addiction Treatment: A Research-Based Guide*. Washington, DC: National Institute on Drug Abuse, 2000.

National Institute on Drug Abuse. "Strategic Plan on Reducing Health Disparities." June 6, 2007. http://www.drugabuse.gov/StrategicPlan/HealthStratPlan.html.

National Institute on Drug Abuse. "National Institute on Drug Abuse." April 4, 2008. http://www.nida.nih.gov/.

National Institute of Environmental Health Sciences. "Environmental Health Topics." n.d. http://www.niehs.nih.gov/health/topics/index.cfm.

National Institute of Environmental Health Sciences. "National Institute of Environmental Health Sciences." n.d. http://www.niehs.nih.gov/.

National Institute of General Medical Sciences. "Minority Biomedical Research Support." December 17, 2007. http://www.nigms.nih.gov/minority/mbrs.html.

National Institute of General Medical Sciences. "Minority Access to Research Careers." January 2, 2008. http://www.nigms.nih.gov/minority/marc.html.

National Institute of General Medical Sciences. "Minority Programs." April 9, 2008. http://www.nigms.nih.gov/minority.

National Institute of General Medical Sciences. "National Institute of General Medical Sciences." April 9, 2008. http://www.nigms.nih.gov/.

National Institute of Mental Health. "Five-Year Strategic Plan for Reducing Health Disparities." n.d. http://www.nimh.nih.gov/about/strategic-planning-reports/nimh-five-year-strategic-plan-for-reducing-health-disparities.pdf.

National Institute of Mental Health. "National Institute of Mental Health." April 9, 2008. http://www.nimh.nih.gov/.

National Institute of Neurological Disorders and Stroke. "Five-Year Strategic Plan on Health Disparities." July 11, 2007. http://www.ninds.nih.gov/about_ninds/plans/disparities.htm.

National Institute of Neurological Disorders and Stroke. "National Institute of Neurological Disorders and Stroke." n.d. http://www.ninds.nih.gov/.

National Institutes of Health. "National Institutes of Health." n.d. http://www.nih.gov/.

National Library of Medicine. "Finding Aid to the Leonidas H. Berry Papers, 1907–1982." November 1, 2006. http://www.nlm.nih.gov/hmd/manuscripts/ead/berry.html.

National Medical Association. "The National Medical Association: The Conscience of American Medicine." 2006. http://www.nmanet.org.

National Organization for the Professional Advancement of Black Chemists and Chemical Engineers. "NOBCChE: National Organization for the Professional Advancement of Black Chemists and Chemical Engineers." 2008. http://www.nobcche.org/.

National Science Foundation. "Science and Engineering Doctorate Awards: 2004." http://www.nsf.gov/statistics/nsf06308/pdf/tables.pdf.

National Science Foundation. "Commission on the Advancement of Women and Minorities in Science, Engineering and Technology Development (CAWMSET)." August 24, 2005. http://www.nsf.gov/od/cawmset.

National Science Foundation. "Sampling of Active Programs by Target Audience or Activity." June 26, 2006. http://www.nsf.gov/od/sampling_activeprograms/ sampling.jsp.

National Science Foundation. "National Science Foundation." February 8, 2008. http://www.nsf.gov/.

National Society of Black Physicists. "National Society of Black Physicists." n.d. http://nsbp.org/.

Network of Minority Research Investigators. "Network of Minority Research Investigators (NMRI)." n.d. http://nmri.niddk.nih.gov/.

The NIDA Clinical Toolbox: Science-Based Materials for Drug Abuse Treatment Providers. n.d. http://www.nida.nih.gov/tb/clinical/clinicaltoolbox.html.

NIH Black Scientists Association. "NIH Black Scientists Association." n.d. http://www1.od.nih.gov/oir/sourcebook/comm-adv/black-sci.htm.

Norfolk State University. "Norfolk State University." n.d. http://www.nsu.edu/.

Norfolk State University. "Research@NSU." n.d. http://www.nsu.edu/researchatnsu/ index.html.

Norman, John C. *Cardiac Surgery*. New York: Appleton-Century-Crofts, 1967.

North Carolina A&T State University, Division of Research and Economic Development. "Centers & Institutes." 2006. http://www.ncat.edu/~divofres/ centers.

North Carolina A&T State University. "North Carolina A&T State University." n.d. http://www.ncat.edu/.

North Carolina Central University. "North Carolina Central University." 2007. http://www.nccu.edu/.

North Carolina Central University. "Research at NCCU." 2007. http://www.nccu. edu/research/.

Oak Ridge Associated Universities. "About ORAU: Diversity in Action." n.d. http://www.orau.org/diversity/.

Oak Ridge Associated Universities. "Oak Ridge Associated Universities." n.d. http:// www.orau.org/.

Oak Ridge Institute for Nuclear Studies. "Our Commitment to Diversity." n.d. http://see.orau.org/Diversity.aspx.

Organ, Claude H., and Margaret Kosiba, eds. *A Century of Black Surgeons: The U.S.A. Experience*. Norman, OK: Transcript Press, 1987.

Partnership for Minority Advancement in the Biomolecular Sciences. "Who We Are." n.d. http://www.unc.edu/pmabs/whoweare.html.

Patten, William. *The Evolution of the Vertebrates and Their Kin*. Philadelphia, PA: P. Blakiston's Son & Co., 1912.

Physicists of the African Diaspora. "Who Are the Black Physicists?" May 27, 1997. http://www.math.buffalo.edu/mad/physics/physics-peeps.html.

Pierce, Chester M. *Basic Psychiatry*. New York: Appleton-Century-Crofts, 1971.

Pierce, Chester M. "The Formation of the Black Psychiatrists of America." In *Racism and Mental Health; Essays*, edited by Charles V. Willie, Bernard M. Kramer, and Patricia P. Rieker. Pittsburgh, PA: University of Pittsburgh Press, 1973.

Pierce, Chester M. *Capital Punishment in the United States*. New York: AMS Press, 1976.

Pierce, Chester M. *Television and Behavior*. Beverly Hills, CA: Sage Publications, 1978.

Pierce, Chester M. *The Mosaic of Contemporary Psychiatry in Perspective*. New York: Springer-Verlag, 1991.

PositiveProfiles.com., "About PMHI." n.d. http://www.positiveprofiles.com/content/about/tier_2/about_landing.asp\#mission.

Prairie View A&M University. "Prairie View A&M University." 2003. http://www.pvamu.edu/pages/1.asp.

Prairie View A&M University. "Research Centers." 2003. http://www.pvamu.edu/pages/634.asp.

Prairie View Solar Observatory. "Prairie View Solar Observatory." n.d. http://www.pvamu.edu/cps/.

The Provident Foundation. "History: Provident Hospital." 2000–2008. http://www.providentfoundation.org/history.

Quality Education for Minorities Network. "Quality Education for Minorities." April 2008. http://qemnetwork.qem.org/.

Rebbeck, Timothy R., Chanita Hughes Halbert, and Pamela Sankar. "Genetics, Epidemiology, and Cancer Disparities: Is It Black and White?" *Journal of Clinical Oncology* 24, 14 (May 10, 2006): 2164–2169.

Robinson, Louise. *The Black Millionaire*. New York: Pyramid Books, 1972.

Salzman, Jack, David Lionel Smith, and Cornel West, eds. *Encyclopedia of African-American Culture and History*. New York: MacMillan, 1996.

Sammons, Vivian Ovelton. *Blacks in Science and Medicine*. New York: Hemisphere Publishing, 1990.

Satcher, David. *Oral Health in America: A Report of the Surgeon General*. 2000. http://profiles.nlm.nih.gov/NN/B/B/J/T/segments.html.

Satcher, David. "Call to Action to Prevent Suicide." U.S. Department of Health and Human Services. January 4, 2007. http://www.surgeongeneral.gov/library/calltoaction/calltoaction.htm.

Satcher, David. "Call to Action to Promote Sexual Health and Responsible Sexual Behavior." U.S. Department of Health and Human Services. January 5, 2007. http://www.surgeongeneral.gov/library/sexualhealth/default.htm.

SEE Science and Everyday Experiences. "Delta Sigma Theta and DREF Implement SEE." 2004. http://www.deltasee.com.

Sellers, Sherill L., Jean Roberts, Levi Giovanetto, Katherine Friedrich, and Caroline Hammargren. *Reaching All Students: A Resource Book for Teaching in Science, Technology, Engineering and Mathematics (STEM)*. n.d. http://www.cirtl.net/DiversityResources/resources/resource-book/contents.html

Sickle Cell Disease Association of America. "About SCDAA." 2005. http://www.sicklecelldisease.org/info/index.phtml.

Sickle Cell Disease Association of America. "What Is Sickle Cell Disease?" 2005. http://www.sicklecelldisease.org/about_scd/index.phtml.

Significant Opportunities in Atmospheric Research and Science. "About SOARS." April 8, 2008. http://www.soars.ucar.edu/.

Smedley, Brian D., Adrienne Y. Stith, and Alan R. Nelson, eds. *Unequal Treatment: Confronting Racial and Ethnic Disparities in Health Care*. Washington, DC: National Academies Press, 2003.

Society of Black Academic Surgeons. "Welcome to the Society of Black Academic Surgeons." 2005. http://www.sbas.net.

Society for Neuroscience. "Diversity in Neuroscience." 2008. http://www.sfn.org/index.cfm?pagename=DiversityInNeuroscience.

Society for Neuroscience. "Society for Neuroscience." 2008. http://www.sfn.org/.

South Carolina State University. "Research & Outreach." n.d. http://www.scsu.edu/researchoutreach.aspx.

South Carolina State University. "Savannah River Environmental Sciences Field Station." n.d. http://www.cnrt.scsu.edu/fieldstation/.

South Carolina State University. "South Carolina State University." 2008. http://www.scsu.edu/.

Southern Regional Education Board Doctoral Scholars Program. "About the Program." 1999–2005. http://www.sreb.org/programs/dsp/process/about_the_program.asp.

Southern Regional Education Board. "Southern Regional Education Board." 1999–2008. http://www.sreb.org/.

Southern University and A&M College System. "Agricultural Research and Extension Center." 2003. http://www.suagcenter.com.

Southern University and A&M College System. "Southern University and A&M College." 2006. http://web.subr.edu/.

Spangenburg, Ray, and Kit Moser. *African Americans in Science, Math, and Invention*. New York: Facts On File, 2003.

Spelman College. "Center for Biomedical and Behavioral Research (RIMI)." 2004. http://www.spelman.edu/academics/research/rimi/.

Spelman College. "Spelman College." 2004. http://www.spelman.edu/.

Spurlock, Jeanne, ed. *Black Psychiatrists and American Psychiatry*. Washington, DC: American Psychiatric Association, 1999.

Student National Medical Association. "Welcome to SNMA." 2006–2007. http://www.snma.org/.

Sullivan Commission. "Missing Persons: Minorities in the Healthcare Workforce: A Report of the Sullivan Commission on Diversity in the Healthcare Workforce." September 20, 2004. http://www.jointcenter.org/healthpolicy/docs/ SullivanExecutiveSummary.pdf.

"The 10 Top Careers for Blacks in the '90s." *Ebony*. February 1999. http://findarticles.com/p/articles/mi_m1077/is_n4_v44/ai_7044940/pg_1.

Tennessee State University Digital Library. "Meharry Medical College (1876–)." n.d. http://www.tnstate.edu/library/digital/meharry.htm.

Tennessee State University. "Research at TSU." n.d. http://www.tnstate.edu/ interior.asp?mid=77.

Tennessee State University. "Tennessee State University." n.d. http://www.tnstate. edu/

Texas Southern University. "Research Center for Biotechnology and Environmental Health." 2002. http://www.tsu.edu/academics/science/research/nasa.asp.

Texas Southern University. "Welcome to Texas Southern University." January 8, 2008. http://www.tsu.edu/.

Thomas, Avis J., Lynn E. Eberly, George Davey Smith, James D. Neaton, and Jeremiah Stamler. "Race/Ethnicity, Income, Major Risk Factors, and Cardio-vascular Disease Mortality." *American Journal of Public Health* 95, 8 (August 2005): 1417–1423.

Thomas, Vivien T. *Pioneering Research in Surgical Shock and Cardiovascular Surgery*. Philadelphia: University of Pennsylvania Press, 1985.

Thurgood Marshall College Fund. "Philip Morris USA/Thurgood Marshall Scholarship Fund." 2004. http://www.thurgoodmarshallfund.org/ scholarships/pm.htm.

Tiner, John H. *100 Scientists Who Shaped World History*. San Mateo, CA: Bluewood Books, 2000.

Tougaloo College. "The Tougaloo Center for Undergraduate Research." 2006. http://www.tougaloo.edu/content/academics/programs/undresearch.htm.

Tougaloo College. "Tougaloo College." 2006. http://www.tougaloo.edu/.

Tuskegee University. "Research." 2003–2008. http://www.tuskegee.edu/Global/category.asp?C=34615&nav=menu200_15.

Tuskegee University. "School of Veterinary Medicine." 2003–2008. http://www.tuskegee.edu/Global/category.asp?C=41703.

Tuskegee University. "Tuskegee University." 2003–2008. http://www.tuskegee. edu/.

Tyson, Neil de Grasse. *Merlin's Tour of the Universe*. New York: Columbia University Press, 1989.

Tyson, Neil de Grasse. *Universe Down to Earth*. New York: Columbia University Press, 1994.

Tyson, Neil de Grasse. *Just Visiting This Planet*. St. Charles, MO: Main Street Books, 1998.

Tyson, Neil de Grasse. *One Universe: At Home in the Cosmos*. Washington, DC: Joseph Henry Press, 2000.

Tyson, Neil de Grasse. *The Sky Is Not the Limit: Adventures of an Urban Astrophysicist*. New York: Doubleday, 2000.

Tyson, Neil de Grasse. *Origins: Fourteen Billion Years of Cosmic Evolution*. New York: W. W. Norton, 2004.

United Negro College Fund Special Programs Corporation. "United Negro College Fund Special Programs Corporation." 2005–2008. http://www.uncfsp.org/spknowledge/default.aspx?page=home.default.

University of Arkansas at Pine Bluff, Aquaculture and Fisheries. "Aquaculture/Fisheries—Center of Excellence." August 5, 2004. http://www.uaex.edu/aqfi/.

University of Arkansas at Pine Bluff. "University of Arkansas at Pine Bluff." 2008. http://www.uapb.edu/.

University of California Office of the President. "MESA USA." 2008. http://mesa.ucop.edu/about/mesausa.html.

University of Colorado at Boulder Department of Computer Science. "Clarence (Skip) Ellis, Professor." n.d. http://www.cs.colorado.edu/~skip/Home.html.

University of the District of Columbia. "Center of Excellence for Renewable Energy." n.d. http://www.udc.edu/cere/index.htm.

University of the District of Columbia. "University of the District of Columbia." 2007. http://www.udc.edu/.

University of Maryland Baltimore County. "The Meyerhoff Scholarship Program." 2005. http://www.umbc.edu/meyerhoff/.

University of Maryland, Department of Physics. "Sylvester J. Gates Jr." 2003. http://www.physics.umd.edu/people/faculty/gates.html.

University of Maryland Eastern Shore. "Academics and Research." August 31, 2007. http://www.umes.edu/Academic/index.aspx.

University of Maryland Eastern Shore. "University of Maryland Eastern Shore." August 31, 2007. http://www.umes.edu/.

University of Maryland Eastern Shore. "Association of Research Directors, Inc." November 2007. http://www.umes.edu/ard/Default.aspx?id=11342.

University of Texas Medical Branch Department of Microbiology and Immunology. "Faculty: Clifford W. Houston, Ph.D." 2004–2005. http://microbiology.utmb.edu/faculty/houston.shtml.

University of the Virgin Islands. "Research and Public Service." n.d. http://www.uvi.edu/pub-relations/uvi/home.html.

University of the Virgin Islands. "University of the Virgin Islands." n.d. http://www.uvi.edu/.

University Studies at North Carolina A&T University. "Joseph L. Graves, Jr., Ph.D." September 2007. http://www.ncat.edu/~univstud/faculty.html.

U.S. Department of Agriculture, Cooperative State Research, Education and Extension Service, "Evans-Allen Program Formula Grant." February 19, 2008. http://www.csrees.usda.gov/business/awards/formula/evansallen.html.

U.S. Department of Education. "Minority Science and Engineering Improvement Program." January 25, 2008. http://www.ed.gov/programs/iduesmsi/index.html.

U.S. Department of Education. "Star Schools Program." May 1, 2007. http://www.ed.gov/programs/starschools/index.html.

U.S. Department of Energy. "Minority Educational Institution Student Partnership Program." http://www.doeminorityinternships.org/.

U.S. Department of Energy. "U.S. Department of Energy." http://www.energy.gov/.

U.S. Department of Health & Human Services. "David Satcher (1998–2002)." January 4, 2007. http://www.surgeongeneral.gov/library/history/biosatcher.htm.

U.S. Department of Veterans Affairs. "Central Alabama Veterans Health Care System, East Campus." October 2, 2007. http://www1.va.gov/directory/guide/facility.asp?ID=141&dnum=ALL.

Ventures Scholars Program. "Welcome to the Ventures Scholars Program." 2006. http://www.venturescholar.org/.

Virginia State University. "Research." 2008. http://www.vsu.edu/pages/152.asp.

Virginia State University. "Virginia State University." 2008. http://www.vsu.edu/pages/1.asp.

Warner Research Group, Louisiana State University. "Isiah M. Warner, Ph.D." 1998–2004. http://www.chem.lsu.edu/imw/group/warner.htm.

Warren, Wini. *Black Women Scientists in the United States*. Bloomington: Indiana University Press, 1999.

Watson, Wilbur H. *Against the Odds: Blacks in the Profession of Medicine in the United States*. New Brunswick, NJ: Transaction Publishers, 1999.

Wayne State University, "Center for Urban and African American Health." 2008. http://www.med.wayne.edu/intmed/CUAAH/cuaah.htm.

Wayne State University. "Wayne State University." 2008. http://www.wayne.edu/.

West Virginia Division of Culture and History. "John C. Norman Jr." 2008. http://www.wvculture.org/history/norman.html.

West Virginia State University. "West Virginia State University." 2008. http://www.wvstateu.edu/.

Winston-Salem State University. "Biomedical Research Infrastructure Center." 2005. http://www.wssu.edu/WSSU/UndergraduateStudies/College+of+Arts+and+Sciences/Biomedical+Research+Infrastructure+Center.

Winston-Salem State University. "Winston-Salem State University." 2008. http://www.wssu.edu/wssu.

Witkop, Bernhard. "Percy Lavon Julian." National Academy of Sciences, *Biographical Memoirs* 52 (1980): 223–266.

Wright, Charles H. *The National Medical Association Demands Equal Opportunity: Nothing More, Nothing Less*. Southfield, MI: Charro Book Co., 1995.

Wright, Louis T. *The Treatment of Fractures*. Philadelphia, PA: W. B. Saunders Co., 1938.

Wynes, Charles E. *Charles Richard Drew: The Man and the Myth*. Urbana: University of Illinois Press, 1988.

Xavier University of Louisiana. "Center for Undergraduate Research." n.d. http://www.xula.edu/CUR/.

Xavier University of Louisiana. "Division of Clinical and Administrative Sciences: About the Clinical Trials Unit." n.d. http://newsite.xula.edu/cop/clinicaltrials.php.

Xavier University of Louisiana. "Xavier University of Louisiana." n.d. http://www.xula.edu/

General Index

acetyl peroxide, 161

actin, 140

actinomycetes, 70

actinomycin, 46

Adams, Eugene W. (Veterinary Pathologist), **4–5**, 222–223

adenosine triphosphate (ATP), 257

Adolescent Medicine HIV/AIDS Research Network, 236

Adolescent Trials Network, 236

Advanced Research Projects Agency Network (ARPANET), 72

aeroacoustics, 103, 104

Aerolysin Cytotoxic Enterotoxin (ACT), 117

Aeromonas hydrophila, 117, 275

African Americans
  and autoimmune diseases, 482
  disproportionate incidence of trauma and illness among, 490–491
  hospitals of, 370–371, **371** (photo)
  and organ transplantation, 482
  reproductive health care of, 488–489
  scientific contributions of, 1–3
  See also Asthma; Cancer; Diabetes; HIV/AIDS; Medical Careers for Blacks; Medical Education for Blacks; Obesity; Science Careers for Blacks; Science Education for Blacks; sexually transmitted diseases (STDs); Sickle Cell Disease

aging, biology of, 95, 96

Airborne LIDAR Topographic Mapping System (ALTMS), 6

alcoholism, 144–145

Alcorn, George E., Jr. (Physicist), **5–7**, 279, 438

alicyclic compounds, 79–80

Alzheimer, Alois, 88

American Cancer Society, 146

American Red Cross (ARC), 61–62

A-methopterin, **46**

amino acids, 57, 65, 110
  threonine, 201, 202

amino sugars, 530

analytical chemistry, 148

anastomosis, 189

Anderson, Charles E. (Meteorologist), **7–9**, 248

Anderson, Gloria L. (Physical Chemist), **9–10**, 267

Anderson, Michael P. (Astronaut), **10–13, 12** (photo), 438, 444

Andrew, John A., 404

antibiotics, 31, 46, 214

antioxidants, 98

Apollo 13 mission, 34

Argonne National Library, 154, 173, 192, 204

aromatic hydrocarbons, 24–25, 203

artificial hearts, implantation of, 167

asthma, **218–220, 219** (photo), 233, 471, 482–483
  studies related to development of, 503–504

astronauts, 172, 437–438
  and biofeedback training, 54–55
  See also National Aeronautics and Space Administration (NASA), Astronaut Program

Selected Topical Index

Institutions

Alabama A&M University Center for Forestry and Ecology, 265

Alabama State University, 218, **288–289**

Alfred P. Sloan Foundation, **289–291, 291** (photo), 373

American Association for the Advancement of Science (AAAS), 150, 154, 155, 280, **291–293**

and the Delta SEE (Science and Everyday Experiences) Connection, 293

Minority Scientists Network, 292

Minority Writers Internship, 292

work of with Delta Sigma Theta Sorority, 293

American Association for Cancer Research (AACR), **293–295**

Minorities in Cancer Research (MICR) subgroup, 294–295

American Chemical Society (ACS), 157, **295–297, 297** (photo)

Committee on Minority Affairs (CMA), 295–296, 297

American College of Veterinary Pathologists (ACVP), **298–299**

American Dental Education Association (ADEA), **299–301, 300** (photo)

Minority Dental Faculty Development (MDFD), 300

Minority Medical Education Program, 299–300

American Geological Institute (AGI), **301–302**

American Institute of Biological Sciences (AIBS), diversity programs of, **302–304**

American Medical Association (AMA), 8, 48, **304–305**

Minority Affairs Consortium (MAC), 304–305

American Medical Student Association (AMSA), **305–307**

American Physical Society (APS), **307–309, 308** (photos)

Committee on Minorities (COM), 307–309

American Psychological Association (APA), **309–310**

American Society for Cell Biology (ASCB), **310–312**

Minority Affairs Committee (MAC), 311–312

sponsorship of the E. E. Just Lecture, 312

American Society for Microbiology (ASM), **312–314**

diversity committees of, 313–314

Association of American Medical Colleges (AAMC), **315–317, 317** (photo)

Summer Medical and Dental Education Program (SMDEP), 300–301, 315

Association of Black Anthropologists (ABA), **317–318**

Association of Black Cardiologists (ABC), 226, 229, **319–320**

Center for Women's Heath, 244, 320

Association of Black Psychologists (ABP), **320–321**

Association of Research Directors (ARD), 1890 Land Grant Universities, **321–323**

About the Author

Charles W. Carey Jr. holds an MS in history from Virginia Polytechnic Institute and State University. A former professor of history at several colleges and universities in Virginia, he is an independent scholar working out of his home in Lynchburg. His published works include biographical dictionaries about African American political leaders and American scientists.